Harnessing Green and Circular Skills for Digital Transformation

Patricia Ordóñez de Pablos
University of Oviedo, Spain

Muhammad Anshari
Universiti Brunei Darussalam, Brunei

Mohammad Nabil Almunawar
Universiti Brunei Darussalam, Brunei

A volume in the Advances in Computer and
Electrical Engineering (ACEE) Book Series

Published in the United States of America by
    IGI Global
    Engineering Science Reference (an imprint of IGI Global)
    701 E. Chocolate Avenue
    Hershey PA, USA 17033
    Tel: 717-533-8845
    Fax: 717-533-8661
    E-mail: cust@igi-global.com
    Web site: http://www.igi-global.com

Library of Congress Cataloging-in-Publication Data

CIP DATA PROCESSING

2024 Engineering Science Reference
ISBN(hc) 9798369328651 | ISBN 9798369349670(sc) | eISBN 9798369328668

This book is published in the IGI Global book series Advances in Computer and Electrical Engineering (ACEE) (ISSN: 2327-039X; eISSN: 2327-0403)

British Cataloguing in Publication Data
A Cataloguing in Publication record for this book is available from the British Library.

For electronic access to this publication, please contact: eresources@igi-global.com.

Advances in Computer and Electrical Engineering (ACEE) Book Series

Srikanta Patnaik
SOA University, India

ISSN:2327-039X
EISSN:2327-0403

MISSION

The fields of computer engineering and electrical engineering encompass a broad range of interdisciplinary topics allowing for expansive research developments across multiple fields. Research in these areas continues to develop and become increasingly important as computer and electrical systems have become an integral part of everyday life.

The **Advances in Computer and Electrical Engineering (ACEE) Book Series** aims to publish research on diverse topics pertaining to computer engineering and electrical engineering. **ACEE** encourages scholarly discourse on the latest applications, tools, and methodologies being implemented in the field for the design and development of computer and electrical systems.

COVERAGE

- Computer Architecture
- Computer Hardware
- Chip Design
- Programming
- VLSI Design
- Analog Electronics
- Qualitative Methods
- VLSI Fabrication
- Digital Electronics
- Applied Electromagnetics

IGI Global is currently accepting manuscripts for publication within this series. To submit a proposal for a volume in this series, please contact our Acquisition Editors at Acquisitions@igi-global.com or visit: http://www.igi-global.com/publish/.

Titles in this Series

701 East Chocolate Avenue, Hershey, PA 17033, USA
Tel: 717-533-8845 x100 • Fax: 717-533-8661
E-Mail: cust@igi-global.com • www.igi-global.com

Editorial Advisory Board

Table of Contents

Section 2

Green Development

Section 3

Digital Transformation

Detailed Table of Contents

Section 1

Sustainability and Sustainable Development

The sustainable development goals (SDGs), which provide a broad framework for addressing mankind's interconnected concerns, are critical in guiding global efforts towards attaining sustainable growth. This book chapter delves into the broad depth of the sustainable development goals (SDGs) along with how these could dramatically alter the direction of humanity and build an economically equitable and wealthy society. The current research investigates the historical evolution, background, significance, key consequences via case studies, and multiple implications about the sustainable development goals (SDGs) to address pressing global concerns such as reducing poverty, safeguarding the environment, equity in society, and growth in the economy. The chapter explores the prospects and challenges of achieving the SDGs while advocating towards a more integrated, holistic approach to global development for a more prosperous and sustainable future. It highlights the importance of teamwork and inclusive practices.

In the contemporary landscape of rapid technological advancement and escalating environmental concerns, the imperative to harmonize digital innovation with sustainable practices has become paramount. This chapter delves into the realm of merging green practices with digital innovation to cultivate sustainable synergy, elucidating how this integration holds the potential to revolutionize industries, mitigate environmental degradation, and propel us towards a more resilient future. Through interdisciplinary collaboration and longitudinal studies, this research aims to assess the long-term impacts and effectiveness of green practices and digital innovation initiatives on sustainability outcomes. By exploring the myriad applications of merging green practices with digital innovation across various domains, from renewable energy and waste management to sustainable urban development and conservation efforts, this chapter seeks to inspire stakeholders to embrace this transformative approach and collaborate towards building a more sustainable and prosperous future.

    Dharmbir Prasad, Asansol Engineering College, India
    Rudra Pratap Singh, Asansol Engineering College, India
    Jatin Anand, Asansol Engineering College, India
    Ranadip Roy, Sanaka Educational Trust's Group of Institutions, Durgapur, India
    Md. Irfan Khan, IAC Electricals Pvt. Ltd., Kolkata, India

This study outlines sustainable agriculture practices in Simdega District, India, emphasizing the critical role of agriculture using the renewable energy. With a focus on long-term environmental, social, and economic viability, the study employs a multidisciplinary approach, integrating field surveys, policy analysis, and literature review. In the agriculture industry, including renewable energy solutions may improve resource efficiency, lower greenhouse gas emissions, and foster climate resilience. Additionally, effective post-harvest processing technology like solar dryers and biomass-based systems may be powered by renewable energy reducing food loss and enhancing the quality and marketability of agricultural products. Increased production, water conservation and soil health may all be achieved by using sustainable agricultural practices including organic farming, precision agriculture and agro-forestry.

    Aliasan, Universitas Islam Negeri Raden Fatah Palembang, Indonesia
    Kusnadi, Universitas Islam Negeri Raden Fatah Palembang, Indonesia
    Muzaiyanah Muzaiyanah, Universitas Islam Negeri Raden Fatah Palembang, Indonesia
    Abdur Razzaq, Universitas Islam Negeri Raden Fatah Palembang, Indonesia

This study examines the ethical considerations and challenges related to digital technology in higher learning institutions, with a focus on intellectual property rights, database management, and the use of digital technology in education. The literature review and bibliometric analysis reveal a growing body of research focused on these topics, indicating the increasing importance of digital ethics in higher education. The study highlights the need for higher learning institutions to take a proactive and systematic approach to addressing digital ethics, by implementing appropriate policies and procedures, providing education and training to students, faculty, and staff, and promoting a culture of responsible and ethical technology use. The study also provides recommendations for higher learning institutions to promote digital ethics, including the development and implementation of comprehensive policies and procedures, ongoing education and training, and the establishment of a culture of digital ethics.

Section 2

Green Development

    Asfand Yar, Universiti Brunei Darussalam, Brunei
    Mahani Hamdan, Universiti Brunei Darussalam, Brunei
    Muhammad Anshari, Universiti Brunei Darussalam, Brunei

The term "Green" instantly sparks green scenery of nature relating to plants, lush fields, forests, and all types of flora. This study is a requisite effort to harness green education enabled with green technological skills and concepts in the digital arena. It will cover the analysis of the necessities of green initiatives in the context of prevailing climate challenges, and eco-friendly opportunities presented with digital change, emphasize the vital role of digital literacy to meet the demands of the green skills job market, discuss the principles and methods of green education and offers proposals to integrate green skills in the curriculum, address obstacles in the integration of green education and technology with digital green innovation and recommend policy interventions and guidelines to develop green innovation education web.

Chapter 6
    Dharmbir Prasad, Asansol Engineering College, India
    Rudra Pratap Singh, Asansol Engineering College, India
    Jatin Anand, Asansol Engineering College, India
    Ranadip Roy, Sanaka Educational Trust's Group of Institutions, Durgapur, India
    Md. Irfan Khan, IAC Electricals Pvt. Ltd., Kolkata, India

An innovative initiative for sustainable Anganwadi education transformation uses renewable energy sources like wind energy to transform early childhood education. This concept provides Anganwadi centres a reliable and environmentally friendly power supply through the use of wind turbines. The use of wind energy not only lowers carbon footprints but also gives kids a practical educational chance to understand the advantages of renewable resources. By establishing a sustainable learning environment, this innovative approach hopes to improve student attendance and academic results. For all the children and communities, the authors see a cleaner, brighter future and wind power is a key component of this shift. In the study the electricity produced is 16,959,313kW/year. The extra energy produced is sold to the grid. The return on investment is 60.2% and the simple payback year is 1.53 years. The annual energy sold to the grid is 16,956,392 kWh.

Chapter 7
    Muafi Muafi, Universitas Islam Indonesia, Indonesia
    Yoga Religia, Universitas Pembangunan Nasional Veteran Yogyakarta, Indonesia
    Yussi Ramawati, Atma Jaya Catholic University of Indonesia, Indonesia

This research investigates the adoption of green e-commerce among SMEs in Indonesia through the lens of the technology-organization-environment (TOE) framework. Using a quantitative approach with 126 SME owners who have adopted green e-commerce, the study finds that technology, organization, and the environment significantly influence green e-commerce adoption. Specifically, SMEs are more likely to adopt green e-commerce when they perceive it as useful and aligned with their values, receive organizational support, and face pressure from customers and competitors. Contrary to expectations, the owner's education level, product type, and duration of operations do not significantly impact the adoption decision. The study contributes to theory by reaffirming the TOE framework's relevance in predicting green e-commerce adoption and provides practical insights for stakeholders to enhance SMEs' green business practices and digital transformation efforts.

    Balaji Gopalan, CMS Business School, Bangalore, India
    Rupesh Kumar Sinha, CMS Business School, Bangalore, India
    V. Vinoth Kumar, CMS Business School, Bangalore, India

There has been a paradigm shift in how businesses manufacture products. Inter-firm manufacturing is a relatively new paradigm. This paper examines inter-firm manufacturing and presents an analytical framework in the light of a circular economy and green supply chain management. In developed countries, industry leadership is associated with manufacturing. Industry leaders are taking measures to encourage and prioritize manufacturing and establish new economies and business ecosystems across various industry sectors. This may be in the area of Information and communication technologies, pharma industries, 3D printing, food industries, housing, energy and utilities, businesses and financial services, and media. Today, various industries are shifting towards eco-friendly and sustainable businesses that align with circular economies and green supply chain management. For that purpose, a different analysis, one that associates performance metrics with an exergy analysis of industries in alignment with a circular economy and green supply chain management is necessary.

Section 3

Digital Transformation

    Rigoberto García-Contreras, National School of Higher Education, National Autonomous
        University of Mexico, Mexico
    David Valle-Cruz, National Autonomous University of Mexico, Mexico
    Rodrigo Sandoval-Almazán, National Autonomous University of Mexico, Mexico

Artificial intelligence is growing exponentially, revolutionizing society, and approaching a virtual point called the "Singularity." This chapter explores the complex relationship between artificial intelligence, human rights, and their impact on social behavior and ethos. By proposing a framework and analyzing international cases, the authors provide examples of the challenges and opportunities arising from this interaction. Artificial intelligence presents enormous opportunities and potential benefits, but it also raises serious concerns about the risks associated with it. This research reveals the dual nature of artificial intelligence, which acts as a double-edged sword in societal impact. Like any emerging and exponential technology, it takes time and conscious thought to understand and manage the potential impact of artificial intelligence on society and human rights. This chapter highlights the need for an informed approach to the implementation of artificial intelligence to ensure the protection of human rights while harnessing the potential of artificial intelligence for social progress.

Zuraihan Masri, Universiti Brunei Darussalam, Brunei
Mohammad Nabil Almunawar, Universiti Brunei Darussalam, Brunei
Muhammad Anshari, Universiti Brunei Darussalam, Brunei
Fairul Rizal Rashid, Universiti Brunei Darussalam, Brunei

The massive development of digital technology accelerated the pace of disruption in almost every industry, creating immense ambiguity and continuing to accelerate uncertainty in the business environment. The essentiality for an organization to adapt to rapid digital transformation led businesses to remain competitive and relevant in the industry. With the rise of the pandemic Covid 19, creating more challenges for organizations in the effort to improve digital maturity. This study focuses on digital transformation and its impact on an organization's performance while narrowing down the research to the telecommunication industry in the Brunei Darussalam context. The contribution of this study is expected to fill the gap in the literature regarding antecedents of a successful digital transformation.

Ahmad Huzaimi Johari, Universiti Brunei Darussalam, Brunei
Annie Dayani Ahad, Universiti Brunei Darussalam, Brunei
Muhammad Anshari, Universiti Brunei Darussalam, Brunei

The COVID-19 pandemic has triggered a significant surge in online shopping across various contexts, influencing the buying behaviors of consumers, particularly those engaged in online and social media-based transactions. This study aims to investigate the impact of gender disparities, customer location, sustainable development goals (SDG) alignment, and digital transformation on consumers' online buying behaviors. The research adopts qualitative methods, employing online interviews to collect primary data. The findings highlight that contemporary consumers exhibit the ability to assess choices and make informed decisions. Notably, factors influencing online shopping behavior encompass influences from close social circles, predominantly family members and friends, as well as virtual social constructs like social network friends. The study emphasizes the crucial role of SDGs and digital transformation in shaping and understanding these evolving consumer behaviors.

Section 4

Business, Management, and Digital Transformation

    Naizatul Hakimah Abdullmalek, Universiti Brunei Darussalam, Brunei
    Thuraya Farhana Said, Universiti Brunei Darussalam, Brunei
    Muhammad Anshari, Universiti Brunei Darussalam, Brunei

The study is a case-based analysis of a merging Telco organisation that created uncertainties for many stakeholders. A qualitative research method was deployed in order to examine whether knowledge sharing could be used to ease and reduce uncertainties in facilitation in ensuring employee readiness, where objectives such as finding out factors to influence communication in ensuring change readiness and finding out the role of knowledge sharing as a potential platform for effective communication in times of organisational change and uncertainties were examined. In addition, the study also employed bibliographic analysis of the published articles on knowledge transfer and organisational change to track the trends of the topic and determine its recency. This paper is expected to give insights on the role of knowledge sharing and its significance in the context of organisational change especially from developing country's perspective.

    Dwi Kartikasari, Universiti Brunei Darussalam, Brunei

This study aims to reveal how well two PLS-SEM statistical technologies—WarpPLS and SmartPLS—work for testing attitude theory with different types of relationships: linear and nonlinear. Non-probability sampling collects 786 internet customers from the digital marketplace. In the linear relationships between the theory of reasoned action baseline (attitudes and subjective norms) and online buying intention, SmartPLS and WarpPLS deliver similar loadings, reliability, validity, and path coefficients. WarpPLS is more effective in validating the nonlinear relationship of consumer ethnocentrism to attitudes toward imports, but SmartPLS is more comprehensive in providing robustness and advanced features. Teachers should educate students on the importance of testing linearity in the required preliminary checks. This step helps them choose the suitable software algorithm and get more accurate results and reports. This study is limited to the default parameter and standard application; future works can explore more advanced settings and complex path models.

    Muhammad Azmi Sait, Universiti Brunei Darussalam, Brunei
    Muhammad Anshari, Universiti Brunei Darussalam, Brunei
    Mohammad Nabil Almunawar, Universiti Brunei Darussalam, Brunei
    Masairol Masri, Universiti Brunei Darussalam, Brunei

This study examines demographic factors and personal innovativeness to information technologies (PIIT) among Brunei Darussalam's digital wallet users. Analyzing data from 181 respondents, it explores the influence of gender, age, and adopter category on PIIT levels. Results show no significant correlation between gender and PIIT levels, challenging gender-based assumptions. Age groups also exhibit no significant association with PIIT levels, contrary to expectations. However, the adopter category demonstrates a significant relationship with PIIT levels, highlighting the impact of adoption behavior. Tailored marketing, product design, and policy interventions are needed for digital inclusion. Findings of this study have implications for academia, industry, and policymaking, providing insights into technology adoption behaviors in the digital wallet domain.

Preface

INTRODUCTION

New and emerging digital technologies are transforming people's lives and businesses. Governments and companies have to develop innovative strategies and make key decisions for the successful transition for the digital age. New sets of skills (digital, circular, green) will be crucial for the new labour market and for strengthening competitiveness of companies and countries. These new technologies will help to tackle climate change challenges and achieve climate-neutral economies too (Almunawar *et al.,* 2023; European Commission, 2024a; Ordóñez *et al.,* 2023).

In the European Union, the Digital Education Action Plan (2021-2027) has two main priorities: Priority 1: Fostering the development of a high-performing digital education ecosystem; and Priority 2: Enhancing digital skills and competences for the digital transformation. This plan supports the European Skills Agenda, the "2030 Digital Compass: the European way for the Digital Decade" and the European Social Pillar Action Plan (European Commission, 2024b).

It is important to explore how governments and businesses use digital technologies to provide workers and citizens with the new skills required to success in the digital and green transition.

CONTENTS OF THE BOOK

The book offers a unique opportunity for international dialogue about approaches, methodologies, and tools for the transformation of education in the digital era, with special focus on green education, circular skills, digital skills and sustainability. It promotes the visibility of new digital technologies for education, create an international scientific platform for active collaboration on digital and green education and accelerate innovation in education technologies. Additionally, the book examines the advances and best practices in new and emerging information technologies for accessible and inclusive education. Finally, the book explores ways of putting circular visions into effect in higher education institutions and trigger the transformation of these institutions to adapt to the digital market. It examines the use of circular visions in cities, countries, and regions too.

The book discusses initiatives, policies and cases to support technology-use and digital competence development in education systems around the world. It stimulates debate about experiences and challenges at national/regional/international level and cover different stakeholders: academic staff, researchers, students, administrators, policymakers, procurement professionals, local and regional authorities and more.

The book explores how green education and advanced information technologies can be applied in the education sector to create more climate neutral and green economies and societies. It analyses how to apply circular visions in cities, countries, and regions. The chapters of the book address how green education and digital creation can boost the creation of new jobs, build circular economies and societies, and increase the inclusiveness of citizens. It is important to design and implement new skills (circular o green skills) to move towards the circular economy.

Thanks to its innovative topics (education, circular economy, circular skills, digital tools, green economy) and approaches, geographical focus (international focus, with special attention to Asian region) and methodologies (empirical studies, case studies and comparative studies), the book will be a reference for students (undergraduate and postgraduate), academics, business leaders, policymakers, circular economy experts and green economy experts.

The book, structured in 4 sections, has a collection of 14 chapters addressing key topics for digital transformation: artificial intelligence, digital ethics, digital innovation, digital transformation, education, green e-commerce, green education, green energy, green skills, knowledge management, SDGs, sustainable development and more.

Next, we present a summary of contents for each section.

Section I: Sustainability and Sustainable Development

Chapter 1, titled "Charting the Path to Global Prosperity: Unveiling the Impact and Promise of Sustainable Development" (by K. Balaji) states that "the Sustainable Development Goals (SDGs), which provide a broad framework for addressing mankind's interconnected concerns, are critical in guiding global efforts towards attaining sustainable growth. This book chapter delves into the broad depth of the Sustainable Development Goals (SDGs) along with how these could potentially utilise to dramatically alter the direction of humanity and build an economically equitable and wealthy society. The current research investigates the historical evolution, background, significance, key consequences via case studies and multiple implications about the Sustainable Development Goals (SDGs) to address pressing global concerns such as reducing poverty, safeguarding the environment, equity in society, and growth in the economy. The chapter delves explores the prospects and challenges of achieving the SDGs while advocating towards a more integrated, holistic approach to global development for a more prosperous and sustainable future. It highlights the importance of teamwork and inclusive practices".

Chapter 2 titled "Application in Merging Green Practices with Digital Innovation to Create Sustainable Synergy" (by Ariq Idris Annaufal, April Lia Dina Mariyana and Muafi Muafi) affirms that "in the contemporary landscape of rapid technological advancement and escalating environmental concerns, the imperative to harmonize digital innovation with sustainable practices has become paramount. This article delves into the realm of merging green practices with digital innovation to cultivate sustainable synergy, elucidating how this integration holds the potential to revolutionize industries, mitigate environmental degradation, and propel us towards a more resilient future. Through interdisciplinary collaboration and longitudinal studies, this research aims to assess the long-term impacts and effectiveness of green practices and digital innovation initiatives on sustainability outcomes. By exploring the myriad applications of merging green practices with digital innovation across various domains, from renewable energy and waste management to sustainable urban development and conservation efforts, this article seeks to inspire stakeholders to embrace this transformative approach and collaborate towards building a more sustainable and prosperous future".

Chapter 3, titled "Renewable Energy for Agriculture Sustainability Conservations: A Step towards Green Revolution" (by Dharmbir Prasad, Rudra Pratap Singh, Jatin Anand, Ranadip Roy and Md. Irfan Khan) discusses the results of a study on "sustainable agriculture practices in Simdega District, India, emphasizing the critical role of agriculture using the renewable energy. With a focus on long-term environmental, social and economic viability, the study employs a multidisciplinary approach, integrating field surveys, policy analysis and literature review. In the agriculture industry, including renewable energy solutions may improve resource efficiency, lower greenhouse gas emissions and foster climate resilience. Additionally, effective post-harvest processing technology like solar dryers and biomass-based systems may be powered by renewable energy reducing food loss and enhancing the quality and marketability of agricultural products. Increased production, water conservation and soil health may all be achieved by using sustainable agricultural practices including organic farming, precision agriculture and agro-forestry".

Chapter 4 titled "Digital Ethics in Higher Learning Institutions: Challenges and Fostering Responsible Practices" (by Aliasan Aliasan, Kusnadi Kusnadi, Muzaiyanah Muzaiyanah and Abdur Razzaq) presents a study that explores "the ethical considerations and challenges related to digital technology in higher learning institutions, with a focus on intellectual property rights, database management, and the use of digital technology in education. The literature review and bibliometric analysis reveal a growing body of research focused on these topics, indicating the increasing importance of digital ethics in higher education. The study highlights the need for higher learning institutions to take a proactive and systematic approach to addressing digital ethics, by implementing appropriate policies and procedures, providing education and training to students, faculty, and staff, and promoting a culture of responsible and ethical technology use. The study also provides recommendations for higher learning institutions to promote digital ethics, including the development and implementation of comprehensive policies and procedures, ongoing education and training, and the establishment of a culture of digital ethics".

Section II: Green Development

Chapter 5 titled "Green Education to Promote Green Technological Skills" (by Muhammad Asfand yar, Mahani Hamdan and Muhammad Anshari) states that "the term 'Green' instantly sparks green scenery of nature relates to plants, lush fields, forests, and all types of flora. This study is a requisite effort to harness green education enabled with green technological skills and concepts in the digital arena. It will cover the analysis of the necessities of green initiatives in the context of prevailing climate challenges, and eco-friendly opportunities presented with digital change, emphasize the vital role of digital literacy to meet the demands of the green skills job market, discuss the principles and methods of green education and offers proposals to integrate green skills in the curriculum, address obstacles in the integration of green education and technology with digital green innovation and recommend policy interventions and guidelines to develop green innovation education web".

Chapter 6 titled "Green Energy Supply to Pre-school Cluster for Sustainable Anganwadi Educational Transformation" (by Dharmbir Prasad, Rudra Pratap Singh, Jatin Anand, Ranadip Roy and Md. Irfan Khan) affirms that "an innovative initiative for sustainable Anganwadi education transformation uses renewable energy sources like wind energy to transform early childhood education. This concept provides Anganwadi centres a reliable and environmental friendly power supply through the use of wind turbines. The use of wind energy not only lowers carbon footprints but also gives kids a practical educational chance to understand the advantages of renewable resources. By establishing a sustainable learning environment, this innovative approach hopes to improve student attendance and academic results. For all the children and communities, we see a cleaner, brighter future and wind power is a key component of this shift. In the study the electricity produced is 16,959,313kW/year. The extra energy produced is sold to the grid. The return on investment is 60.2% and the simple payback year is 1.53 year. The annual energy sold to the grid is 16,956,392 kWh".

Chapter 7 titled "Identification of Green E-Commerce Adoption among SMEs Based on the TOE Framework with Demographics as Control Variables: Identification of Green E-Commerce Adoption among SMEs Based on the TOE Framework" (by Muafi Muafi, Yoga Religia and Yussi Ramawati) presents the results of a research that explores "the adoption of green e-commerce among SMEs in Indonesia through the lens of the TOE (Technology-Organization-Environment) framework. Using a quantitative approach with 126 SME owners who have adopted green e-commerce, the study finds that technology, organization, and the environment significantly influence green e-commerce adoption. Specifically, SMEs are more likely to adopt green e-commerce when they perceive it as useful and aligned with their values, receive organizational support, and face pressure from customers and competitors. Contrary to expectations, the owner's education level, product type, and duration of operations do not significantly impact the adoption decision. The study contributes to theory by reaffirming the TOE framework's relevance in predicting green e-commerce adoption and provides practical insights for stakeholders to enhance SMEs' green business practices and digital transformation efforts".

Chapter 8 titled "Analyzing Inter-firm Manufacturing for a Circular Economy and Green Supply Chain Management" (by Balaji Gopalan, Rupesh Sinha and Vinoth V) states that "there has been a paradigm shift in how businesses manufacture products. Inter-firm manufacturing is a relatively new paradigm. This paper examines inter-firm manufacturing and presents an analytical framework in the light of a circular economy and green supply chain management. In developed countries, industry leadership is associated with manufacturing. Industry leaders are taking measures to encourage and prioritize manufacturing and establish new economies and business ecosystems across various industry sectors. This may be in the area of Information and communication technologies, pharma industries, 3D printing, food industries, housing, energy and utilities, businesses and financial services, and media. Today, various industries are shifting towards eco-friendly and sustainable businesses that align with circular economies and green supply chain management. For that purpose, a different analysis, one that associates performance metrics with an exergy analysis of industries in alignment with a circular economy and green supply chain management is necessary".

Section III: Digital Transformation

Chapter 9 "The Singularity is near?: Unraveling Artificial Intelligence, Ethos, and Human Rights in the Era of Emerging Digital Transform" (by Rigoberto Garcia-Contreras, David Valle-Cruz and Rodrigo Sandoval-Almazán) observes that "artificial intelligence is growing exponentially, revolutionizing society, and approaching a virtual point called the "Singularity." This paper explores the complex relationship between artificial intelligence, human rights, and their impact on social behavior and ethos. By proposing a framework and analyzing international cases, we provide examples of the challenges and opportunities arising from this interaction. Artificial intelligence presents enormous opportunities and potential benefits, but it also raises serious concerns about the risks associated with it. This research reveals the dual nature of artificial intelligence, which acts as a double-edged sword in societal impact. Like any emerging and exponential technology, it takes time and conscious thought to understand and manage the potential impact of artificial intelligence on society and human rights. This paper highlights the need for an informed approach to the implementation of artificial intelligence to ensure the protection of human rights while harnessing the potential of artificial intelligence for social progress".

Chapter 10 "Digital Transformation on Organizational Performance: A Literature Review Analysis" (by Zuraihan Masri, Mohammad Almunawar, Muhammad Anshari and Fairul Rizal Rashid) states that "the massive development of digital technology accelerated the pace of disruption in almost every industry, creating immense ambiguity and continue to accelerate uncertainty in business environment. The essentiality for an organization to adapt to rapid digital transformation led businesses to remain competitive and relevant in the industry. With the rise of the pandemic Covid 19, creating more challenges for organizations in the effort to improve digital maturity. This study focuses on digital transformation and its impact on an organization's performance while narrowing down the research to the telecommunication industry in the Brunei Darussalam context. The contribution of this study is expected to fill the gap in the literature regarding antecedents of a successful digital transformation".

Chapter 11 "Examining the Impact of Gender Differences, Sustainable Urbanism, and Digital Transformation on Online Consumer Buying Behavior: A Perspective Towards SDG Alignment" (by Ahmad Johari, Annie Dayani Ahad and Muhammad Anshari) affirms that "the COVID-19 pandemic has triggered a significant surge in online shopping across various contexts, influencing the buying behaviors of consumers, particularly those engaged in online and social media-based transactions. This study aims to investigate the impact of gender disparities, customer location, Sustainable Development Goals (SDG) alignment, and digital transformation on consumers' online buying behaviors. The research adopts qualitative methods, employing online interviews to collect primary data. The findings highlight that contemporary consumers exhibit the ability to assess choices and make informed decisions. Notably, factors influencing online shopping behavior encompass influences from close social circles, predominantly family members and friends, as well as virtual social constructs like social network friends. The study emphasizes the crucial role of SDGs and digital transformation in shaping and understanding these evolving consumer behaviors".

Section IV: Business, Management and Digital Transformation

Chapter 12 titled "Organisational Change and Knowledge-Sharing Strategies in Managing Risks" (by Naizatul Hakimah Abdullmalek, Thuraya Farhana Said and Muhammad Anshari) discusses a study that "is a case-based analysis of a merging Telco organisation that created uncertainties for many stakeholders. A qualitative research method was deployed in order to examine whether knowledge sharing could be used to ease and reduce uncertainties in facilitation in ensuring employee readiness, where objectives such as finding out factors to influence communication in ensuring change readiness and finding out the role of knowledge sharing as a potential platform for effective communication in times of organisational change and uncertainties were examined. In addition, the study also employed bibliographic analysis of the published articles on knowledge transfer and organisational change to track the trends of the topic and determine its recency. This paper is expected to give insights on the role of knowledge sharing and its significance in the context of organisational change especially from developing country's perspective".

Chapter 13 titled "Comparing PLS-SEM Statistical Technologies for Educating the Importance of Linearity: Attitude Theory Validation in Digital Marketplace" (by Dwi Kartikasari) presents the results of a study that "aims to reveal how well two PLS-SEM statistical technologies—WarpPLS and SmartPLS—work for testing attitude theory with different types of relationships: linear and nonlinear.

Non-probability sampling collects 786 internet customers from the digital marketplace. In the linear relationships between the theory of reasoned action baseline (attitudes and subjective norms) and online buying intention, SmartPLS and WarpPLS deliver similar loadings, reliability, validity, and path coefficients. WarpPLS is more effective in validating the nonlinear relationship of consumer ethnocentrism to attitudes toward imports, but SmartPLS is more comprehensive in providing robustness and advanced features. Teachers should educate students on the importance of testing linearity in the required preliminary checks. This step helps them choose the suitable software algorithm and get more accurate results and reports. This study is limited to the default parameter and standard application; future works can explore more advanced settings and complex path models".

Finally, chapter 14 titled "Investigating the Impact of Demographic Factors on Personal Innovativeness in Digital Wallet Usage: An Exploratory Study" (by Muhammad Azmi Sait, Muhammad Anshari and Mohammad Almunawar, Masairol Masri) presents the results of a study that "examines demographic factors and personal innovativeness to information technologies (PIIT) among Brunei Darussalam's digital wallet users. Analyzing data from 181 respondents, it explores the influence of gender, age, and adopter category on PIIT levels. Results show no significant correlation between gender and PIIT levels, challenging gender-based assumptions. Age groups also exhibit no significant association with PIIT levels, contrary to expectations. However, adopter category demonstrates a significant relationship with PIIT levels, highlighting the impact of adoption behavior. Tailored marketing, product design, and policy interventions are needed for digital inclusion. Findings of this study have implications for academia, industry, and policymaking, providing insights into technology adoption behaviors in the digital wallet domain".

Patricia Ordóñez de Pablos
The University of Oviedo, Spain

Muhammad Anshari
Universiti of Brunei Darussalam, Brunei Darussalam

Mohammad Nabil Almunawar
Universiti of Brunei Darussalam, Brunei Darussalam

REFERENCES

Almunawar, N., Ordóñez de Pablos, P., & Anshari, M. (2023). *Digital Transformation for Business and Society: Contemporary Issues and Applications in Asia*. Routledge. doi:10.4324/9781003441298

Almunawar, N., Ordóñez de Pablos, P., & Anshari, M. (2023). *Sustainable Development and the Digital Economy: Human-centricity, Sustainability and Resilience in Asia*. Routledge. doi:10.4324/9781003388753

European Commission. (2024a), *European Climate Pact*. EC. https://climate-pact.europa.eu/priority-topics/green-skills_en

European Commission. (2024a). *Digital European Plan (2021-2027)*. EC. https://education.ec.europa.eu/focus-topics/digital-education/action-plan

Ordóñez de Pablos, P., Almunawar, N., & Anshari, M. (2023a). *Developing Skills and Competencies for Digital and Green Transitions*. IGI-Global. doi:10.4018/978-1-6684-9089-1

Ordóñez de Pablos, P., Almunawar, N., & Anshari, M. (2023b). *Perspectives on the Transition Toward Green and Climate Neutral Economies in Asia*. IGI-Global. doi:10.4018/978-1-6684-8613-9

Section 1
Sustainability and Sustainable Development

Chapter 1
Charting the Path to Global Prosperity:
Unveiling the Impact and Promise of Sustainable Development

K. Balaji

iD https://orcid.org/0000-0002-3065-3294

Presidency University, Banglore, India

ABSTRACT

The sustainable development goals (SDGs), which provide a broad framework for addressing mankind's interconnected concerns, are critical in guiding global efforts towards attaining sustainable growth. This book chapter delves into the broad depth of the sustainable development goals (SDGs) along with how these could dramatically alter the direction of humanity and build an economically equitable and wealthy society. The current research investigates the historical evolution, background, significance, key consequences via case studies, and multiple implications about the sustainable development goals (SDGs) to address pressing global concerns such as reducing poverty, safeguarding the environment, equity in society, and growth in the economy. The chapter explores the prospects and challenges of achieving the SDGs while advocating towards a more integrated, holistic approach to global development for a more prosperous and sustainable future. It highlights the importance of teamwork and inclusive practices.

INTRODUCTION

The Sustainable Development Goals (SDGs) constitute an internationally endorsed framework containing socioeconomic as well as ecological elements which seeks to tackle humanity's complex and interconnected challenges. The United Nations adopted the SDGs as part of the 2030 Plan on Sustainability in September 2015. It serves as a call to action to every nation, both developed and developing, in order to increase wealth while protecting the environment (Pham-Troffer M et al., 2020). The Sustainable Development Goals (SDGs) are a collection of ambitious goals including eliminating poverty, guaran-

DOI: 10.4018/979-8-3693-2865-1.ch001

teeing good health and happiness, supporting equitable and accessible education, accomplishing gender equality, speeding up growth in the economy, supporting sustainable cities and communities, maintaining biodiversity, combating climate change, and building peace and justice (O'Byrne D, et al., 2015).

BACKGROUND AND HISTORY OF THE SDGs

The Sustainable Development Goals (SDGs) constitute a comprehensive and ambitious framework for global development, building on prior worldwide agreements and demonstrating a shared commitment to solving critical global concerns.

As we reach the halfway mark of the 2030 Agenda for Sustainable Development and conduct the initial Global Stocktake under the Paris Agreement, which focuses on implementing SDG 13 concerning climate action, we find that only 15% of the SDG targets are being met. Disappointingly, none of the targets within SDG 13 show significant progress, and global emissions continue to rise steadily (UN DESA &UNFCCCA,2024).

The global community is confronting a crisis in sustainable development. The 2024 Financing for Sustainable Development Report underscores that financing challenges lie at the core of this crisis, threatening the achievement of the Sustainable Development Goals (SDGs) and efforts to address climate change (United Nations General Assembly, 2023). While there remains a window of opportunity to salvage the SDGs and avert a climate disaster, it is rapidly narrowing.

The report highlights significant and growing financing gaps for sustainable development. Estimates from international organizations and other sources converge around the need for an additional $4 trillion in investment annually for developing countries. This represents a more than 50% increase over pre-pandemic estimates (DESA &FSDO,2024). The formulation and acceptance of the SDGs represent a concerted global effort to encourage environmental sustainability reduce poverty, and create equitable development around the world (Pradhan P et al,2017). Blockchain-based smart contracts represent a cutting-edge development in both finance and technology. They constitute autonomous agreements that carry out their obligations without the assistance of intermediaries (K. Balaji,2024)

In Rio de Janeiro, the United Nations Conference on Environment and Development, often known as the Earth Summit, was held (Rio Earth Summit,1992). It resulted in Agenda 21, a comprehensive plan of action to achieve sustainable development on a global, national, and local scale The Millennium Development Goals (MDGs) were developed in 2000 as a collection of eight global objectives largely focusing on reducing poverty, education, gender equality, child mortality, maternal health, avoiding illness, sustainability of the environment, and worldwide collaborations (Purvis B. D,2019). These targets, which were set by world leaders, led global development activities from 2000 to 2015.The United Nations Conference on Sustainable Development, often known as Rio+20, was held in Rio de Janeiro to evaluate progress since the 1992 Earth Summit. The purpose of the conference was to reaffirm political commitment to sustainable development and to examine the global sustainable development agenda. Rio+20 provided the framework for drafting a new set of goals to replace the Millennium Development Goals. To propose a proposal for the SDGs, the Open Working Group on Sustainable Development Goals was formed (Rodríguez García AM, et al.,2019). The proposal comprised seventeen objectives and 169 targets that addressed social, economic, and environmental issues.

The United Nations General Assembly officially adopted the 2030 Agenda for Sustainable Development, which includes the 17 SDGs, in September 2015. The plan of action has been agreed upon by 193 member countries, indicating a global commitment to achieve sustainable development by 2030. Nations have begun attempting to connect national policies, strategies, and budgets with the SDGs since their inception (Sachs JD et al.,2021). Globally, society is today confronted with serious problems related to the economy, society, and the environment. The UN (United Nations) approved the seventeen Sustainable Development Goals (SDGs) in 2015 to tackle various worldwide challenges in a globally cross-border level as well as achieve a more environmentally sound as well as happier future for everyone (United Nations, 2015). Every Sustainable Development Goal (SDG) comprises metrics which are employed to track the achievement of the targets (United Nations, 2017). Individual targets do not exist in isolation, instead they impact as well as related to the others (Sachs JD, 2012); every objective tackle ecological emotional, social, as well as economic issues (Anita N,2011)). It is crucial to understand the way individuals around this globe see, embrace, as well as assess the Sustainable Development Goals (SDGs). In this regard, various polls were undertaken during the past few years, yielding different outcomes. Although worldwide recognition regarding the Sustainable Development Goals has risen in comparison with their earlier version, the Millennium Development Targets (Kabeer N, 2016), 63% of those surveyed from a study of 28 European nations indicated they were unaware about these goals. Around the world, 50% of individuals have heard of the Sustainable Development Goals, or SDGs (Chatterjee S,2015); yet just 1% were extremely knowledgeable regarding the SDGs (Rakesh Kumar Maurya,2015). Additionally, there are also regional variances in the evaluation of one's own objectives.

Combating climate change, outstanding health and happiness along with excellent education are viewed as especially essential universally (Schober P, et al., 2018). According to another survey, the most significant Sustainable Development Goals are 'zero hunger,' 'clean water and sanitation,' and 'no poverty' (Bhattacharya S, et al., 2023).

The younger generation, in specific, were more probable to be aware of the Sustainable Development Goals and high-quality education is very essential to individuals (United N,2014). Generally, individuals all across the globe are enthusiastic regarding the Sustainable Development Goals' content (Hanson et al., 2023). The educational system plays a critical role in promoting consciousness regarding the Sustainable Development Goals as well as imparting abilities and principles which contribute to more sustainable conduct. As a result, the United Nations Educational, Scientific, and Cultural Organisation (UNESCO) has created instructional goals towards the Sustainable Development Goals (SDGs) in order to assist both educators and pupils (UNESCO, 2017). Higher academic institutions are particularly essential in this context because they develop the coming generations of individuals whom are going to make an important effect on the sustainability of the world (Celine Dorathy MB, 2011). Universities, via teaching as well as impact significantly support the accomplishment of a wide variety goals SDGs. Additionally, there has been a significant expansion in sustainability curricula in institutions in the past few years, particularly an emphasis on the views of students (Rodrguez-Garca et al., 2019); yet, there is significant variation amongst programmes (O'Byrne et al., 2015). Although the current boom in environmentalism in educational institutions, student exhibit a widespread lack of understanding of the Sustainable Development Goals (Zamora-Polo et al., 2019). Higher education institutions, in particular, bear an important accountability in shaping generations to come (Scoones I.1999), individuals (Burda Michael, Wyplosz Charles, 2009), experts (Christen Marius et al., 2022), as well as philosophers within different fields of study (Diemer Arnaud, 2019).

In addition to educating the coming generations of individuals who is most certainly essential aspect, institutions contribute significantly to accomplishing the Sustainable Development Goals via investigations, public involvement, and educational policy (Fergus Andrew &Rowney Julie,2005).

Although high-ranking positions within society may be attained without a university education, educational institutions offer expertise and technical abilities that considerably boost an individual's probability of attaining a such a socially pertinent position (Guan T et al., 2019). At this point, yet, there seems to be a dearth of credible global studies which investigates the perspectives of both natural and environmental sciences learners about the different the Sustainable Development Goals The present investigation aims to bridge the worldwide gap in research by examining the perspectives of environmental students from various nations on the SDGs. The goal is to establish how significant the Sustainable Development Goals are important to pupils across every nation.

PURPOSE OF THE CHAPTER

The purpose of this chapter is

i.   To comprehensively analyse the significance, impacts, and possibilities of the Sustainable Development Goals (SDGs).
ii. To explain whether the SDGs have influenced worldwide growth through case studies, quantitative data, and examples of effective programmes aligned with these goals.
iii. To provide stakeholders, policymakers, corporations, non-governmental organisations, and individuals with recommendations on how they may assist achieve the SDGs.

RESEARCH METHODOLOGY

The research methodology for the review book chapter "Charting the Path to Global Prosperity: Unveiling the Impact and Promise of Sustainable Development" involves a systematic literature review approach. Ethical considerations will be upheld throughout the review process, with a focus on transparency and rigor in data selection and analysis. The resulting synthesis will provide valuable insights into the current state, challenges, and opportunities in advancing sustainable development goals and promoting global prosperity.

Focus of the Chapter

Different Approaches in Defining Sustainable Development

Sustainable development is frequently depicted in various perspectives (directives, regions, as well as sectors). Specific component descriptions as well as connections between them, on the other hand, vary among authors. Further components of sustainable development, including organisational issues, a future-oriented viewpoints, societal requirements, society, or morals, may be separated as independent elements as well as incorporated into a few of those three primary elements (Inglehart R., 1995).

According to (Jabareen's, 2008, pp. 179) comprehensive assessment of the available research on this aspect of sustainable development, the terms used for the description of the term are ambiguous. Additionally, there is no consensus regarding what ought to be ecological or the means to make sustainable development a reality. The identical situation is true regarding the ecological base, that tends to be a nebulous term that covers the natural world needed to sustain life as well as financial transactions (which affects the planet), in addition to a greater perspective on daily life (International Monetary Fund, 2021).

Considering a long-term developmental standpoint to consideration is frequent yet not organised, despite the fact that the concept is widely considered as an essential component of sustainability (the requirements of current as well as future generations). In the end, two elements ought to be emphasised which are less usually addressed in contemporary literary works: moral and cultural considerations (Kaiser HF,1960).To summarise, the philosophy of sustainable development often appears in the context of a variety of fundamental and further elements which aren't always suitable with one another; they were tend to not be readily apparent; they ought to are a variable in terms and occasionally vary significantly according to the contributor's direction. Yet it may be said that there is some agreement upon the three fundamental concurrent aspects of sustainable growth: social, economic, and ecological, which are now supplemented with three more aspects addressing requirements, permanent vision, including organisational problems.

linkages across all of the fundamental elements of sustainability are commonly regarded as significant; nevertheless, the manner of assessment of those linkages remained uncertain (Kioupi V & Voulvoulis N, 2020). The significance of one's own qualities and multiple approaches to sustainable growth are best conveyed visually in the Figure 1.

Figure 1. Ways of presenting the basic three dimensions of SD and their importance in mutual relations
Source: [Joumard 2011a, p. 60]

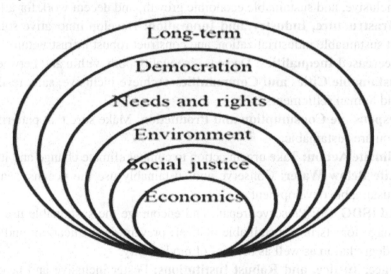

The above figure 1 tailored to reflect the sort of interplay across every dimension, as well as their order of importance as well as relationships (weaker, stronger, or systemic). It clearly reflects the need of Sustainable Development goals to promote economic development, social justice, environment, protect need and rights of citizens, support democracy for future generations.

Goals for Sustainable Development (SDGs): The United Nations

The United Nations (UN) established 17 Sustainable Development Goals (SDGs) to address global issues and establish a more equitable and sustainable world. These goals cover a wide range of societal, economic, and ecological issues (Lampert M & Papadongonas P,2016). The following is a list of the 17 SDGs:

- **SDG 1: No Poverty:** Remove all forms of poverty worldwide.
- **(SDG 2) Zero Hunger:** Encourage sustainable agriculture, attain food security, and put an end to hunger.
- **SDG 3:** Ensuring healthy lifestyles and promoting well-being for all at all ages is about good health and well-being.
- **SDG 4: Quality Education**: Ensure inclusive and equitable quality education and encourage possibilities for lifelong learning for everyone.
- **SDG 5: Gender Equality**: Enable all women and girls and attain gender equality.
- **SDG 6: Clean Water and Sanitation**: Guarantee universal access to and sustainable management of water and sanitation.
- **SDG 7:** Ensure that everyone has access to modern, cheap, dependable, sustainable, and clean energy.
- **(SDG 8) Decent Work and Economic Growth:** Encourage full and productive employment, consistent, inclusive, and sustainable economic growth, and decent work for all.
- **(SDG 9) Infrastructure, Industry, and Innovation:** Develop innovative solutions, encourage inclusive and sustainable industrialization, and construct robust infrastructure.
- **(SDG 10) Decreased Inequalities:** Decrease inequality both within and between nations.
- **SDG 11: Sustainable Cities and Communities**: Achieve inclusive, safe, resilient, and sustainable cities and human settlements.
- **SDG 12: Responsible Consumption and Production**: Make sure that patterns of consumption and production are sustainable.
- **(SDG 13) Climate Action:** Take urgent action to combat climate change and its impacts.
- **(SDG 14) Life Below Water**: Conserve and sustainably use the oceans, seas, and marine resources for sustainable development.
- **Life on Land (SDG 15)**: Preserve, repair, and encourage the sustainable use of terrestrial ecosystems; manage forests in a sustainable manner; prevent desertification; and stop, reverse, and reverse land degradation as well as the loss of biodiversity.
- **SDG 16: Peace, Justice, and Robust Institutions:** Foster inclusive and peaceful societies for sustainable development; guarantee universal access to justice; and establish inclusive, efficient, and responsible institutions at all levels.
- **Partnerships for the Goals (SDG 17):** Reinvigorate the global partnership for sustainable development and strengthen the mechanisms of implementation.

These goals, which place a special focus on sustainable and equitable growth, aim to tackle the interconnected problems that the world encounters, such as inequalities, poverty, damage to the environment, along with the promotion of peace and prosperity for everyone.

Contribution of Global Nations Towards Achieving the Sustainable Development Goals (SDGs)

According to the UN Intergovernmental Committee of Experts, the Sustainable Development Goals (SDGs) will require "trillions of dollars per annum" in total. Though it provides a broad global estimation, this fails to demonstrate the fact that the Sustainable Development Goals were viable or the amount for achieving are going to cost for any given country (Lozano R,2006). The Organisation for Development's report examines developing nations having populations of over one million individuals, a minimum 1% of whom live in severe poverty.

The yearly expenses of meeting the 2030 Agenda for Sustainable Development goals on health, education, and poverty is estimated to be US$148 billion within nations with low revenues alone (Lozano R et al,2023). The result depends upon the respective nation's overall poverty gap—that is, the amount of money required for bringing everybody from poverty (Sustainable Development Goals Report (2023) as shown in the figure 2.

Figure 2. Contribution of global nations towards achieving the sustainable development goals (SDGs)
Source: *UN Global Sustainable Development Goals Report (2023).*

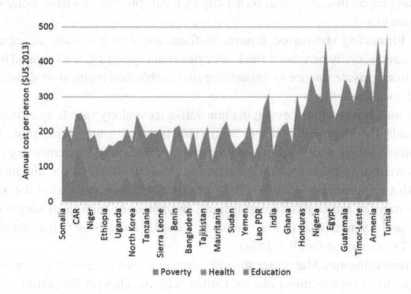

Figure 2 depicts the estimations of the UN Intergovernmental Committee of Experts. The yearly expenditure of meeting the 2030 Agenda for Sustainable Development goals for health, education, and poverty is estimated to be US$148 billion in low-income countries alone. This depends on the respective nation's general poverty gap that is, the amount of money required for bringing everybody away from poverty.

Models for Achieving Sustainable Development Goals (SDGs)

Achieving the Sustainable Development Goals (SDGs) requires a variety of methods and strategies customised to individual settings and difficulties around the globe (Nilsson M et.al (2016). Among the most successful models for promoting the Sustainable Development Goals (SDGs) around the world are:

- **Integrated Policy Frameworks:** A growing number of nations are implementing integrated policy frameworks to link national strategies to the Sustainable Development Goals These structures include inter-ministerial collaboration, participation of stakeholders, and cross-sector policy coherence to ensure that the government's actions are in line with the aims.
- **Public-Private Partnerships (PPPs):** Collaboration among governments, corporations, and non-profit organisations is critical to attaining the Sustainable Development Goals (SDGs). public-private partnerships bring together assets, experience, and creativity from several industries to carry out long-term goals like building infrastructure, educational institutions, healthcare, as well as green energy ventures.
- **Local and Community-Led Initiatives:** It is critical to strengthen the local population and community organisations. Bottom-up strategies for improvement that include involvement of communities, building capacities, as well as ownership by locals provide inclusion along with connection to local requirements.
- **Innovative Financing strategies**: Innovative financing strategies such as impact investments, green bonds, and socially beneficial funds are critical in supporting SDG-related initiatives. These approaches draw private finance to projects for sustainable development while providing financial rewards and social benefit.
- **Technology and Innovation**: Leveraging innovative technology speeds up advancement towards the Sustainable Development Goals (SDGs). This involves using digital tools for data gathering, distribution, along with tracking of progress, in addition to implementing environmentally friendly innovations in fields such as green power, the agricultural sector, and medicine.
- **South-South Cooperation**: South-South cooperation, which encourages collaboration as well as information transfer across developing nations, promotes the transfer of successful procedures, experience, and resources to tackle common obstacles as well as collaboratively achieve the Sustainable Development Goals (SDGs).
- **Global Partnerships and Multilateralism:** Fostering worldwide collaboration as well as solidarity via international organisations like the United Nations. These collaborations allow the flow of thoughts, assets, and skills in order to collaboratively tackle worldwide issues.

Importance and Relevance of the SDGs in the Context of Global Development

The Sustainable Development Goals (SDGs) are highly pertinent and essential in light of global growth for a variety of factors.

- **A Universal Agenda for Shared Prosperity:** The Sustainable Development Goals (SDGs) provide an international structure that crosses national boundaries and brings together nations, industries, businesses, and people in a collaborative effort to accomplish collective objectives. Experts talk about interconnected challenges and emphasise the importance of collaborating jointly to generate wealth which helps humanity.

- **All-encompassing and Holistic Approach:** The seventeen Sustainable Development Goals (SDGs) cover a wide range of issues, including gender equality, poverty, education, health, and climate action. This presents a holistic approach that recognises the interdependence of the social, economic, and environmental facets of sustainability.

- **Priority for Sustainable Development:** The Sustainable Development Goals (SDGs) put an important priority on sustainable development, particularly attempts to fulfil today's needs while jeopardising the capacity of coming generations to fulfil their own. They advocate for an equilibrium among advancement for humans and global health by emphasising the importance of prosperity, inclusion in society, and safeguarding the environment.

- **Handling Global concerns:** Poverty, famine, inequality, climate change, and damage to the environment were just some of the pressing worldwide problems addressed by these objectives. By providing specific goals and metrics, the Sustainable Development Goals (SDGs) drive attempts to relieve these difficulties and set the way for sustainable and equitable growth.

- **Mobilising Resources and Action:** With response to the Sustainable Development Goals governments, corporations, individuals, and civil society collectively adopt actions. These encourage the gathering of resources, investments in novel concepts, ultimately implementation.

- **Monitoring and Accountability:** One of the Sustainable Development Goals' key features is the structure it provides for assessing progress and holding stakeholders accountable. Regular disclosure, data collection, and assessment aid in the appraisal of advancement, evaluation of gaps, and transparency in the achievement of goals.

- **Policymaking and Decision Making:** The Sustainable Development Goals (SDGs) has had an effect on both domestic as well as international policies, guiding organisations and governments in their choices & setting priorities processes. They encourage the implementation of sustainable development principles with policy structures across all stages to create long-range plans for positive transformation.

- **inclusion and Leave No One Behind:** The Sustainable Development Goals (SDGs) promote inclusiveness by ensuring that improvements serve everyone, irrespective of gender, age, colour, or socioeconomic status. They put a high value on fairness, equal treatment, and providing equal accessibility to opportunities for all.

Case Studies and Examples Highlighting Successful Initiatives Aligned With Specific SDGs

1. **SDG 1 - No Poverty:** Bangladesh, Brazil, India, Kenya, and Peru have each implemented innovative poverty reduction initiatives with remarkable success. In Bangladesh, the Grameen Bank Microfinance Program, spearheaded by Muhammad Yunus, empowers impoverished individuals, particularly women, by providing small loans to kickstart small businesses, leading to improved living standards for millions. Meanwhile, Brazil's Bolsa Familia Conditional Cash Transfer Program tackles poverty and inequality head-on, offering financial aid to low-income families based on children's school attendance and healthcare utilization, resulting in significant improvements in health and education outcomes. In India, the National Rural Employment Guarantee Act (NREGA)

provides crucial support by guaranteeing 100 days of wage employment annually to rural house-holds, fostering rural development and social inclusion through infrastructure projects. Kenya's M-Pesa Mobile Money Transfer system has revolutionized financial inclusion, enabling millions, including the impoverished, to access formal financial services and participate in the economy via mobile phones, thus significantly reducing poverty in rural and underserved areas. Similarly, Peru's Juntos Conditional Cash Transfer Program has effectively targeted vulnerable populations in remote regions, reducing poverty rates and enhancing social indicators like education and healthcare access.

2. **Sustainable Development Goal (SDG) 2 - Zero Hunger**: In the pursuit of Sustainable Development Goal (SDG) 2: Zero Hunger, several impactful case studies offer insights into successful strategies for addressing food insecurity and malnutrition worldwide. In Brazil, the Zero Hunger Program (Fome Zero) implemented a range of initiatives, including school feeding programs, agricultural support for small-scale farmers, and cash transfers to vulnerable households, resulting in significant reductions in hunger and poverty rates. Similarly, Ethiopia's Productive Safety Net Program (PSNP) has provided food and cash transfers to millions of chronically food-insecure households while simultaneously investing in community assets and resilience-building activities, leading to improved food security and livelihoods. India's National Food Security Act guarantees subsidized food grains to approximately two-thirds of the population, ensuring access to essential nutrition for millions of marginalized individuals. In Rwanda, the Girinka Program has distributed dairy cows to low-income households, enhancing nutrition and income generation opportunities, while also promoting social cohesion and environmental sustainability. Lastly, the United Nations World Food Programme's (WFP) initiatives, such as school feeding programs and food assistance in humanitarian crises, have played a crucial role in alleviating hunger and malnutrition globally.

3. **SDG 3 - Good Health and Well-being:** Gavi, the Vaccine Alliance, is a notable effort trying to advance SDG 3—Good Healthcare and Well-being—by increasing the availability of immunisation in nations with low incomes, thus drastically lowering infant mortality rates. Gavi is critical in supplying vaccines and strengthening worldwide medical systems. Gavi has effectively provided universal distribution of vaccines that save lives to infants in some of the globe's disadvantaged areas by cooperating with various groups such as governments, health organisations, and funders. Gavi makes sure that vaccines reach those who need them the most through smart alliances and creative funding structures, achieving significant achievements in reducing infectious diseases and child death rates globally. Gavi's activities have had an enormous effect. The alliance's initiatives have succeeded in a significant rise in immunisation protection, protecting thousands of children from fatal diseases. Gavi has enhanced accessibility to key vaccines while also strengthening healthcare facilities and competencies in developing nations by strengthening systems of healthcare.

4. **Sustainable Development Goal (SDG) 4 - Quality Education:** In the pursuit of Sustainable Development Goal (SDG) 4: Quality Education, various case studies showcase effective strategies for enhancing educational access, equity, and quality worldwide. Finland's education system stands out for its emphasis on equity, teacher professionalism, and student-centred learning approaches, leading to consistently high levels of student performance and well-being. In Rwanda, the government's commitment to education reform, including investments in infrastructure, teacher training, and curriculum development, has resulted in significant improvements in enrolment rates and learning outcomes. Furthermore, the Escuela Nueva model in Colombia has transformed education by promoting active learning, community involvement, and student-centred pedagogies, particularly

in rural areas, leading to improved academic achievement and social inclusion. In Pakistan, the Teach For All initiative recruits and trains recent graduates to teach in underserved communities, addressing educational inequities and empowering both students and teachers. Lastly, the PISA-D project in Vietnam has leveraged technology and innovative teaching methods to enhance students' digital literacy skills, preparing them for success in the digital age. These case studies illustrate diverse approaches to promoting quality education, emphasizing the importance of equitable access, teacher capacity building, community engagement, and innovation in achieving SDG 4 and ensuring inclusive and equitable education for all.

5. **Sustainable Development Goal (SDG) 5 - Gender Equality:** In the context of Sustainable Development Goal (SDG) 5: Gender Equality, several compelling case studies highlight efforts to address gender disparities and promote women's empowerment globally. Iceland's pioneering gender equality policies, including parental leave provisions and quotas for corporate boards, have significantly narrowed the gender gap in political representation and economic participation, setting a global standard for gender equality. In Rwanda, post-genocide reforms prioritized women's inclusion in decision-making processes, resulting in the world's highest percentage of female parliamentarians and notable advancements in women's rights and opportunities. The Self-Employed Women's Association (SEWA) in India has empowered millions of informal sector women workers through collective organizing, access to financial services, and skill development, fostering economic independence and social empowerment. Additionally, the HeForShe campaign, initiated by UN Women, engages men and boys as allies in the fight for gender equality, promoting transformative gender norms and behaviours worldwide. Finally, the Malala Fund's advocacy for girls' education, particularly in regions affected by conflict and poverty, has catalysed investments in girls' schooling and activism, amplifying voices for gender equality and social change. These case studies underscore the multifaceted nature of gender equality efforts, emphasizing the importance of policy reform, grassroots mobilization, cross-sectoral collaboration, and global advocacy in advancing SDG 5 and creating a more inclusive and equitable world for all genders.

6. **SDG 6 - Clean Water and Sanitation:** Water.org, the world's a charitable organisation, exhibits SDG 6—Clean Water and Sanitation initiatives through concentrating on offering healthy water as well as sanitation services in impoverished nations. The group's programmes strengthen people by easing access to cheap funding for water and sanitation remedies, with the goal of addressing the widespread issue of lacking access to clean water and proper sanitation services. Water.org has allowed people in need to receive micro financing enabling the construction of water and sanitation infrastructure via creative ways of financing such as Water Credit, supporting permanent remedies to water shortages and inadequate hygiene.

7. **Sustainable Development Goal (SDG) 7 - Ensure access to affordable, reliable, sustainable, and modern energy:** In pursuit of Sustainable Development Goal (SDG) 7: Ensure access to affordable, reliable, sustainable, and modern energy for all, numerous case studies demonstrate innovative approaches to expanding energy access while advancing sustainability and affordability. The introduction of off-grid solar solutions in rural areas of Sub-Saharan Africa, such as through programs like Lighting Africa, has empowered millions of households with access to clean and sustainable energy, enhancing livelihoods, health outcomes, and educational opportunities. In India, the government's ambitious renewable energy targets and policies, including the Jawaharlal Nehru National Solar Mission and the Ujwal DISCOM Assurance Yojana, have accelerated the adoption of solar and wind power, driving down costs and reducing dependence on fossil fuels. Similarly,

Costa Rica's commitment to renewable energy, supported by investments in hydropower, wind, and geothermal resources, has enabled the country to achieve nearly 100% renewable electricity generation, demonstrating the feasibility of a transition to clean energy at a national scale. Meanwhile, the introduction of innovative financing mechanisms, such as green bonds and impact investment funds, has mobilized capital for renewable energy projects in emerging markets, facilitating their deployment and scalability.

8. **Sustainable Development Goal (SDG) 8- Decent Work and Economic Growth:** In the pursuit of Sustainable Development Goal (SDG) 8: Decent Work and Economic Growth, a multitude of case studies exemplify initiatives aimed at fostering inclusive and sustainable economic development while promoting decent employment opportunities for all. Germany's dual vocational training system stands as a model for providing high-quality skills training and apprenticeships, effectively bridging the gap between education and employment and nurturing a skilled workforce crucial for economic growth. Meanwhile, in Bangladesh, the Ready-Made Garments (RMG) industry has been pivotal in providing employment opportunities, particularly for women from rural areas, contributing significantly to the country's economic growth and poverty reduction efforts. In the technology sector, initiatives such as the Silicon Savannah in Kenya have catalysed innovation and entrepreneurship, creating job opportunities and driving economic diversification. Furthermore, social enterprises like Grameen Bank in Bangladesh and BRAC in multiple countries have demonstrated the potential of microfinance and social entrepreneurship in empowering marginalized communities, fostering economic resilience, and promoting sustainable livelihoods.

9. **Sustainable Development Goal (SDG) 9- Infrastructure, Industry, and Innovation**: In the realm of Sustainable Development Goal (SDG) 9: Infrastructure, Industry, and Innovation, a multitude of case studies exemplify transformative initiatives aimed at fostering inclusive and sustainable industrialization, promoting innovation, and enhancing infrastructure development worldwide. China's Belt and Road Initiative (BRI) stands out as one of the largest infrastructure development projects in history, facilitating connectivity and economic cooperation across Asia, Africa, and Europe through investments in transportation, energy, and telecommunications infrastructure. Meanwhile, the Green Climate Fund's support for renewable energy projects in developing countries, such as the Solar Home System program in Bangladesh, has not only expanded access to clean energy but also fostered local entrepreneurship and economic growth. In the realm of innovation, initiatives like Silicon Valley in the United States and Silicon Savannah in Kenya have become global hubs for technological innovation and entrepreneurship, driving economic diversification and job creation. Furthermore, the Fourth Industrial Revolution technologies, including artificial intelligence, blockchain, and the Internet of Things, hold promise for revolutionizing industries and addressing pressing global challenges, as demonstrated by initiatives like Estonia's e-Residency program and Rwanda's drone delivery system for medical supplies. Additionally, public-private partnerships, such as the Global Infrastructure Facility (GIF) and the World Bank's Private Sector Window, have mobilized investments for infrastructure development projects in emerging economies, bridging financing gaps and facilitating sustainable development. Moreover, initiatives aimed at enhancing digital connectivity, such as Google's Loon project and Facebook's Aquila initiative, have expanded internet access to remote and underserved communities, unlocking opportunities for education, entrepreneurship, and economic empowerment.

10. **Sustainable Development Goal (SDG) 10- Reduced Inequalities:** In the pursuit of Sustainable Development Goal (SDG) 10: Reduced Inequalities, various case studies showcase innovative

strategies and transformative initiatives targeting disparities within and among nations. The Nordic model, seen in countries like Sweden and Denmark, emphasizes progressive taxation and robust social safety nets, leading to lower income inequality and improved social mobility. Bhutan's Gross National Happiness Index prioritizes holistic well-being, guiding policies to reduce disparities and enhance social cohesion, resulting in significant progress in poverty reduction. South Africa's Black Economic Empowerment policy addresses historical injustices, albeit with ongoing challenges in achieving equity. Efforts like Landesa's work on securing land rights for women in India and Tanzania empower marginalized communities, reducing inequalities in resource access. Global partnerships like the SDGs foster collective action, emphasizing integrated approaches to address economic, social, and political dimensions of inequality, ensuring inclusive development for all.

11. **SDG 11- Sustainable Cities and Communities:** The Indian government's Smart Cities Mission incorporates an ambitious plan to build cities that are citizen-centric, environmentally friendly, as well as proficient in technology, in accordance with SDG 11—Sustainable Cities and Communities. Such transformational goal involves urban areas that prioritise effective urban planning, infrastructure development, and improving the standard of life for citizens. This initiative's initiatives aim to use technology, innovation, and strategic thinking to develop cities that aren't just smart as well as more environmentally friendly and equitable.

12. **Sustainable Development Goal (SDG) 12 - Responsible Consumption and Production:** In the context of Sustainable Development Goal (SDG) 12: Responsible Consumption and Production, various case studies highlight innovative strategies and transformative initiatives aimed at fostering sustainable consumption and production practices globally. Sweden's circular economy model stands out, employing recycling, waste-to-energy facilities, and producer responsibility schemes to drastically reduce landfill waste and resource use while generating renewable energy. Japan's "3R" initiative emphasizes waste minimization and resource efficiency through policies and public awareness campaigns, resulting in significant waste reduction and increased recycling rates. Transitioning to sustainable agriculture, as seen in Brazil's agroecology projects and Denmark's organic farming, prioritizes biodiversity and soil health while reducing food production's environmental impact. Circular fashion initiatives promote closed-loop systems and reduce textile waste, while electronics initiatives address social and environmental impacts through fair labor practices and responsible sourcing. Sharing economy platforms like Airbnb reduce resource consumption associated with ownership, fostering more sustainable consumption patterns.

13. **SDG 13 - Climate Action - Renewable Energy Initiatives**: International Solar Alliance (ISA): Initiatives like the International Solar Alliance (ISA) are examples of activities associated with the Sustainable Development Goals 13—Climate Action, with an emphasis on increasing the worldwide implementation of solar power and renewable energy sources. The International Solar Alliance (ISA), an initiative involving renewable-rich nations, intends to combat climate change by exploiting renewable energy capacity and supporting massive solar energy installation. The International Solar Alliance (ISA) seeks to expedite the worldwide shift to renewable and renewable energies by enabling collaboration amongst member nations, exchanging successful models, as well as mobilising financing and innovation. Renewable energy programmes, especially the International Solar Alliance, have had an important effect on climate action. The ISA has aided in the decrease of carbon dioxide emissions and reliance on fossil fuels through encouraging the use of solar power and green energy sources, therefore aiding to worldwide efforts to battle global warming. The alliance's lobbying and joint efforts have resulted in higher expenditures in clean

energy initiatives, advances in solar energy systems, including a proliferation many possibilities for participating nations' sustainable economic growth. The ISA is establishing the road towards a more environmentally friendly and climate-resilient tomorrow by encouraging the utilisation of renewable energy sources.

14. **Sustainable Development Goal (SDG) 14 - Life Below Water:** In the realm of Sustainable Development Goal (SDG) 14: Life Below Water, numerous case studies showcase innovative strategies and collaborative endeavours to conserve and sustainably manage marine and coastal ecosystems globally. Marine protected areas (MPAs) like the Great Barrier Reef Marine Park in Australia and the Chagas Marine Protected Area in the Indian Ocean play a vital role in preserving biodiversity and critical habitats, enhancing ecosystem resilience to climate change. Sustainable aquaculture initiatives, such as the Marine Stewardship Council's certification scheme and integrated multi-trophic aquaculture (IMTA) systems in Norway, ensure seafood production while minimizing coastal ecosystem impacts. Efforts to combat marine pollution, including global advocacy campaigns and initiatives like the Ocean Clean-up Project, raise awareness and promote waste management solutions. Global partnerships like the SDGs and CBD facilitate international cooperation in addressing marine conservation challenges, emphasizing integrated approaches for safeguarding life below water for current and future generations.

15. **Sustainable Development Goal (SDG) 15 - Life on Land:** Various case studies highlight innovative strategies and collaborative endeavours in advancing Sustainable Development Goal (SDG) 15: Life on Land, globally. Costa Rica's Payment for Ecosystem Services (PES) program incentivizes forest conservation, yielding substantial reforestation and habitat restoration. European rewilding projects, like the Nature Reserve in the Netherlands and the Knepp Estate in the UK, exhibit successful landscape restoration and species reintroduction. Global initiatives combatting illegal wildlife trade, such as the Global Tiger Initiative and Elephant Protection Initiative, mobilize international cooperation against poaching. Efforts like REDD+ and FSC certification promote sustainable forestry, balancing conservation with socio-economic needs. International frameworks like SDGs and CBD foster collective action, highlighting the imperative for integrated approaches in preserving terrestrial ecosystems and biodiversity for future generations.

16. **SDG 16 - Peace, Justice, and Strong Institutions**: United Nations peacekeeping missions contribute significantly to the achievement of SDG 16—Peace, Justice, and Strong Institutions—by working to safeguard harmony and safety in areas experiencing conflicts around the globe. Through employing peacekeeping forces, aiding solving conflicts, safeguarding individuals, and assisting in re-establishing of system law and order as well as stable leadership, these operations strive to achieve security, equity, and better government structures in vulnerable regions.

The impact of United Nations Peacekeeping Operations has proven substantial across a variety of crisis zones around the world. These operations have been critical in averting war escalated situations, safeguarding communities at risk, and fostering circumstances for a sustainable peace. UN peacekeeping deployments have helped to develop sustainable organisations, promote human rights, and ensure the maintenance of the rule of the law in unstable and conflict-prone areas by encouraging discourse, settling disagreements, and supporting in after-conflict reconstruction endeavours. Furthermore, these initiatives have served a critical role in helping the reintegration of displaced individuals as well as allowing the building of democratic and transparent governing systems. UN peacekeeping missions continues making vital contributions to establishing global peace, justice, and improved structures by their initiatives.

17. **Sustainable Development Goal (SDG) 17 - Partnerships for the Goals:** In the pursuit of Sustainable Development Goal (SDG) 17: Partnerships for the Goals, numerous case studies demonstrate the transformative potential of collaborative efforts and global partnerships in advancing sustainable development and achieving the SDGs. The Global Alliance for Vaccines and Immunization (GAVI), a public-private partnership, has played a pivotal role in increasing access to life-saving vaccines in low-income countries, resulting in significant reductions in child mortality rates and contributing to progress towards SDG 3 (Good Health and Well-being). Similarly, the Global Fund to Fight AIDS, Tuberculosis, and Malaria has mobilized resources and coordinated efforts among governments, civil society, and the private sector to combat infectious diseases, saving millions of lives and accelerating progress towards SDG 3. Moreover, the Sustainable Development Solutions Network (SDSN), a global initiative launched by the United Nations, brings together academia, policymakers, and civil society to promote research, knowledge sharing, and practical solutions for sustainable development challenges, advancing progress across multiple SDGs.

Small and Medium Industries, Entrepreneurship, and Start-Up's Contribution to Sustainable Development Goals

i.   **Grameen Bank (Bangladesh):** Grameen Bank, founded by Muhammad Yunus, provides microfinance services to empower impoverished individuals, particularly women, to start small businesses. This initiative addresses SDG 1 (No Poverty) by providing access to financial services for the unbanked population, contributing to poverty alleviation and economic empowerment. Moreover, Grameen Bank promotes SDG 5 (Gender Equality) by focusing on women's economic inclusion, as the majority of its borrowers are women. By providing opportunities for entrepreneurship and income generation, Grameen Bank also supports SDG 8 (Decent Work and Economic Growth), fostering economic growth and job creation in rural areas of Bangladesh.

ii. **Solar Sister (Africa):** Solar Sister recruits and trains women entrepreneurs to sell solar products in rural African communities, providing clean energy access and economic opportunities. This initiative directly addresses SDG 7 (Affordable and Clean Energy) by increasing access to clean and sustainable energy solutions, thereby improving living standards and reducing reliance on fossil fuels. Furthermore, Solar Sister promotes SDG 5 (Gender Equality) by empowering women as agents of change and economic development, enabling them to generate income and contribute to their households' well-being. Additionally, by creating jobs and fostering entrepreneurship, Solar Sister contributes to SDG 8 (Decent Work and Economic Growth), particularly in underserved rural areas where employment opportunities are limited.

iii. **Fairphone (Netherlands):** Fairphone produces ethically sourced and modular smartphones, promoting fair labour practices, responsible mining, and electronic waste reduction. This initiative addresses SDG 12 (Responsible Consumption and Production) by promoting sustainable consumption patterns and reducing the environmental impact of electronic products. Fairphone also contributes to SDG 8 (Decent Work and Economic Growth) by prioritizing fair wages and working conditions throughout its supply chain, thereby supporting decent livelihoods for workers. Furthermore, by advocating for transparency and accountability in the electronics industry, Fairphone promotes SDG 16 (Peace, Justice, and Strong Institutions), fostering responsible business practices and corporate accountability.

iv. **M-KOPA Solar (Kenya):** M-KOPA Solar offers pay-as-you-go solar energy systems to off-grid households, enabling access to clean and affordable energy. This initiative directly contributes to SDG 7 (Affordable and Clean Energy) by increasing energy access in underserved areas, thereby improving living standards and enhancing economic opportunities. Moreover, M-KOPA Solar supports SDG 1 (No Poverty) by providing affordable energy solutions to low-income households, reducing their reliance on expensive and polluting energy sources. Additionally, by creating jobs and stimulating local entrepreneurship in the renewable energy sector, M-KOPA Solar contributes to SDG 8 (Decent Work and Economic Growth), fostering economic development and poverty reduction.

v. **Embrace Innovations (India):** Embrace Innovations develops low-cost infant warmers for premature babies in resource-constrained settings, addressing neonatal mortality rates. This initiative directly supports SDG 3 (Good Health and Well-being) by providing life-saving medical devices to vulnerable populations, thereby reducing infant mortality rates and improving health outcomes. Furthermore, Embrace Innovations contributes to SDG 9 (Industry, Innovation, and Infrastructure) by leveraging technology and innovation to develop affordable healthcare solutions, promoting sustainable development and resilience in healthcare systems. Additionally, by addressing healthcare disparities and improving access to essential medical devices, Embrace Innovations supports SDG 10 (Reduced Inequalities), fostering inclusive and equitable healthcare for all.

Challenges and Obstacles Faced in Implementing the SDGs

Implementing the Sustainable Development Goals (SDGs) is a complicated and varied undertaking fraught with difficulties and setbacks, such as:

- **Inadequate financial resources impede SDG implementation**; many poor countries have budget limits, debt burdens, as well as competing goals. Furthermore, global economic uncertainty, including recessions, emergencies, as well as market volatility, has an impact on funding accessible to SDG projects, influencing both national and global development programme allocation.

- **Data and monitoring are major obstacles for SDG monitoring**: underdeveloped countries suffer with inadequate comprehensive data infrastructure and acquiring trustworthy information throughout metrics. The challenges faced in harmonising information across industries, regions, as well as levels of governance continue to impede the establishment of efficient surveillance systems at the national and international levels, affecting methods for reporting.

- **Policy and institutional challenges obstruct SDG integration**: many nations suffer with integrating varied government policies considering the targets' interrelated character, necessitating coordinated efforts and inter-ministerial coordination. Improving the capacity of institutions across the national and local levels is critical, but many countries face challenges such as insufficient governance systems, laws and regulations, as well as administration abilities, which impede successful execution of the Sustainable Development Goals.

- **Socioeconomic and environmental difficulties limit SDG achievement**: addressing poverty, gender, and educational inequities, as well as having access to resources, pose significant barriers to equitable growth. Furthermore, environmental issues such as climate change, pollution, deforestation, and depletion of resources impede long-term progress, necessitating new methods to balancing economic expansion and environmental protection.

- **Global partnerships and cooperation encounter challenges:** geopolitical conflicts, trade disputes, and differing national interests can stymie joint attempts by governments, international organisations, non-profit organisations, including the private sector to achieve common SDG goals. Moreover, significant stakeholders' involvement and participation are critical for the Sustainable Development Goals achievement, but problems remain in successfully incorporating marginalised populations and local communities, stifling developmental programmes' development.
- **Unexpected difficulties:** unexpected difficulties such as pandemics, disputes, as well as catastrophic events interrupt developmental goals, drawing focus and funds away from achieving the Sustainable Development Goals. Furthermore, fluctuations in political leadership, policy focus, as well as system of governance raise concerns about the sustainability as well as momentum of SDG projects, demanding adaptive deployment solutions.

Promises and Potential of SDGs for Future Generations

The Sustainable Development Goals (SDGs) offer a comprehensive framework for global progress, addressing crucial aspects like poverty eradication, education, healthcare, environmental preservation, and gender equality. This holistic approach paves the way for a fair and inclusive future. Through multilateral partnerships, involving nations, international organizations, non-profits, and businesses, the SDGs promote collective responsibility in tackling shared challenges like climate change and poverty. With a long-term vision set for achievement by 2030, the SDGs emphasize handling present issues while laying the groundwork for future generations to thrive in a fair, ecologically responsible world. Inclusivity lies at the core, ensuring equal opportunities regardless of background, while fostering innovation and progress towards sustainable solutions. Ultimately, pursuing the SDGs establishes a legacy of accountability, ensuring a responsibly managed planet for generations to come.

Strategies for Overcoming Challenges in Achieving the SDGs

To overcome the hurdles of reaching the Sustainable Development Goals (SDGs), multiple approaches to tackle numerous obstructions are required. Following are some essential strategies for overcoming these barriers:

- **Improved Financing and Resource Mobilisation:** Promote more money from a variety of sources, such as national budgets, private investments, foreign aid, and novel finance arrangements. Encourage collaboration among governments, corporations, donors, as well as non-profit organisations in order to harness funds along with match investment with SDG objectives.
- **Better Data and Monitoring Systems:** Increase national statistical capacity regarding gathering, analysing, and presenting data on the Sustainable Development Goals metrics. To improve accuracy of information as well as availability, encourage the use of solutions based on technology such as online tools and content-sharing systems.
- **Policy Integration and Institutional Strengthening:** Incorporate the Sustainable Development Goals (SDGs) into national policies, development plans, and strategies in order to ensure consistency throughout industries along with different levels of control. Improve the capacity of institutions and governance frameworks to promote successful SDG-related initiative execution as well as evaluation.

- **Addressing Inequality and Environmental Challenges:** Prioritise specific initiatives that tackle income, education, healthcare, and accessibility to resource disparity gaps. Adopt environmentally friendly procedures and regulations to protect the natural world, resist global warming, and preserve ecosystems.
- **Global Partnerships and Cooperation:** Improve global collaboration, alliances, and initiatives for sharing knowledge across governments, international organisations, the private sector, and civil society. Encourage teamwork and collaborative action to tackle international problems including climate change, migration, and global health crisis situations.
- **Empowerment and Inclusivity:** Empower marginalised communities, women, youth, and vulnerable groups through engaged participation with decision-making and equal opportunity. Encourage equitable policies that prioritise equal chances for education, healthcare, and economic opportunity for all members of community.
- **Resilience and Preparedness for Uncertain Circumstances:** Create emergency strategies and adaptable strategies to deal with unexpected events such as epidemics, natural catastrophes, and geopolitical upheavals. At the local, national, and global levels, enhance social security systems, emergency response structures, and Resilience-building initiatives.
- **Innovation and Technology Promotion:** Leverage the power of creativity, investigation, including technology to provide sustainable solutions, enhance effectiveness, and overcome inequalities in healthcare, education, energy access, and infrastructure development.

POLICY IMPLICATIONS AND RECOMMENDATIONS

The policy implications highlight the critical importance of incorporating the Sustainable Development Goals into national policies and plans throughout sectors, creating consistency and inter-ministerial collaboration. This combination guarantees that governments prioritise sustainable development goals, build strong finance arrangements with collaboration, as well as invest in information systems for improved tracking and well-informed making choices. Furthermore, policy should encourage international collaboration including collaborations for collective progress, as well as inclusivity, social fairness, and climate action.

Recommendations focus on ensuring policy compliance particularly the Sustainable Development Goals (SDGs) throughout all levels of government, particularly an emphasis on creative finance, strong systems for data, and equitable practices. Improving policies regarding the environment, strengthening marginalised people, including promoting international cooperation are critical foundations for driving advancement towards the Sustainable Development Goals (SDGs). Educational and awareness efforts ought to encourage sustainable principles, creating the groundwork for an accountable and successful future in line with the SDGs.

FUTURE RESEARCH DIRECTIONS

Future research should concentrate on three key domains in order to improve our understanding and execution of the Sustainable Development Goals (SDGs). To begin, additional studies should be conducted to assess the success of legislative convergence and alignment efforts at the national and international levels. It involves evaluating how various nations implement the Sustainable Development Goals into their policies, the obstacles they confront, and the effective techniques they use to solve them. It will be critical to recognise efficient procedures regarding inter-ministerial collaboration as well as the influence of policy cohesion on the Sustainable Development Goals attainment.

Secondly, additional research should look into innovative financing structures and how they affect SDG implementation. It will be beneficial to investigate the success factors and challenges to public-private partnerships, impact investment, and other innovative financing strategies. Furthermore, investigating the role of technology and data-driven approaches in tracking advancement towards the SDGs, as well as finding gaps in information accessibility and dependability, will be critical for informed choices as well as successful policies modifications. Additionally, studies ought to concentrate on measuring long-term socioeconomic and ecological effects of SDG-oriented policies, actions, and collaborations in order to direct upcoming sustainable development plans.

CONCLUSION

The Sustainable Development Goals (SDGs) are a revolutionary system for attaining global prosperity while attempting at tackling humanity's diverse concerns. The path to achieving these objectives will include collaborative efforts, policy alignment, creative finance, and inclusive approaches throughout all industries. As we travel down this road, it comes to clear that successful execution is dependent on coordinated policies, strong information systems, and collaborative relationships across governments, corporations, non-profit organisations, and global organisations. In order to advance the Sustainable Development Goals (SDGs), it is critical to embrace sustainability, equality, and environmental stewardship while building global collaboration. These goals' potential resides not only in their effect on present difficulties, but also in their ability to design a sustainable, equitable, and prosperous future for future generations. As a result, ongoing dedication, research-driven initiatives, and collective effort are critical in mapping the way towards sustainable development through the achievement of the SDGs.

REFERENCES

Andrew, F., & Julie, R. (2005). Sustainable development: Lost meaning and opportunity? *Journal of Business Ethics*, 60(1), 17–27. doi:10.1007/s10551-005-2927-9

Anita, N. (2011). India's progress toward achieving the Millennium development goal. *Indian Journal of Community Medicine*, 36(2), 85–92. doi:10.4103/0970-0218.84118 PMID:21976790

Arnaud, D. (2019). Six key drivers for sustainable development. *International Journal of Environmental Sciences & Natural Resources*, 18(4), 555–994.

Balaji, K. (2024). The Nexus of Smart Contracts and Digital Twins Transforming Green Finance With Automated Transactions in Investment Agreements: Leveraging Smart Contracts for Green Investment Agreements and Automated Transactions. *Harnessing Blockchain Digital Twin Fusion for Sustainable Investments*. IGI Global.

Bhattacharya, S. (2023). Localising the gender equality goal through urban planning tools in South Asia. *Journal of South Asia*, 2, 45.

Burda, M. & Wyplosz, C. (2009). Macroeconomics: A European text. Oxford: Oxford University Press. 2, 28.

Celine Dorathy, M. B. (2011). Carbon Emission-An Emerging Issue in Corporate Governance. *Journal of Commerce and Management Thought*, 2(3), 451–461.

Chatterjee, S. (2015). Assessing India's Progress in Achieving the Millennium Development Goals: Key Drivers of Inter-state Variations. *United Nations Economic and Social Commission for Asia and the Pacific (ESCAP). South and South-West Asia Office*, 20, 25.

DESA FSDO. (2024), Financing for Development. *Financing for Sustainable Development Report 2024*. UN. https://desapublications.un.org/publications/financing-sustainable-development-report-2024

Financing for Development. (2015). *Report of the third International Conference on Financing for Development*, http://www.undocs.org/A/CONF.227/20

Guan, T., Meng, K., Liu, W., & Xue, L. (2019). Public attitudes toward Sustainable Development Goals: Evidence from five Chinese cities. *Sustainability (Basel)*, 11(20), 57–93. doi:10.3390/su11205793

Hanson, Ranson, M. K., Oliveira-Cruz, V., & Mills, A. (2023). Expanding access to priority health interventions: A framework for understanding the constraints to scaling-up. *Journal of International Development*, 15(1), 1–14. doi:10.1002/jid.963

Inglehart, R. (1995). Public support for environmental protection: Objective problems and subjective values in 43 societies. *PS, Political Science & Politics*, 28(1), 57–72. doi:10.2307/420583

International Monetary Fund. (2021). *World Economic Outlook: managing divergent recoveries*. IMF. https://www.imf.org/en/Publications/WEO/weo-database/2021/April

Kabeer, N. (2016). Leaving No One Behind: The Challenge of Intersecting Inequalities. ISSC, IDS and UNESCO, Challenging Inequalities: Pathways to a Just World, *World Social. Scientific Reports*, 22, 55–58.

Kaiser, H. F. (1960). The application of electronic computers to factor analysis. *Educational and Psychological Measurement*, 20(1), 141–151. doi:10.1177/001316446002000116

Kioupi, V., & Voulvoulis, N. (2020). Sustainable Development Goals (SDGs): Assessing the contribution of higher education programmes. *Sustainability (Basel)*, 12(17), 67–71. doi:10.3390/su12176701

Lampert, M., & Papadongonas, P. (2016). *Towards 2030 Without Poverty: increasing knowledge of progress made and opportunities for engaging frontrunners in the world population with the global goals*. OxFamSol. https://oxfamsol.be/sites/default/files/documents/towards_2030_without_poverty-glocalities2016-2-new.pdf

Lozano, R. (2006). Incorporation and institutionalization of SD into universities: Breaking through barriers to change. *Journal of Cleaner Production*, 14(9–11), 787–796. doi:10.1016/j.jclepro.2005.12.010

Lozano, R., Lukman, R., Lozano, F. J., Huisingh, D., & Lambrechts, W. (2023). Declarations for sustainability in higher education: Becoming better leaders, through addressing the university system. *Journal of Cleaner Production*, 48, 10–19. doi:10.1016/j.jclepro.2011.10.006

Lu, Y., Nakicenovic, N., Visbeck, M., & Stevance, A.-S. (2015). Policy: Five priorities for the UN Sustainable Development Goals. *Nature*, *520*(7548), 433. doi:10.1038/520432a PMID:25903612

Marius, C., & Schmidt, S. (2022). A formal framework for conceptions of sustainability – a theoretical contribution to the discourse in sustainable development. *Sustainable Development*, *20*(6), 400–410.

Nilsson, M., Griggs, D., & Visbeck, M. (2016). Policy: Map the interactions between Sustainable Development Goals. *Nature*, *534*(7607), 320–322. doi:10.1038/534320a PMID:27306173

O'Byrne, D., Dripps, W., & Nicholas, K. A. (2015). Teaching and learning sustainability: An assessment of the curriculum content and structure of sustainability degree programs in higher education. *Sustainability Science*, *10*(1), 43–59. doi:10.1007/s11625-014-0251-y

Pham-Truffert, M., Metz, F., Fischer, M., Rueff, H., & Messerli, P. (2020). Interactions among Sustainable Development Goals: Knowledge for identifying multipliers and virtuous cycles. *Sustainable Development (Bradford)*, *28*(5), 1236–1250. doi:10.1002/sd.2073

Pradhan, P., Costa, L., Rybski, D., Lucht, W., & Kropp, J. P. (2017). A systematic study of Sustainable Development Goal (SDG) Interactions. *Earth's Future*, *5*(11), 1169–1179. doi:10.1002/2017EF000632

Purvis, B., Mao, Y., & Robinson, D. (2019). Three pillars of sustainability: In search of conceptual origins. *Sustainability Science*, *14*(3), 681–695. doi:10.1007/s11625-018-0627-5

Rakesh Kumar, M. (2015), National Implementation of the SDG. *SDG Monitoring India 2015*. UN. https://unstats.un.org/sdgs/.../Presentation--4.3-Implementation-of-SDG-Monitoring--I

Rodríguez-García, A.-M., López Belmonte, J., Agreda Montoro, M., & Moreno-Guerrero, A.-J. (2019). Productive, structural and dynamic study of the concept of sustainability in the educational field. *Sustainability (Basel)*, *11*(20), 5613. doi:10.3390/su11205613

Sachs, J. D. (2012). From millennium development goals to sustainable development goals. *Lancet*, *379*(9832), 832–2206. doi:10.1016/S0140-6736(12)60685-0 PMID:22682467

Sachs, J. D. (2021). Sustainable Development Report 2021: the decade of action for the Sustainable Development Goals. Cambridge University Press.

Schober, P., Boer, C., & Schwarte, L. A. (2018). Correlation coefficients: Appropriate use and interpretation. *Anesthesia and Analgesia*, *126*(5), 1763–1768. doi:10.1213/ANE.0000000000002864 PMID:29481436

Scoones, I. (1999). New ecology and the social sciences: What prospects for a fruitful engagement. *Annual Review of Anthropology*, *28*(1), 479–507. doi:10.1146/annurev.anthro.28.1.479

UN DESA & UNFCCCA. (2024). Reinforcing the 2030 Agenda and eradicating poverty in times of multiple crises: the effective delivery of sustainable, resilient and innovative solutions. *Global Expert Group Meeting in preparation for HLPF*. UN. https://sdgs.un.org/sites/default/files/202401/Draft%20CN_EGM%20for%20SDG13%20at%202024%20HLPF_as%20of%2031%20Jan.pdf

United Nations. (2014). *The Millennium Development Goals Report 2014*. UN. https://unctad.org/en/PublicationsLibrary/wir2014_en.pdf

United Nations General Assembly. (2023), Economic and Social Council Progress towards the Sustainable Development Goals: Towards a Rescue Plan for People and Planet, *United Nations General Assembly report 2023*,143, https://sdgs.un.org/sites/default/files/202304/SDG_Progress_Report_Special_Edition_2023_ADVANCE_UNEDITED_VERSION.pdf

ADDITIONAL READINGS

Global Sustainable Development Report. (2023). UN. https://sdgs.un.org/gsdr/gsdr2023

The Sustainable Development Goals Report. (2023). DESA. https://reliefweb.int/report/world/sustainable-development-goals-report-2023-special-edition?gad_source=1&gclid=Cj0KCQiAtOmsBhCnARIsAG-Pa5yagFb88OzzRC6fqQHNyu5iIlR0HDUap0y60co9NdMQvCYvpD8vhpZEaAhmxEALw_wcB

KEY TERMS AND DEFINITIONS

Economic Expansion: Economic expansion refers to the increase in a country's production of goods and services over time. It involves the growth of an economy measured by indicators such as Gross Domestic Product (GDP), employment rates, investment, and consumption.

International Monetary Fund (IMF): The International Monetary Fund is an international organization established to promote global monetary cooperation, exchange stability, and balanced economic growth.

Poverty Alleviation: Poverty alleviation refers to efforts aimed at reducing and ultimately eradicating poverty. It involves implementing strategies and policies to improve the living standards, access to basic needs, and economic opportunities for people living in poverty.

Public Policy: Public policy refers to the actions and decisions made by governments or other authorized bodies to address public issues or concerns.

Social Justice: Social justice refers to the fair and equitable distribution of resources, opportunities, and rights in society.

Sustainable Development Goals (SDGs): The sustainable development goals are a set of 17 global goals adopted by the United Nations in 2015 as part of the 2030 Agenda for Sustainable Development. They serve as a universal call to action to end poverty, protect the planet, and ensure that all people worldwide enjoy peace and prosperity by 2030.

United Nations (UN): The United Nations is an intergovernmental organization founded in 1945 to promote international cooperation, peace, and security among nations.

Zero Hunger: Zero Hunger is one of the Sustainable Development Goals (Goal 2) that aims to end hunger, achieve food security, improve nutrition, and promote sustainable agriculture.

Chapter 2
Application in Merging Green Practices With Digital Innovation to Create Sustainable Synergy

Ariq Idris Annaufal
Universitas Islam Indonesia, Indonesia

April Lia Dina Mariyana
Universitas Islam Indonesia, Indonesia

Muafi Muafi
Universitas Islam Indonesia, Indonesia

ABSTRACT

In the contemporary landscape of rapid technological advancement and escalating environmental concerns, the imperative to harmonize digital innovation with sustainable practices has become paramount. This chapter delves into the realm of merging green practices with digital innovation to cultivate sustainable synergy, elucidating how this integration holds the potential to revolutionize industries, mitigate environmental degradation, and propel us towards a more resilient future. Through interdisciplinary collaboration and longitudinal studies, this research aims to assess the long-term impacts and effectiveness of green practices and digital innovation initiatives on sustainability outcomes. By exploring the myriad applications of merging green practices with digital innovation across various domains, from renewable energy and waste management to sustainable urban development and conservation efforts, this chapter seeks to inspire stakeholders to embrace this transformative approach and collaborate towards building a more sustainable and prosperous future.

DOI: 10.4018/979-8-3693-2865-1.ch002

INTRODUCTION

In the contemporary landscape of rapid technological advancement and escalating environmental concerns, the imperative to harmonize digital innovation with sustainable practices has become paramount. The convergence of green principles with digital technologies offers a promising pathway towards addressing pressing ecological challenges while fostering economic growth and societal well-being (Singh et al, 2023; Garcia et al, 2024). This article delves into the realm of merging green practices with digital innovation to cultivate sustainable synergy, elucidating how this integration holds the potential to revolutionize industries, mitigate environmental degradation, and propel us towards a more resilient future.

The escalating climate crisis, coupled with resource depletion and biodiversity loss, underscores the urgent need for transformative action across all sectors of society. In response, businesses, governments, and individuals are increasingly recognizing the importance of adopting sustainable practices to minimize their ecological footprint. Concurrently, the proliferation of digital technologies, including artificial intelligence, Internet of Things (IoT), blockchain, and data analytics, presents unprecedented opportunities for efficiency gains, resource optimization, and environmental monitoring (Van and Au, 2020; Chauchan et al, 2022).

By harnessing the power of digital innovation, organizations can streamline operations, optimize resource utilization, and reduce waste generation, thereby enhancing their environmental sustainability. However, the true potential of digital transformation lies not only in optimizing existing processes but also in catalyzing systemic change through the integration of green principles. This entails reimagining business models, product design, supply chains, and consumption patterns to align with the imperatives of sustainability.

Moreover, the synergy between green practices and digital innovation extends beyond mere operational efficiency to encompass broader societal benefits. From smart grids and energy management systems to precision agriculture and sustainable mobility solutions, the integration of digital technologies enables the creation of resilient infrastructures and eco-friendly services that enhance quality of life while minimizing environmental impact.

In this article, we explore the myriad applications of merging green practices with digital innovation across various domains, ranging from renewable energy and waste management to sustainable urban development and conservation efforts. By elucidating real-world examples and emerging trends, we aim to inspire stakeholders to embrace this transformative approach and collaborate towards building a more sustainable and prosperous future. Through collective action and strategic investments in green digital solutions, we can unlock new opportunities for innovation, foster inclusive growth, and pave the way for a regenerative economy that thrives within planetary boundaries.

LITERATURE REVIEW

The term "green practices" encompasses actions aimed at diminishing environmental impact, such as eco-friendly purchasing and recycling. Wang (2013) adopts a broader interpretation based on the definition provided by, wherein green practices extend beyond mere environmental protection to emphasize waste reduction as a means to minimize environmental footprint (Wang, 2013). Digital technology has emerged as a transformative force, reshaping numerous facets of our lives and fundamentally altering business operations (Attaran, 2020). Within the realm of digital transformation (DT), digital technology serves as the cornerstone for organizational evolution and innovation. It empowers businesses to streamline processes, optimize resource utilization, and introduce novel value propositions (Du et al., 2023). Through the utilization of digital tools and platforms, enterprises can gather and analyze extensive datasets, facilitating data-driven decision-making and personalized customer experiences. Furthermore, digital technology fosters agile and collaborative workflows, dismantling traditional barriers and enabling organizations to swiftly adapt to market dynamics (Maran et al., 2022). It holds the potential to redefine business models, enhance customer engagement, and drive operational excellence. Organizations that adeptly leverage the capabilities of digital technology in their digital transformation journey are primed to thrive in the digital age.

The integration of green practices and sustainability has emerged as a significant driving force behind the adoption of sustainable practices across various industrial sectors (Dües et al., 2013). This strategic implementation holds promise for enhancing sustainability outcomes within industries. Thorlakson et al. (2018) underscore the pivotal role of the global supply chain in addressing environmental, social, and economic challenges highlighted by the United Nations' Sustainable Development Goals (SDGs). The 17 SDGs, formulated by the United Nations to advance global sustainable development across economic, environmental, and social dimensions, emphasize the imperative of engaging supply chains in fostering sustainable practices (Thorlakson et al., 2018; Brockhaus et al., 2019). Heightened concerns over environmental and social impacts, including resource depletion, environmental degradation, and climate change, have spurred governments, communities, and corporations to prioritize actions aimed at mitigating ecological and social challenges (Yildiz Çankaya & Sezen, 2019).

In the context outlined above, sustainable synergy refers to the harmonious integration and mutually reinforcing interaction between green practices and digital innovation to achieve enduring environmental, social, and economic benefits. It involves leveraging the complementary strengths of sustainable principles and digital technologies to create value that is greater than the sum of their individual parts.

Green Practices on Sustainability

Green practices encompass a broad spectrum of strategies, initiatives, and behaviors aimed at reducing environmental impact, conserving natural resources, and promoting ecological sustainability (Ercantan and Eyupoglu, 2022; Haleem et al, 2023). These practices are rooted in the recognition of the finite nature of Earth's resources and the urgent need to mitigate the adverse effects of human activities on the planet's ecosystems. From individual actions to corporate policies and governmental regulations, green practices play a pivotal role in shaping sustainable development trajectories and fostering a harmonious relationship between human societies and the natural world (Martin et al, 2016).

At the heart of green practices lies the principle of environmental stewardship, which entails responsible management and preservation of natural resources such as water, air, land, and biodiversity. This often involves adopting practices that minimize resource consumption, such as energy-efficient technologies, water conservation measures, and sustainable land management practices. By reducing the demand for finite resources and minimizing waste generation, green practices contribute to the long-term resilience of ecosystems and help mitigate the negative impacts of climate change (Perkumienė et al, 2023; Yang et al, 2022).

Furthermore, green practices encompass efforts to promote renewable energy sources and reduce reliance on fossil fuels, which are major contributors to greenhouse gas emissions and air pollution. Transitioning to renewable energy sources such as solar, wind, and hydroelectric power not only reduces carbon emissions but also enhances energy security and fosters economic development. Additionally, green practices encompass sustainable transportation initiatives, such as promoting public transit, carpooling, biking, and walking, to reduce greenhouse gas emissions from the transportation sector and alleviate traffic congestion (Yang et al, 2022).

Moreover, green practices extend beyond environmental considerations to encompass social and economic dimensions of sustainability. For example, sustainable agriculture practices prioritize soil health, biodiversity conservation, and water quality while promoting fair labor practices and supporting local economies. Similarly, green building practices focus on energy efficiency, materials conservation, and indoor air quality to create healthier and more sustainable built environments. By integrating social, environmental, and economic considerations, green practices contribute to the creation of more resilient and equitable societies that thrive within the boundaries of the planet's ecosystems (Martin et al, 2016).

In summary, green practices are integral to advancing sustainability goals by promoting responsible stewardship of natural resources, reducing environmental impact, and fostering resilience and equity in human societies. Whether at the individual, community, corporate, or governmental level, embracing green practices is essential for building a sustainable future for current and future generations.

Digital Innovation on Sustainability

Digital innovation is rapidly emerging as a powerful force in advancing sustainability goals by leveraging cutting-edge technologies to address pressing environmental challenges. From data analytics and artificial intelligence to blockchain and Internet of Things (IoT) devices, digital innovation offers novel solutions for monitoring, managing, and mitigating environmental impacts across various sectors. By harnessing the transformative potential of digital technologies, organizations and policymakers can optimize resource use, improve operational efficiency, and foster sustainable practices that promote ecological resilience and long-term prosperity (Darmayanti et al, 2023; Yang and Jin, 2023).

One key area where digital innovation is driving sustainability is in environmental monitoring and conservation efforts. Remote sensing technologies, satellite imagery, and drones equipped with advanced sensors enable real-time monitoring of environmental parameters such as air and water quality, deforestation rates, and wildlife habitats. These data-driven insights empower conservationists and policymakers to make informed decisions and implement targeted interventions to protect endangered species, preserve critical ecosystems, and combat illegal logging, poaching, and habitat destruction (Chisom et al, 2024).

Moreover, digital innovation is revolutionizing resource management and energy efficiency through the deployment of smart grid systems, energy management platforms, and IoT-enabled devices. Smart meters, sensors, and automation technologies allow utilities and consumers to optimize energy consumption, reduce waste, and lower greenhouse gas emissions. Additionally, blockchain technology is being utilized to create transparent and secure systems for tracking and verifying the origin and sustainability credentials of renewable energy sources, such as solar and wind power, thereby incentivizing investment in clean energy infrastructure and accelerating the transition to a low-carbon economy (Chisom et al, 2024).

Furthermore, digital innovation is reshaping transportation systems and urban infrastructure to promote sustainable mobility and reduce reliance on fossil fuels. Ride-sharing platforms, electric vehicles, and autonomous transportation systems are revolutionizing the way people move within cities, reducing traffic congestion, air pollution, and carbon emissions. Similarly, urban planning and design are being informed by data-driven insights and predictive analytics to create more walkable, bikeable, and transit-oriented communities that prioritize human well-being, environmental sustainability, and social equity (Yildiz Çankaya & Sezen, 2019).

In addition to environmental conservation and resource management, digital innovation is also driving sustainability across supply chains, manufacturing processes, and product lifecycle management. Technologies such as big data analytics, artificial intelligence, and digital twins enable companies to optimize production processes, minimize waste, and design products with a smaller environmental footprint. By embracing circular economy principles, which prioritize resource efficiency, reuse, and recycling, businesses can create value from waste streams, extend product lifecycles, and minimize environmental impact while enhancing economic resilience and competitiveness.

In conclusion, digital innovation holds immense promise for advancing sustainability goals by enabling data-driven decision-making, optimizing resource use, and fostering innovation across various sectors of society. By harnessing the power of digital technologies to address environmental challenges, we can create a more sustainable and resilient future for generations to come. However, realizing this vision requires collaboration, innovation, and concerted efforts from governments, businesses, academia, and civil society to leverage digital innovation as a force for positive change in pursuit of a more sustainable world.

Framework Model

Figure 1. Impact of green practices and digital innovation on sustainable synergy

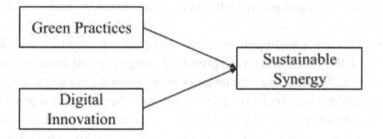

METHODOLOGY

In supporting the hypotheses that have been made regarding the causes of climate change, this research can be completed using quantitative techniques through a mini review. The topic of this research brings an important role in tackling climate change. This research aims to see the importance of Green Practices and Digital Innovation in creating Sustainable Synergy. Conducting a survey of stakeholders and transportation users is an appropriate research method to deepen the topic of climate change.

Result

The convergence of green practices with digital innovation offers a promising pathway towards addressing pressing ecological challenges while fostering economic growth and societal well-being. This integration holds the potential to revolutionize industries, mitigate environmental degradation, and propel us towards a more resilient future.

Green practices encompass a broad spectrum of strategies aimed at reducing environmental impact, conserving natural resources, and promoting ecological sustainability. From individual actions to corporate policies and governmental regulations, these practices play a pivotal role in shaping sustainable development trajectories and fostering a harmonious relationship between human societies and the natural world. By embracing green practices, we can promote responsible stewardship of natural resources, reduce environmental impact, and foster resilience and equity in human societies.

Digital innovation, on the other hand, is rapidly emerging as a powerful force in advancing sustainability goals by leveraging cutting-edge technologies to address pressing environmental challenges. From data analytics and artificial intelligence to blockchain and Internet of Things devices, digital innovation offers novel solutions for monitoring, managing, and mitigating environmental impacts across various sectors. By harnessing the transformative potential of digital technologies, organizations and policymakers can optimize resource use, improve operational efficiency, and foster sustainable practices that promote ecological resilience and long-term prosperity.

The integration of green practices and digital innovation holds promise for enhancing sustainability outcomes within industries and across supply chains. By reimagining business models, product design, supply chains, and consumption patterns to align with the imperatives of sustainability, organizations can streamline operations, optimize resource utilization, and reduce waste generation, thereby enhancing their environmental sustainability. Moreover, the synergy between green practices and digital innovation extends beyond mere operational efficiency to encompass broader societal benefits, including the creation of resilient infrastructures and eco-friendly services that enhance quality of life while minimizing environmental impact.

In conclusion, by elucidating real-world examples and emerging trends, this article aims to inspire stakeholders to embrace the transformative approach of merging green practices with digital innovation. Through collective action and strategic investments in green digital solutions, we can unlock new opportunities for innovation, foster inclusive growth, and pave the way for a regenerative economy that thrives within planetary boundaries. It is imperative that governments, businesses, academia, and civil society collaborate to leverage digital innovation as a force for positive change in pursuit of a more sustainable world.

DISCUSSION

The application of both green practices and digital innovation holds immense potential for fostering sustainable synergy, where the integration of these two approaches amplifies their impact and creates a virtuous cycle of environmental, social, and economic benefits. By combining the principles of responsible resource management with cutting-edge technologies, organizations and societies can achieve greater efficiency, resilience, and sustainability across various domains.

One of the key areas where green practices and digital innovation intersect is in the realm of smart energy management. By deploying IoT devices, sensors, and advanced analytics, energy systems can be optimized for efficiency, reducing waste and emissions while promoting the integration of renewable energy sources. For example, smart grid technologies enable real-time monitoring and control of electricity distribution, allowing for dynamic pricing mechanisms and demand response programs that incentivize energy conservation and grid stability. Additionally, blockchain-enabled energy trading platforms empower consumers to buy and sell renewable energy directly, fostering decentralized and sustainable energy ecosystems.

Moreover, green building practices augmented by digital innovation are revolutionizing the construction industry, leading to the emergence of sustainable, energy-efficient buildings that prioritize occupant comfort and environmental performance. Building information modeling (BIM) software allows architects and engineers to design and simulate structures with optimal energy efficiency and material use, while IoT-enabled sensors monitor indoor air quality, temperature, and lighting levels to optimize building performance and occupant well-being. Furthermore, digital twins enable real-time monitoring and predictive maintenance of building systems, prolonging asset lifespan and reducing maintenance costs while minimizing environmental impact.

In the realm of sustainable transportation, the convergence of green practices and digital innovation is driving the transition towards low-carbon, multimodal mobility solutions. Electric vehicles (EVs) powered by renewable energy sources are becoming increasingly prevalent, aided by advances in battery technology, charging infrastructure, and vehicle-to-grid (V2G) integration. Meanwhile, smart mobility platforms and ride-sharing apps optimize transportation networks, reduce congestion, and promote modal shifts towards public transit, cycling, and walking, thereby reducing emissions and improving urban air quality.

Furthermore, the application of green practices and digital innovation extends beyond individual sectors to encompass broader systemic transformations that promote circularity, resilience, and inclusivity. For example, digital platforms and blockchain technologies enable transparent and traceable supply chains, fostering accountability and ethical sourcing practices while reducing waste and promoting resource efficiency. Similarly, digital marketplaces for sharing, renting, and repurposing goods promote circular consumption patterns that minimize waste and extend product lifecycles, contributing to a more sustainable and circular economy.

In conclusion, the application of green practices and digital innovation towards sustainable synergy represents a transformative approach to addressing complex sustainability challenges. By harnessing the complementary strengths of these two approaches, organizations and societies can unlock new opportunities for innovation, collaboration, and positive impact, ultimately paving the way for a more sustainable and resilient future for all. However, realizing this vision requires concerted efforts from stakeholders across sectors to embrace innovation, collaboration, and collective action in pursuit of shared sustainability goals.

CONCLUSION

In the pursuit of sustainability, the convergence of green practices with digital innovation offers a promising pathway towards addressing pressing environmental challenges while fostering economic growth and societal well-being. Through the harmonious integration of responsible resource management strategies with cutting-edge technologies, organizations and societies can achieve greater efficiency, resilience, and sustainability. The discussion above has highlighted the transformative potential of this integration across various domains, from smart energy management and green building practices to sustainable transportation solutions and circular economy initiatives. However, while significant progress has been made, there are still numerous opportunities for future research and exploration.

Future research should prioritize interdisciplinary collaboration between scholars, practitioners, and policymakers to explore the complex interactions between green practices, digital innovation, and sustainability outcomes. By integrating insights from diverse fields such as environmental science, engineering, economics, sociology, and information technology, researchers can develop holistic approaches to addressing sustainability challenges and maximizing the benefits of synergistic integration. Longitudinal studies are needed to assess the long-term impacts and effectiveness of green practices and digital innovation initiatives on sustainability outcomes. By tracking trends and trajectories over time, researchers can identify key drivers of success, barriers to implementation, and unintended consequences, informing the design of more effective policies, programs, and strategies for sustainable development. Understanding the social and behavioral dynamics underlying the adoption and diffusion of green practices and digital innovation is essential for driving meaningful change at scale. Research should explore factors influencing individual and organizational decision-making, stakeholder engagement strategies, and mechanisms for promoting behavior change, trust, and collaboration in sustainability initiatives.

Limitation

Organizations need to adapt their business models, product designs, and operational processes to align with sustainability imperatives. This requires investing in digital technologies for resource optimization, waste reduction, and environmental impact monitoring. Companies that embrace this transformation stand to gain a competitive edge by meeting consumer demand for sustainable products and services while reducing costs and enhancing resilience.

As industries evolve towards sustainability-driven practices, there is a growing need for workforce development and capacity building. Educational institutions and training programs should incorporate sustainability principles and digital literacy into their curricula to prepare future professionals for the changing job market. This includes training in data analytics, IoT technologies, renewable energy systems, and circular economy principles.

In summary, the convergence of green practices with digital innovation presents a transformative opportunity to address pressing environmental challenges while driving economic growth and societal well-being. However, realizing the full potential of this integration requires coordinated action from businesses, governments, academia, investors, and civil society to overcome barriers, drive innovation, and create a more sustainable future for all.

REFERENCES

Anh, N. V., & Cheng, A. Y. (2020). Supply Chain Optimization in the Digital Age: A Big Data Analytics Perspective on Resilience and Efficiency. *AI, IoT and the Fourth Industrial Revolution Review, 10*(2), 11–18. https://scicadence.com/index.php/AI-IoT-REVIEW/article/view/15

Attaran, M. (2020). Digital technology enablers and their implications for supply chain management. Supply Chain. *Forum Int. J., 21*, 158–172.

Brockhaus, S., Petersen, M., Michael Knemeyer, A. (2019). The promise: signaling sustainability in supply chain relationships. *Logistik im Wandel der Zeit – Von der Produktionssteuerung zu vernetzten Supply Chains (Changing times - from production control to networked supply chains)*. Springer Fachmedien Wiesbaden, Wiesbaden.

Chauhan, C., Parida, V., & Dhir, A. (2022). Linking circular economy and digitalisation technologies: A systematic literature review of past achievements and future promises. *Technological Forecasting and Social Change, 177*, 121508. doi:10.1016/j.techfore.2022.121508

Chisom, O. N., Biu, P. W., Umoh, A. A., Obaedo, B. O., Adegbite, A. O., & Abatan, A. (2024). Reviewing the role of AI in Environmental Monitoring and Conservation: A data-driven revolution for our planet. *World Journal of Advanced Research and Reviews, 21*(1), 161–171. doi:10.30574/wjarr.2024.21.1.2720

Dharmayanti, N., Ismail, T., Hanifah, I. A., & Taqi, M. (2023). Exploring Sustainability Management Control System and eco-innovation Matter Sustainable Financial Performance: The role of supply chain management and digital adaptability in Indonesian context. *Journal of Open Innovation, 9*(3), 100119. doi:10.1016/j.joitmc.2023.100119

Dües, C. M., Tan, K. H., & Lim, M. (2013). Green as the new Lean: How to use Lean practices as a catalyst to greening your supply chain. *Journal of Cleaner Production, 40*, 93–100. doi:10.1016/j.jclepro.2011.12.023

Ercantan, O., & Eyupoglu, S. (2022). How do green human resource management practices encourage employees to engage in green behavior? perceptions of university students as prospective employees. *Sustainability (Basel), 14*(3), 1718. doi:10.3390/su14031718

Haleem, A., Javaid, M., Singh, R. P., Suman, R., & Qadri, M. A. (2023). A pervasive study on green manufacturing towards attaining sustainability. *Green Technologies and Sustainability, 1*(2), 100018. doi:10.1016/j.grets.2023.100018

Martin, J.-L., Maris, V., & Simberloff, D. S. (2016). The need to respect nature and its limits challenges society and conservation science. *Proceedings of the National Academy of Sciences of the United States of America, 113*(22), 6105–6112. doi:10.1073/pnas.1525003113 PMID:27185943

Perkumienė, D., Atalay, A., Safaa, L., & Grigienė, J. (2023). Sustainable Waste Management for clean and safe environments in the recreation and tourism sector: A case study of Lithuania, Turkey and Morocco. *Recycling, 8*(4), 56. doi:10.3390/recycling8040056

Sanchez-García, E., Martínez-Falcó, J., Marco-Lajara, B., & Manresa-Marhuenda, E. (2024). Revolutionizing the circular economy through new technologies: A new era of sustainable progress. *Environmental Technology & Innovation, 33*, 103509. doi:10.1016/j.eti.2023.103509

Singh, P. K., Khatake, P., Gori, Y., Parmar, A., Shivakumar, P., Anandhi, R. J., & Kareem, S. H. (2023). Harmonizing innovation: The path to sustainable design and production. *E3S Web of Conferences*. IEEE. doi:10.1051/e3sconf/202345301025

Thorlakson, T., De Zegher, J. F., & Lambin, E. F. (2018). Companies' contribution to sustainability through global supply chains. *Proceedings of the National Academy of Sciences of the United States of America, 115*(9), 2072–2077. doi:10.1073/pnas.1716695115 PMID:29440420

Wang, Y. F., Chen, S.-P., Lee, Y.-C., & Tsai, C.-T. S. (2013). Developing green management standards for restaurants: An application of green supply chain management. *International Journal of Hospitality Management*, *34*(1), 263–273. doi:10.1016/j.ijhm.2013.04.001

Yang, M., Chen, L., Wang, J., Msigwa, G., Osman, A. I., Fawzy, S., Rooney, D. W., & Yap, P.-S. (2022). Circular Economy Strategies for combating climate change and other environmental issues. *Environmental Chemistry Letters*, *21*(1), 55–80. doi:10.1007/s10311-022-01499-6

Yildiz Çankaya, S., & Sezen, B. (2019). Effects of green supply chain management practices on sustainability performance. *Journal of Manufacturing Technology Management*, *30*(1), 98–121. doi:10.1108/JMTM-03-2018-0099

Zhang, Y., & Jin, S. (2023). How does Digital Transformation Increase Corporate Sustainability? the moderating role of top management teams. *Systems*, *11*(7), 355. doi:10.3390/systems11070355

Chapter 3
Renewable Energy for Agriculture Sustainability Conservations:
A Step Towards Green Revolution

Dharmbir Prasad
https://orcid.org/0000-0002-9010-9717
Asansol Engineering College, India

Rudra Pratap Singh
https://orcid.org/0000-0001-7352-855X
Asansol Engineering College, India

Jatin Anand
Asansol Engineering College, India

Ranadip Roy
https://orcid.org/0000-0003-2111-2581
Sanaka Educational Trust's Group of Institutions, Durgapur, India

Md. Irfan Khan
IAC Electricals Pvt. Ltd., Kolkata, India

ABSTRACT

This study outlines sustainable agriculture practices in Simdega District, India, emphasizing the critical role of agriculture using the renewable energy. With a focus on long-term environmental, social, and economic viability, the study employs a multidisciplinary approach, integrating field surveys, policy analysis, and literature review. In the agriculture industry, including renewable energy solutions may improve resource efficiency, lower greenhouse gas emissions, and foster climate resilience. Additionally, effective post-harvest processing technology like solar dryers and biomass-based systems may be powered by renewable energy reducing food loss and enhancing the quality and marketability of agricultural products. Increased production, water conservation and soil health may all be achieved by using sustainable agricultural practices including organic farming, precision agriculture and agro-forestry.

DOI: 10.4018/979-8-3693-2865-1.ch003

INTRODUCTION

Simdega district centrally located in India thrives on agriculture, not merely as an economic pursuit but as an integral way of life for its residents. The agricultural sector holds a pivotal role in supporting the livelihoods of a significant proportion of the local population. Despite its agricultural prominence, Simdega encounters challenges akin to those experienced globally-issues of environmental degradation, resource depletion and the impacts of climate change. The system proposed in this study includes the use of solar as a primary source and grid as the secondary. The grid used in this study purchases as well as sells the energy enduring for a sustainable development in the area. The proposed system does not uses a storage unit as the grid been installed fulfils any need for the use of electricity and also a step towards reducing the capital cost for setting up the system. Jharkhand's Simdega district is home to a wide variety of year-round crops, including grains like rice, maize, and wheat; oilseed crops like Niger, tori, mustard, and groundnut; pulses like black gram, pigeon pea, chickpea and pea; vegetables like lady finger, cowpea, potato, and tomato; and fruits like papaya, mango, guava and jackfruit (Abot, 2020). There are continuous efforts to boost agricultural output through programs like artificial insemination centres for cattle to improve milk yield, despite obstacles including dependency on rain-fed agriculture and poor irrigation infrastructure as shown in Table 1. The temperature and terrain of the district enable a range of crops to be cultivated in certain locations according to the fertility and composition of the soil. In Simdega area, sustainable farming methods are essential for maximizing agricultural productivity and enhancing lives. The gases controlled using the system are carbon dioxide, nitrogen oxide and sulphur dioxide.

Table 1. Initiatives for agriculture taken in India

Sl.	Agricultural segmentation	Sustainable Initiatives	Location	Date	Reference
1.	Integrated Portal for Farming Investment	The development of the "Krishi Nivesh Portal"	India	February 29, 2024	The Hindu Business Line
2.	To promote agricultural exports from India	Value-added millet products.	India	March 6, 2024	ANI News
3.	Smart agricultural practices	Aims to uplift and empower rural communities.	Jharsuguda, Odisha.	February 28,2024	Times of India
4.	leveraging technology and market research	Aligning existing agricultural policies with the UN Sustainable Development Goals.	India	October 18, 2021.	The Economic Times
5.	Capsber Agrisciences	Sustainable farming practices for greener future	India	February 29,2024	The Economic Times
6.	Diagnosis of plant disease severity	Digitizing agriculture with AI, ML and IOT	India	February 5,2022	Nature
7.	Effective farm methods	Precision Farming SaaS	India	September 23, 2023	Agriculture post
8.	Modernising and transforming our farming practices	Agri-drone technology	India	December 23, 2023	Hindustan Times
9.	Region specific smart agricultural technologies	IOT	India	January 21, 2024	MDPI
10.	Weed removal	Robotics	India	March 20, 2023	MDPI

Paper Layout: Rest of the paper is organised as follows - energy potential assessment, problem statement, research reviews of green revolution, sustainable agriculture practices, and mathematical formulation, modelling for re powered farming, energy requirements for agricultural, results and finally study concluded.

Energy Potential Assessment at Site

The Indian state of Jharkhand is home to Simdega, which is extremely important to the area because of its cultural, historical land economic contributions. The customs of several tribal groups, such as the 57,000 person Oraon, Mundaand Kharia, are deeply woven into the district's unique cultural fabric. Each community contributes its own traditions, rituals and creative creations, resulting in a vivid mosaic of Indian cultural expressions that highlights the peaceful coexistence of many ethnic groupings. Simdega's economy is centred on agriculture, which is made possible by the area's rich soil and pleasant environment. Simdega District covers 3761.20 km² in total as mapping depicted in Figure 1. In addition to providing for the local population, this agricultural environment is essential to Jharkhand's total food output. The region is proud of its natural beauty and attracts tourists seeking a tranquil vacation. Simdega's biodiversity includes a large range of flora and fauna, highlighting the region's ecological significance and amplifies the allure of its surroundings. Simdega's commitment to social and economic development is exemplified by a number of initiatives, particularly those that improve the lives of indigenous populations. The district's endeavours in the domains of education, healthcare and the establishment of sustainable livelihoods bear witness to its dedication to the overall welfare of its inhabitants. The climate in Simdega is mild and pleasant. In Simdega, it rains very little in the summer and predominantly in the winter. The Koppen-Geiger climate classification places this climate in the Csa category. Simdega experiences 25.1°C temperature on average every year. The average annual rainfall is 1450 mm. December had the least amount of precipitation, averaging 3 mm. With an average of 410 mm, August is when the precipitation peaks. With a temperature of 33.0°C, May is the hottest month of the year. December is the coldest month of the year with a temperature of 17.9°C. Out of the total land 134,024.33 hectares of usable land, 16,367 hectares is irrigated while 117,657.33 hectares is unirrigated.

Figure 1. Location of Simdega, Jharkhand for agricultural sustainability

To satisfy its load requirement, Simdega district, like many other places, depends on a combination of energy resources. Geographical features, economic conditions and environmental issues can all affect the availability of energy supplies. Simdega is in the state of Jharkhand, which is well-known for having large coal deposits. Power stations that burn coal may be a substantial source of energy. There may be possibilities for hydropower generation in the area's rivers and other bodies of water. Because of Simdega's unique geographic location and plenty of sunshine, solar energy may be a practical renewable energy source. To capture solar energy, photovoltaic panels are put in place. Wind energy may also be included in the energy mix, depending on regional wind patterns. Electricity may be produced by installing wind turbines. Biomass which includes agricultural leftovers may be burned to produce biogas or utilized in other processes to generate electricity. In order to fulfil Simdega's energy demands, the electrical grid infrastructure's dependability and availability are essential. Energy from several sources may be sent and distributed to end consumers more easily with improved grid connection. Managing the load demand requires both encouraging energy conservation measures and putting into effect energy-efficient activities. This covers programs including those that encourage the use of energy-efficient lighting, appliances and industrial procedures.Location-based mapping involves the utilization of geographical characteristic information for the visualization of data on maps, offering valuable context and insights across diverse domains. The location of Simdega district can be known from the co-ordinates 22.62°N latitude and 84.52°E longitude.

Table 2. Meteorological resources of study site favourable for weather conditions

Month	Clearness index	Daily radiation (kWh/m^2/day)	Average wind speed (m/s)	Daily temperature (°C)
Jan	0.629	4.460	3.950	16.640
Feb	0.653	5.320	4.310	20.370
Mar	0.628	5.930	4.720	25.810
Apr	0.622	6.510	4.390	30.790
May	0.576	6.330	4.190	32.790
Jun	0.431	4.760	4.880	29.870
Jul	0.355	3.910	5.040	26.420
Aug	0.356	3.780	4.720	25.820
Sep	0.420	4.100	4.110	25.150
Oct	0.560	4.760	3.410	22.830
Nov	0.623	4.550	3.300	19.220
Dec	0.643	4.330	3.540	16.340

The charts of solar GHI resource data, which shows the amount of solar radiation received by a surface horizontal to the ground, is important for assessing the solar energy potential of a site and designing the appropriate solar energy system for the site as can be observed from Table 2 and Figure 2. GHI is a crucial parameter in solar energy applications, especially in the field of photovoltaic and solar thermal systems. It provides information about the amount of solar energy available at a specific location, considering all components of solar radiation. For the clearness index is highest for the month of February with index of 0.653 and lowest month for Julywith 0.355 and the daily radiation data is measured in kWh/m²/day having peak month for the month of April with a value of 6.510 and the lowest month for the month of August having a value of 3.780

Figure 2. Meteorological characteristics for the proposed energy system of agriculture supply

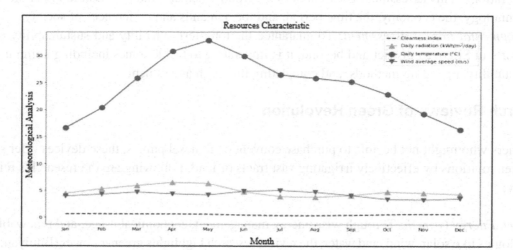

The efficiency and performance of PV solar panels can be strongly impacted by temperature. A number of variables, such as the surrounding environment, solar radiation and solar array design, affect the temperature of PV panels. PV modules feature a temperature coefficient, which expresses how much the module's power output drops as the temperature rises. Usually, the temperature coefficient is given as a percentage (%/°C) of the temperature. When the temperature rises, a positive temperature coefficient means that the power output falls. PV modules' efficiency tends to decline with increasing temperature. The month of May had the highest temperature ever recorded 32.790°C, while the month of December had the lowest with 16.340°C.

The speed record for November is the lowest at 3.300 m/s, while the maximum speed is 5.040 m/s for July. Dust and other particles that might collect on the surface of the PV panels could be carried by the wind under windy and dusty conditions. Due to a decreased capacity to absorb sunlight, this might result in a decrease in the quantity of energy created. Cleaning may be required often in these circumstances. Although wind does not directly contribute to the production of electricity in solar systems, wind speed can have an indirect impact on the total amount of energy generated in these systems. The average wind speed in the area is 4.213 m/s.

Problem Statement

A problem statement for sustainable agricultural development identifies a specific issue or difficulty that impedes environmentally friendly farming techniques or food production systems. It is simply defining the problem's background and relevance, laying the groundwork for focused solutions to improve the sustainability of agricultural operations.

– *System technical compatibility:* The economic, environmental, and social advantages of using solar energy in the area are demonstrated by the successful completion of solar-powered projects for irrigation, electrification, and the production of green electricity in the Simdega district.

– *Economic feasibility evaluation:* A concept, project, or solution's economic feasibility is evaluated by considering a number of factors, including operational, legal, financial and technological considerations. This assessment is essential to ascertain whether a plan is feasible given the state of technology, the economy, the time period, and the demands and preferences of society.

– *Environmental impact assessment:* To guarantee the long-term viability and sustainability of solar efforts in Simdega district and beyond, it is imperative to tackle issues including community acceptability, operating methods, and completing thorough assessment.

Research Reviews of Green Revolution

For farmers who might not be able to purchase conventional diesel pumps, these devices offer sustainable water solutions by effectively irrigating vast tracts of land. Following are the research's related to the study:

(a). Green Energy Growth: Through wise energy management, economical usage, and renewable technologies like solar, wind, and water, the review research highlights greener power (Bhuiyan, 2022). While tackling challenges like CEP and FFC, the research places a strong emphasis on ICTs and sustainable NR management for green growth in KBEs (Wang et al., 2023).

(b). Digital Transformation: Investigating the relationship between Industry 4.0 and sustainability, the study highlights the significance of sustainability in intelligent manufacturing as well as their tight relationship (Furstenau et al., 2020). The study examines how employee performance on digital strategy goals is impacted by IEO, indicating that risk-taking and proactiveness have favourable effects while creativity has negative effects (Ritala et al., 2021). The research presents novel examples of waste management digitalization in Indonesia and other countries, showing how old approaches are being replaced by the CE using digital platforms (Kurniawan et al., 2022). The study examines the REMs industry in China and discovers beneficial connections between DT, SD, and ES. For competitiveness and sustainability, ES and DT integration is essential (Guan et al., 2023). The study does an extensive literature assessment on industrial digitalization, including suggestions for future lines of inquiry and managerial and scholarly insights (Matt et al., 2023). Greenhouse gas emissions and cost savings from digitalization support the objectives of the circular economy (Kurniawan et al., 2023). ES, DT, and SD were shown to have substantial positive correlations in the PLS-SEM study that examined ES's influence on DT and SD in China's REMs industry (Guan et al., 2023). According to the study, there is a general expectation that digital technology would drastically change cities, infrastructure, buildings, architecture, and construction. It also maps out many images of digital construction (Braun & Kropp, 2023). By mentoring staff members, supporting learning, and advocating for the circular economy, lean leadership nurtures a culture of continuous improvement with an emphasis on coaching, empowerment, and respect (Gatell & Avella, 2024). The study examines how natural resource usage and e-commerce affect green growth in fifteen developing Asian nations, highlighting the positive effects of foreign investment and e-commerce as well as the negative implications of urbanization and mineral consumption (Sun et al., 2024). This research explored the intricate relationship between media, cultural industries and

their impact on mineral resource efficiency through an extensive analysis spanning from 2000 to 2020 across ten major global CO2 emitters (Liu et al., 2024). Ecological sustainability and mitigating climate change are given special attention in this research, which examines China's natural resources, technological innovation, and economic growth (Zhang & Xie, 2024).

(c). Circular Economy: In order to demonstrate way to BDA meets the goals of the circular economy by boosting competitiveness and societal value, the study looks at five case studies in emerging nations (Modgil et al., 2021). In order to bring waste management and the circular economy into line with the UN SDGs, the study looks at how COVID-19 affects the SDGs (Sharma et al., 2021). The study aspired to develop a theoretical model linking key resources for I4.0 adoption, sustainable production and circular economy (Bag et al., 2021). The present analysis reveals that research in this domain is fragmented across interdisciplinary fields (Chauhan et al., 2022). In line with responsible consumption, reducing environmental effect, and Vietnamese low-carbon goals, the research focuses on SMEs using CE for sustainable development (Chowdhury et al., 2022). Real technical and economic change is needed to achieve carbon neutrality. Through the decoupling of growth from resource depletion, the CE promotes regenerative economic cycles (Kurniawan et al., 2022). The study investigates the relationship between AM and the CE (Hettiarachchi et al., 2022). Considering the social and environmental crisis being faced and since we know that MNEs are highly pressured toward financial performance researchers, managers and investors should be predominantly oriented to an agenda that encompasses social and environmental sustainability and how they can also align with financial enhancement of the firm (de Oliveira et al., 2023). Implementing circular economy initiatives in business activities is essential for improving the organization's efficiency through resource management as well as protecting the environment (James et al., 2023). The paper discusses Industry 4.0 social challenges and offers solutions. Job loss, a lack of skilled workers, a lack of IT know-how, managerial support, cyber security, and goal alignment are major obstacles (Upadhyay et al., 2023). Intensive collaborative research accentuates the significance of devising solutions tailor-made for MSW concerns (Munir et al., 2023).

(d). Conservation of Agriculture: The authors used a proven research method to collect published articles from reputable databases such as WoS, Scopus and Google Scholar. The authors sought to answer three research questions using SMEs (Truant et al., 2024). The discipline of assessing impacts of changes in farm practice using the 10 indicator structure (later 11) has been helpful in that it permitted science-based, quantitative and qualitative environmental, social, economic and commercial assessments to be made within a single structure (Pretty et al., 2008). The Australian Bureau of Agricultural and Resource Economics have defined similar sustainability indicators of farm performance using a similar methodology and annual farm survey data as employed here (ABARE, 1999) (Dillon et al., 2010). The CA-based cropping system and holistic system approach not only conserves natural resources but also helps in producing more at low costs, improves soil health, promotes timely planting and ensures crop diversification, reduces environmental pollution and adverse effects of climate change on cereal systems in IGP (Jat et al., 2021). The concept of sustainable agriculture is predicated on a delicate balance of maximizing crop productivity and maintaining economic stability, while minimizing the utilization of finite natural resources and detrimental environmental impacts (Chel & Kaushik, 2011). The idea is to identify a set of thresholds that any agricultural production strategy must meet beyond which unsustainable trends caused by the farming systems and associated rage rating of more than 1 for farmer satisfaction and resource conservation is required for a farm to be sustainable technologies would lead to tipping-

point phenomena (Koohafkan et al., 2012). The first concerned practitioners' different understandings of modernization. Indeed, the practitioners on the ground showed extremely heterogeneous understandings of modernization (Knickel et al., 2017).

Sustainable Agriculture Practices

There are sixteen sustainable farming techniques that have been defined by the Council on Energy, Environment and Water. Although acceptance varies, there has been improvement in areas such as organic farming in Sikkim and zero-budget natural farming in Andhra Pradesh (The Times of India, 2023). The government encourages natural farming, which uses age-old, chemical-free techniques, to address these problems. This encourages a variety of bacterial communities in the soil, which improves plant development, resistance to environmental stressors and natural insect resistance (The Wire, 2023). There will be pressure on agriculture to meet future targets, so innovation will be important. Participating in bio fuel will provide farmers with an opportunity to improve economic efficiency. It will also create competition between food and fuel producers for valuable crops (S&P Global, 2023). Economic inequities grew as a result of concentration in some areas, which marginalized small farmers. The revolution accidentally increased wealth disparity in the dairy industry while attempting to increase rural incomes and food supply (Mint, 2023). In contrast, Mizoram, Kerala and Andhra Pradesh, Madhya Pradesh and West Bengal excel in sustainability thanks to better infrastructure and agricultural diversification (The News India Express, 2023).

India, a leader in the Green Revolution, now has to modernize agriculture in a way that is sustainable. In order to maintain environmental sustainability in the twenty-first century, this essay examines the possible advantages and difficulties of incorporating electric tractors into Indian farming techniques (The Sunday Guardian, 2023). Two of the most important issues facing the 21st century are climate change and food poverty. Heat waves and droughts are examples of climate-related occurrences that have an influence on agriculture and increase food demand due to population expansion and dietary changes. Farmers adjust to reduce climate risk, but a comprehensive strategy is required. In light of climatic issues, agricultural productivity has to rise by 60% by 2050 to fulfil food demand (The Hindu, 2023). The Indian agriculture sector has been inching close to achieving these figures on the back of the green revolution and tech-backed agriculture solutions that are integrally playing a key role in making sustainable agriculture a reality (The Financial Express, 2023). This vital economic sector is also part of the problem as it contributes 17% to greenhouse gas emissions, produced especially by intensive farming characterized by efficient processes that maximize production yield (Vatican News, 2023).

Mathematical Formulation

Understanding and assessing the risks associated with farming requires the use of mathematical models, which help farmers use resources optimally to increase produce while lowering expenses and environmental effect. When exposed to sunlight, arrays of panels continually generate power. Three critical parameters affect the design of a PV cell: the idealist factor, short-circuit current and open-circuit voltage. The output current produced by the PV panel is calculated by equation (1) (Bharathi & Sasikumar, 2021),

$$I_0 = I_{irr} - I_{01}\left(e^{\left(\frac{(V_0+IR_1)}{\left(N_a \times \frac{kT}{q}\right)}\right)^{-1}} - \left(\frac{V_0+IR_1}{R_2}\right)\right) \qquad (1)$$

where, I_0: output current, I_{01}: reverse diode current, V_0: output voltage, N: PV cell number, a: ideality factor, $\frac{kT}{q}$: Boltzmann constant.

The inverter synchronizes the AC output with the local electrical grid's frequency and phase in addition to converting DC electricity to AC voltage. Furthermore, a MPPT technology that optimizes the energy harvest from PV panels by adjusting voltage and current levels to the panels' maximum power point, is frequently included in inverters. The converter's efficiency is represented by equation (2) (Hassan et al., 2023),

$$\eta_{ec} = \frac{P_{opc}}{P_{ipc}} \qquad (2)$$

where, η_{ec}: converter efficiency, P_{opc}: output power of the converter, Pi_{pc}: input power of the converter.

The goal of reducing agriculture's dependency on energy is to increase energy efficiency in the use of machinery, fertilizer and land management practices. But because of the rebound effect, these developments can paradoxically lead to a rise in energy usage. This happens when manufacturers choose more energy-intensive processes as a result of efficiency advancements, which raises the amount of energy used. Agriculture energy efficiency is represented by the equation (3) (Han & Zhou, 2024),

$$EF_{it} = \frac{OEI_{it}}{AEI_{it}} \qquad (3)$$

where, EF_{it}: agriculture energy efficiency around region i in t year, OEI_{it}: agricultural energy input at the optimal production frontier around region i in year t, AEI_{it}: actual agricultural energy input in i region for year t .

The NPC of a system is the total present value, discounted to present value, of all costs incurred during the system's lifetime for its acquisition, implementation, operation, and maintenance, less any savings or benefits realized during that same period. This system is given by the equation (4) (Pal & Mukherjee, 2021),

$$NPC = \frac{TC_{an.cos}}{C_{RF}\left(i, R_{project}\right)} \qquad (4)$$

where, NPC: net present cost, $TC_{an.cos}$: total annualized cost (\$/year), C_{RF}: capital recovery factor.

The levelized COE is given by the equation (5) (Pal & Mukherjee, 2021),

$$LCOE = \frac{TC_{ancos}}{E_{ser}}$$ (5)

where, *LCOE*: levelized cost of energy, TC_{ancos}: total annualized cost (\$/year), E_{ser}: total electrical load served per year (kWh/year).

Modelling for RE Powered Farming

Farmers may increase their resistance to agricultural hazards, increase profitability, and use resources more efficiently by utilizing mathematical models to guide their decision-making.

Current System: JGF5+F75, Simdega, Jharkhand 835223, India's power demands are satisfied. The annual cost of energy for operation is presently \$6,039.

Proposed System: We intend to add 680 kW of PV, this would cut the running costs to -\$103,172 per year. The investment has a payback period of 4.58 years and an IRR of 21.7%.

Block diagrams provide an emphasis on learning and simplicity. The system modelling is illustrated in Figure 3.

Figure 3. Block diagram using grid/solar pv/converter and electric load for agriculture supply

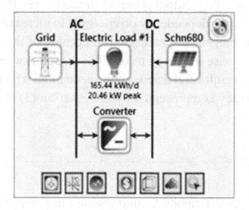

This components description illustrate agriculatural power supply. It entails outlining each component's features, capabilities and interactions with other parts within the overall structure:

(a). PV Module: Photovoltaic power generation is the process of using photovoltaic cells also commonly called solar cells to convert sunlight into electricity. The PV model used here is Schneider ConextCoreXC 680kW with Generic PV with a rated capacity of 680.08 kW and comes under flat plate category. The capital cost for the unit is 500,000\$ and the cost for the O&M is 10\$. The temperature coefficient for the PV system is 0.4100 while it has operating temperature of 45°C. The system has derating factor of 96% and an efficiency of 17.30%.

(b). Power Converter: In a photovoltaic system, an inverter's main job is to change the direct current produced by the solar panels into alternating current. AC is used by most electrical equipment and the power grid. The inverter synchronizes the generated AC with the utility grid in PV systems

that are connected to the grid. This enables extra energy to be supplied back into the grid and through net metering, the system owner may get paid or earn credits. PV system's total efficiency is enhanced by inverters. Superior inverters enhance the system's overall performance by converting DC to AC with the least amount of energy loss. Inverters can occasionally be found in hybrid systems that combine solar energy with backup power sources like batteries or generators. The energy transfer between these various parts is controlled by the inverter. The capacity of converter used here is 50,000 kW as to transmit maximum energy to the grid without the losses because there is no battery used to store the energy. The capital and replacement of the converter used is $300.

(c). Grid Connectivity: A growing alternative is the distributed grid, which generates electricity closer to the point of consumption, frequently utilizing renewable sources. The issues posed by intermittent energy sources such as solar and wind power must be addressed in order to integrate renewable energy into the system. In order to manage these difficulties, energy storage systems and advanced grid technology are important. Digital technology is used by smart grids to improve reliability, efficiency and performance. The grid power price is 0.100 $/kWh and the grid net excess price is 0.050 $/kWh. Better control of the supply and demand for energy is made possible by their ability to provide two-way communication between utilities and customers. To provide a steady and dependable electricity supply, grid stability is essential. Demand variations, abrupt changes in generation and fault-related disturbances are a few examples of the variables that might affect stability.

Energy Requirements for Agricultural

The goal of sustainable agriculture is to meet society's current food and textile demands while preserving the capacity of present or future generations to meet their own needs. Being a large power user, agriculture has a number of issues that impact the availability of resources. Observation for the present study is summarised as in the succeeding sections:

(i). Energy Consumption: Every piece of machinery, input, and end product used in agriculture has energy. In order to bring agriculture closer to sustainability, energy analysis can be used to optimize energy consumption and boost energy efficiency. It also makes it possible to quantify the amounts of energy required for agricultural output. In this analysis, Table 3-4 present electricity produced and it shows that the PV produces maximum electricity which is 1,160,751 kWh/year and it produces 97.7% of the total electricity while the electricity purchased from the grid is around 27,592 kWh/year which contributes to only 2.32% of the total electricity which is 1,188,343 kWh/year. Figure 4 shows load profile under various circumstances. For energy systems, an electrical summary could provide a snapshot of essential details about the electrical infrastructure, power generation methods, distribution networks and patterns of energy consumption.

Table 3. Energy production summary at the proposed energy system of agriculture load supply

Production	kWh/year	%
Schneider ConextCoreXC 680kW with Generic PV	1,160,751	97.7
Grid purchases	27,592	2.32
Total	1,188,343	100

Figure 4. Load characteristics under various agricultural conditions

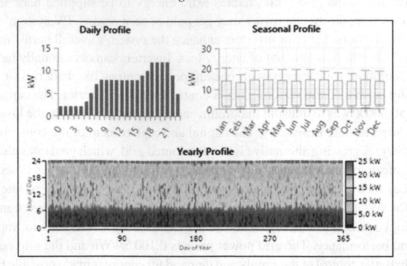

Table 4. Energy consumption results for proposed energy system of agriculture load supply

Consumption	kWh/year (%)	Consumption	kWh/year (%)
AC primary load	60,386 (5.34%)	Excess Electricity	183 (0.0154%)
DC primary load	0 (0%)	Unmet Electric Load	0(0%)
Deferrable load	0 (0%)	Capacity Storage	0 (0%)
Grid sales	1,069,919 (94.7%)	Renewable Fraction	97.6(%)
Total	1,130,305 (100%)	Max. Renewable Penetration	105 (%)

(ii). Power Demand Estimation: The goal of this study is to model and forecast the energy consumption in one of the village of Indian agriculture, which is a crucial component of production. Following are results compilation given below:

(a). Electrical Summary: Photovoltaic systems offer a renewable and sustainable source of electricity generation, harnessing the abundant energy of the sun to produce clean electricity with minimal environmental impact. Figure 5 shows the electricity produced from the renewable source used. The microgrid requires 3101 kWh/day and has a peak of 646 kW. In the proposed system, it shows the generation sources serving the electrical load.

Figure 5. Characteristics for energy consumption and production

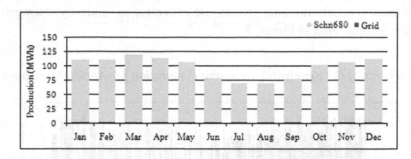

From Table 5, it can be clearly analysed that the renewable fraction has 97.6% value and the maximum renewable penetration is 105% because it represents the extent to which the solar renewable energy contributes to the overall energy mix in the area for Schneider ConextCoreXC 680kW with Generic PV.

Table 5. Renewable Penetration for Energy Production

Quantity	Value
Renewable fraction (%)	97.6
Maximum renewable penetration (%)	105

(b). Variation of Power Demand and Generation: The characteristics acts as an aid in this researchin a wide range of scientific and technical domains by providing essential insights into how systems, signals, and variables interact over time as presented in Figure 6.

Figure 6. Characteristics of the Combined Heat and Power uror Agriculture Supply

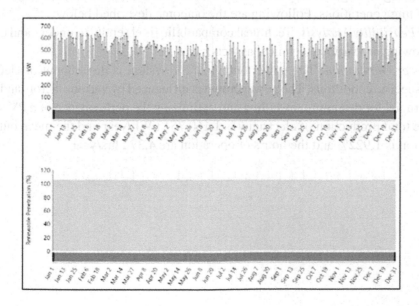

The objective of this approach is to improve sustainability in the agriculture industry by decreasing the dependence on fossil fuels, minimizing greenhouse gas emissions and maybe lowering the operating expenses for farmers as presented in Figure 7.

Figure 7. Characteristics of the Renewable Resource Penetration for Agriculture Supply

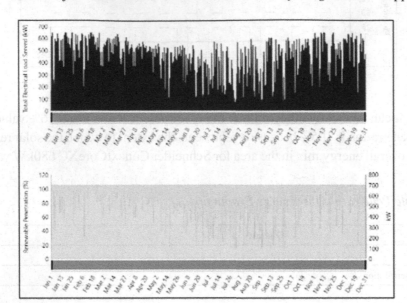

RESULTS AND DISCUSSION

The debate surrounding the climate, water, land, energy and food nexus revolves around the agricultural sector. The primary goal in creating a sustainable agriculture sector is to feed the growing global population while minimizing its negative effects on the environment and protecting the most valuable natural resources for coming generations. Following are the outcome described below:

(i). Technical Feasibility Analysis: Technical compatibility is essential to understand efficient system integration. Following are various technical aspects:

(a). Solar Power Generation: The power output of PV system is the amount of electrical power it generates under specific conditions. The power output is influenced by various factors and understanding these factors is crucial for designing, installing and optimizing the performance of a PV system as given in Table 6-7. The total production of electricity is 1,160,751 kWh/year and the mean output is 133 kW. The PV penetration is 1,922% and the hours of operation are 4,372 hrs/year.

Table 6. Electricity Production for Running Various Equipment's in Agricultural Work

Quantity	Value
Rated Capacity (kW)	680
Mean Output (kW)	133
Mean Output (kWh/d)	3,180
Capacity Factor (%)	19.5
Total Production (kWh/year)	1,160,751
Dedicated Converter (kW)	680

Table 7. Power Output Chart for Proper Utilization in the Agricultural Fields

Quantity	Value
Minimum output (kW)	0
Maximum output (kW)	680
PV Penetration (%)	1,922
Hours of operation (hrs/year)	4,372
Levelized Cost ($/kWh)	0

Figure 8. Characteristics for Solar Power Generation and Power Converter Performance

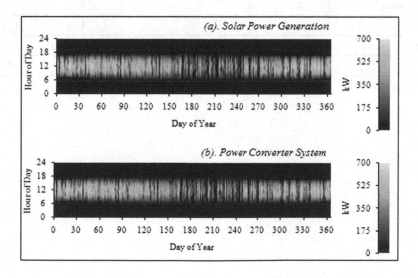

A photovoltaic system's daily power production may be estimated by considering factors including a gradual rise in power at sunrise, a peak output at solar noon and a decrease in power at nightfall due to varying levels of irradiance. Figure 8 shows the power output characteristics of the PV with power converter performance. Actual production is influenced by panel efficiency, system architecture and site conditions. For precise estimations, use solar modelling software that includes the precise location and panel parameters.

(b). Power Converter Simulation Output: In a renewable energy system, power converters provide energy produced by solar or wind turbines into a form that may be used locally or connected to the grid. It improves the integration of renewable energy sources by ensuring effective power transmission and system stability as given in Table 8-9 and Figure 9. The mean output of the inverter is 126 kW, capacity factor is 0.252%and losses are 58,038 kWh/year.

Table 8. Converter Power Output for Grid Utilization

Quantity	Inverter
Power capacity (kW)	50,000
Mean output power (kW)	126
Minimum output power(kW)	0
Maximum output power(kW)	646
Capacity factor (%)	0.252

Table 9. Energy Exchange by Converter for Better Efficiency

Quantity	Inverter
Hours of operation (hrs/year)	4,372
Energy out (kWh/year)	1,102,713
Energy In (kWh/year)	1,160,751
Losses (kWh/year)	58,038

Figure 9. System Converter Output Characteristics for Agricultural Power Supply

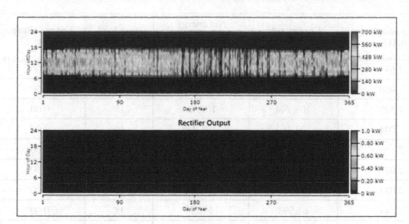

(c). Grid Integrated Interfacing: When demand exceeds supply, customers and the system trade energy by buying electricity and selling excess renewable energy. Credits for extra energy can be put back into the grid thanks to net metering. During times of low renewable output, reliance on the grid for power increases. In the energy markets, utilities make transactions easier. Technologies for smart grids maximize energy flow and encourage the incorporation of renewable. The dynamics in the changing energy environment emphasize sustainability and carbon reduction, with variations depending on local rules and resource availability as presented in Table 10. From the value below, it can analyse that the highest grid purchase is in made in the month of March which is 107,436 kWh while the maximum energy is also sold in the month of March which is 109,744 kWh. Vegetables like Cucumber, Cucumber, Bitter gourd, Gourd, Luffa, Petah, Spinach, Cauliflower, Brinjal, Okra, Arabic Mirchi Tomato are grown in the month of March which requires more energy for production so, the maximum energy is purchased in the month of March. The annual energy sold is 1,069,919 kWh.

Table 10. Grid Integrated Power Bidirectional Supply

Month	Energy purchased (kWh)	Energy sold (kWh)	Net energy purchased (kWh)	Peak load (kW)	Energy charge ($)	Demand charge ($)
January	2,692	101,625	-98,933	20	0.00	0.00
February	2,080	101,331	-99,251	17	0.00	0.00
March	2,309	109,744	-107,436	19	0.00	0.00
April	2,204	103,463	-101,259	19	0.00	0.00
May	2,159	96,303	-94,143	19	0.00	0.00
June	2,013	71,017	-69,004	19	0.00	0.00
July	2,024	61,511	-59,486	19	0.00	0.00
August	2,319	61,598	-59,279	18	0.00	0.00
September	2,233	69,599	-67,366	18	0.00	0.00
October	2,448	93,113	-90,664	17	0.00	0.00
November	2,492	97,715	-95,223	19	0.00	0.00
December	2,618	102,900	-100,282	18	0.00	0.00
Annual	27,592	1,069,919	-1,042,327	20	$103,190.42	0.00

Figure 10. Characteristics of the Energy Purchased and Sold Through Grid for Agricultural Activity

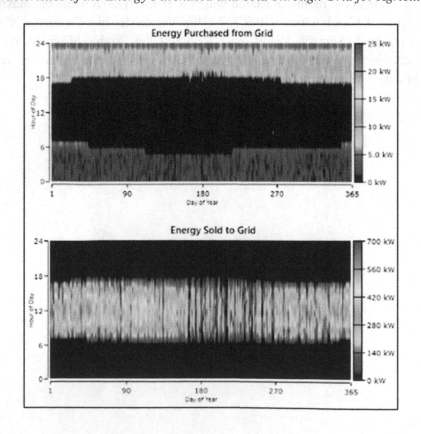

A grid purchase daily profile shows the amount of power purchased from the grid over the course of a day, highlighting demand variations. Figure 10 shows the characteristics of the energy purchased and sold through grid while Figure 11 shows the grid purchase daily profile. Demand peaks denote strong demand, whilst demand troughs denote low demand. Peaks often happen in the morning and evening, coinciding with everyday tasks like cooking and housekeeping. Recognizing these trends facilitates effective energy management.

Figure 11. Grid Purchase Daily Profile for Agriculture Energy Supply

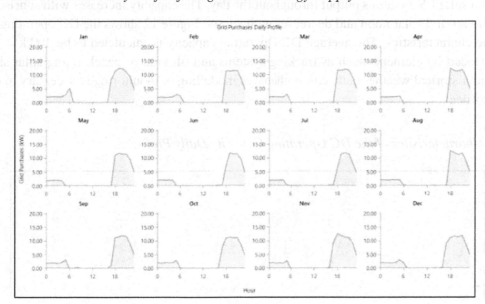

Table 11. Results for Renewable Output by Load for Crop Management

Capacity based matrices for agrarian tasks	
Capacity based metrics	Value (%)
Nominal renewable capacity divided by total nominal capacity	100
Usable renewable capacity divided by total capacity	100
Renewable output by load for crop management	
Peak values	Value (%)
Renewable output divided by load (HOMER standard)	105
Renewable output divided by total generation	100
One minus non-renewable output divided by total load	100
Energy based analysis for rural activities	
Energy-based metrics	Value (%)
Total renewable production divided by load	103
Total renewable production divided by generation	97.7
One minus total non-renewable production divided by load	100

The amount or proportion of renewable energy in a certain energy system or grid is measured as renewable penetration. It shows how much of the total energy generated comes from renewable sources. When evaluating sustainability and environmental effect, this statistic is essential as shown in Table 11. Achieving greater energy independence, lowering dependency on fossil fuels, promoting climate change mitigation and moving toward cleaner energy all depend on increasing the share of renewable energy. Effective integration of renewable is necessary to achieve considerable penetration, overcoming issues like grid stability and intermittency.

The DC operational capacity daily profile shows how changes in system features, weather and sunshine affect a solar PV system's output throughout the day. The capacity increases with sunrise, reaches its maximum around solar noon and decreases with sunset. Figure 12 shows the DC operating capacity daily profile characteristics. The average DC Operating capacity is calculated to be 300 kW. The profile is influenced by elements such as tracking systems and tilt kind of panel. Using solar simulation software and historical weather data, comprehensive modelling or monitoring is necessary to obtain an accurate profilee.

Figure 12. Characteristics of the DC Operating Capacity Daily Profile

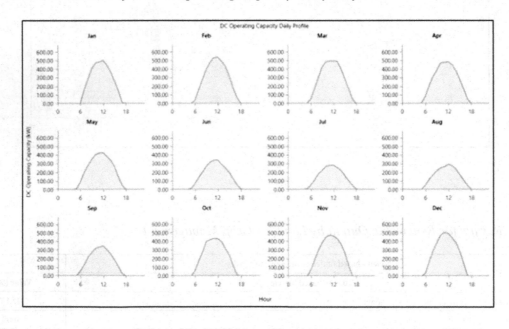

A solar PV system's daily profile for AC primary load and needed operational capacity is determined by a number of factors, such as system design, solar irradiation and patterns of energy consumption. Figure 13 showcases the AC required operating capacity daily profile characteristics. It's crucial to remember that the real profiles will rely a lot on the location's unique qualities, the kind of energy required and the efficiency and design of the solar PV system.

Figure 13. Characteristics of AC Required Operating Capacity Daily Profile

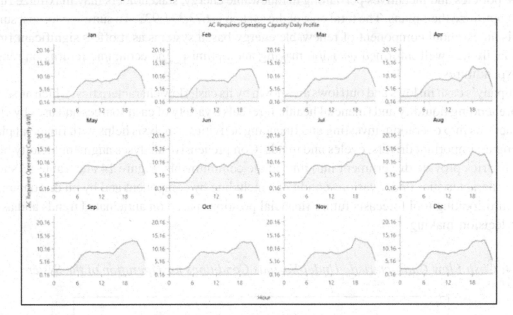

(ii). Economic Viability Analysis: A graphic depiction or table that shows varying rates or prices for various goods, services, or activities is called a rate chart as given in Table 12. It offers a methodical means of communicating expenses, levies, or fees related to certain goods or activities. Rate charts are frequently used to communicate with people in a variety of situations and sectors.

Table 12. Rate Chart Comparison Data Analysis for Farm Operations

Financial Aspects	Data
Discount rate (%)	8.00
Inflation rate(%)	2.00
Real Interest Rate (%)	5.9
Project Lifetime(Years)	25.00

Assessment of the initial investment assists in determining the expenses related to installing renewable energy sources, such solar or wind power. When weighing their investment alternatives, decision-makers must be aware of these expenses. Evaluation of operational costs makes it possible to look closely at the costs associated with continuing operations, such as upkeep, repairs and replacement parts for renewable energy systems. Examining the expenses associated with producing energy from renewable sources against conventional fossil fuel-based energy sources can provide light on the competitiveness and economic feasibility of renewable technologies.

Cost analysis assists by contrasting the initial investment with the anticipated savings or income from the production of renewable energy. This measure is crucial for determining if renewable energy projects are financially feasible and appealing. By knowing the financial effects of different government subsidies, policies and incentives pertaining to renewable energy, stakeholders may maximize financial gains and optimize their plans. The total cost of the system is 673,331.92$. To summarise, cost summary analysis is an essential component of renewable energy-based systems as it offers significant financial insights, facilitates well informed decision making and optimises the economic returns on renewable energy expenditures.

A company's cash inflows and outflows are shown by its cash flow characteristics, which are essential for comprehending liquidity and financial health. It reveals a variety of cash sources and uses by classifying transactions into operating, investing and financing activities. Analysis helps with financial planning by pointing up important drivers, cycles and trends. Comprehensive analyses augment lucidity however liquidity metrics provide discernment into immediate commitments. Figure 14 and Table 13 show, the cash flow characteristics under various conditions including by component and by nu discounted price. This forward-looking tool forecasts future financial positions based on anticipated trends and assists in strategic decision-making.

Figure 14. Cash Flow Characteristic Under Various Conditions for Operation of the System

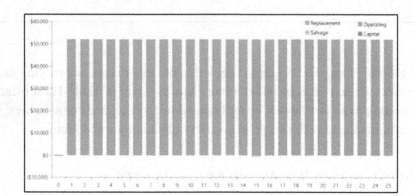

Table 13. Economical Comparison for the Proposed System

Metric	Value
Simple payback (Year)	4.58
Return on Investment (%)	17.8
Internal Rate of Return (%)	21.7
Net Present Value ($)	911,527
Capital Investment ($)	500,300
Annualized Savings ($)	109,211

(iii). Environmental Impact Assessment: Carbon dioxide emissions refer to the release of carbon dioxide gas into the atmosphere and they play a significant role in the context of climate change and environmental sustainability. The carbon dioxide produced here is 138 kg/year, the particular matter here

is 166 kg/year, the sulphur dioxide produced here is 75.6 kg/year and nitrogen dioxide produced here is 37.0 kg/year as can be observed in Table 14. The emissions here are basically produced because of the grid been installed as the electricity bought from the distribution network in grid-connected PV-storage microgrids may indirectly contribute to carbon dioxide emissions in the power grid.

Table 14. Emissions Reduction for Environmental Impact Assessment

Quantity	Value
Carbon Dioxide (kg/year)	414
Carbon Monoxide (kg/year)	0
Unburned Hydrocarbons (kg/year)	0
Particulate Matter (kg/year)	166
Sulphur Dioxide (kg/year)	75.6
Nitrogen Oxides (kg/year)	37.0

This outcome refer to Figure 15 indicates the precise values given to the decision variables in order to maximize the objective function and guarantee the best possible performance or efficiency within the parameters of the problem under consideration. In Table 15, the NPC calculated using the formula is -$833,463and COE is -$0.0570. The annual operating cost is -$103,172. The initial capital for setting up the system is $500,300and the renewable fraction is 97.6%.

Table 15. Optimization Result for Energy Supply to Agricultural Requirements

			Schn 680 (kW)	Schn 680-MPPT (kW)	Grid (kW)	Converter (kW)	Dispatch	NPC ($)	COE ($)	Operating Cost ($/year)	Initial Capital ($)	Renewable Fraction (%)
			680	680	999,999	50,000	CC	-$833,463	-$0.0570	-$103,172	$500,300	97.6
					999,999		CC	$78,064	$0.100	$6,039	$0.00	0

Figure 15. Comparative Optimization Characteristics for Sustainable Energy Growth

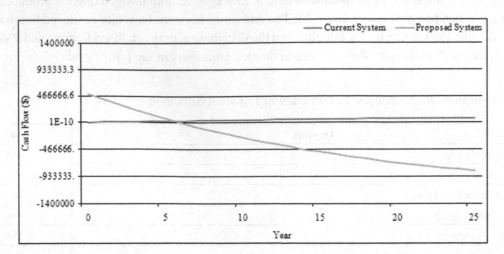

CONCLUSION

Grid analysis assesses the efficiency and dependability of electrical networks, taking into account demand patterns, load distribution, and renewable energy integration. Similarly, PV analysis evaluates the efficacy of solar power systems, concentrating on crucial aspects such as solar irradiation, panel orientation, and shading in order to maximize performance. PV power generation is the pivotal process of converting sunlight into electricity through photovoltaic cells. The global solar monthly and daily profiles encapsulate the intricate variation in solar energy availability worldwide. Dependent on factors such as Earth's tilt, latitude and climate conditions, these profiles provide a holistic view of solar energy patterns. The total energy produced by the PV panels is 1,160,751 kWh/year. Simulation tools further refine the accuracy of these profiles, offering location-specific insights crucial for the development of sustainable energy solutions. In essence, the understanding of these diverse facets is imperative for navigating the complex landscape of renewable energy, emissions reduction and the evolving dynamics of global energy systems. In conclusion to this the present worth of the proposed system is estimated to be $751,396 while the annual worth is $58,124. The return on investment for the project is 19,378.35% just because of the energy being sold to the grid but if the proposed system is utilized for the sustainable agriculture practice it will find its worth. The carbon dioxide produced here is 138 kg/year. Thus there are no health hazards caused due to the proposed system.

REFERENCES

Abot, M. D. 2020. Factors influencing adoption of artificial insemination by smallholder livestock farmers in dryland production systems of Kenya *(Doctoral dissertation, University of Nairobi)*.

Bag, S., Yadav, G., Dhamija, P., & Kataria, K. K. (2021). Key resources for industry 4.0 adoption and its effect on sustainable production and circular economy: An empirical study. *Journal of Cleaner Production, 281*, 125233. doi:10.1016/j.jclepro.2020.125233

Bharathi, K., & Sasikumar, M. (2021). Power flow control based on bidirectional converter for hybrid power generation system using microcontroller. *Microprocessors and Microsystems*, *82*, 103950. doi:10.1016/j.micpro.2021.103950

Bhuiyan, M. R. A. (2022). Overcome the future environmental challenges through sustainable and renewable energy resources. *Micro & Nano Letters*, *17*(14), 402–416. doi:10.1049/mna2.12148

Braun, K., & Kropp, C. (2023). Building a better world? Competing promises, visionsand imaginaries-in-the-making of the digitalization of architecture and construction. *Futures*, *154*, 103262. doi:10.1016/j.futures.2023.103262

Chauhan, C., Parida, V., & Dhir, A. (2022). Linking circular economy and digitalisation technologies: A systematic literature review of past achievements and future promises. *Technological Forecasting and Social Change*, *177*, 121508. doi:10.1016/j.techfore.2022.121508

Chel, A., & Kaushik, G. (2011). Renewable energy for sustainable agriculture. *Agronomy for Sustainable Development*, *31*(1), 91–118. doi:10.1051/agro/2010029

Chowdhury, S., Dey, P. K., Rodríguez-Espíndola, O., Parkes, G., Tuyet, N. T. A., Long, D. D., & Ha, T. P. (2022). Impact of organisational factors on the circular economy practices and sustainable performance of small and medium-sized enterprises in Vietnam. *Journal of Business Research*, *147*, 362–378. doi:10.1016/j.jbusres.2022.03.077

de Oliveira, R. T., Ghobakhloo, M., & Figueira, S. (2023). Industry 4.0 Towards Social and Environmental Sustainability in Multinationals: Enabling Circular Economy, Organizational Social Practices and Corporate Purpose. *Journal of Cleaner Production*, *430*, 139712. doi:10.1016/j.jclepro.2023.139712

Dillon, E. J., Hennessy, T., & Hynes, S. (2010). Assessing the sustainability of Irish agriculture. *International Journal of Agricultural Sustainability*, *8*(3), 131–147. doi:10.3763/ijas.2009.0044

Furstenau, L. B., Sott, M. K., Kipper, L. M., Machado, E. L., Lopez-Robles, J. R., Dohan, M. S., Cobo, M. J., Zahid, A., Abbasi, Q. H., & Imran, M. A. (2020). Link between sustainability and industry 4.0: Trends, challenges and new perspectives. *IEEE Access : Practical Innovations, Open Solutions*, *8*, 140079–140096. doi:10.1109/ACCESS.2020.3012812

Gatell, I. S., & Avella, L. (2024). Impact of Industry 4.0 and circular economy on lean culture and leadership: Assessing digital green lean as a new concept. *European Research on Management and Business Economics*, *30*(1), 100232. doi:10.1016/j.iedeen.2023.100232

Guan, L., Li, W., Guo, C., & Huang, J. (2023). Environmental strategy for sustainable development: Role of digital transformation in China's natural resource exploitation. *Resources Policy*, *87*, 104304. doi:10.1016/j.resourpol.2023.104304

Han, H., & Zhou, Z. (2024). The rebound effect of energy consumption and its determinants in China's agricultural production. *Energy*, *290*, 129961. doi:10.1016/j.energy.2023.129961

Hassan, Q., Sameen, A. Z., Salman, H. M., & Jaszczur, M. (2023). Large-scale green hydrogen production via alkaline water electrolysis using solar and wind energy. *International Journal of Hydrogen Energy*, *48*(88), 34299–34315. doi:10.1016/j.ijhydene.2023.05.126

Hettiarachchi, B. D., Brandenburg, M., & Seuring, S. (2022). Connecting additive manufacturing to circular economy implementation strategies: Links, contingencies and causal loops. *International Journal of Production Economics, 246*, 108414. doi:10.1016/j.ijpe.2022.108414

James, A. T., Kumar, G., James, J., & Asjad, M. (2023). Development of a micro-level circular economy performance measurement framework for automobile maintenance garages. *Journal of Cleaner Production, 417*, 138025. doi:10.1016/j.jclepro.2023.138025

Jat, H. S., Datta, A., Choudhary, M., Sharma, P. C., & Jat, M. L. (2021). Conservation Agriculture: Factors and drivers of adoption and scalable innovative practices in Indo-Gangetic plains of India–a review. *International Journal of Agricultural Sustainability, 19*(1), 40–55. doi:10.1080/14735903.2020.1817655

Knickel, K., Ashkenazy, A., Chebach, T. C., & Parrot, N. (2017). Agricultural modernization and sustainable agriculture: Contradictions and complementarities. *International Journal of Agricultural Sustainability, 15*(5), 575–592. doi:10.1080/14735903.2017.1373464

Koohafkan, P., Altieri, M. A., & Gimenez, E. H. (2012). Green agriculture: Foundations for biodiverse, resilient and productive agricultural systems. *International Journal of Agricultural Sustainability, 10*(1), 61–75. doi:10.1080/14735903.2011.610206

Kurniawan, T. A., Maiurova, A., Kustikova, M., Bykovskaia, E., Othman, M. H. D., & Goh, H. H. (2022). Accelerating sustainability transition in St. Petersburg (Russia) through digitalization-based circular economy in waste recycling industry: A strategy to promote carbon neutrality in era of Industry 4.0. *Journal of Cleaner Production, 363*, 132452. doi:10.1016/j.jclepro.2022.132452

Kurniawan, T. A., Othman, M. H. D., Hwang, G. H., & Gikas, P. (2022). Unlocking digital technologies for waste recycling in Industry 4.0 era: A transformation towards a digitalization-based circular economy in Indonesia. *Journal of Cleaner Production, 357*, 131911. doi:10.1016/j.jclepro.2022.131911

Kurniawan, T. A., Othman, M. H. D., Liang, X., Goh, H. H., Gikas, P., Kusworo, T. D., Anouzla, A., & Chew, K. W. (2023). Decarbonization in waste recycling industry using digitalization to promote net-zero emissions and its implications on sustainability. *Journal of Environmental Management, 338*, 117765. doi:10.1016/j.jenvman.2023.117765 PMID:36965421

Liu, Y., Yu, Y., Huang, Y., & Guan, W. (2024). Utilizing the resources efficiency: Evidence from the impacts of media industry and digitalization. *Resources Policy, 88*, 104346. doi:10.1016/j.resourpol.2023.104346

Matt, D. T., Pedrini, G., Bonfanti, A., & Orzes, G. (2023). Industrial digitalization. A systematic literature review and research agenda. *European Management Journal, 41*(1), 47–78. doi:10.1016/j.emj.2022.01.001

Mint, (August 14, 2023). *Indian agriculture must balance profits with sustainable practices.* https://www.livemint.com/opinion/first-person/indian-agriculture-must-balance-profits-with-sustainable-practices-11691889108165.html (Accessed on: December 18, 2023).

Modgil, S., Gupta, S., Sivarajah, U., & Bhushan, B. (2021). Big data-enabled large-scale group decision making for circular economy: An emerging market context. *Technological Forecasting and Social Change, 166*, 120607. doi:10.1016/j.techfore.2021.120607

Munir, M. T., Li, B., Naqvi, M., & Nizami, A. S. (2023). Green loops and clean skies: Optimizing municipal solid waste management using data science for a circular economy. *Environmental Research*, 117786. PMID:38036215

Pal, P., & Mukherjee, V. (2021). Off-grid solar photovoltaic/hydrogen fuel cell system for renewable energy generation: An investigation based on techno-economic feasibility assessment for the application of end-user load demand in North-East India. *Renewable & Sustainable Energy Reviews*, *149*, 111421. doi:10.1016/j.rser.2021.111421

Pretty, J., Smith, G., Goulding, K. W. T., Groves, S. J., Henderson, I., Hine, R. E., King, V., Van Oostrum, J., Pendlington, D. J., Vis, J. K., & Walter, C. (2008). Multi-year assessment of Unilever's progress towards agricultural sustainability II: Outcomes for peas (UK), spinach (Germany, Italy), tomatoes (Australia, Brazil, Greece, USA), tea (Kenya, Tanzania, India) and oil palm (Ghana). *International Journal of Agricultural Sustainability*, *6*(1), 63–88. doi:10.3763/ijas.2007.0323

Ritala, P., Baiyere, A., Hughes, M., & Kraus, S. (2021). Digital strategy implementation: The role of individual entrepreneurial orientation and relational capital. *Technological Forecasting and Social Change*, *171*, 120961. doi:10.1016/j.techfore.2021.120961

Sharma, H. B., Vanapalli, K. R., Samal, B., Cheela, V. S., Dubey, B. K., & Bhattacharya, J. (2021). Circular economy approach in solid waste management system to achieve UN-SDGs: Solutions for post-COVID recovery. *The Science of the Total Environment*, *800*, 149605. doi:10.1016/j.scitotenv.2021.149605 PMID:34426367

Sun, L., Li, X., & Wang, Y. (2024). Digital trade growth and mineral resources In developing countries: Implications for green recovery. *Resources Policy*. 88, pp. 104338. S&P Global, (August 3, 2023). *Future Farming: Agriculture's Role in a More Sustainable India*. https://www.spglobal.com/en/research-insights/featured/special-editorial/look-forward/future-farming-agriculture-s-role-in-a-more-sustainable-india (Accessed on: December 18, 2023).

The News India Express. (August 18, 2023). *India's agriculture sustainability at risk*. https://www.newindianexpress.com/xplore/2023/aug/18/indiasagriculture-sustainability-at-risk-2606814.html (Accessed on: December 18, 2023).

The Sunday Guardian. (October 14, 2023). *The Green Revolution in India: Harnessing Electric Tractors for Sustainable Agriculture*. https://sundayguardianlive.com/business/the-green-revolution-in-india-harnessing-electric-tractors-for-sustainable-agriculture (Accessed on: December 18, 2023).

The Times of India. (May 4, 2023). *Embracing sustainable agriculture: A virtuous cycle of prosperity*. https://timesofindia.indiatimes.com/blogs/voices/embracing-sustainable-agriculture-a-virtuous-cycle-of-prosperity/ (Accessed on: December 18, 2023).

The Wire. (July 21, 2023). *How Natural Farming Can Revive India's Farmlands and Ensure Sustainable Agriculture*.https://thewire.in/agriculture/how-natural-farming-can-revive-indias-farmlands-and-ensure-sustainable-agriculture (Accessed on: December 18, 2023).

Truant, E., Giordino, D., Borlatto, E., & Bhatia, M. (2024). Drivers and barriers of smart technologies for circular economy: Leveraging smart circular economy implementation to nurture companies' performance. *Technological Forecasting and Social Change*, *198*, 122954. doi:10.1016/j.techfore.2023.122954

Upadhyay, A., Balodi, K. C., Naz, F., Di Nardo, M., & Jraisat, L. (2023). Implementing industry 4.0 in the manufacturing sector: Circular economy as a societal solution. *Computers & Industrial Engineering*, *177*, 109072. doi:10.1016/j.cie.2023.109072

Vatican News. (December 04, 2023). *COP28: Sustainable agriculture is antidote to climate change.* https://www.vaticannews.va/en/world/news/2023-12/cop28-sustainable-agriculture-antidote-to-climate-change.html (Accessed on: December 18, 2023).

Wang, Z., Huang, Y., Ankrah, V., & Dai, J. (2023). Greening the knowledge-based economies: Harnessing natural resources and innovation in information and communication technologies for green growth. *Resources Policy*, *86*, 104181. doi:10.1016/j.resourpol.2023.104181

Zhang, H., & Xie, Y. (2024). Assessing natural resources, rebounding trends, digital economic structure and green recovery dynamics in China. *Resources Policy*, *88*, 104482. doi:10.1016/j.resourpol.2023.104482

Chapter 4
Digital Ethics in Higher Learning Institutions:
Challenges and Fostering Responsible Practices

Aliasan
Universitas Islam Negeri Raden Fatah Palembang, Indonesia

Kusnadi
Universitas Islam Negeri Raden Fatah Palembang, Indonesia

Muzaiyanah Muzaiyanah
Universitas Islam Negeri Raden Fatah Palembang, Indonesia

Abdur Razzaq
iD https://orcid.org/0000-0002-8267-5700
Universitas Islam Negeri Raden Fatah Palembang, Indonesia

ABSTRACT

This study examines the ethical considerations and challenges related to digital technology in higher learning institutions, with a focus on intellectual property rights, database management, and the use of digital technology in education. The literature review and bibliometric analysis reveal a growing body of research focused on these topics, indicating the increasing importance of digital ethics in higher education. The study highlights the need for higher learning institutions to take a proactive and systematic approach to addressing digital ethics, by implementing appropriate policies and procedures, providing education and training to students, faculty, and staff, and promoting a culture of responsible and ethical technology use. The study also provides recommendations for higher learning institutions to promote digital ethics, including the development and implementation of comprehensive policies and procedures, ongoing education and training, and the establishment of a culture of digital ethics.

DOI: 10.4018/979-8-3693-2865-1.ch004

INTRODUCTION

In the context of higher education institutions like universities and colleges, digital ethics can be defined as the moral principles and values that guide the use, development, and governance of digital technologies within the academic environment (Anshari et al., 2022). The necessity of addressing digital ethics in higher learning institutions is vital as technology becomes universal in education. This research aims to examine challenges and propose strategies for fostering responsible digital practices in higher learning education (Alas et al., 2016). While, the ethical implications of data collection are irresistible. Learning management systems, educational apps, and online assessments result in the collection of vast amounts of student data, raising concerns about privacy and potential misuse. This study assesses an ethical guideline for data management in educational settings (Hamdan et al., 2020; Hasmawati, 2020).

Furthermore, intellectual property rights in digital learning are another crucial consideration. Students and faculty create and share digital content, raising challenges related to copyright, plagiarism, and fair use. The research aims to provide guidance on promoting responsible practices and respecting intellectual property rights (Huda et al., 2016).

Digital ethics extends to the responsible use of information and technology. This study explores the ethical implications of social media, online communication, and information literacy (Mulyani et al., 2021). It investigates the role of higher education institutions in educating students about responsible digital citizenship. Fostering responsible digital practices can create a more equitable and ethical learning environment (Sait & Anshari, 2021).

The chapter begins with an introduction emphasizing the importance of digital ethics in higher education. It then reviews relevant literature, focusing on data management, intellectual property rights, and responsible technology use. The methodology, analysis, and discussion follow, concluding with reflections on key findings and implications for future research and implementation.

LITERATURE REVIEW

This section describes with a comprehensive literature review of critical themes that underpin the ethical landscape in higher learning institutions. It delves into three pivotal topics: Intellectual Property Rights, Data Management, and Responsible Technology Use (Almunawar & Anshari, 2024; Mulyani et al., 2019). The integration of digital tools and platforms in academia has given rise to ethical considerations that demand attention (Razzaq et al., 2018; Al-Sharif, 2013). As the study navigates the issue of intellectual property, it explores the challenges associated with preservation creative outputs, including research papers, presentations, and multimedia resources. Simultaneously, the ethical implications of data collection and analysis in educational settings are scrutinized, focusing on concerns related to privacy, consent, and the responsible management of vast student datasets (Barzman et al., 2021). The literature review also discusses the discourse surrounding the responsible use of information and technology, examining the multifaceted dimensions of social media, online communication, and information literacy (Samiha et al., 2021). By critically engaging with the existing body of knowledge on these topics, this section lays the foundation for an understanding of the ethical imperatives in the digital landscape of higher education.

Intellectual Property Rights

Intellectual Property Rights (IPR) constitute a cornerstone in the realm of higher education, intricately woven to safeguard the creative endeavors and innovations emerging from students, faculty, and institutions (Sattiraju et al., 2022; Anshari et al., 2021). Central to this framework are copyright laws, which serve as guardians of original works, encompassing diverse forms of expression such as written compositions, musical compositions, and artistic creations. Through the grant of exclusive rights, copyright empowers creators to control the reproduction, distribution, adaptation, and display of their work, thereby fostering an environment that respects and protects the myriad expressions of intellectual ingenuity (Hawkridge et al., 2010).

Transitioning seamlessly, patents emerge as another critical dimension within the realm of IPR, offering protection to inventors and encouraging innovation. Unlike copyright, which shields creative expressions, patents are dedicated to safeguarding inventions (Anshari & Sumardi, 2021). By conferring exclusive rights, patents empower inventors to control the usage, sale, and importation of their innovations for a limited period, incentivizing inventiveness without the fear of unauthorized duplication. This dual-layered protection system, combining copyright and patents, ensures that both creative expressions and groundbreaking inventions within higher education are shielded from undue replication (Samiha et al., 2022).

Complementing the protective of IPR, trademarks play a pivotal role in the identification and differentiation of goods or services. Serving as distinctive symbols, trademarks contribute to the establishment of brand identity and consumer trust (Kashyap & Agrawal, 2020). By safeguarding the reputation and goodwill associated with a specific brand or product, trademarks foster an environment where educational institutions, faculty, and students can confidently engage in creative pursuits, knowing that their intellectual contributions are shielded from misrepresentation or unauthorized use (Japar & Anshari, 2023).

Furthermore, as we navigate the realm of trade secrets, the focus shifts to the confidential information that bestows a competitive advantage (Anshari et al., 2015). This layer of protection ensures that institutions can safeguard proprietary information critical to their success, fostering an atmosphere that not only encourages creativity but also upholds ethical principles surrounding intellectual property. These interconnected dimensions of IPR collectively form a vital framework that strengthens the setting of higher education, encouraging innovation while maintaining ethical standards.

Ethical Guidelines of IPR

In the domain of IPR within higher education, ethical considerations serve as a foundational element. Institutions traversing this complex landscape are obligated to unwaveringly adhere to ethical guidelines, fostering an environment that upholds the principles of acknowledging authorship, endorsing fair use, and rigorously preventing plagiarism (Lazariuc & Lozovanu, 2021).

The first is the principle of respecting authorship, highlighting the importance of recognizing and referencing the originators of ideas and works. This practice not only upholds the integrity of academic pursuits but also ensures that due credit is accorded where it is rightfully deserved. Seamlessly transitioning, the concept of fair use emerges as a critical ethical consideration, allowing restricted utilization of copyrighted materials for educational purposes without explicit permission. However, it is imperative to guarantee that such usage is transformative and does not compromise the original work's market value (Maya et al., 2023).

The ethical landscape further unfolds with a focus on the imperative of avoiding plagiarism, emphasizing the crucial role of academic honesty in preventing intellectual misappropriation. Simultaneously, the principle of proper attribution reinforces the ethical conduct of crediting original creators, even when incorporating ideas or works with modifications. Additionally, obtaining permission from the copyright holder becomes obligatory when employing copyrighted materials in ways that surpass the confines of fair use (Pratiwi et al., 2023).

Extending beyond ethical considerations pertaining to the utilization of existing intellectual property, the paradigm shifts towards the proactive protection of creative output. This involves concrete actions such as registering trademarks and patents, highlighting the ethical obligation to protection originality and innovative contributions. The narrative concludes with an educational imperative, emphasizing the importance of educating both students and faculty about intellectual property rights and the ethical use of copyrighted materials. This educational emphasis is pivotal in cultivating a culture within the academic community that values respect, responsibility, and ethical conduct. The ethical guidance for intellectual property rights in higher education intricately weaves a fabric that not only preserves academic integrity but also fosters a culture of responsible and respectful engagement with intellectual creations (Sun et al., 2021).

Data Management

Data management in higher learning institutions is a critical aspect of digital ethics. With the increasing use of technology in education, institutions are collecting and storing vast amounts of personal data about students, faculty, and staff. Proper data management practices are essential to ensure the privacy, security, and integrity of this data. This includes implementing appropriate data governance policies, such as data classification and access controls, to prevent unauthorized access and data breaches. It also involves ensuring that data is stored and transmitted securely, using encryption and other data protection measures (Ahmad et al., 2022).

Data management practices in higher learning institutions should also align with ethical principles around data collection, storage, and usage. This includes obtaining informed consent from individuals before collecting their data, providing transparency about how data is used and shared, and ensuring that data is used for legitimate educational purposes only. Furthermore, institutions should provide individuals with the ability to access, correct, and delete their data at any time (Ali et al., 2021). By adhering to ethical principles around data management, higher learning institutions can build trust with their stakeholders and maintain their reputation as responsible and trustworthy organizations.

In addition to ethical considerations, higher learning institutions should also consider the legal and regulatory requirements around data management. This includes complying with respective laws and regulations which impose specific data protection and privacy requirements on educational institutions. Institutions should also establish clear data management policies that align with industry best practices and standards. By implementing robust data management practices that align with ethical and legal requirements, higher learning institutions can ensure the responsible use of data, protect the privacy and security of their stakeholders, and maintain their reputation as ethical and trustworthy organizations (Chan, 2023).

Responsible Technology Use

Responsible technology use is an essential aspect of digital ethics in higher learning institutions. With the increasing use of technology in education, institutions must ensure that technology is used in a way that promotes ethical behavior and respect for individuals' rights. This includes implementing appropriate technology policies that align with ethical principles around data privacy, security, and accessibility. For example, institutions should implement appropriate access controls to prevent unauthorized access to sensitive data and ensure that technology is accessible to all individuals, regardless of their abilities or disabilities (Anshari et al., 2021).

Responsible technology use also involves promoting digital citizenship and literacy among students, faculty, and staff. This includes educating individuals about the responsible use of technology, such as avoiding cyberbullying, respecting intellectual property rights, and using technology in a way that promotes positive social interactions. By promoting digital citizenship and literacy, higher learning institutions can help to create a culture of responsible technology use that promotes ethical behavior and respect for individuals' rights.

Responsible technology use is also essential for maintaining the integrity and reputation of higher learning institutions in the context of ethical considerations. This includes protecting against cyber threats, such as data breaches and hacking, which can compromise the security and privacy of sensitive data. It also involves ensuring that technology is used in a way that promotes academic integrity, such as preventing cheating and plagiarism. By implementing robust technology policies and promoting digital citizenship and literacy, higher learning institutions can ensure the responsible use of technology, protect the privacy and security of their stakeholders, and maintain their reputation as ethical and trustworthy organizations.

METHODOLOGY

The methodology for this study involves a comprehensive literature review and bibliometric analysis to identify and analyze the relevant literature on digital ethics in higher learning institutions, with a focus on intellectual property rights, database management, and use of digital technology in education. The literature review involved a systematic search of relevant databases, such as Scopus, ProQuest, and JSTOR, using keywords such as "digital ethics", "intellectual property rights", "database management", and "digital technology in education". The search was limited to peer-reviewed articles, book chapters, and conference proceedings published in English between 2010 and 2023. The bibliometric analysis involved using tools such as VOSviewer to identify trends, themes, and networks in the literature, as well as to analyze the citation patterns and impact of key studies and authors. The data were analyzed using qualitative and quantitative methods, such as thematic analysis and statistical analysis, to identify key findings and trends. By using a rigorous and systematic methodology, this study aims to provide a comprehensive and nuanced understanding of digital ethics in higher learning institutions and to inform the development of policies and practices that promote ethical behavior and respect for individuals' rights.

ANALYSIS & DISCUSSION

The literature review and bibliometric analysis reveal several key findings related to digital ethics in higher learning institutions (see Figure 1). First, intellectual property rights are a critical aspect of digital ethics, as higher learning institutions must ensure that individuals' ideas, creations, and innovations are respected and protected. This involves implementing appropriate policies and procedures for copyright, patents, and trademarks, as well as providing education and training to students, faculty, and staff about the importance of intellectual property rights.

While, database management is an essential component of digital ethics in higher learning institutions. Proper database management practices are necessary to ensure the privacy, security, and integrity of sensitive data, such as personal information and research data. This includes implementing appropriate data governance policies, such as data classification and access controls, as well as ensuring that data is stored and transmitted securely.

Finally, the use of digital technology in education raises important ethical considerations related to digital equity, accessibility, and pedagogy (Anshari et al., 2016a). Higher learning institutions must ensure that technology is used in a way that promotes ethical behavior and respect for individuals' rights, while also providing equitable access to technology and ensuring that technology is accessible to all individuals, regardless of their abilities or disabilities.

Digital ethics is a complex and multifaceted issue in higher learning institutions, with several key areas of concern, including intellectual property rights, database management, and use of digital technology in education (Anshari et al., 2016b). The literature review and bibliometric analysis reveal a growing body of research focused on these topics, indicating the increasing importance of digital ethics in higher education.

The analysis also suggests that higher learning institutions must take a proactive and systematic approach to addressing digital ethics, by implementing appropriate policies and procedures, providing education and training to students, faculty, and staff, and promoting a culture of responsible and ethical technology use.

Figure 1. Bibliometric visualization results
(Source: Authors' Compilation, 2024)

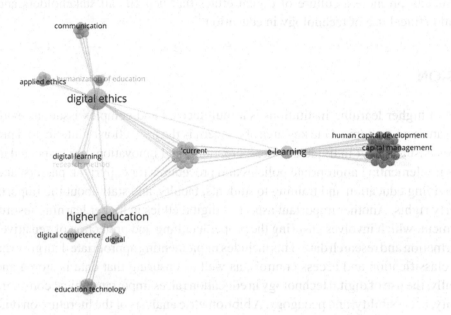

In terms of discussion, the findings raise several important questions and issues for higher learning institutions to consider. For example, how can institutions ensure that intellectual property rights are respected and protected, while also promoting openness and collaboration in research and education? How can institutions ensure that database management practices are ethical and secure, while also providing access to data for research and other purposes? How can institutions ensure that digital technology is used in a way that promotes ethical behavior and respect for individuals' rights, while also providing equitable access to technology and ensuring that technology is accessible to all individuals?

Based on the literature review and bibliometric analysis, higher learning institutions undertake various strategic measures to foster digital ethics (Anshari et al., 2017). Firstly, they develop and implement robust policies and procedures concerning intellectual property rights, database management, and the use of digital technology in education. These policies undergo regular review and updates to align with contemporary ethical and legal standards. Secondly, institutions provide continuous education and training to students, faculty, and staff, emphasizing digital ethics, intellectual property rights, and responsible technology use. Tailored to specific stakeholder needs, this education contributes to a nuanced understanding of ethical considerations. Thirdly, a culture of digital ethics is cultivated through open communication, collaboration, and dialogue, facilitated by forums and platforms for discussion. Fourthly, institutions ensure the ethical and secure management of databases by implementing robust data governance policies, including data classification and access controls. Fifthly, they champion digital equity and accessibility, striving to make technology available to all, irrespective of abilities or disabilities, through accommodations and support. Lastly, institutions engage in continual dialogue and collaboration on digital ethics by participating in professional networks, attending conferences, and contributing to the broader discourse within higher education.

By engaging in ongoing dialogue and collaboration around these questions and issues, higher learning institutions can promote a culture of digital ethics that benefits all stakeholders and ensures the responsible and ethical use of technology in education.

CONCLUSION

Digital ethics in higher learning institutions is a multifaceted and complex issue, as evidenced by the extensive literature on the topic. One key area of concern is the protection of intellectual property rights, which involves ensuring that individuals' ideas, creations, and innovations are respected and protected. This includes implementing appropriate policies and procedures for copyright, patents, and trademarks, as well as providing education and training to students, faculty, and staff about the importance of intellectual property rights. Another important aspect of digital ethics in higher learning institutions is database management, which involves ensuring the proper handling and protection of sensitive data, such as personal information and research data. This includes implementing appropriate data governance policies, such as data classification and access controls, as well as ensuring that data is stored and transmitted securely. Finally, the use of digital technology in education raises important ethical considerations related to digital equity, accessibility, and pedagogy. A bibliometric analysis of the literature on this topic reveals a growing body of research focused on the use of digital technology in teaching and learning, as well as the need for institutions to ensure that technology is used in a way that promotes ethical behavior and respect for individuals' rights. By addressing these ethical considerations, higher learning institutions can promote a culture of responsible and ethical technology use that benefits all stakeholders.

REFERENCES

Ahmad, K., Maabreh, M., Ghaly, M., Khan, K., Qadir, J., & Al-Fuqaha, A. (2022). Developing future human-centered smart cities: Critical analysis of smart city security, Data management, and Ethical challenges. *Computer Science Review*, *43*, 100452. doi:10.1016/j.cosrev.2021.100452

Al-Sharif, M. A. B. (2023). ETHICAL ISSUES WITH TECHNOLOGY IN HIGHER EDUCATION. *Integrating Technology Into Student Affairs (# 9 SAPPI Series)*, (9), 69.

Alas, Y., Anshari, M., Sabtu, N. I., & Yunus, N. (2016). Second-chance university admission, the theory of planned behaviour and student achievement. *International Review of Education*, *62*(3), 299–316. doi:10.1007/s11159-016-9558-5

Ali, M., & Abdel-Haq, M. K. (2021). Bibliographical analysis of artificial intelligence learning in Higher Education: is the role of the human educator and educated a thing of the past? In *Fostering Communication and Learning With Underutilized Technologies in Higher Education* (pp. 36–52). IGI Global. doi:10.4018/978-1-7998-4846-2.ch003

Almunawar, M. N., & Anshari, M. (2024). Customer acceptance of online delivery platform during the COVID-19 pandemic: The case of Brunei Darussalam. *Journal of Science and Technology Policy Management*, *15*(2), 288–310. doi:10.1108/JSTPM-04-2022-0073

Anshari, M., Alas, Y., & Guan, L. S. (2016b). Developing online learning resources: Big data, social networks, and cloud computing to support pervasive knowledge. *Education and Information Technologies, 21*(6), 1663–1677. doi:10.1007/s10639-015-9407-3

Anshari, M., Alas, Y., & Guan, L. S. (2017). Pervasive knowledge, social networks, and cloud computing: E-learning 2.0. *Eurasia Journal of Mathematics, Science and Technology Education, 11*(5), 909–921. doi:10.12973/eurasia.2015.1360a

Anshari, M., Alas, Y., Sabtu, N. P. H., & Hamid, M. S. A. (2016a). Online Learning: Trends, issues and challenges in the Big Data Era. *Journal of E-learning and Knowledge Society, 12*(1).

Anshari, M., Alas, Y., Yunus, N., Sabtu, N. I., & Hamid, M. H. (2015). Social customer relationship management and student empowerment in online learning systems. *International Journal of Electronic Customer Relationship Management, 9*(2-3), 104–121. doi:10.1504/IJECRM.2015.071711

Anshari, M., Almunawar, M. N., Masri, M., & Hrdy, M. (2021). Financial technology with AI-enabled and ethical challenges. *Society, 58*(3), 189–195. doi:10.1007/s12115-021-00592-w

Anshari, M., Almunawar, M. N., & Razzaq, A. (2021). Developing talents vis-à-vis fourth industrial revolution. [IJABIM]. *International Journal of Asian Business and Information Management, 12*(4), 20–32. doi:10.4018/IJABIM.20211001.oa2

Anshari, M., & Sumardi, W. H. (2020). Employing big data in business organisation and business ethics. *International Journal of Business Governance and Ethics, 14*(2), 181–205. doi:10.1504/IJBGE.2020.106349

Anshari, M., Syafrudin, M., Fitriyani, N. L., & Razzaq, A. (2022). Ethical responsibility and sustainability (ERS) development in a metaverse business model. *Sustainability (Basel), 14*(23), 15805. doi:10.3390/su142315805

Barzman, M., Gerphagnon, M., Aubin-Houzelstein, G., Baron, G. L., Benard, A., Bouchet, F., & Mora, O. (2021). Exploring digital transformation in higher education and research via scenarios. *Journal of Futures Studies, 25*(3), 65–78.

Hamdan, M., Ahmad, N., Jaidin, J. H., & Anshari, M. (2020). Internationalisation in Brunei's higher education and its policy implications: Case study of Universiti Brunei Darussalam. *TEST Engineering and Management, 83*, 764–779.

Hasmawati, F., Samiha, Y. T., Razzaq, A., & Anshari, M. (2020). Understanding nomophobia among digital natives: Characteristics and challenges. *Journal of Critical Reviews, 7*(13), 122–131.

Hawkridge, D., Armellini, A., Nikoi, S., Rowlett, T., & Witthaus, G. (2010). Curriculum, intellectual property rights and open educational resources in British universities—And beyond. *Journal of Computing in Higher Education, 22*(3), 162–176. doi:10.1007/s12528-010-9036-1

Huda, M., Anshari, M., Almunawar, M. N., Shahrill, M., Tan, A., Jaidin, J. H., & Masri, M. (2016). Innovative teaching in higher education: The big data approach. *Tojet*, 1210-1216.

Kashyap, A., & Agrawal, R. (2020). Scale development and modeling of intellectual property creation capability in higher education. *Journal of Intellectual Capital, 21*(1), 115–138. doi:10.1108/JIC-09-2018-0168

Lazariuc, C., & Lozovanu, E. (2021). Intellectual property in the context of global ethics. [EEJRS]. *Eastern European Journal for Regional Studies*, *7*(1), 218–229. doi:10.53486/2537-6179.7-1.11

Maya, Y., Putri, R. W., & Davey, O. M. (2023, May). Toward the Legal Aspect on Developing Academics Intellectual Property Rights in University. In *3rd Universitas Lampung International Conference on Social Sciences (ULICoSS 2022)* (pp. 17-29). Atlantis Press. 10.2991/978-2-38476-046-6_3

Mulyani, M. A., Razzaq, A., Sumardi, W. H., & Anshari, M. (2019, August). Smartphone adoption in mobile learning scenario. In *2019 International Conference on Information Management and Technology (ICIMTech)* (Vol. 1, pp. 208-211). IEEE..

Japar, D. F. I. P. M., & Anshari, M. (2023). Potential and challenges of the Metaverse on future businesses. In *Metaverse applications for new business models and disruptive innovation* (pp. 102-119). IGI Global.

Mulyani, M. A., Yusuf, S., Siregar, P., Nurihsan, J., Razzaq, A., & Anshari, M. (2021, August). Fourth industrial revolution and educational challenges. In *2021 International Conference on Information Management and Technology (ICIMTech)* (Vol. 1, pp. 245-249). IEEE. 10.1109/ICIMTech53080.2021.9535057

Pratiwi, A. C., Pertiwi, N. R. L., & Al Baihaqi, A. H. (2023). The Importance of Understanding Intellectual Property Rights from a Legal Perspective and Its Benefits for Society. *Proceedings vof Islamic Economics. Business, and Philanthropy*, *2*(2), 100–120.

Razzaq, A., Samiha, Y. T., & Anshari, M. (2018). Smartphone habits and behaviors in supporting students self-efficacy. *International Journal of Emerging Technologies in Learning*, *13*(2), 94. doi:10.3991/ijet.v13i02.7685

Sait, M. A., & Anshari, M. (2021). Industrial Revolution 4.0: A New Challenge to Brunei Darussalam's Unemployment Issue. [IJABIM]. *International Journal of Asian Business and Information Management*, *12*(4), 33–44. doi:10.4018/IJABIM.20211001.oa3

Samiha, Y. T., Handayani, T., Razaq, A., Fithriyah, M., Fitri, A., & Anshari, M. (2022, March). Implementation of Education 4.0 as sustainable decisions for a sustainable development. In *2022 International Conference on Decision Aid Sciences and Applications (DASA)* (pp. 846-850). IEEE. 10.1109/DASA54658.2022.9765080

Samiha, Y. T., Handayani, T., Razzaq, A., Fitri, A., Fithriyah, M., & Anshari, M. (2021, November). Sustainability of Excellence in Education 4.0. In *2021 Sustainable Leadership and Academic Excellence International Conference (SLAE)* (pp. 1-5). IEEE. 10.1109/SLAE54202.2021.9788095

Sattiraju, V. K., Pandey, R., Pallela, R., Sircar, A., Ligade, V. S., Muragundi, P. M., & Janodia, M. D. (2022). Intellectual property rights policies of higher education institutions (HEIs) in India: A cross-sectional study. *Journal of Science and Technology Policy Management*, *13*(4), 837–848. doi:10.1108/JSTPM-01-2021-0002

Sun, X., Zhou, X., Wang, Q., Tang, P., Law, E. L. C., & Cobb, S. (2021). Understanding attitudes towards intellectual property from the perspective of design professionals. *Electronic Commerce Research*, *21*(2), 521–543. doi:10.1007/s10660-019-09378-z

Section 2
Green Development

Chapter 5
Green Education to Promote Green Technological Skills

Asfand Yar
Universiti Brunei Darussalam, Brunei

Mahani Hamdan
ⓘ https://orcid.org/0000-0003-3859-4433
Universiti Brunei Darussalam, Brunei

Muhammad Anshari
ⓘ https://orcid.org/0000-0002-8160-6682
Universiti Brunei Darussalam, Brunei

ABSTRACT

The term "Green" instantly sparks green scenery of nature relating to plants, lush fields, forests, and all types of flora. This study is a requisite effort to harness green education enabled with green technological skills and concepts in the digital arena. It will cover the analysis of the necessities of green initiatives in the context of prevailing climate challenges, and eco-friendly opportunities presented with digital change, emphasize the vital role of digital literacy to meet the demands of the green skills job market, discuss the principles and methods of green education and offers proposals to integrate green skills in the curriculum, address obstacles in the integration of green education and technology with digital green innovation and recommend policy interventions and guidelines to develop green innovation education web.

INTRODUCTION

This is the fourth industrial revolution era based on digitalization, digital technology, tools, and transformation where all economic growth and social drivers merely depend on technological innovation. The upcoming era will be called the fifth industrial revolution, the green digital revolution, a merger of ecology, technology, sociology, science, math, and economics. The response to the evolutionary green revolution becomes more dynamic to encompass and develop the moderation strategies for green technology and setting for a green future. Modern online technologies have more eco-friendly operations, in

DOI: 10.4018/979-8-3693-2865-1.ch005

structuring the perfect bond between sustainable practices and digital green revolution. The education system works as a catalyst to make changes in society. The mode of incorporation of eco-sustainable measures with green expertise into educational programs is an emergent trend in academic circles to foster eco-vision and green skills among educators and learners for green and sustainable preparations. Education as a service sector has the potential to transform the education process (teaching-learning) with eco-friendly tools, techniques, policies, and strategies to develop the green education model and conducive environment for children (Aithal & Rao, 2016). Green education is a diverse range of green initiatives, from early childhood to university education to provoke green efforts for a green future through educational policies, administrative tools, real-world base knowledge models, infrastructural settings, and dynamic engagements of the community. Green education, integrating green technological solutions and sustainable development practices as part of the educational curriculum, can adopt the established bond between man and nature. The purposes, theories, and skills of ecological education can be part of school syllabus by opting green curriculum to improve the learning and understanding attitude towards science and facilitate students to realize their responsibilities for environmental protection (Tan, 2004). Green innovation holds the node of digital technology and green sustainability pursuing the ability and power of the digital revolution. The complexity of the situation demands multi-dimensional schemes that can condense the externalities of digital infrastructures as electronic wastes, and carbon capture as the prime objective while promoting sustainable decisions and green digital solutions. Green education grapples and accentuates the activities, initiatives, and practices in education for student awareness regarding environmental issues, climate change, global warming, glacier melting, water scarcity, tsunami, sea level rise, cloudburst, urban flooding, droughts, deforestation, natural resource depletion, smog, air quality, soil erosion, sustainable development programs, biodiversity, green energy, preservation, and conservation strategies. The dual challenges of intensifying climate threats on the globe and digital innovation, demand green education as a decisive force to shape the sustainable future landscape. The key objective of green education is to educate young minds to develop a learning attitude, drive a sense of responsibility, and train them with skills for mature actions to preserve a sustainable environment for green contribution and innovation in the digital arena. Environment and natural resource management courses, ecological informatics, climate justice debates, environment-related science exhibitions, green clubs, sustainable thematic projects, and reuse, reduce, and recycle projects can motivate thoughtful and critical thinking concerning the gravity of environmental and climate challenges. Green education is raising a sense of responsible adoption of nature and connection with natural fabric and has the intention to groom young people, educate educators, to develop a sense among the community, about environmental concerns for their contribution to a sustainable and green future. The evolving panorama of the digital era and the merger of the digital and green revolutions have surfaced with a novel front. As global voices are grappling with climate challenges, resource scarcity, and biodiversity loss, the importance of green novelty has been enunciated with low pitch. Although the digital revolution has greatly shaped climate actions by opening new avenues to promote, be aware, and engage in sustainable arrangements, however, this unprecedented urgency plea for the ropes and hopes from digital transformation to consider environmental perils at a rapid pace and through inventive technological smart solutions. The realization of this call requires a potential task force fostered with green skills and ample green education. Green skills are vital to foster green resilience, digital transition, and emerging trends in green labor markets. This chapter is an attempt to discover a synergetic bond among green revolution, green education, and green skills to drive shared development for a sustainable future along with digital transformative support.

BACKGROUND AND SIGNIFICANCE

Green education, environmental education, and sustainable education are similar terminologies rooted in the late 20th century about movements that raised awareness for the environment. The 1970 momentous events of the UN conference on the human environment in Stockholm and the publication of Rachel Cordon's "Silent Spring" encouraged global attention to green issues and provided the foundation for green education. Green education as the catalytic agent has developed a multidimensional approach, methods, strategies, and initiatives to foster and promote eco-literacy through multidisciplinary prospects to galvanize and prepare the citizens to get mandatory knowledge, and skills, and adopt the necessary values for the smooth transition towards green living. Green education has significantly raised awareness about environmental sustainability, and green adoption through the provision of reliable, and accurate information about human activities and climate threats, devising adaptive modes, and advising resilient capacities to protect mankind from environmental and climate hazards.

Keystone for Green Education

The regions across the globe are confronting climate coercions and global warming unprecedently alarm the human future on Earth. The juncture of ecological fronts and the push for the reshaping of a sustainable future provides a holistic basis for the development and design of green education. Green education can excel in conventional academic domains, with the incorporation of sustainable notions, themes, approaches, and actions. The maturity in green education is critical to cultivating an ideology that stimulates practical actions for the active performance of green tasks. The education system has opted into a hybrid mode during COVID-19, and this transformation from a conventional to a hybrid mode of operation has become effective in the teaching and learning process. The outcome of the research explores the impact of how green computing practices and information technology-based teaching and learning can bring revolutionary reforms in the education sector. The findings describe that information technology-based teaching-learning practices and green computing practices pledge the eco-friendly performance for a green educational setup that reconnects students, educators, the community, and the market with nature (Podder, Karuppiah, Thomas, & Samanta, 2022). There is a need to anchor a coherent set of **objective principles** and **methods** of green education in a green digital transformation context. The foundation of green education can be created on interdisciplinary lines that incorporate concepts and examples of diverse subjects. It can develop attentive morality in the use of **"digital sobriety"** to reduce digital impacts for a sustainable future of this planet. There is sufficient policy space in the development of a **"thinking system"** that can impulse inclusive insights for the digital green innovative decisions aligned with environmental and social domains for sustainable responses. The thinking system encourages young minds to think critically and rationally in fathoming the system of environment, society, and economy for long-term policy actions, probable outcomes, and potential impacts on green initiatives. Green education emphasizes an inclusive and multi-approach that can develop a modern **curriculum of "green digital skill"** for the promotion of green practices and adoption of green principles. Integration of digital and social sciences to enterprise with the technology industry can deliver an advanced outlook to educators to enrich green awareness for green digital solutions. Students and the community can actively learn and teach more about recycling ideas, reuse designs, and reduce methods through E-waste solution programs. Vocational courses based on green, clean, affordable, sustainable, and renewables can develop a deep connection with green nature and boost energy efficient systems in practicing and promoting the ethos of green future and eco-friendly living. Green education is committed to designing such strategies that can mitigate the negative environmental impacts. These core principles of green education guarantee the provision of a new responsible generation that is critical towards environmental disasters. The combination of core principles and key concepts of green education within a green policy framework can blend economic growth and ecological factors for a promising green and resilient future. The key aspiration of green education is for students to act as strong footings to the policymakers, educators, and active learners in understanding socio-economic, and eco-techno complexities and enable the students as active social change agents in fostering a green future.

Pillars of Green Education

The structure green educational system consists of green schools, green curriculum, green training, and green communities. The embryonic trend of green schools with a reformed system based on eco-education is to develop and promote green education. Green education by practicing smart digital tools and digital platforms benefits students, and educators, and rapidly regulates the educational environment. The construction of green boundaries in educational institutes as useful learning helps students' connectivity with nature. The empirical results of a study illustrate that green governance at the university level can boost students' learning, teachers' performance, and employee satisfaction to support sustainable projects (Leal Filho et al., 2019). The vision to establish green schools is to make sure that all the schools from kindergarten to secondary level should attain certification. The green school views a whole institution method, by developing an inclusive learning environment like green classrooms, teaching methodologies, co-curricular activities, school management, facilities, and functions to teach, learn, and guide the students and learners about climate and environmental challenges. There are vibrant efforts to develop science and technological societies integrated along with digital transformations in the education sector. A study exhibits that digital technologies can provide digital thinking solutions by robust digital teaching and administration to address the challenges to green school establishment (Qiu, Chen, & Ng, 2023). Green education pieces of training show significant impacts on student's concepts, behavior, and attitude for a future sustainable environment. A survey study using a Likert scale revealed a positive correlation showing that the students who received a university education in environment-related disciplines are more voluntary in green movements (Boca & Saraçlı, 2019). The existing trend to establish green schools is facing challenges of high reconstruction costs, outdated mode of school governance, poor management efficiencies, insufficient infrastructure, and less information on green areas among students and educators. The goal of establishing green schools is to foster knowledge and skills among students of all ages about sustainable practices. The green school approach practices the revolutionary concepts that all students irrespective of their gender, social status, family background, and cultural disparities should enable them to gain general awareness, ample information, mandatory knowledge, essential skills, and learning tools with collaborative and unity minds for a possible green future. The ACES project, with 11 European and Latin American universities has effectively applied green curriculum. UNESCO is working hard to establish green schools with a new global theme "Education for Sustainable Development-2030" to make climate-ready students across the globe. The second pillar of green education is the development of a green curriculum with the vision to adopt an extensive method that can incorporate climate education in vocational and technical school syllabi, teachers' professional and skill development green training courses, green careers, teacher resources, and pedagogical courses. The development of a green curriculum should include a green outlook, green concepts, and sustainable practices, that encourage the students and educators to successfully apply digital tools with green skills and be capable of addressing the modern complex challenges for the practice of digital sustainable solutions for human benefits. According to UNESCO analysis, knowledge, skill, and conceptual gaps in textbooks of more than a hundred countries' national curricula, regarding green, sustainable, climate, and environmental perspectives. A sizeable number of students in educational institutions across the globe are lacking in green education knowledge and understanding of basic sustainable activities and green actions. The content and context of teacher's training model should cover theoretical, productive, moral, and research spheres (Bonil, Calafell, Granados, Junyent, & Tarín, 2012). The issue becomes grimmer, on the part of teacher's competence, interdisciplinary knowledge depth, and understanding of green drivers. Practical modes of green education and pragmatic co-curricular activities like school gardening, and exhibitions on 3R processes can enrich students' wisdom on green engagements and sustainable knowledge. Key findings of a systematic review of the literature show that a positive correlation exists between students' performance and green spaces within and around educational institutions (Browning & Rigolon, 2019). The modern green curriculum should encompass mitigating and adaptative strategies in the teacher guide, methodology, and training for early childhood classes to the post-secondary level to engage educators and students about the areas of ecology, economy, technology, and society and inspire them to sustainable actions. The course outline both for teachers and educators should focus on lessons and strategies on the importance of fresh water and conservation, ecological benefits of forests, conservation themes, nature, and biodiversity subjects, skills, and adaptive use of solar as a source of energy, and clean practices for adoption of sustainability in daily life. The inclusion of green skills at elementary school levels can increase environmentally sustainable practices by adoption of 3R strategy. The objective of a green curriculum is to design the student learning outcomes to transform the economy, environment, and society for a sustainable development future by adoption, promotion, and execution of green practices. The efforts to design and develop the novel green curriculum can be piloted by experienced interdisciplinary specialists and expert authors on socio-economic, socio-political, and socio-psychological subjects and themes like the post-carbon economy, climate crisis, climate justice, climate anxiety, and green revolution to develop green skills on compassion, rational decision-making, and public advocacy ranks. The third and foremost pillar of green education is the development of professional teacher training and skill modules based on climate actions, green knowledge, and sustainable actions with the vision to provide a support system to increase the institutional capacity, of the education sector. The fourth pillar of green education is the development of green communities giving opportunities to the public by educating them with green skills, sustainable actions, and preserving attitudes in community centers. Global Rivers Environmental Education Network (Green) is an international organization that works for community networking and provides a roadmap for the development of local-based green projects.

Digital Transformation

The dynamic digital swing shows a vibrant thrive in social communication, economic conditions, and business operations covers the inclusivity of digital tools in human activities from online health services to online education, from banking to e-commerce, from water sensors in agriculture to blockchain in the environment conservation, and from chatbot customer service to informed data-based policy decisions, and governance infrastructure. This digital transformation has objectives of new business models, enlarging productivity, boosting operational efficacy, improving consumer satisfaction, amplifying connectivity, resource recovery, cost cutting, and encouraging change and reform. Better-quality access to the right information from digital flux, modernized organizational operations based on data-driven decisions, new digital innovative markets, and workplaces are the substantial advantages of this digital spring. Green information technology is an attempt to consume resources effectually and operatively to minimize the impacts of organizational procedures on the environment. A qualitative study explores that green information technology is being adopted and practiced in the Philippines' higher education sector with approaches including paperless digital record systems, resourceful IT tools and equipment, secure e-waste disposal, 3R strategy, sustainable courses, and awareness programs (Hernandez, 2020). Besides the challenges such as the surge of energy, greenhouse gas emissions, and a glut of electronic waste management, digital transformations have remarkable successful stories like smart agriculture techniques and drip irrigation water systems to boost bumper crop harvest with water management, conservation, and food preservation strategies. The fruitful digital transformation believes in a visionary and committed leadership having thriving strategies and resourceful labor to respond to the changing trends of competitive digital markets, innovative economies, and customer needs. Data accessibility is the backbone of developing digital solutions in the digital ecosystem based on training and testing of algorithms. The results of the empirical study analyze that digital transformation remarkably sponsors considerable innovative green businesses with the favorable roles of government financial inputs and incentives in the form of subsidies, tax exemption policy, and investment in research and development (Feng, Wang, Song, & Liu, 2022). Thus, digital transformation like a vital force, compels the stakeholders to devise new business strategies and design modern business models to perform according to the needs of the developing digital era.

Green Education and Digital Transformation

In the modern digitalized era, the digital landscape deals with the practical application of various kinds of digital tools, utilization of digital platforms, operate digital and online resources, to initiate, assist, engage, collaborate, navigate, and accelerate the efforts for knowledge gain and skill learning both for teachers and students in the domain of green education. This can help educators create dynamic learning classroom environments and design participating situations by using advanced audio-video teaching aids and tools like simulated and augmented reality where students are vibrantly able to absorb the penetration of the ecosystem. Digital transformation develops a sense of realization and ownership that encourages students to play their role actively with clear devotion and deliberate actions in preservation, conservation, and sustainable activities. Digital platforms offer worldwide innovation, collaborations, and exchanges on "think green and go green" notions. The traditional educational setup and learning techniques for green and sustainability can never fulfill the sustainable development goals and green tasks, and here the inclusion of digital transformation comes in educational settings to provide the updated version in terms of extensive online resources, synergistic tools, immersive practices for student teaching learning milieu. Digital transformation becomes productive in the green education system when educators and learners are capable enough to practice digital pedagogical models and tools proficiently, to improve student learning outcomes for green solutions with quality and better institutional setup. Technical and vocational training institutions with digital resources can provide an opportunity for learners to demonstrate their creativity for green skills and respond to forthcoming youth unemployment soon. Digitally innovative tools and technologies are embracing by university graduates and serving researchers in academia to collect real-time data, of environmental statistics and simulated experiments on climate indicators like air quality, smog intensity, water quality, deforestation, weather patterns, temperature fluctuations, rain and flood forest for policy inputs and data-driven based informed decisions. Digital technology resets the tailored needs and pace of self-learning to harness the potential of digital transformation for a green future landscape.

Nexus of Green Sustainability and Digital Transformation

As the digital space is rising exponentially and digital technology expanding and driving the entire economic circle, there are grave ecological footprints in terms of digital pollution like carbon emissions, extensive energy consumption, and e-waste generation also become intensified. A study "Towards digital sobriety" by Frederic Bordage, claims that for the digital galaxy to function, it costs 75 million data centers as servers, 34 billion user terminals like smartphones, mobile phones, laptops, tablets, desktop computers, projectors, TV sets, and 1.5 billion communication networks as Wi-Fi points, Routers, and network sockets. A "shift project" report on the environmental impact of digital technology narrates that digital technologies have carbon footprints, and their share is nearly 4% in global greenhouse gas emissions. In this scenario, the digital revolution appears as a paradox, that in one way provides tools to deal on environmental fronts, while deepening the risks associated with it. Thus, the prime aim of the green revolution is to navigate this puzzle to combat digital pollution by reducing emission footprints because of digital advancement. Digital transformation has a strong potential to grasp the environment confronted through innovative green technologies, green and clean energy efficient systems for powerful data centers, and a 3R strategy for waste products. Cloud computing platforms, teleconference tools such as Zoom, webinar, skype, remote sense technology, virtual exchanges like virtual test drives, Internet of technologies, Artificial intelligence, and machine learning tools can effectively be adept to enable remote work, lessen and safe disposal of e-waste, and energy consumption to harness ecological benefits along with scalable, flexible, accessible, inclusive, hybrid, and normalized solutions in the digital revolution. Digital transformations provide enough support for resource optimization and reduction in e-waste, Internet of Things technologies consist of devices like digital meters, and industry base sensors for mechanical efficiency and resource optimization by collection and identification of important, accurate, and precise data. Digital alternative tools can be leveraged as an instrumental factor for green alternative digital solutions by adopting innovative patterns to attain global sustainable goals. The shift from physical to digital products and services as digital alternatives like e-books foster the environmental efforts for sustainability, and consumer accessibility, lessen energy use, and curtail paper waste. Digital transformations have brought radical eco-friendly steps in businesses, to decrease deforestation, by accepting the transition from paperless to accelerating digitalization. Blockchain tools and technologies are encouraging green practices to promise safety, responsibility, transparency, and accountability in supply chain management by controlling and tracking real-time data visualizations. The smart green supply-chain management system is improving green applications by opening green processes and dealing with green affairs with digital transformation. A study suggests that a green smart chain management system as a mediating agent can enhance green performance along with digital transformation (Lerman, Benitez, Müller, de Sousa, & Frank, 2022). 3D printers are capable enough to produce spare parts and cut inventory costs. Big data analytics, to detect and uncover data trends and patterns in an energy management system, can help in spotting excessive resource consumption, and waste creation, predict the outcomes, and evaluate the performance of green projects to enhance operational efficiency based on data-driven decisions and improve the efficiency of green energy sources. E-vehicles under digital technology are accelerating the shift in the transportation sector to optimize traffic and manage logistics and freight systems in digital mode. Green education in an effective transformation mode can harness sustainable digital solutions. The inclusion of green education and digital skills is the promising paradigm swing for a sustainable and resilient planet. Thus, green education should come to play with substantial role in balancing the equation between digital transformations and environmental pollution pledging that digital solutions are significant to own environment stewards and, a positive contribution to Earth's sustainable landscape and green future along with digital progress. Nevertheless, the integration of green education and digital transformation has enhanced collaborative digital green networking and information access among diverse cultures and communities to exchange ideas. Thus, the transition pace towards green innovation can accelerate with the fusion of green and digital skills.

Urge for Green Innovation in Digital Times

The urgency for green innovation is rooted in the imperative call to deal with imminent climate threats, without compromising technological spread and economic growth. World intensified threat of climate calamity calls urgent need to start green innovative steps to deliver mitigating solutions to man-made pollution problems on Earth. The digital green revolution keeps its pace to reshape the global village. The inclusion of sustainable practices in this digital transformation process is a need of time. Digital transformation can provide tools to conserve the environment, manage energy consumption, and reduce e-waste. In the 21st century, the green revolution has emerged as a vital force and key driver that can respond actively and critically by designing processes and systems for smooth economic growth trajectory and environment preservation, leveraging digital technologies to open the path for a sustainable future view. Green innovative practices can reconcile the in-demand prerequisites of emergent digital green economies along with the essentials of environmental stewardship. Green innovation is vital to support and attain sustainable development goals. Under the umbrella of green innovation and digital transformation, the introduction and practical use of smart technologies for preserving and conserving green nature brings global determination into line. Green education and digital transformation can be possible as a catalyst for the growth of the green and digital economy. The Green Revolution can foster the establishment of green markets having green products and services for the greener circular economy, where green regulations can be applicable to drive eco-friendly and technology consumer businesses. Green skills have gained the attention of eyeballs and emerged as vibrant instruments for green stewards and entrepreneurship in this unfolding digital age. Green skills have the expertise that can extend resource efficiency and sponsor sustainable efforts. Green skills under the spectrum of green education, incorporate an extensive range of capabilities, from the practical experience of the renewable energy system to the buildup of ideas and awareness about green innovation through data science, tools, and analytics. Green skills from design to disposal exemplify the best abilities to practice digital tools like climate and energy data analytics for the implementation of green strategies by digital designs, sustainable techniques by software solutions, and to contribute to environmental stewardship. The demand for green skills is driven by regulatory conditions, market forces, and social trends to attain sustainable visions. The new models of green businesses are rising, spotting the fact that the digital-driven decisions related to green sustainable incorporation need time to operate the market for consumer compliance. The emerging trends of the green market are demanding green experts and professionals equipped with a range of digital tools and green skills to practice sustainable decision processes. The industry deems the thrust to align the diverse job market with in-demand green skills to reach the environmental objectives and sustainable development goals decisively. The green energy market needs energy data analysts using big data techniques that can regulate and enhance the efficiency of green and clean energy sources. Green skills are being considered as the backbone of a green circulation economy where humans can enjoy the benefits of economy, ecology, and technology equally by making digital literate. In traditional meaning, digital literacy is the adeptness to use digital alternative tools effectively and efficiently for analysis, and interpretation of data. Digital literacy i.e. the digital learning platforms provides a strong foundation to develop expertise and a toolkit for maintaining green skills by applying digital technologies to attain green targets and sustainable commitments. Green skills with digital transformation have a central role in steering the global green and digital economy which is expanding because of exponential digital growth associated with risks and gains for a green future. In a nutshell, the desire for green education in the digital phase by pulling off digital tools and digital platforms, and opening new horizons of industrial style, business models, customer-oriented markets, and economic structures are to reduce carbon emissions, improve resource efficiency, data-driven decision-making and digital based innovative solutions that promise green future.

Challenges Associated With Green Innovation and Digital Transformations

A study in China found that businesses switching to digital transformation has meaningful and positive effects in terms of resource allocation, strengthening economic growth, regulations on the environment, pollution reduction, and reinforcement of institutional capacity on the promotion of green innovation (Wang, Yan, & Ou, 2023). As the digital transformation has evolved and reshaped the economy, ecology, and society, there are certain challenges confronted green education in the digital transformative phase such as outdated educational models, quality of standard curriculum, worthy professionals, competency of teachers, financial controls, legal affairs, cybersecurity, digital literacy, digital divide, investment costs, market regulations, business models, capacity gaps, and job creations in the rapid evolution of digital economics under digital transformations and green skills for green momentum. Green and sustainable development strategies ensure the upgradation of digital transformations, and digital economies in the digital age. The results of the reviewed study between digitally transformed businesses and green initiatives narrate that digitally transformed enterprises effectively promote green culture and upgrade digital economies (Yu, 2023). The adoption of digital alternatives for digital and green solutions requires data-driven decision-making to set up initial costs in a rapidly digitally changing scenario. The initial cost to set, develop, and implement green projects is relatively expensive with high upfront investments and longer payoff periods, this becomes a crucial state for marginal groups, small and medium enterprises, modest organizations, limited companies, and small-scale businesses to find reasonable solutions with low financial capital, short term profit return strategy, and unskilled digital workforce to harness digital alternatives with green solutions. The rapid swing of the fourth industrial digital revolution demands digital and data literacy for young minds to cultivate a green environment. Discrepancies in digital and green skills affect the green market's mobility, operational costs, and business efficiency. As a preemptive measure, the inclusion of digital and environmental literacy in green education is vital to fulfill global commitments and to cope with inequalities. The integration of digital-induced tools and green practices to harness and implement digital transformation for an eco-friendly future makes an intricate system that can meddle with the geo-political, geo-economics, cultural, and social parameters among global partners. There should come robust education, vocational, labor, and industrial policies with market regulatory, legal, and institutional frameworks that can propose the policy interventions and tools to facilitate the green markets for a trained and updated digital literate workforce in the adoption of green and digital skills to promote a culture of sustainable practices.

Modernize Perspective of Green Education

The modern and revolutionary perspective of green education has gained much attention among academia, environmental groups, policymakers, and governments worldwide. The evolutionary concept of green has changed and is reflected according to social needs and priority trends. Green education grips a conceivable vision that can reshape and evolve our conceptions about sustainable future design and adopt environmental stewardship with a modern digital alternative approach. Green jobs are gaining pivotal focus in policy circles, political discussions, and economic spheres. A community educator with experience in environmental education and justice fields stated that green jobs will improve sustainable society settings shortly together with a STEM-equipped workforce (Griswold, 2013). Green innovation or novelty designates new courses, methods, and tools that can reduce climate and environmental effects notably with the inclusion of green targets, and offers changes in patterns of production, procedure, and consumption. The Green Revolution comprehends the technologies and practices intending to develop, promote, and manage energy-efficient systems, and waste reductions for green living. Green Skills deals with the knowledge, expertise, and capabilities to make proficient young minds that can contribute to a green economy and sustainability by designing, implementing, and managing plans and projects. The skills extend from scientific, mathematical, technical, engineering, and vocational courses to awareness programs and workshops. Green education encompasses conventional educational policies, plans, initiatives, and strategies to develop innovative curricula and syllabi to equip the students' skulls with innovative green skills to foster green solutions. A multi-dimensional policy is essential that can integrate green and digital skills to extend the impression of green education on digitalized sustainability. Green education aims to encourage the conceptual debate among interdisciplinary related themes on economics, ecology, technology, and other social elements and appreciate the critical thinking styles and problem-solving attitudes in young minds to paramount effective green and sustainable environmental principles, practices, processes, problems, and active solutions by digital means. Green education demands a holistic and multidimensional movement to manage balance and integration among education, environment, economy, digital technology, and sustainability. Green education supports the thinking system to understand, and analyze complex ecological and social relations, to develop critical and problem-solving minds, and to design innovative digital solutions. A study devised a sustainable engineering system and leadership model taken from the thinking system approach to improve the communications between leaders and teams in cross-cultural exchange by the use of information technology to attain green and sustainable digital transformation (Kroculick, 2022). Open resources of green education allow citizens to actively participate in the public decision process for the establishment of sustainable communities. The modern notion of green education promotes inclusivity and focuses the cross-cultural challenges, values cultural worth, and accepts and respects cultural diversity. In a nutshell, the modernized perspective of green education accentuates the development of green landscape, the importance of green knowledge, and digital skills, values the thinking system based on critical, problem-solving, and innovative young minds, balances interdisciplinary themes, engages the public, and respects cultural diversity.

Successful Cases

There are indications from the decisions of numerous multinational companies and organizations like "Unilever" and "Ikea" that they are drastically introducing and redefining their operational parameters by practicing diverse versions of digital tools in operational wings of their businesses and by implementing small grids, energy-efficient systems, and zero-waste techniques to focus on sustainable economic solutions and to reinforce resilient efforts for the green journey. "Coca-Cola" is being become a leader in the water industry by adopting a recycling of bottles strategy known as "World Without Waste". Businesses like "Loop" pull digital technologies and establish digital platforms to promote the 3R strategy to improve physical and capital resources, and tackle wastes according to the novel principles of green skills circular economy. Amsterdam and Singapore have developed green and smart city programs through digital drives to practice urban-based green solutions. The Solar Decathlon is a US energy department that provides a competitive and challenging platform for the young generation to apply knowledge and skills in building and designing low-carbon, energy-efficient, and sustainable homes powered by renewables and promote innovation in designing green infrastructure. The engineering discipline is preparing young graduates to create sustainable products by introducing them to the concepts of risk management, principles of green chemistry, and estimations of life cycles. The challenges of Eco-car, Green Building, living building, and green chemistry encourage researchers to design and promote innovative and sustainable solutions in the transport, housing, and chemical sectors. Green energy solutions in the form of wind, geothermal, and small hydro are increasing renewables share in national grids across the globe and accelerating the transition pace towards clean energy. Gamification and game-based learning activities also provide interaction and action to increase awareness of the concepts, train the practices of green education, and develop responsible behavioral changes.

Literature Echo for Green Education

In the last decade, the term green education has gained incredible acknowledgment and eyeball attention worldwide to foster sustainable practices and environmental awareness by designing student learning outcomes based on green curricula to understand green skills. The literature articulates that green education grasps a continuum of activities with a multi-dimensional approach, like the formation of a green educational system, establishment of green institutional infrastructure, development of green syllabus, green staffing, green professionals, community engagement, promotion of green initiatives, strategies for green infrastructure, smart and digital tools, green information technologies, green computing, green skills, green workforce, green taskforce, green clubs, green job markets, and practical green based learning projects consists of sustainability practices, conservation concepts, and preservation themes for students, educators, and community learning. The literature sheds light on the traditional education system is in the initial stages of the adoption of green education, green curriculum, green campus, green strategies, and green practices with the collaboration of international organizations in different regions across the globe. It is evident from the academic literature that green education shows remarkable positive impacts on the young generation's behavior towards nature, feelings for ecology, awareness about environmental issues, perceptions of green ideas, thinking for green solutions, learning green skills, understanding green concepts, tackling green challenges, and voluntary participation in favor of green innovations, sustainable initiatives, green societies, and green circular economies. Some studies highlight that green education also boosts academic performance, mental health, and personalized learning of university students. The studies on digital transformation claim that digital literacy becomes a key factor in the promotion of green education and skills and digital tools are beneficial to attain sustainable development goals by the adoption of smart agro-water technologies, green-clean energy-efficient systems, modeling and designing of green products, and sustainable practices. Digital tools are being practiced in the establishment, management, and extension of green schools under the UNESCO green school program. The process of digital transformation provides accessibility to big data networks to develop Internet of things-smart systems to address the climate challenges and create prospects for future sustainable green societies. The joint venture of green innovation and digital transformation is necessary for the building of green and digital infrastructure, knowledge of digital literacy, training of green skilled human resource, commencing of community-based green educational and technology projects, creation of green job markets, and flow of green digital circular economy.

Policy Recommendation for Green Education

Green education and digital literacy depend on the design of the digital value chain, the development of digital networks, socioeconomic status, institutional capacity building, and market bottlenecks. Effective policy measures can translate the policy vision into policy outcomes, and thus policy intrusions always have a substantial role in overcoming the social-based digital divide, to guide market actors in the development, adoption, and promotion of digitalized green solutions. On the policy front, a comprehensive and robust policy framework should be designed to integrate the strategies for eco-design, green education, skills, and digital literacy with green mission and vision and to attain green goals. The policy sphere should entail legal binding, regulatory standards, economic parameters, procurement strategies, research tools, digital advocacy programs, and voluntary approaches. There should be a policy-sinking approach for education, digital, climate, labor, and industrial policies. Green policy should be digitalized, and digital policy should be green, i.e. policy cohesion and coherence to reinforce the green transition, and digital transformations should be practiced. For a profitable green-digital nexus, green stakeholders should engage in digital applications, and on the same lines, digital players should be included in green activities. There should be use of the power of online learning and sharing platforms containing green courses to gain acceleration of green education impact for the global audience and to attain targets of global sustainability by harnessing digital transformation. Data analytics and the development of immersive technologies such as VR and AR to scale up green skills and to provide support in developing the skills to understand complex real-world situations by simulation of ecological challenges and sustainable practices should be experienced. There should be policy initiatives to promote eco-digital literacy for effective and responsible use of digital tools and digital p to develop essential green skills curricula according to the demands of green markets and to meet the needs of the 21st century. The responsible use of digital tools will be helpful in the provision of tracking, monitoring, and evaluating the real-time progress of green projects based on a data-driven decision-making process. The curriculum should be formulated to insert sustainable concepts with digital alternative adeptness to make capable and groom the generation that can drive sustainable force and balance technology with ecology. There should be incorporation of environment and digital literacy in vocational school curricula with student learning outcomes containing green education, green skills, use of digital tools, and environmentally, and digitally responsible citizens in the evolving digital age for a green future. There should be training in professional development courses for educators and teachers to learn and develop the skills of integrating digital tools and technologies in teaching practices as teacher's aides and effective resources. There should be policy interventions in education, labor, and industrial policies to develop a collaborative approach between vocational schools and industry. Financial push such as green funds, subsidy schemes, and tax incentives like carbon credits can attract investors to improve the fiscal landscape and reinforce the governments to accelerate the green agenda. There should be a realistic allocation of financial and physical resources in the development of green digital infrastructures, green digital integration, coordinated mechanisms, and policy advocacy, for green commitments. There should be policy mechanisms in education and digital policies that guide to combat the social divide causing the digital divide and promote digital equity to ensure the accessibility of green skills and digital literacy among all students. There should be greener and more resilient efforts in the digital sector by investing more in renewables and clean energy efficient digitalized infrastructure and building bridges by cross-cutting strategies between green innovation and digital transformation. Governments should assist in engaging green and digital stakeholders and provide ease in regulations for B2B plugs to encourage zero-carbon schemes. Governments should induce the civil society, and non-profit organizations by investing more in research and innovative activities of recycling, repairing, reducing, and reusing to open the drive and develop public-private partnership projects, plans, and programs in green education promotion and green digital literacy adoption.

CONCLUSION

Technology and humanity can coexist together. A dual shift of green and digital is vital to combat the climate crisis. Green innovation can integrate the common goals between digital and climate domains by linking the paramount dots between ecology and technology and bridging the gap among economy, ecology, technology, and sustainability to mitigate the carbon impacts of digital progress and to influence the digital solutions of technology to promote green trends. Green education is a torchbearer with a convergence of digital renovation, paved with vivid corridors furnished with green innovative skills to groom young minds for navigating and shaping the green world. Ecological thinking patterns are vital for the expansion of green schools' trends to enhance green initiatives. Green education and digital theories such as Cornerstone propose revolutionary principles, methods, techniques, and tools to educate, engage, encourage, and empower the young bloods to cope with the climate and environmental enigmas to unlock a proactive sustainable future panorama. In today's complex world green innovations, digital modernizations, and sustainable practices are being considered as promising futures for harmonized stability among economy, ecology, and technology.

REFERENCES

Aithal, P., & Rao, P. (2016). Green education concepts & strategies in higher education model. *International Journal of Scientific Research and Modern Education (IJSRME) ISSN (Online)*, 2455-2563.

Boca, G. D., & Saraçlı, S. (2019). Environmental education and student's perception, for sustainability. *Sustainability (Basel)*, *11*(6), 1553. doi:10.3390/su11061553

Bonil, J., Calafell, G., Granados, J., Junyent, M., & Tarín, R. M. (2012). A training model for progress in curriculum greening. *Profesorado. Revista de Currículum y Formación del Profesorado*, *16*(2), 145–163.

Browning, M. H., & Rigolon, A. (2019). School green space and its impact on academic performance: A systematic literature review. *International Journal of Environmental Research and Public Health*, *16*(3), 429. doi:10.3390/ijerph16030429 PMID:30717301

Feng, H., Wang, F., Song, G., & Liu, L. (2022). Digital transformation on enterprise green innovation: Effect and transmission mechanism. *International Journal of Environmental Research and Public Health*, *19*(17), 10614. doi:10.3390/ijerph191710614 PMID:36078329

Griswold, W. (2013). Community education and green jobs: Acknowledging existing connection. *Adult Learning*, *24*(1), 30–36. doi:10.1177/1045159512467322

Hernandez, A. A. (2020). Green IT adoption practices in education sector: a developing country perspective. In Waste Management: Concepts, Methodologies, Tools, and Applications (pp. 1379-1395): IGI Global. doi:10.4018/978-1-7998-1210-4.ch063

Kroculick, J. B. (2022). Enabling Green Digital Transformation through a Sustainable Systems Engineering Leadership Model. *Paper presented at the INCOSE International Symposium*. INCOSE. 10.1002/iis2.12896

Leal Filho, W., Will, M., Salvia, A. L., Adomssent, M., Grahl, A., & Spira, F. (2019). The role of green and Sustainability Offices in fostering sustainability efforts at higher education institutions. *Journal of Cleaner Production*, *232*, 1394–1401. doi:10.1016/j.jclepro.2019.05.273

Lerman, L. V., Benitez, G. B., Müller, J. M., de Sousa, P. R., & Frank, A. G. (2022). Smart green supply chain management: A configurational approach to enhance green performance through digital transformation. *Supply Chain Management*, *27*(7), 147–176. doi:10.1108/SCM-02-2022-0059

Podder, S. K., Karuppiah, M., Thomas, B., & Samanta, D. (2022). Research initiative on sustainable education system: Model of balancing green computing and ict in quality education. Paper presented at the *2022 Interdisciplinary Research in Technology and Management (IRTM)*. IEEE. 10.1109/IRTM54583.2022.9791758

Qiu, Y., Chen, Q., & Ng, P. S. J. (2023). Research on the Spillover Effects of Digital Transformation on the Sustainable Growth of Green Schools. *Proceedings of Business and Economic Studies*, *6*(6), 16–23. doi:10.26689/pbes.v6i6.5749

Tan, M. (2004). Nurturing scientific and technological literacy through environmental education. *Kokusai Kyoiku Kyoryoku Ronshu*, *7*(1), 115–131.

Wang, C., Yan, G., & Ou, J. (2023). Does digitization promote green innovation? Evidence from China. *International Journal of Environmental Research and Public Health*, *20*(5), 3893. doi:10.3390/ijerph20053893 PMID:36900903

Yu, A. (2023). Research and prospect of enterprise digital transformation and green innovation. *Industrial Engineering and Innovation Management*, *6*(11), 12–22.

Chapter 6
Green Energy Supply to Pre-School Cluster for Sustainable Anganwadi Educational Transformation

Dharmbir Prasad
iD https://orcid.org/0000-0002-9010-9717
Asansol Engineering College, India

Ranadip Roy
iD https://orcid.org/0000-0003-2111-2581
Sanaka Educational Trust's Group of Institutions, Durgapur, India

Rudra Pratap Singh
iD https://orcid.org/0000-0001-7352-855X
Asansol Engineering College, India

Md. Irfan Khan
IAC Electricals Pvt. Ltd., Kolkata, India

Jatin Anand
Asansol Engineering College, India

ABSTRACT

An innovative initiative for sustainable Anganwadi education transformation uses renewable energy sources like wind energy to transform early childhood education. This concept provides Anganwadi centres a reliable and environmentally friendly power supply through the use of wind turbines. The use of wind energy not only lowers carbon footprints but also gives kids a practical educational chance to understand the advantages of renewable resources. By establishing a sustainable learning environment, this innovative approach hopes to improve student attendance and academic results. For all the children and communities, the authors see a cleaner, brighter future and wind power is a key component of this shift. In the study the electricity produced is 16,959,313kW/year. The extra energy produced is sold to the grid. The return on investment is 60.2% and the simple payback year is 1.53 years. The annual energy sold to the grid is 16,956,392 kWh.

DOI: 10.4018/979-8-3693-2865-1.ch006

INTRODUCTION

The Indian government supports Anganwadi centres through the Ministry of Women and Child Development. They get money, training and monitoring to assure high-quality service delivery and program execution. Pre-school cluster for sustainable Anganwadi education transformation is essential. This innovative study's only goal is to install wind turbines in Anganwadi facilities in order to take advantage of the region's abundant wind energy. These wind turbines, which offer kids educational opportunities in along with electricity, are a symbol of growth and sustainability. This project seeks to install in young minds, an interest for sustainability, in addition to electricity. A steady electricity supply from wind turbines improves the educational atmosphere. Additionally, it significantly lowers these institutions' carbon impact, saving the environment for all. This Darbhanga project is a step toward a cleaner, brighter future rather than just a technological change. By developing a foundation for a generation that appreciates and protects our world, it represents a dedication to education, sustainability and community empowerment.

Paper Layout: The remaining work is divided into the following sections: problem statement, research gap and contribution, mathematical modeling, potential access for energy harvesting, system modelling for Anganwadi center, results and discussion and conclusions. The Conclusion Sections mark the end result of the present study.

Potential for Sustainable Anganwadi Electricity Supply

Wind turbines are positioned carefully in open, elevated spaces to capture wind energy in the Darbhanga district of Bihar. With the rotation of the blades, these turbines transform the kinetic energy of the wind into mechanical energy. A generator of turbine subsequently transforms this mechanical energy into electrical energy. The generated AC electricity is incorporated into the nearby power system, providing clean, renewable energy to homes and businesses. In Darbhanga, wind energy boosts the region's economic and energy independence by lowering carbon emissions, promoting sustainable development and reducing dependency on fossil fuels. Its energy access location mapping is shown in Figure 1. In the Indian state of Bihar, Darbhanga is considered as a significant city in North Bihar and is the state's fifth largest city and Municipal Corporation. The Anandbagh Palace was located inside the Darbhanga Raj, the 16[th]century estate that had the city as its capital. The climate of Darbhanga is humid subtropical. There are three distinct seasons that it experiences: winter, summer and rainy seasons. The hottest month is May, when highs of 43°C are recorded. The district of Darbhanga experiences an average of 1142.3 mm of rainfall annually, with the monsoon season contributing to about 92% of this total. As wind turbine technology continues to progress, even regions with moderate wind speeds can now produce energy. This provides Darbhanga an opportunity to increase the amount of renewable energy production. By utilizing these advantages, Darbhanga could grow into a centre for wind energy production, helping the state meet its energy needs while achieving its goals for sustainable development.

Figure 1. Location mapping for sustainable Anganwadi education center

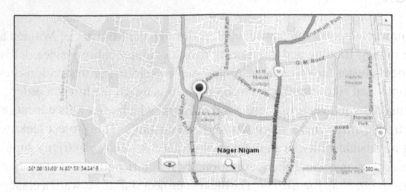

Paper layout: The remaining work is divided into the following sections: problem statement, research gap and contribution, mathematical modeling, potential access for energy harvesting, system modeling for Anganwadi center, results and conclusions.

Problem Statement

The issue statement focuses on establishing green energy solutions to power Anganwadi facilities, which would ensure consistent availability to electricity for lighting, heating, cooling, and powering electronic devices. The study seeks to accomplish the following objectives:

(i). Technical feasibility: Green energy solutions for powering pre-school clusters, notably Anganwadi facilities, require various technical considerations to assure their viability and efficacy.

(ii). Economical evaluation: The economic study of integrating wind turbines with the grid to power pre-school clusters, notably Anganwadi facilities, include determining, the project's financial viability and cost-effectiveness.

(iii). Environmental impact assessment: The environmental impact assessment of integrating wind turbines with the grid to power pre-school clusters, particularly Anganwadi facilities, entails assessing the project's possible environmental consequences.

This evaluation guides decision-making, regulatory compliance and stakeholder involvement, ensuring that environmental factors are included into the planning, design and execution of wind energy projects to power pre-school clusters.

Solution Methodology

Starting with a thorough analysis of the region's energy needs, the procedure next looks at different green energy sources that make sense for the area, taking affordability and practicality into account. Careful planning is then required for the design, acquisition, and installation of renewable energy systems when the best option has been determined. After receiving training in system operation and maintenance, staff members are guaranteed to use resources efficiently.

Figure 2. Schematic diagram showing various parameters with their effect

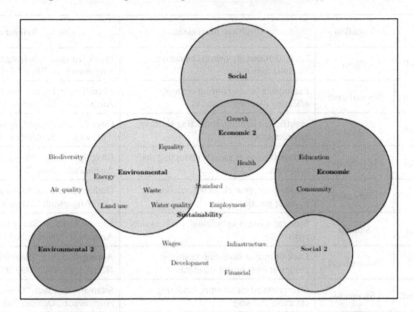

For pre-school clusters like Anganwadis, implementing a sustainable energy solution entails a methodical strategy meant to satisfy the unique energy requirements of these educational establishments while reducing environmental impact. Ongoing progress is facilitated by ongoing monitoring and assessment, and community involvement initiatives raise awareness and support. In the end, this approach helps to revolutionize education while also giving pre-school clusters a sustainable energy source. Figure 2 shows the schematic explanation of how the various parameters would be affecting the existing problems faced by the Anganwadi centers as shown in Table 1. As from the figure, we can see that social with the economic would affect growth and health of the Anganwadi centers while the social with economic would affect education and community. There are various effects of environment such as wages, development, infrastructure, financial, waste, equality, air quality. The environmental has diverse changes, it would also affect but in a diversify manner resulting in a sustainable green energy growth.

Table 1. Anganwadi centers problem explanation

Sl.	Anganwadi Center	Location	Problem Statement	Reference
1.	ABC Anganwadi	Patna	Lack of electricity access, hindering teaching aids usage	Patna Tribune, "Challenges Faced by Anganwadis in Bihar", July 2023
2.	XYZ Anganwadi	Muzzafarpur	Inadequate heating during winters, affecting children's comfort	Muzaffarpur Times, "Winter Woes at XYZ Anganwadi", December 2022
3.	LMN Anganwadi	Gaya	Insufficient lighting, impacting learning environment	Gaya Gazette, "Lighting Issues at LMN Anganwadi", September 2023
4.	PQR Anganwadi	Bhagalpur	Unreliable power supply, disrupting daily activities	Bhagalpur Daily, "Power Woes at PQR Anganwadi", June 2023
5.	DEF Anganwadi	Darbhanga	Limited access to clean water, affecting hygiene practices	Darbhanga Chronicle, "Water Challenges at DEF Anganwadi", August 2023
6.	GHI Anganwadi	Saharsa	Structural issues in building, posing safety risks	Saharsa Herald, "Safety Concerns at GHI Anganwadi", November 2022
7.	JKL Anganwadi	Aurangabad	Lack of proper sanitation facilities, compromising health standards	Aurangabad Post, "Sanitation Problems at JKL Anganwadi", May 2023
8.	MNO Anganwadi	Sitamarhi	Overcrowded classrooms, hindering effective teaching	Sitamarhi Sentinel, "Overcrowding at MNO Anganwadi", October 2023
9.	UVW Anganwadi	Nawada	Poor ventilation, leading to discomfort and health issues	Nawada News, "Ventilation Problems at UVW Anganwadi", February 2023
10.	OPQ Anganwadi	Jehanabad	Unsafe playground equipment, posing injury risks	Jehanabad Journal, "Safety Concerns at OPQ Anganwadi", August 2023
11.	STU Anganwadi	Samastipur	Lack of transportation facilities, affecting attendance	Samastipur Chronicle, "Transportation Challenges at STU Anganwadi", March 2023
12.	VWX Anganwadi	Araria	Inadequate food supplies, impacting nutrition programs	Araria Times, "Food Shortages at VWX Anganwadi", November 2022
13.	YZA Anganwadi	Katihar	Pest infestation, compromising cleanliness and hygiene	Katihar Gazette, "Pest Problems at YZA Anganwadi", June 2023
14.	BCD Anganwadi	Nalanda	Limited access to educational technology, hindering modern teaching methods	Nalanda News, "Technology Challenges at BCD Anganwadi", May 2023
15.	EFG Anganwadi	Kishanganj	Lack of trained staff, affecting quality of education	Kishanganj Herald, "Staff Shortages at EFG Anganwadi", February 2023
16.	HIJ Anganwadi	Supaul	Unsafe drinking water sources, posing health risks	Supaul Post, "Water Safety Concerns at HIJ Anganwadi", October 2023
17.	KLM Anganwadi	Banka	Limited access to healthcare services, impacting child well-being	Banka Bulletin, "Healthcare Challenges at KLM Anganwadi", September 2023
18.	NOP Anganwadi	Siwan	Language barriers for non-Hindi speaking children, affecting communication	Siwan Sentinel, "Language Challenges at NOP Anganwadi", January 2023
19.	QRS Anganwadi	Munger	Lack of proper waste management, leading to environmental pollution	Munger Messenger, "Waste Issues at QRS Anganwadi", April 2023

Research Gap and Contribution

The issue statement focuses on establishing green energy solutions to power Anganwadi facilities, which would ensure consistent availability to electricity for lighting, heating, cooling, and powering electronic devices. This study seeks to accomplish the following objectives:

(i). Environment Friendly Way of Child Education: Suraj Mandhare, the Maharashtra Education Commissioner, will meet with experts on Monday to discuss the merger of Anganwadis and elementary schools in the state, as proposed by the National Education Policy 2020 (The Indian Express, 2024). ECCE is seen as a predecessor to formal education. Preschool years serve an important role in preparing children for their future schooling. A successful ECCE increases enrolment, reduces dropouts in the early years, and helps children develop foundational literacy and numeracy skills in the early grades (The Times of India, 2022). To achieve such a lofty ambition, the Indian education system must be revived and reconfigured in order to satisfy the important targets and goals (SDGs) of the 2030 Agenda for Sustainable Development (Sarvgyan, 2024). The new policy intends to universalize education from pre-school to secondary level by 2030, with 100% GER in school education, and to reintegrate 2 crore out-of-school children into the mainstream (Organizer, 2020). Indore's Anganwadi centres will be converted into pre-schools after the district administration chose to 'improve' the quality and level of education at government-run institutions (The Times of India, 2023).On Wednesday, Rajasthan's Deputy Chief Minister Diya Kumari announced a substantial initiative to further the development of Anganwadi facilities in the region. According to the official release, this entailed sanctioning the transition of 6204 tiny Anganwadi into model Anganwadi facilities (Financial Express, 2024). The National Education Policy proposed that Anganwadi personnel receive pedagogy training in order to bring teaching levels at these rural pre-schools up to par with those at city playschools and nursery schools (Edugraph, 2024).

(ii). Sustainable Energy Transformation: The study of sustainability patterns using a range of environmental, social, and economic indicators allows policymakers to quantify the importance of each UAS and aids in the development of a stronger UAS governance program (Valenica et al., 2022). This article examines the technological and economic benefits of integrating a PSHP with a grid-connected solar renewable system (Bhimaraju et al., 2023). With increased concerns about environmental impact and the need for resilience in the global economy, there is a strong demand for SC designs that can adapt to unexpected changes while being competitive and sustainable (Fakheri et al., 2022). This research offers a multi-criteria intelligent approach employing fuzzy logic, quantitative data, and experts' views to compute the Sustainability Index 4.0 of an SSC in the PV industry while considering the influence of I4.0 and digital technologies (Mastrocinque et al., 2022). Based on patent transfer data for green technologies in Yangtze River Delta cities, this paper examines the structural characteristics and evolutionary pattern of the spatial linkage network of the region's intercity GITT using social network analysis, as well as the key regional classifications and roles (Yan et al., 2024). This paper analysed and evaluated the dynamic stability and operational problems that modern power systems with highly high VRE generation face (Ahmed et al., 2023). The paper offers a grid-connected DES that combines AD and gasification technologies in the KW management sector to fulfil future energy demands and meet sustainable development goals (Huang & Xu, 2023). This work provides a complete bibliometric evaluation of energy transition and green finance, utilizing a quantitative approach to identify recent and emerging trends. The literature on the energy transition-green finance relationship appeared in 2012 and increased significantly beginning in 2019 (Xu et al., 2024). Adopting sustainable standards for green hydrogen is critical to promote a responsible and sustainable approach to hydrogen generation (Blohm &Dettner, 2023). The research investigates the intersection between the PSM abilities required to support innovation and strategic sustainability objectives (Picaud-Bello et al., 2024).

*(iii).Green Energy Supply Chain:*The introduction of RES, which has the ability to be enhanced with modern communication and information technologies, as well as efficient design and planning, all contribute to the current worldwide visualization of SGs (Khalid, 2024). The shift to the new ''smart''

era necessitates the use of smart technology through comprehensive and efficient energy management functions (Thomas et al., 2018). The scientific paper proposes a strategy for optimizing a home's energy management system (Ma & Poursoleiman, 2022). The paper employs an umbrella review to understand current trends and adoption dynamics in GSCM by methodically combining prior evaluations (Islam et al., 2023).

(iv). Renewable Energy Trading: This work offered an optimization model for the P2P energy trading grid, which included DGs such as PV, wind turbines, and battery storage, as well as a central battery on the local grid (Sahebi et al., 2023). This paper provided a complete assessment of P2P energy sharing and trading, including trading price models, decision-making in dynamic trading behaviour, and agent-based synergistic teamwork (Zhou & Lund, 2023). The Chinese government intends to implement renewable energy development policies based on CET, including FIP and RPS in the power business, to encourage the growth of renewable energy (Ma et al., 2024). The success of the P2P energy trading market and a decrease in CO2 emissions necessitate expanded and active participation from market players (Amin et al., 2020). This paper presents an innovative demand response-based energy allocation strategy combined with usage-based invoicing in the P2P energy trading market, addressing the inherent issues provided by the irregular nature of DERs (Ahmed et al., 2024). This study proposed seven potential grid-connected and off-grid HRES to fulfil the electrical demand of a university campus (MUET, Jamshoro) in Sindh, Pakistan, using HOMER software (Manoo et al., 2024). This work tackled the complicated task of optimum energy trading in cooperative microgrids, taking into account non-renewable, renewable, and hybrid renewable energy supplies (Ullah et al., 2024). As integrated energy and carbon trading markets emerge, the interrelationships among CIES stakeholders become more complex and dynamic (Zang et al., 2024).

Mathematical Modelling

Wind turbines in a system powered by renewable energy use the kinetic energy of the wind to create electricity. A generator located in the tower's nacelle is connected to a rotor that spins as the wind blows through the turbine blades. The grid's integration of wind power makes it possible to full fill societal demands for electricity while maintaining environmental sustainability. The power law or logarithmic profile is used to normalize the value at this height to the hub height that the designer has selected. This is represented by the equation (1)-(2) (Babatunde et al., 2022).

$$Vh = V_m \left(\frac{\ln\left[\dfrac{H_{hh}}{S_{rl}}\right]}{\ln\left[\dfrac{H_m}{S_{rl}}\right]} \right) \tag{1}$$

where, V_h: wind speed at the proposed hub height, V_m: wind speed measured at H_m height of anemometer, H_{hh}: hub height, S_{rl}: surface roughness length and H_m: height of the anemometer.

$$V_h = V_m \left(\frac{H_{hh}}{H_m} \right)^{\beta} \tag{2}$$

where, V_h: wind speed at the proposed hub-height, V_m: wind speed measured at height of anemometer, H_{hh}: hub height, β: power law exponent and Hm height of the anemometer.

The output power by the wind turbine is represented by the equation (3) (Babatunde et al., 2022),

$$P_{opw} = \frac{\rho}{\rho_0} \times P_{w-stp} \tag{3}$$

where, P_{opw}: output power by the wind turbine, ρ: real air density, $\rho0$: air density at standard temperature and pressure and Pw-$_{stp}$: wind turbine output at standard temperature and pressure.

Surplus energy may be distributed around areas to balance supply and demand by connecting renewable power facilities to the grid. Furthermore, the grid enables the deployment of energy storage technologies, such as pumped hydro and batteries, which store excess renewable energy for periods of low output. This facilitates the shift to a cleaner and more robust energy infrastructure while also enabling a dependable and sustainable electricity supply, lowering dependency on fossil fuels and minimizing environmental effect. The TNPC of the grid is evaluated only based on net energy purchased is represented by the equation (4) (Elkadeem et al., 2024),

$$TNPC_{GRID} = \sum_{n=1}^{N_{project}} \frac{E_{g,p}.C_{g,p} - E_{g,s}.C_{g,s}}{(1+r)^n} \tag{4}$$

where, $TNCP_{GRID}$: total net present cost, $N_{project}$: project lifetime, n: number of years, $E_{g,p}$: energy purchased from the grid annually, kWh/year $C_{g,p}$: energy purchase price from the grid, \$/kWh, $E_{g,s}$: energy sold from the grid annually, kWh/yr, $C_{g,s}$: energy sellback to the grid, \$/kWh and r: real discount rate, %.

It is a statistic used to calculate the lifetime cost of producing electricity from a certain source, taking into account all expenditures incurred throughout the plant's lifespan, such as building, operation, maintenance, fuel and finance. The LCOE of the system is represented by the equation (5) (Elkadeem et al., 2024),

$$LCOE = \frac{TNPC.CRF(r,n)}{E_{aaec}} \tag{5}$$

where, $LCOE$: levelized cost of energy, $TNCP$: total net present cost, CRF: capital recovery factor, % r: real discount rate, %, n: number of years and E_{aaec}: average annual electricity consumption, kWh/yr.

The simple payback time is a basic and uncomplicated method for determining a project's financial feasibility, with shorter payback periods typically suggesting greater investment prospects. The project's simple payback period is represented by the equation (6) (Elkadeem et al., 2024),

$$Pa_p = \frac{TNPC}{R_{ars}} \tag{6}$$

where, Pa_p: project simple payback period, *TNCP*: total net present cost and R_{ars}: annual revenue of the system, $/year

Energy Harvesting Potential Access

For a wind turbine-based renewable energy system data on global horizontal irradiance (GHI), wind speed, temperature and are essential. Table 2 illustrates average solar GHI for Darbhanga GHI ranges between 4.020 kWh/m²/day and 7.070 kWh/m²/day. It is maximum for the month of May and minimum for the month of December. The average GHI is 5.28 kWh/m²/day for the proposed site. Figure 3 illustrates the average wind speed data for the different months of a year for Darbhanga. The wind speed is highest in July 5.210m/s. The wind speed is minimum in November 3.010 m/s. The annual average wind speed is 4.36 m/s. Figure 3 also illustrates the monthly average temperature data for the different months of a year. The temperature is maximum 34.030°C for the month of May and minimum 15.980°C for the month of January. The annual average temperature is 25.98°C. The system's overall performance, reliability and efficiency are determined by all of these factors considered collectively.

Table 2. Meteorological resources of proposed Darbhanga Anganwadi center

Month	Clearness index	Daily radiation (kWh/m²/day)	Average wind speed (m/s)	Daily temperature (°C)
Jan	0.621	4.060	3.930	15.980
Feb	0.681	5.250	4.520	19.800
Mar	0.696	6.390	4.960	25.900
Apr	0.671	6.980	4.980	31.420
May	0.638	7.070	4.760	34.030
Jun	0.521	5.880	5.120	33.710
Jul	0.416	4.630	5.210	30.170
Aug	0.448	4.730	4.950	29.120
Sep	0.477	4.520	4.620	27.770
Oct	0.631	5.070	3.100	25.500
Nov	0.704	4.750	3.010	21.300
Dec	0.653	4.020	3.200	17.070

Figure 3. Meteorological characteristics for sustainable Anganwadi center

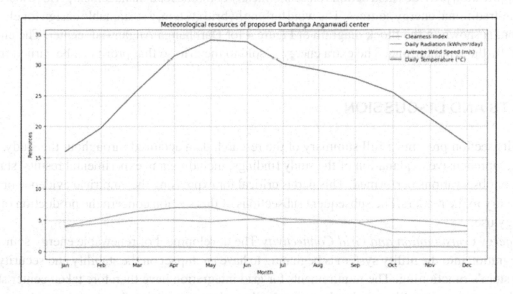

System Modeling for Anganwadi Center

Green and sustainable electricity is produced by the components of the current study working together. The output is produced by the HOMER Pro software tools. By simulating the engineering and financial sustainability of distributed energy systems connected to a standard grid, this makes it possible to build least-cost electrical systems and risk-mitigation solutions.

Figure 4. Schematic for sustainable Anganwadi child education center

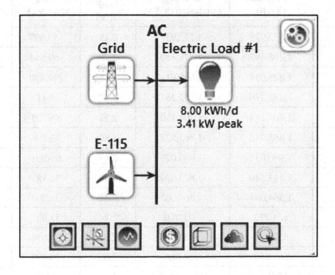

The application provides instructions on economically combine load management, grid resources and renewable-traditional energy sources. The wind turbine hybrid system, a sustainable design for electricity generation, is shown in the block diagram of Figure 4 for Darbhanga Anganwadi center. The energy is produced by the wind turbine. The extra energy is sold to the grid so that profit can be earned from it.

RESULTS AND DISCUSSION

The results section presents a full summary of the research data acquired throughout the study. It provides a comprehensive explanation of the study findings, including any experimental results, statistical analysis, or observations performed. This part is critical for expressing the empirical evidence or results of the inquiry to the readers.The subsequent subsections of this section concern the production of power and energy use:

*(i). Energy Consumption and Grid Connectivity:*The development of renewable energy sources and their integration into the utility system is beginning to have an impact on the stability and security of the power system's functioning. The requirements for grid integration have therefore taken center stage as renewable energy sources like wind turbines gradually replace conventional power plants. Average load demand, peak load and load factor of 21,452kWh/day, 9,138.0kW and 0.1, respectively. In accordance, Table 3-4 provides a summary of the results for energy consumption and the shift to green energy. Figure 5-6 shows the grid commercial details for the sustainable Anganwadi center located at Darbhanga. The details are organized below per month of the year. Energy of 127 kWh is purchased from the grid each year, whereas 16,956,393 kWh are sold to grid for the sustainable Anganwadi center located at Darbhanga.

Table 3. Green energy transition results for Anganwadi center located at darbhanga

Month	Energy purchased (kWh)	Energy sold (kWh)	Net energy purchased (kWh)	Peak load (kW)	Energy charge ($)	Demand charge ($)	Total charge ($)
January	20.9	1,153,978	-1,153,957	2.19	-57,697	NR	-57,697
February	12.0	1,398,892	-1,398,880	2.28	-69,643	NR	-69,643
March	6.21	1,828,617	-1,828,611	1.85	-91,430	NR	-91,430
April	11.5	1,782,376	-1,782,364	2.37	89,118	NR	89,118
May	7.17	1,704,118	-1,704,110	2.27	85,205	NR	85,205
June	5.95	1,863,933	-1,863,927	1.80	93,196	NR	93,196
July	9.68	1,980,038	-1,980,029	2.48	99,001	NR	99,001
August	9.81	1,823,640	-1,823,630	2.37	91,181	NR	91,181
September	2.49	1,564,064	-1,564,062	2.49	78,203	NR	78,203
October	12.0	621,772	-621,760	2.74	31,087	NR	31,087
November	21.1	553,156	-553,135	2.53	27,656	NR	27,656
December	7.98	681,808	-681,800	3.05	34,090	NR	34,090
Annual	127	13,956,392	-16,956,266	3.05	847,807	NR	847,807

Table 4. Energy Consumption optimization results for Anganwadi Center located at Darbhanga

Consumption	kWh/year (%)	Consumption	kWh/year (%)
AC primary load	2,920 (0.0172%)	Excess electricity	0 (0%)
DC primary load	0 (0%)	Unmet electric load	0 (0%)
Deferrable load	0 (0%)	Capacity storage	0 (0%)
Grid sales	16,956,393(100%)	Renewable fraction	100 (%)
Total	16,959,313(100%)	Maximum renewable penetration	100 (%)

Figure 5. Characteristics for Load demand daily, seasonal and yearly profile of Anganwadi

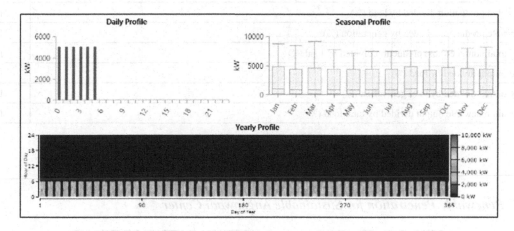

Figure 6. Characteristics for net electricity produced of Anganwadi center

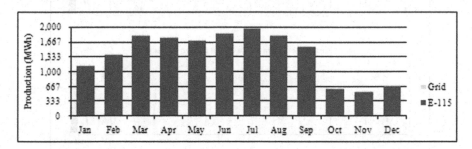

*(ii). Optimization of Green Energy Generation:*PV penetration is the term used to describe the quantity of PV solar electricity generated inside a particular area, such as a nation, region, or electric grid. Instantaneous renewable output divided by load, as shown in Figure 7 and Table 5, is a ratio that compares the amount of electricity generated from renewable resources at a specific time with the amount of power consumed concurrently by the electric load for the sustainable Anganwadi center in Darbhanga. Figure

7 shows the electricity produced for the Anganwadi beneficiary. An increased percentage denotes a more sustainable and environmentally friendly mix of energy. By dividing the instantaneous non-renewable by the load, one may find the percentage of energy that is not derived from non-renewable sources at any given time. In addition, the ratio that indicates the percentage of power generated by renewable sources (wind, solar, hydro, etc.) at a given time in relation to the overall amount of electricity generated is instantaneous renewable output divided by generation.

Table 5. Renewable energy generation penetration for Anganwadi Center located at Darbhanga

Parameters	Value
Nominal renewable capacity divided by total nominal capacity (%)	100
Usable renewable capacity divideed by total capacity (%)	100
Total renewable production divided by load (%)	100
Total renewable production divided by generation (%)	100
One minus total nonrenewable production divided by load (%)	100
Renewable output divided by load (%)	100
Renewable output divided by total generation (%)	100
One minus nin renewable output divided by total load (%)	100

Figure 7. Renewable Penetration for Sustainable Anganwadi Center

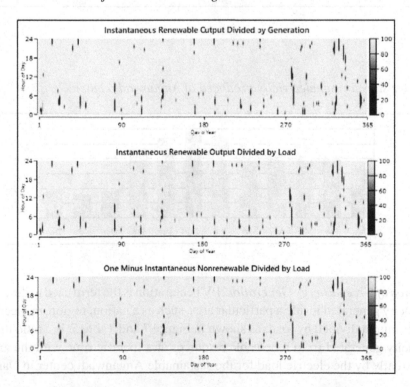

This is the proportion of total electrical capacity that comes from PV solar systems. Policymakers, energy planners and grid operators need to consider PV penetration in order to balance and control the variability of renewable energy sources like solar power. Figure 8 is the characteristics curve for grid purchase daily profile kW for the different months of a year for the sustainable Anganwadi center in Darbhanga.

Figure 8. Grid energy sales daily profile for the Sustainable Anganwadi Center

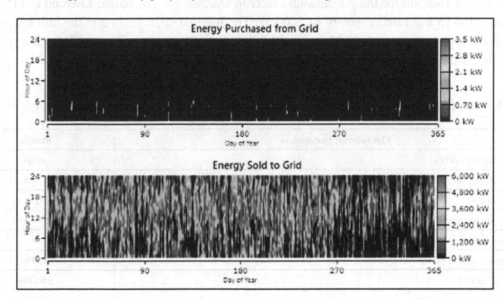

However, Figure 9 is the characteristics curve for grid sales daily profile kW for the different months of a year for the sustainable Anganwadi center in Darbhanga.

Figure 9. Grid energy sales daily profile for the Sustainable Anganwadi Center

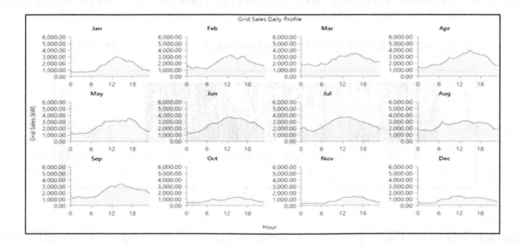

(a). Wind Power Generation: Wind turbines generate electricity by capturing the wind's kinetic energy with rotor blades, which turn a shaft connected to a gearbox. The gearbox increases shaft speed, spinning a generator that converts mechanical energy to electrical energy through electromagnetic induction. This creates AC current, converted to DC current within the turbine. The electricity travels through internal cables to a substation, where its voltage is boosted to match the grids. From there, it enters the larger power grid for distribution to homes and businesses. This process harnesses renewable wind energy, providing a clean source of electricity for various applications. Table 6consist the wind turbine specifications information for the Anganwadi center in Darbhanga. The name: Enercon E-115 [3MW] abbreviated asE-115 has rated capacity of 300 kW. The lifetime is 20 years and the hub height is 122 m. The capital, replacement and O&M cost is $1,300,000.00 $1,300,000.00 and $260.00, respectively. Figure 10 shows the characteristics curve of wind turbine power output.

Table 6. Wind turbine module configuration and power generation for Anganwadi Center

Operational parameters	Results
Total Rated Capacity (kW)	600
Mean power output (kW)	1,936
Capacity factor (%)	32.3
Total energy production (kWh/year)	16,959,186
Minimum power output (kW)	0
Maximum power output (kW)	6,000
Wind penetration (%)	580,794
Hours of operation (hours/year)	8,612
Levelized cost of energy ($/kWh)	0.00677

The output data for the wind turbine utilized to generate power is shown in Table 6. Over a year, the wind turbine produces16,959,186kWh for the Anganwadi center. Levelized cost is0.00677$/kWh indicating the system's cost-effectiveness. There are 8,612 hours of operation every year for the Anganwadi center.

Figure 10. Power generation characteristics of wind turbine for sustainable Anganwadi

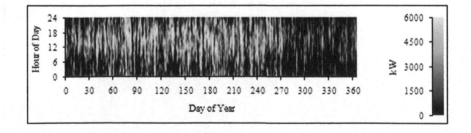

The characteristic curve illustrates the E-115 power output monthly averages kW on x-axis and months on y-axis. Figure 10 shows the wind turbine power output profile for the proposed Anganwadi center.

The characteristics curve is plotted against E-115 power output average profile on y-axis and hour on x-axis for the different months of the year.

(iii). Economical Aspect Optimization: The graph illustrates inflation rates, which are important to take into account while analyzing the costs and profits related to energy projects and investments. The flow and comparison analysis for a sustainable Anganwadi center are shown in Figure 11. The characteristic curve shows the nominal cash flow and the cost type. The capital, replacement, O&M, fuel, salvage and total cost of each component in the operational circuit for the sustainable Anganwadi center are shown in Table 7-9. Figure 12 shows the system effect on the economic sector. From this we can clearly analyse that how the system would be reducing the current costs of running the Anganwadi electric needs.

Figure 11. Economical Anganwadi Center

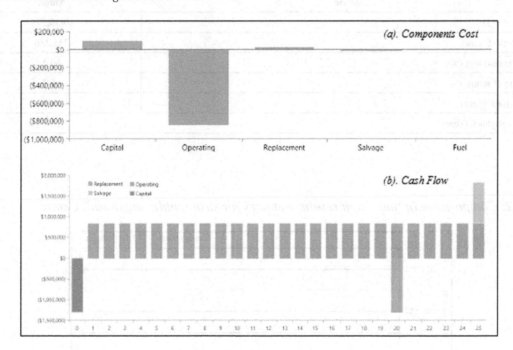

Table 7. Rate chart details of the proposed sustainable Anganwadi Center

Banking rate	Value
Discount rate (%)	8.00
Inflation rate (%)	2.00
Annual capacity storage (%)	0.00
Project lifetime (years)	25.00

Table 8. Cost Summary Details of the Proposed Sustainable Anganwadi Center

Component	Capital ($)	Replacement ($)	O&M ($)	Salvage ($)	Total ($)
Enercon E-115 [3MW]	1,300,000.0	414,449.56	3,361.15	233,568.90	1,484,241.81
Grid	0.00	0.00	10,960,038.58	0.00	10,960,038.58
System	1,300,000.0	414,449.56	10,956,677.42	233,568.90	9,475,796.77

Table 9. Comparative Economics Analysis Results for Sustainable Anganwadi Center

Metric	Value
Present worth ($)	9,479,571
Annual worth ($/year)	733,286
Return on investment (%)	60.2
Internal rate of return (%)	65.2
Simple payback (year)	1.53
Discounted payback (year)	1.66

Figure 12. Comparative optimization results summary for sustainable Anganwadi Centre

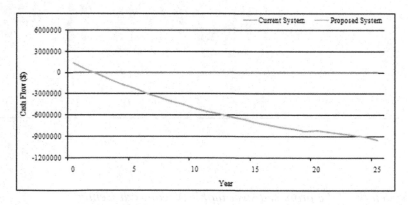

(iv). Assessment of Environmental Impact: The harmful gases produced by the power supply system are shown in Table 10. For human health, these gases are dangerous. Long-term inhalation of these gases can cause bronchial infections, lung cancer and other ailments. Carboxyhemoglobin, which is toxic to the body, is produced when blood hemoglobin and carbon dioxide combination.

Table 10. Emissions analysis details for proposed sustainable Anganwadi Center

Quantity	Value
Carbon Dioxide	7.99 (kg/year)
Carbon Monoxide	0 (kg/year)
Unburned Hydrocarbons	0 (kg/year)
Particular Matter	0 (kg/year)
Sulfur Dioxide	0.347 (kg/year)
Nitrogen Oxides	0.170 (kg/year)

CONCLUSION

Technical, economic and environmental details should be added. The use of renewable energy solutions to power pre-school clusters has great potential for the long-term reform of Anganwadi education. This effort not only addresses the critical demand for reliable energy sources in both rural and urban regions, but it also corresponds with larger environmental aims. The effective deployment of green energy supply to pre-school clusters involves collaborative efforts from a variety of stakeholders. Adequate financing, technical assistance, and capacity building activities are required to overcome hurdles and ensure the sustainability of these programs. Anganwadi centres may contribute to environmental conservation efforts by switching to green energy sources like solar, wind, or biomass. This will reduce their carbon footprint and dependency on non-renewable energy. The overall electricity production of the proposed system is 16,959 MWh/year with emissions of 7.09 kg/year. The NPC of the system is calculated to be $3,775 while the O&M and LCOE are $292/year and $0.100/kWh. The IRR and the ROI are 65% and 60% while the simple payback for the system is 1.5 year.

REFERENCES

Ahmed, F., Al Kez, D., McLoone, S., Best, R. J., Cameron, C., & Foley, A. (2023). Dynamic grid stability in low carbon power systems with minimum inertia. *Renewable Energy*, *210*, 486–506. doi:10.1016/j.renene.2023.03.082

Ahmed, S. A., Huang, Q., Zhang, Z., Li, J., Amin, W., Afzal, M., Hussain, J., & Hussain, F. (2024). Optimization of social welfare and mitigating privacy risks in P2P energy trading: Differential privacy for secure data reporting. *Applied Energy*, *356*, 122403. doi:10.1016/j.apenergy.2023.122403

Amin, W., Huang, Q., Umer, K., Zhang, Z., Afzal, M., Khan, A. A., & Ahmed, S. A. (2020). A motivational game-theoretic approach for peer-to-peer energy trading in islanded and grid-connected microgrid. *International Journal of Electrical Power & Energy Systems*, *123*, 106307. doi:10.1016/j.ijepes.2020.106307

Babatunde, O. M., Munda, J. L., & Hamam, Y. (2022). Off-grid hybrid photovoltaic–micro wind turbine renewable energy system with hydrogen and battery storage: Effects of sun tracking technologies. *Energy Conversion and Management*, *255*, 115335. doi:10.1016/j.enconman.2022.115335

Behl, A., Sampat, B., Gaur, J., Pereira, V., Laker, B., Shankar, A., Shi, Y., & Roohanifar, M. (2024). Can gamification help green supply chain management firms achieve sustainable results in servitized ecosystem? An empirical investigation. *Technovation, 129*, 102915. doi:10.1016/j.technovation.2023.102915

Bhimaraju, A., Mahesh, A., & Nirbheram, J. S. (2023). Feasibility study of solar photovoltaic/grid-connected hybrid renewable energy system with pumped storage hydropower system using abandoned open cast coal mine: A case study in India. *Journal of Energy Storage, 72*, 108206. doi:10.1016/j.est.2023.108206

Blohm, M., & Dettner, F. (2023). Green hydrogen production: Integrating environmental and social criteria to ensure sustainability. *Smart Energy, 11*, 100112. doi:10.1016/j.segy.2023.100112

Edugraph (September 30, 2024). *National Education Policy recommends pedagogy training for Anganwadi workers to raise teaching standards.* https://www.telegraphindia.com/edugraph/national-education-policy-recommends-pedagogy-training-for-anganwadi-workers-to-raise-teaching-standards/cid/1969946.

Elkadeem, M. R., Kotb, K. M., Sharshir, S. W., Hamada, M. A., Gabr, I. K., Hassan, M. A., Worku, M. Y., Abido, M. A., Ullah, Z., Hasanien, H. M., & Selim, F. F. (2024). Optimize and analyze a large-scale grid-tied solar PV-powered SWRO system for sustainable water-energy nexus. *Desalination, 579*, 117440. doi:10.1016/j.desal.2024.117440

Fakheri, S., Bahrami-Bidoni, Z., Makui, A., Pishvaee, M. S., & Gonzalez, E. D. S. (2022). A sustainable competitive supply chain network design for a green product under uncertainty: A case study of Iranian leather industry. *Socio-Economic Planning Sciences, 84*, 101414. doi:10.1016/j.seps.2022.101414

Financial Express. (2024). *Deputy CM of Rajasthan Diya Kumari of Rajasthan approved the transformation of 6204 mini Anganwadis into model centres.* https://www.financialexpress.com/jobs-career/education-deputy-cm-of-rajasthan-diya-kumari-of-rajasthan-approved-the-transformation-of-6204-mini-anganwadis-into-model-centres-3407650/..

Huang, Y., Shi, Y., & Xu, J. (2023). Integrated district electricity system with anaerobic digestion and gasification for bioenergy production optimization and carbon reduction. *Sustainable Energy Technologies and Assessments, 55*, 102890. doi:10.1016/j.seta.2022.102890

Islam, M. S., Islam, M. S., Khan, T., Akhter, R., Rahman, S. M., Ara, H., Thurasamy, R., & Hoque, I. (2023). Umbrella Review in Green Supply Chain Management (GSCM): Developing Models for adoption and sustaining GSCM. *Environmental Challenges*, 100820.

Khalid, M. (2024). Smart grids and renewable energy systems: Perspectives and grid integration challenges. *Energy Strategy Reviews, 51*, 101299. doi:10.1016/j.esr.2024.101299

Ma, J., & Poursoleiman, R. (2022). Optimization of the home energy system in presence of price fluctuation and intermittent renewable energy sources in grid-connected and islanded modes. *Sustainable Energy Technologies and Assessments, 54*, 102875. doi:10.1016/j.seta.2022.102875

Ma, X., Pan, Y., Zhang, M., Ma, J., & Yang, W. (2024). Impact of carbon emission trading and renewable energy development policy on the sustainability of electricity market: A stackelberg game analysis. *Energy Economics, 129*, 107199. doi:10.1016/j.eneco.2023.107199

Manoo, M. U., Shaikh, F., Kumar, L., & Arıcı, M. (2024). Comparative techno-economic analysis of various stand-alone and grid connected (solar/wind/fuel cell) renewable energy systems. *International Journal of Hydrogen Energy*, *52*, 397–414. doi:10.1016/j.ijhydene.2023.05.258

Mastrocinque, E., Ramírez, F. J., Honrubia-Escribano, A., & Pham, D. T. (2022). Industry 4.0 enabling sustainable supply chain development in the renewable energy sector: A multi-criteria intelligent approach. *Technological Forecasting and Social Change*, *182*, 121813. doi:10.1016/j.techfore.2022.121813

Moniruzzaman, M., Yassine, A., & Benlamri, R. (2023). Blockchain and cooperative game theory for peer-to-peer energy trading in smart grids. *International Journal of Electrical Power & Energy Systems*, *151*, 109111. doi:10.1016/j.ijepes.2023.109111

Organizer. (2020). *Cabinet Approves NEP 2020 – Paves way for transformational reforms in school and higher education in the country.* https://organiser.org/2020/07/29/129578/bharat/cabinet-approves-national-education-policy-2020-paving-way-for-transformational-reforms-in-school-and-higher-education/..

Picaud-Bello, K., Schiele, H., Koch, V., & Francillette, M. (2024). Innovation through sustainability: Identifying purchaser skills fostering green innovation. *Cleaner Logistics and Supply Chain*, *10*, 100136. doi:10.1016/j.clscn.2023.100136

Sahebi, H., Khodoomi, M., Seif, M., Pishvaee, M., & Hanne, T. (2023). The benefits of peer-to-peer renewable energy trading and battery storage backup for local grid. *Journal of Energy Storage*, *63*, 106970. doi:10.1016/j.est.2023.106970

Sarvgyan (2024). *Top Features of New Education Policy (NEP) 2020.* https://news.sarvgyan.com/new-education-policy-nep-2020-features..

The Indian Express. (2024). Maharashtra plans integration of Anganwadis and primary schools as per NEP recommendation. https://indianexpress.com/article/cities/mumbai/maharashtra-integration-anganwadis-primary-schools-nep-8900571.

The Times of India. (2022). *Implementation of NEP 2020: Focusing on early childhood learning.* https://timesofindia.indiatimes.com/blogs/voices/implementation-of-nep-2020-focusing-on-early-childhood-learning..

The Times of India. (2023). *15 anganwadis in Indore to be turned into pre-schools.* https://timesofindia.indiatimes.com/city/indore/15-anganwadis-in-indore-to-be-turned-into-pre-schools/articleshow/98109116.cms. (Accessed on: April 4, 2024).

Thomas, D., Deblecker, O., & Ioakimidis, C. S. (2018). Optimal operation of an energy management system for a grid-connected smart building considering photovoltaics' uncertainty and stochastic electric vehicles' driving schedule. *Applied Energy*, *210*, 1188–1206. doi:10.1016/j.apenergy.2017.07.035

Ullah, Z., Qazi, H. S., Alferidi, A., Alsolami, M., Lami, B., & Hasanien, H. M. (2024). Optimal energy trading in cooperative microgrids considering hybrid renewable energy systems. *Alexandria Engineering Journal*, *86*, 23–33. doi:10.1016/j.aej.2023.11.052

Valencia, A., Qiu, J., & Chang, N. B. (2022). Integrating sustainability indicators and governance structures via clustering analysis and multicriteria decision making for an urban agriculture network. *Ecological Indicators*, *142*, 109237. doi:10.1016/j.ecolind.2022.109237

Xu, J., Liu, Q., Wider, W., Zhang, S., Fauzi, M. A., Jiang, L., Udang, L. N., & An, Z. (2024). Research landscape of energy transition and green finance: A bibliometric analysis. *Heliyon*, *10*(3), e24783. doi:10.1016/j.heliyon.2024.e24783 PMID:38314294

Yan, X., Han, Z., Zou, C., & Cheng, C. (2024). Assessing the role of emerging green technology transfer in sustainable development and identification of key regions in Yangtze River Delta region. *Technological Forecasting and Social Change*, *200*, 123099. doi:10.1016/j.techfore.2023.123099

Zhang, M., Yang, J., Yu, P., Tinajero, G. D. A., Guan, Y., Yan, Q., Zhang, X., & Guo, H. (2024). Dual-Stackelberg game-based trading in community integrated energy system considering uncertain demand response and carbon trading. *Sustainable Cities and Society*, *101*, 105088. doi:10.1016/j.scs.2023.105088

Zhou, Y., & Lund, P. D. (2023). Peer-to-peer energy sharing and trading of renewable energy in smart communities - trading pricing models, decision-making and agent-based collaboration. *Renewable Energy*, *207*, 177–193. doi:10.1016/j.renene.2023.02.125

APPENDIX

List of Abbreviations

AD Anaerobic Digestion
CET Clean Energy Target
CIES Clean Energy and Carbon Intensity Reduction
DERs Distributed Energy Resources
DES Distributed Energy System
ECCE Early Childhood Care and Education
FIP Feed-in Premium
GITT Greater Intercity Transportation Network
GSCM Green Supply Chain Management
IRR Internal rate of return
KW Kitchen Waste
LCOE Levelized cost of energy
MUET Mehran University of Engineering and Technology
NPC Net-present cost
P2P peer-to-peer
PSHP Pumped Storage Hydropower Plant
PSM Public Service Motivation
ROI Return of Interest
RPS Renewable Portfolio Standard
SDGs Sustainable Development Goals
VRE Variable Renewable Energy

Chapter 7
Identification of Green E-Commerce Adoption Among SMEs Based on the TOE Framework With Demographics as Control Variables

Muafi Muafi
Universitas Islam Indonesia, Indonesia

Yoga Religia
 https://orcid.org/0000-0002-7496-0819
Universitas Pembangunan Nasional Veteran Yogyakarta, Indonesia

Yussi Ramawati
Atma Jaya Catholic University of Indonesia, Indonesia

ABSTRACT

This research investigates the adoption of green e-commerce among SMEs in Indonesia through the lens of the technology-organization-environment (TOE) framework. Using a quantitative approach with 126 SME owners who have adopted green e-commerce, the study finds that technology, organization, and the environment significantly influence green e-commerce adoption. Specifically, SMEs are more likely to adopt green e-commerce when they perceive it as useful and aligned with their values, receive organizational support, and face pressure from customers and competitors. Contrary to expectations, the owner's education level, product type, and duration of operations do not significantly impact the adoption decision. The study contributes to theory by reaffirming the TOE framework's relevance in predicting green e-commerce adoption and provides practical insights for stakeholders to enhance SMEs' green business practices and digital transformation efforts.

DOI: 10.4018/979-8-3693-2865-1.ch007

INTRODUCTION

The development of green businesses in the SME sector is increasingly attracting attention from various quarters as it is considered to play a significant role in the success of a country's economy. Currently, the number of SMEs in Indonesia accounts for over 99 percent of the total business units in other sectors, making the majority of the Indonesian population work in the SME sector (Jayani, 2021). Moreover, the number of Internet users in Indonesia is among the largest in the world, with over 204 million users recorded in 2022 (Riyanto, 2022). The trend of Internet users in Indonesia continues to increase annually. Dihni (2021) states that Indonesia has become the country with the largest retail sales through e-commerce in Southeast Asia. Currently, SMEs in developing countries face various obstacles that are different from SMEs in developed countries. One of the reasons is the topic of e-commerce adoption among SMEs, which has only recently received attention in academic circles, so that many still view it as a threat, not an opportunity, for SMEs in developing countries (Nasution et al., 2021).

Recent findings suggest that green e-commerce will be the sole future of retail sales for SMEs (Lal & Chavan, 2019; Martínez et al., 2020). Green e-commerce is an online business practice that focuses on minimizing the environmental impact of e-commerce activities (Jalil et al., 2024). This covers various aspects, from selecting sustainable products, environmentally friendly packaging, to energy efficient shipping. Green e-commerce presents a unique potential that SMEs can leverage for green business development in green marketing. Currently, more and more companies are aware of the environmental impact of company supply chain activities, but almost no research has analysed green e-commerce criteria to evaluate green supplier performance (Liou et al., 2024). In developed countries, green marketing is an integral part of corporate strategy in an era that prioritizes sustainability, aligns with consumer values, and delivers real benefits. Integration with digital marketing increases transparency and engagement, creating a powerful combination and sustainable competitive advantage in the ever-evolving digital and sustainable marketing landscape (Piccolo et al., 2024). However, attention to this matter is still difficult to find in developing countries. Ocloo et al. (2020) note that many SMEs still face challenges in green marketing their products online through green e-commerce. Despite the importance of utilizing e-commerce in SME product marketing, there is still a scarcity of research on e-commerce adoption among SMEs (Ocloo et al., 2020; Yang et al., 2022), especially in developing countries.

From a practical perspective, this research is highly essential due to the need to encourage SMEs to adopt green e-commerce to survive in the current green business transformation. This was emphasized by Teten Masduki, Minister of Cooperatives and SMEs of the Republic of Indonesia, who highlighted that there are still many SMEs in various regions that are not yet connected to the digital ecosystem. In fact, this digital ecosystem will be very useful for achieving green business among SMEs. Apart from that, SMEs need to be motivated to use digital systems for green marketing their products (Kemenkopukm, 2022).

According to Chandra and Kumar (2018); Purwandari et al. (2019), the TOE (Technology-Organization-Environment) framework is considered a robust model for predicting green technology adoption. The TOE framework was initially proposed by Tornatzky and Fleischer (1990) where innovation adoption can be explained through three contexts: technology, organization, and environment. The TOE framework is highly suitable for predicting green technology adoption (including e-commerce) within the organizational scope (Ali et al., 2020). Several pieces of literature state that technology significantly influences e-commerce adoption (Putra & Santoso, 2020; Qalati et al., 2021). When SMEs perceive e-commerce technology as useful, beneficial, and aligned with their values, they are more likely to adopt e-commerce

(Religia et al., 2021). Yeng et al. (2015) argue that the organizational context is the most frequently used context in predicting innovation adoption among SMEs. Some studies find that the organization has a significant impact on e-commerce adoption (Effendi et al., 2020; Qalati et al., 2021). Regarding the environmental context, Qalati et al. (2021); Tripopsakul (2018) found that the environment significantly influences e-commerce adoption. In terms of technology adoption, the environment has a considerable influence on e-commerce usage (Religia, 2022). However, some studies supporting the TOE framework do not exempt it from criticism.

Kam and Tham (2022) dan Stjepić et al. (2021) have criticized the TOE framework, stating that the technological context is not the sole determinant of e-commerce adoption. Chee et al. (2016) present an alternative perspective on organizational context, suggesting that factors such as top management support and organizational readiness can influence e-commerce adoption. These findings are further supported by Sun et al. (2020), who argue that indicators in the organizational context may not always be used to predict technology adoption decisions. In the environmental context, Awa and Ojiabo (2016) found that partner readiness is not a decisive factor in a company's technology adoption, and the same applies to competitive pressures (Hmoud et al., 2023). Even now, it remains challenging to find research addressing the reasons SMEs decide to adopt e-commerce, prompting this study to seek clarification on the matter.

Theoretically, this research is justified to address a research gap that suggests the TOE framework is highly effective in predicting green technology adoption among SMEs, as found by Chandra and Kumar (2018); Purwandari et al. (2019), dan Religia et al. (2021), However Sun et al. (2020); Stjepić et al. (2021); dan Hmoud et al. (2023) found contradictory results. Thus, this research not only provides practical contributions in supporting efforts to drive green e-commerce adoption by SMEs for business survival but also fills theoretical gaps related to the effectiveness of the TOE framework in predicting green e-commerce adoption among SMEs. In broad terms, there are two main research gaps that aim to be addressed in this study, including:

1. Despite the emphasis on the crucial role of the three contexts (technology, organization, and environment) in the TOE framework, criticisms still exist. This research will identify factors in the technological, organizational, and environmental contexts that influence the adoption of green e-commerce by SMEs.
2. Despite the acknowledged potential of using green e-commerce in green marketing SME products, there are still challenges faced by SMEs in developing countries. The research can explore specific obstacles and challenges encountered by SMEs in green marketing their products online on e-commerce platforms.

Based on the discussed points, this research aims to identify the reasons for green e-commerce adoption among SMEs in Indonesia and to test and explain the role of the TOE framework in influencing green e-commerce adoption by SMEs.

BACKGROUND

Green e-commerce is transforming the rules of engagement for SMEs in expanding to foreign green markets through the utilization of automated green digital transaction features (Lian et al., 2022). The use of green e-commerce by SMEs can assist them in exploring new green market potentials and seizing opportunities in previously untouched customer segments (Saridakis et al., 2018). However, recent data indicates that many SMEs have yet to transform their green businesses using e-commerce platforms (Ocloo et al., 2020; Yang et al., 2022). Numerous studies have attempted to identify factors influencing the decision to adopt e-commerce among SMEs, such as Putra and Santoso (2020); Qalati et al. (2021); dan Religia et al. (2021). However, research conducted in developing countries remains limited (Hossain et al., 2023). Yet, SMEs in developing countries face more significant challenges in ICT adoption compared to those in developed countries (Shahadat et al., 2023).

Currently, there are several theories that can be employed to adopt the intention of green e-commerce adoption, such as the Technology Acceptance Model (TAM), Diffusion of Innovation (DoI), and the TOE framework. Research using the TAM theory has been thoroughly discussed by Koksalmis and Gozudok (2021); Pipitwanichakarn and Wongtada (2021); dan Khan et al. (2023). Additionally, the TAM theory is more focused on individual technology adoption (Davis et al., 1989), not organizational adoption. This study attempts to examine SMEs within the organizational scope. The Diffusion of Innovation (DoI) theory introduced by Rogers and Cartano (1962), emphasizes internal and external concepts within the organizational context. Furthermore, the DoI theory is recognized for its superior explanatory ability in explaining technology adoption decisions within the organizational scope compared to other adoption models (Zamani, 2022). However, although the DoI theory has been frequently applied to explain technology adoption among SMEs, its limitation lies in its focus solely on organizational and environmental factors, without considering the technical characteristics of new technologies such as e-commerce (Ghobakhloo et al., 2011). This limitation has been well addressed by the TOE framework, where technology adoption is determined not only by organizational and environmental contexts but Tornatzky and Fleischer (1990) also consider technology context as a primary consideration.

Many studies use the TOE framework to identify the adoption of technologies such as e-commerce, cloud computing, etc. (Ali et al., 2020; Chandra & Kumar, 2018). This research leverages the TOE framework because it is suitable for explaining e-commerce adoption among SMEs within the organizational scope. The TOE framework will be used as the theoretical basis for creating the research model and hypotheses. It is hoped that this study can reaffirm the strength of the TOE framework in aiding the identification of reasons for e-commerce adoption among SMEs.

Technology and Green E-Commerce Adoption

Technology is related to the technological characteristics perceived as relevant to the company's needs. The technological characteristics required by organizations can typically explain the adoption of information technology within an organization (Abed, 2020). The technological context can be seen through perceived usefulness, relative advantages to be gained, and technological compatibility to be adopted Perceived usefulness is related to the company's perception that the adopted technology is expected to enhance company performance (Davis, 1986). Relative advantages pertain to the extent to which the technology to be adopted is better than the idea it will replace (Religia et al., 2021). Compatibility is related to the assumption that the adopted technology aligns with the values held by the organization (Khwaji et al., 2022). When e-commerce is perceived as user-friendly, SMEs are more likely to adopt such e-commerce services (Religia et al., 2021). Previous research has found that technology has a significant impact on e-commerce adoption by SMEs (Effendi et al., 2020; Putra & Santoso, 2020; Qalati et al., 2021).

H1:*Technology significantly and positively influences green e-commerce adoption among SMEs.*

Organization and Green E-Commerce Adoption

Organization is related to the characteristics and resources possessed by the organization to adopt e-commerce. Yeng et al. (2015) explain that organizational characteristics are the most frequently used factors in explaining innovation adoption among SMEs. The organizational context can be observed through top management support and organizational readiness to adopt technology (Abed, 2020; Chau & Deng, 2018). Top management support is related to how managers understand and treat the new technology to be adopted (Maroufkhani et al., 2022). Organizational readiness is related to the resources that the organization possesses to adopt new innovative technology (Chwelos et al., 2001). Several studies indicate that organizations have a significant influence on e-commerce adoption (Effendi et al., 2020; Putra & Santoso, 2020; Qalati et al., 2021).

H2:*Organization significantly and positively influences green e-commerce adoption among SMEs.*

Environment and Green E-Commerce Adoption

The environment is a crucial factor in influencing technology adoption among SMEs (Religia, 2022). In this context, the environment relates to the pressures and support obtained from external parties that influence SMEs to adopt e-commerce. The environment can be explained based on competitive pressure from rivals and the pressure from consumers for organizations to use e-commerce (Bravo et al., 2022; Chau & Deng, 2018). Competitive pressure is related to SMEs' desire to adopt e-commerce due to pressure from similar business competitors who have already adopted e-commerce (Religia et al., 2020). Consumer pressure is related to SMEs' desire to provide more convenient product information and ease of purchasing transactions (Hoang et al., 2021; Zhang et al., 2018). Previous research has found that the environment significantly influences e-commerce adoption (Effendi et al., 2020; Qalati et al., 2021; Tripopsakul, 2018).

H3: *Environment significantly and positively influences green e-commerce adoption among SMEs.*

The theoretical model framework of this research explores the exploratory relationships among the constructs of technology, organizational constructs, and environmental constructs towards the construct of green e-commerce adoption as depicted in Figure 1.

Figure 1. Theoretical model framework

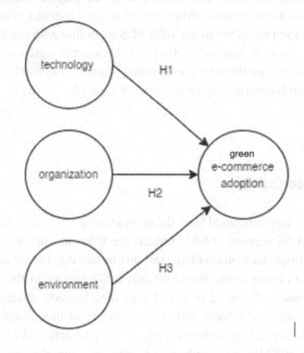

RESEARCH METHODOLOGY

This study utilizes a quantitative, descriptive, cross-sectional research method with primary data sources. The target population is identified as SMEs that have adopted green e-commerce on the Shopee and Tokopedia platforms. The random sampling method is employed to better represent the overall population (Hair et al., 2014). Questionnaires are distributed to prospective respondents, who are SME owners, through an online survey via the Google Forms application (www.docs.google.com). The questionnaires are distributed within WhatsApp groups containing SME operators who have utilized green e-commerce in their green business operations. It is essential to note that the respondents in this study are confirmed SME owners who have adopted green e-commerce. The research constructs are evaluated using 20 statements, with the technology construct consisting of 6 statements, organizational and environmental constructs consisting of 5 statements each, and the green e-commerce adoption construct consisting of 4 statements. Following Malhotra (2009), data measurement in the research is done using a Likert scale from 1, meaning "strongly disagree," to 5, meaning "strongly agree." Additionally, demographic characteristics such as gender, age, and the last education level of SME owners, as well as the number of employees, type of products, and the duration of operations of SMEs, are inquired. Over the 7-month survey period, a complete set of observations is conducted to understand respondents' perspectives on green e-commerce adoption decisions. Based on the distributed questionnaires, 126 respondents completed the survey. This number is considered sufficient as Stevens (1996) states that the estimated sample size with maximum likelihood (ML) should be at least 15 times the number of observed variables.

Several demographic characteristics such as the last education level, type of products, and duration of operations will be used as control variables. Although not the main focus of the study, inserting control variables into the model allows for the estimation of assumed effects to be consistently and stably carried out. This step helps researchers eliminate alternative factors that may be linked to control variables, thus strengthening the causal inference sustainability related to the observed effects (Hair Jr et al., 2021). After data acquisition, it is then analyzed using SEM-PLS modeling with the SmartPLS 3.0 application. The use of SmartPLS is not only to test the relationships between research variables but also to test the external/outer model relationships through confirmatory factor analysis (CFA) and the internal/inner model relationships through bootstrapping (Kaufmann & Gaeckler, 2015).

RESEARCH RESULT

Respondent Characteristics

Respondent Characteristics were obtained from the completed questionnaires, totaling 126 respondents. It is known that more than 66 percent of SME owners are women. This result is consistent with what Nainggolan (2016), mentioned, as women often start businesses due to low family income and support their husbands who work in companies. Based on age, it is known that the majority of SME owners using e-commerce are between 27 and 42 years old, with their last education being high school. This is because, according to Suryono and Pitoyo (2013), the majority of Indonesian graduates prefer to work as experts, while high school graduates often choose to sell products and/or services. It is also known that more than 50 percent of SMEs have only 1 to 3 employees, emphasizing that SMEs in Indonesia are still dominated by Micro Businesses.

Table 1. Respondent characteristics

Characteristics	Criteria	N	Percentage
Gender	Male	42	33,3
	Female	84	66,7
Age	17 to 26 years	27	21,4
	27 to 42 years	61	48,4
	43 to 58 years	38	30,2
Education	Junior High School	33	26,2
	Senior High School	57	45,2
	Undergraduate	36	28,6
Number of Employee	1-3 employees	66	52,4
	3-5 employees	32	25,4
	6-8 employees	28	22,2
Type of Product	Self-made	46	36,5
	Local Made	47	37,3
	Service	33	26,2
Duration of operations	< 5 years	47	37,3
	5 to 10 years	44	34,9
	> 10 years	35	27,8

Note: N = 126 respondents

Based on the type of product, it is known that the majority of SMEs prefer to market locally made products rather than their own products or service offerings. This is due to the fact that producing products or providing services requires sufficient working capital for the production process. The limited production tools and the limited knowledge of SME owners in obtaining product permits are also constraints that lead SMEs to choose not to market their own products (Mersita et al., 2019). Regarding the Duration of operations, most SMEs have been operating through e-commerce for less than 5 years. This is because SMEs started looking at e-commerce after the Covid-19 pandemic, when social distancing policies began to be implemented. A more detailed presentation of respondent characteristics can be seen in Table 1.

Confirmatory Factor Analysis and Discriminant Validity

Confirmatory factor analysis (CFA) in this study is used to assess the convergent validity and reliability of the research data. The convergent validity of this study is measured using the outer loading values on each instrument and the average variance extracted (AVE) values for each construct, while the testing of data reliability is done using Cronbach's alpha (CA) and composite reliability (CR) values. Based on the CFA test results, it is known that all instruments used have values above 0.7, thus acceptable. Hair Jr et al. (2021) explain that the outer loading values of each research instrument used should be at least 0.7. In the AVE test, values of 0.580 for the technology construct, 0.672 for the organization construct, 0.643 for the environment construct, and 0.741 for the e-commerce adoption construct were obtained. Hair Jr et al. (2021) explain that a construct can be considered valid when its value is greater than 0.5. From the convergent validity test based on outer loading and AVE values, it can be said that the research data is convergently valid.

Table 2. VIF, outer loadings, AVE, Cronbach Alpha, and composite reliability

Construct	Indicator	Item*	VIF	Loading	AVE	CA	CR
Technology (TEC)	Perceived usefulness	TEC_1	1,952	0,769	0,580	0,856	0,892
		TEC_2	2,339	0,833			
	Relative advantage	TEC_3	2,083	0,714			
		TEC_4	1,898	0,708			
	Compatibility	TEC_5	2,025	0,802			
		TEC_6	1,908	0,781			
Organization (ORG)	Organizational readiness	ORG_1	2,080	0,818	0,672	0,879	0,911
		ORG_2	2,542	0,860			
		ORG_3	2,227	0,845			
	Top management support	ORG_4	2,501	0,807			
		ORG_5	2,314	0,764			
Environment (ENV)	Competitive pressure	ENV_1	1,820	0,796	0,643	0,862	0,900
		ENV_2	1,842	0,814			
	Consumer pressure	ENV_3	1,848	0,780			
		ENV_4	2,787	0,839			
		ENV_5	2,340	0,779			
Green E-commerce adoption(GCA)	Actual use	GCA_1	2,422	0,867	0,741	0,884	0,920
		GCA_2	2,316	0,861			
	Continuous use	GCA_3	2,006	0,836			
		GCA_4	2,535	0,880			

Note: p < 0.05; AVE = Average Extracted Variance; CR = Composite Reliability; *)research items can be seen in the attachment

Further evaluation of convergent validity is conducted by examining CA and CR values. CA values that approach 1 indicate good internal consistency in the data used, while CR values that approach 1 indicate the accuracy and quality of the constructs used. According to Hair Jr et al. (2021), the minimum limits for CA and CR should be above 0.7. The CA values for each construct in this study turned out to be greater than 0.8, and the CR values were also greater than 0.8, so it can be said that the data used in this study is highly reliable. For more complete results of convergent validity, refer to Table 2.

High levels of multicollinearity can be problematic as it increases the variance of regression coefficients and leads to unstable results. VIF values below 5 are generally acceptable, indicating that the model has been well estimated (Hair Jr et al., 2021). This study has VIF values for all indicators in the model ranging from 1.820 to 2.787. For more details, refer to Table 2.

Discriminant validity assesses how different constructs can be distinguished from each other in a study. Analysis methods like the Fornell-Larcker criterion test are often used to evaluate discriminant validity in the context of CFA. The Fornell-Larcker test results indicate that the square root of AVE for each construct in this study is proven to be larger than the correlations with other constructs in the model. These results clearly indicate the success of discriminant validity. Therefore, it can be said that the data used in this study meets discriminant validity. See Table 3 for more information.

Table 3. Fornell-Larcker criterion

	1	2	3	4
1. Technology	**0,762**			
2. Organization	0,751	**0,820**		
3. Environment	0,658	0,686	**0,802**	
4. Green E-commerce adoption	0,759	0,737	0,737	**0,861**

Analysis of Relationships Among Constructs

Structural model testing was conducted using SEM-PLS analysis with Smart PLS 3.0 tools, and the results are documented in Table 4. The initial step of the analysis involved testing with control variables, namely the last education level, type of product, and duration of operations. The last education level was used as a control variable because of the assumption that the education level of SME owners can influence various aspects of the decision to adopt green e-commerce. The type of product was used as a control variable to understand how the differences in products produced by SMEs can affect their decisions to adopt e-commerce. Additionally, the duration of operations was also used as a control variable because SMEs that have been operating for a longer period may have broader experience, networks, and knowledge, thereby influencing their decisions to adopt green e-commerce. The use of control variables in statistical analysis aims to minimize the influence of other variables that may affect the research or analysis results, allowing for a more accurate isolation of the effects of the variables under investigation The test results revealed that neither the last education level of SME owners, the type of products offered, nor the duration of operations significantly influenced the decision to adopt green e-commerce. The non-significant results of the control variables used indicate the absence of differences in outcomes and the consistency of results from this research model. The second step involved testing without using control variables, and the results are presented in Figure 2 and more comprehensively in Table 4. In the final step, hypothesis testing was conducted by comparing the results of the relationships among constructs using control variables and without control variables, as performed in the first and second steps.

Figure 2. Hypothesis testing results
Note: ***p = <0.001; **p = <0.01; *p = <0.05

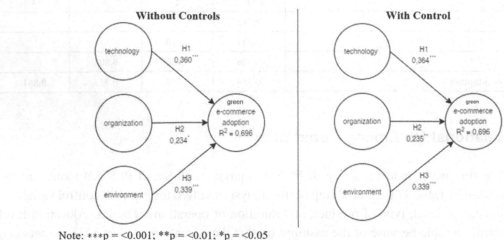

Note: ***p = <0.001; **p = <0.01; *p = <0.05

Based on Figure 2, the results of the hypothesis testing in the study are as follows:

1. Without control variables:
   - H1: (β = 0.360; R^2 = 0.696; p-value < 0.001);
   - H2: (β = 0.234; R^2 = 0.696; p-value > 0.05);
   - H3: (β = 0.339; R^2 = 0.696; p-value < 0.001);
2. With control variables:
   - H1: (β = 0.364; R^2 = 0.696; p-value < 0.001);
   - H2: (β = 0.235; R^2 = 0.696; p-value > 0.01);
   - H3: (β = 0.339; R^2 = 0.696; p-value < 0.001);

The hypothesis testing results indicate that technology significantly and positively influences green e-commerce adoption with a significance level of 0.001, confirming the acceptance of H1. Additionally, organization is found to have a significant positive impact on the decision of SMEs to adopt green e-commerce with a significance level of 0.05, confirming the acceptance of H2. Finally, the environment is known to have a significant positive influence on green e-commerce adoption among SMEs with a significance level of 0.001, confirming the acceptance of H3 in this study. These results hold true both with and without the use of control variables.

The adequacy of this research model is evaluated using the R^2 value. The R^2 value indicates the extent to which the variation in the endogenous variable can be explained or attributed by the exogenous variables present in the model. Generally, the R^2 value ranges from 0 to 1. A higher R^2 value indicates that the model can explain a significant amount of variation in the data. According to Hair Jr et al. (2021), R^2 values between 0.4 and 0.7 indicate strong predictive results. This research model shows an R^2 value of 0.696, indicating that the predictive results of this research model are reliable. The presence of multicollinearity in the model is observed through the variance inflation factor (VIF) values.

Table 4. Results of the test of relationships between constructs

Hypotheses	Relations	Without Controls		With Control		Result
		β	P-Value	β	P-Value	
H1	TEC -> GCA	0,360	0,000	0,364	0,000	Supported
H2	ORG -> GCA	0,234	0,020	0,235	0,007	Supported
H3	ENV -> GCA	0,339	0,000	0,339	0,000	Supported
Control Variable						
	Education -> GCA	-	-	0,058	0,236	Not Supported
	Business Type -> GCA	-	-	-0,025	0,666	Not Supported
	Duration of Operations -> GCA	-	-	0,018	0,756	Not Supported

Note: $R2 = 0.696$; R^2 Adjusted = 0.689; TEC = Technology; ORG = Organization; ENV = Environment; GCA = Green E-Commerce Adoption.

DISCUSSION

The findings of this research support H1, indicating that technology significantly influences the adoption of green e-commerce. The more green e-commerce is perceived as useful, beneficial, and aligned with the operations of SMEs, the more likely SMEs are to continue using green e-commerce in their product sales processes. This result aligns with research stating that SMEs are more likely to adopt e-commerce when it is perceived as useful, beneficial, and aligned with the values embraced by SMEs (Effendi et al., 2020; Putra & Santoso, 2020; Qalati et al., 2021; Religia et al., 2021). These findings suggest that stakeholders in the SME sector can enhance technological awareness among SMEs, including providing education about the benefits of green e-commerce, offering technical support, and emphasizing values relevant to SMEs.

This study supports H2, where the organization is proven to have a significant positive influence on the adoption of green e-commerce. The more SMEs are prepared to use green e-commerce and receive support from top management in using green e-commerce for green marketing, the more likely SMEs are to continue using green e-commerce. This result is consistent with several studies stating that the organization significantly influences the adoption of e-commerce (Effendi et al., 2020; Putra & Santoso, 2020; Qalati et al., 2021). The government is recommended to provide incentives or training to better prepare SMEs for transforming green marketing using green e-commerce. Meanwhile, stakeholders need to ensure top management support in integrating green e-commerce into the green marketing strategy of SMEs.

Similar to H1 and H2, this study also supports H3, where the environmental context has proven to have a significant positive influence on the adoption of green e-commerce among SMEs. The more SMEs experience pressure from their customers and competitors to use green e-commerce, it turns out that it can encourage SMEs to adopt green e-commerce. This result supports the findings of Effendi et al. (2020); Tripopsakul (2018); dan Qalati et al. (2021) where the environment is significantly shown to influence e-commerce adoption. The government and stakeholders in the SME sector are advised to provide support programs, supportive policies, as well as infrastructure and resources that support green e-commerce adoption. Collaboration with industry, academia, and efforts to increase SME awareness of the benefits of green e-commerce is also needed to ensure the success and growth of the SME sector.

Finally, regarding the use of control variables, this research indicates that the owner's education level, the type of products offered, and the duration of operations do not have a significant influence on the decision to adopt green e-commerce. This result demonstrates the consistency of the results from the model used in the study, where with or without control variables, the results provided will remain the same. As stated by Hair Jr et al. (2021), incorporating control variables in the research model can make the study more accurate in evaluating the impact of the variables being studied without being influenced by unwanted interfering factors. This provides a stronger basis for making accurate conclusions and supports the internal validity of this research. Additionally, with an R^2 value of 0.696, it proves that the research model developed in this study provides strong predictive results and can be implemented in further research.

FUTURE RESEARCH DIRECTIONS

Research Implications

The theoretical implications of the research findings provide a significant contribution to the TOE framework and the literature on green e-commerce adoption among SMEs. The finding that technology has a significant positive influence on green e-commerce adoption supports the TOE principle that emphasizes the role of technology in influencing organizational decisions. The proven positive influence of organizational support and top management also supports the structural and social elements in the TOE framework, emphasizing the importance of internal organizational factors in shaping a positive attitude towards green e-commerce adoption. Additionally, the confirmation that the environmental context has a significant positive impact on green e-commerce adoption enriches the TOE framework by considering external pressure from customers and competitors. The results indicating the lack of influence of the owner's education level, type of products, and operational duration provide further understanding of the variability of these factors in the context of green e-commerce adoption in SMEs. Overall, these findings strengthen and complement the TOE framework proposed by Tornatzky and Fleischer (1990), providing a strong theoretical foundation for further research in understanding green e-commerce adoption among SMEs.

Practical implications of the research findings have significant impacts on efforts to enhance green e-commerce adoption among SMEs. The government and stakeholders can direct their efforts to increase technological awareness among SMEs by providing education on the benefits of green e-commerce, technical support, and emphasizing values relevant to SMEs. Additionally, incentives and training provided by the government can help enhance SMEs' readiness to adopt green e-commerce. Furthermore, top management in SME organizations also needs to provide strong support for the use of e-commerce in green marketing. Finally, the government and stakeholders need to understand the influence of the external environment, such as pressure from customers and competitors, in driving green e-commerce adoption by SMEs. Collaborative efforts between industry sectors, academia, and awareness-building initiatives also need to be strengthened to ensure the green growth and green sustainability of the SME sector. A good understanding of the factors influencing green e-commerce adoption among SMEs can provide valuable guidance for the government and stakeholders to design effective policies and support programs.

Research findings suggest that green e-commerce will be the future of retail sales for SMEs. Green e-commerce offers a unique potential for SMEs to develop green businesses and market their products online in a sustainable manner. However, many SMEs still face challenges in adopting green e-commerce. These challenges include a lack of technological awareness, organizational support, and top management support, as well as an unsupportive environmental context. Therefore, collaborative efforts from various parties are needed to increase the adoption of green e-commerce among SMEs. Governments and stakeholders need to raise technological awareness, provide technical support, incentives, and facilities, and strengthen environmental regulations and policies. Top management of SMEs also needs to provide strong support for green e-commerce. By implementing these policies, it is hoped that green e-commerce adoption among SMEs can be increased and sustainable business growth can be encouraged, in line with global commitments to sustainable development.

Limitations of the Study

This research has several limitations involving various aspects. The research method employs a cross-sectional approach and online surveys through Google Forms, as well as questionnaire distribution through WhatsApp groups, which may introduce bias in respondents consisting only of SME owners who have adopted green e-commerce. This could impact the sample's representativeness of the overall SME population. The use of control variables such as the owner's highest education level, product type, and duration of operations, although included in the model, still has the potential for unidentified factors that may influence the results. Additionally, this study does not deeply explore specific factors affecting each construct. While a high R^2 value indicates strong predictions, the research model remains constrained by the variables included. Acknowledging these limitations enriches the understanding of SME green e-commerce adoption while providing guidance for future research to address and delve deeper into these aspects.

Future Research

It is recommended that further research delve into the influence of control variables that have not been proven significant in green e-commerce adoption, such as the owner's education level, product type, and duration of operations, to understand more complex dynamics. Additionally, research could involve a qualitative approach to explore in-depth the specific factors within the constructs of technology, organization, and the environment that influence green e-commerce adoption. The next steps may include longitudinal research to evaluate changes in green e-commerce adoption by SMEs over time, providing a more holistic insight into the dynamics of digital transformation among SMEs.

CONCLUSION

In the development of the SME sector, the adoption of green e-commerce is becoming increasingly important considering the potential green economic growth it can generate (Ekaputri et al., 2018). Despite Indonesia having a significant number of SMEs and the world's largest internet user base, the adoption of green e-commerce among SMEs still faces challenges, and research on this topic is still limited (Jayani, 2021; Ocloo et al., 2020). In theoretical terms, although the TOE framework has been a strong foundation, some other findings criticize the effectiveness of this framework. This suggests lingering doubts about the effectiveness of the TOE framework, prompting this study to contribute to a better understanding of green e-commerce adoption by SMEs, especially in developing countries. The research indicates that technology, organization, and the environment have a positive and significant influence on the adoption of green e-commerce among SMEs. These findings align with previous research and underscore the importance of technology awareness, organizational support, and responsiveness to environmental pressures in driving green e-commerce adoption among SMEs (Chandra & Kumar, 2018; Purwandari et al., 2019; Religia et al., 2021). However, the study also reveals that control variables such as the owner's education level, product type, and duration of operations do not significantly contribute to the decision to adopt green e-commerce.

This research contributes not only theoretically but also practically. Theoretically, it strengthens and complements the foundation of the TOE framework introduced by Tornatzky and Fleischer (1990), providing a solid theoretical basis for further research in understanding the green e-commerce adoption process by SMEs. Practically, the study offers guidance for stakeholders in the SME sector, the government, and researchers to understand the factors influencing green e-commerce adoption and to direct efforts and policies that support the green growth of the SME sector in the digital era.

ACKNOWLEDGMENT

This research was supported by the management department at the Islamic University of Indonesia, UPN "Veteran" Yogyakarta, and Atma Jaya Catholic University of Indonesia.

REFERENCES

Abed, S. S. (2020). Social commerce adoption using TOE framework: An empirical investigation of Saudi Arabian SMEs. *International Journal of Information Management*, *53*(1), 102118. doi:10.1016/j.ijinfomgt.2020.102118

Ali, O., Shrestha, A., Osmanaj, V., & Muhammed, S. (2020). Cloud computing technology adoption: An evaluation of key factors in local governments. *Information Technology & People*, *34*(2), 666–703. doi:10.1108/ITP-03-2019-0119

Awa, H. O., & Ojiabo, O. U. (2016). A model of adoption determinants of ERP within T-O-E framework. *Information Technology & People*, *29*(4), 901–930. doi:10.1108/ITP-03-2015-0068

Bravo, R., Segura, M. G., Temowo, O., & Samaddar, S. (2022). How does a pandemic disrupt the benefits of ecommerce? a case study of small and medium enterprises in the US. *Journal of Theoretical and Applied Electronic Commerce Research*, *17*(2), 522–557. doi:10.3390/jtaer17020028

Chandra, S., & Kumar, K. N. (2018). Exploring factors influencing organizational adoption of augmented reality in e-commerce: Empirical analysis using technology–organization–environment model. *Journal of Electronic Commerce Research*, *19*(3), 237–265.

Chau, N. T., & Deng, H. (2018). Critical determinants for mobile commerce adoption in Vietnamese SMEs: A conceptual framework. *Procedia Computer Science, 138*(1), 433–440. doi:10.1016/j.procs.2018.10.061

Chee, L. S., Suhaimi, B. A., & Quan, L. R. (2016). Understanding the determinants of e-commerce adoption: Evidence from manufacture sector in West Malaysia. *Indian Journal of Science and Technology, 9*(10), 1–8. doi:10.17485/ijst/2016/v9i10/88075

Chwelos, P., Benbasat, I., & Dexter, A. S. (2001). Empirical test of an electronic data interchange adoption model. *Information Systems Research, 12*(3), 304–321. doi:10.1287/isre.12.3.304.9708

Davis, F. D. (1986). Perceived usefulness, perceived ease of use, and user acceptance of information technology. *Management Information Systems Quarterly, 13*(3), 319–340. doi:10.2307/249008

Davis, F. D., Bagozzi, R. P., & Warshaw, P. R. (1989). User Acceptance of Computer Technology: A Comparison of Two Theoretical Models. *Management Science, 35*(8), 982–1003. https://www.jstor.org/stable/2632151. doi:10.1287/mnsc.35.8.982

Dihni, V. A. (2021). *Penjualan E-Commerce Indonesia Diproyeksi Paling Besar di Asia Tenggara pada 2021*. KataData. https://databoks.katadata.co.id/datapublish/2021/09/21/penjualan-e-commerce-indonesia-diproyeksi-paling-besar-di-asia-tenggara-pada-2021

Effendi, M. I., Sugandini, D., & Istanto, Y. (2020). Social media adoption in SMEs impacted by COVID-19: The TOE model. *Journal of Asian Finance. Economics and Business, 7*(11), 915–925. doi:10.13106/jafeb.2020.vol7.no11.915

Ekaputri, S., Sudarwanto, T., & Marlena, N. (2018). Peran Lingkungan Industri, Perilaku Kewirausahaan, Dan Kemampuan Manajerial Terhadap Kinerja Perusahaan Pada Usaha Logam Skala Mikro. *JRMSI-Jurnal Riset Manajemen Sains Indonesia, 9*(1), 1–21. doi:10.21009/JRMSI.009.1.01

Ghobakhloo, M., Arias-Aranda, D., & Benitez-Amado, J. (2011). Adoption of e-commerce applications in SMEs. *Industrial Management & Data Systems, 111*(8), 1238–1269. doi:10.1108/02635571111170785

Hair, J. F., Hult, G. T. M., Ringle, C. M., & Sarstedt, M. (2014). *A Primer on Partial Least Squares Structural Equation Modeling (PLS-SEM)*. SAGE Publications Ltd.

Hair, J. F. Jr, Hult, G. T. M., Ringle, C. M., Sarstedt, M., Danks, N. P., & Ray, S. (2021). *Partial least squares structural equation modeling (PLS-SEM) using R: A workbook*. Springer Nature. doi:10.1007/978-3-030-80519-7

Hmoud, H., Al-Adwan, A. S., Horani, O., Yaseen, H., & Zoubi, J. Z. A. (2023). Factors influencing business intelligence adoption by higher education institutions. *Journal of Open Innovation, 9*(3), 100111. doi:10.1016/j.joitmc.2023.100111

Hoang, T. D. L., Nguyen, H. K., & Thu, N. H. (2021). Towards an economic recovery after the COVID-19 pandemic: Empirical study on electronic commerce adoption of small and medium enterprises in Vietnam. *Management & Marketing, 16*(1), 47–68. doi:10.2478/mmcks-2021-0004

Hossain, M. B., Dewan, N., Senin, A. A., & Illes, C. B. (2023). Evaluating the utilization of technological factors to promote e-commerce adoption in small and medium enterprises. *Electronic Commerce Research*. doi:10.1007/s10660-023-09692-7

Jalil, F., Yang, J., Al-Okaily, M., & Rehman, S. U. (2024). E-commerce for a sustainable future: integrating trust, green supply chain management and online shopping satisfaction. *Asia Pacific Journal of Marketing and Logistics*. doi:10.1108/APJML-12-2023-1188

Jayani, D. H. (2021). *UMKM Indonesia bertambah 1,98% pada 2019*. databoks. https://databoks.katadata.co.id/datapublish/2021/08/12/umkm-indonesia-bertambah-198-pada-2019

Kam, A. J. Y., & Tham, S. Y. (2022). Barriers to e-commerce adoption: Evidence from the retail and food and beverage sectors in Malaysia. *Asian-Pacific Economic Literature*, *36*(2), 32–51. doi:10.1111/apel.12365

Kaufmann, L., & Gaeckler, J. (2015). A Structured Review of Partial Least Squares in Supply Chain Management Research. *Journal of Purchasing and Supply Management*, *21*(4), 259–272. doi:10.1016/j.pursup.2015.04.005

Kemenkopukm, H. (2022). *MenKopUKM kolaborasi dengan Jagoan Internet Marketer bantu UMKM go digital*. https://kemenkopukm.go.id/read/menkopukm-kolaborasi-dengan-jagoan-internet-marketer-bantu-umkm-go-digital

Khan, A. G., Hasan, N., & Ali, M. R. (2023). Unmasking the Behavioural Intention of Social Commerce in Developing Countries: Integrating Technology Acceptance Model. *Global Business Review*, *09721509231180701*, 09721509231180701. doi:10.1177/09721509231180701

Khwaji, A., Alsahafi, Y., & Hussain, F. K. (2022). Conceptual Framework of Blockchain Technology Adoption in Saudi Public Hospitals Using TOE Framework. *International Conference on Network-Based Information Systems*. Kwansei Gakuin University, Japan. 10.1007/978-3-031-14314-4_8

Koksalmis, G. H., & Gozudok, A. (2021). What Impacts E-Commerce Acceptance of Generation Z? A Modified Technology Acceptance Model. In M. Al-Emran & K. Shaalan (Eds.), *Recent Advances in Technology Acceptance Models and Theories* (pp. 57–77). Springer International Publishing. doi:10.1007/978-3-030-64987-6_5

Lal, B., & Chavan, C. R. (2019). A road map: E-commerce to world wide web growth of business world. *Global Journal of Management and Business Research*, *19*(11), 32–36.

Lian, A. T. G., Lily, J., & Cheng, C. T. (2022). The Study of SMEs' E-Commerce Adoption in Sabah and Sarawak. *International Journal of Academic Research in Business & Social Sciences*, *12*(7), 314–326. doi:10.6007/IJARBSS/v12-i7/13900

LiouJ. J.JiangC.LiuS.JiangH.ShaoT. (2024). Selecting Green Suppliers for E-Commerce Enterprises Based on a Hybrid Multiple-Criteria Decision-Making Model. *Available at* SSRN, 1-43. doi:10.2139/ssrn.4770626

Malhotra, N. K. (2009). *Riset Pemasaran Pendekatan Terapan*. PT. Indeks Kelompok Gramedia.

Maroufkhani, P., Iranmanesh, M., & Ghobakhloo, M. (2022). Determinants of big data analytics adoption in small and medium sized enterprises (SMEs). *Industrial Management & Data Systems*, *122*(9), 1–24. doi:10.1108/IMDS-11-2021-0695

Martínez, J. L., Marco, J. N., & Moya, B. R. (2020). Analysis of the adoption of customer facing InStore technologies in retail SMEs. *Journal of Retailing and Consumer Services*, *57*(1), 102225. doi:10.1016/j. jretconser.2020.102225

Mersita, D., Fathoni, A., & Wulan, H. S. (2019). Analysis of Empowerment of Human Resources in Efforts to Optimize The Potential of Human Capital in UMKM. *Journal of Management Information Systems*, *5*(5), 1–8.

Nainggolan, R. (2016). Gender, Tingkat Pendidikan dan Lama Usaha Sebagai Determinan Penghasilan UMKM Kota Surabaya. *Jurnal Kinerja*, *20*(1), 1–12. doi:10.24002/kinerja.v20i1.693

Nasution, M. D. T. P., Rafiki, A., Lubis, A., & Rossanty, Y. (2021). Entrepreneurial orientation, knowledge management, dynamic capabilities towards e-commerce adoption of SMEs in Indonesia. *Journal of Science and Technology Policy Management*, *12*(2), 256–282. doi:10.1108/JSTPM-03-2020-0060

Ocloo, C. E., Xuhua, H., Akaba, S., Shi, J., & Worwui-Brown, D. K. (2020). The Determinant Factors of Business to Business (B2B) E-Commerce Adoption in Small- and Medium-Sized Manufacturing Enterprises. *Journal of Global Information Technology Management*, *23*(3), 1–26. doi:10.1080/10971 98X.2020.1792229

Piccolo, R., Romeo, E. F., & Zarić, S. (2024). Green marketing, brand development and digital strategies: Forging a sustainable future. *KNOWLEDGE-International Journal*, *63*(1), 15–20.

Pipitwanichakarn, T., & Wongtada, N. (2021). Leveraging the technology acceptance model for mobile commerce adoption under distinct stages of adoption. *Asia Pacific Journal of Marketing and Logistics*, *33*(6), 1415–1436. doi:10.1108/APJML-10-2018-0448

Purwandari, B., Otmen, B., & Kumaralalita, L. (2019). Adoption factors of e-marketplace and instagram for micro, small, and medium enterprises (MSMEs) in Indonesia. *Proceedings of 2019 2nd International Conference on Data Science and Information Technology*, Seoul, Republic of Korea. 10.1145/3352411.3352453

Putra, P. O. H., & Santoso, H. B. (2020). Contextual factors and performance impact of e-business use in Indonesian small and medium enterprises (SMEs). *Heliyon*, *6*(1), 1–10. doi:10.1016/j.heliyon.2020. e03568 PMID:32211544

Qalati, S. A., Li, W., Ahmed, N., Mirani, M. A., & Khan, A. (2021). Examining the factors affecting SME performance: The mediating role of social media adoption. *Sustainability (Basel)*, *13*(75), 1–24. doi:10.3390/su13010075

Religia, Y., Surachman, Rohman, F., & Indrawati, N. K. (2020). The antecendence of e-commerce adoption by micro, small, and medium sized enterprise (MSME) with e-commerce training as moderation. *Solid State Technology*, *63*(2), 335–346.

Religia, Y. (2022). The effect of environmental pressures and the covid19 pandemic on the adoption of TikTok by MSMEs: Can MSME engagement moderate? *Journal of International Conference Proceedings*, *5*(5), 285–300. doi:10.32535/jicp.v5i5.2031

Religia, Y., Surachman, S., Rohman, F., & Indrawati, N. (2021). *E-commerce adoption in SMEs: A literature review*. *Proceedings of the 1st International Conference on Economics Engineering and Social Science (InCEESS 2020)*, Bekasi, Indonesia. 10.4108/eai.17-7-2020.2302969

Riyanto, A. D. (2022). *Hootsuite (We are Social): Indonesian Digital Report 2022.*. Hoot Suite. https://andi.link/hootsuite-we-are-social-indonesian-digital-report-2022

Rogers, E. M., & Cartano, D. G. (1962). Methods of Measuring Opinion Leadership. *Public Opinion Quarterly*, *26*(3), 435–441. https://www.jstor.org/stable/2747233. doi:10.1086/267118

Saridakis, G., Lai, Y., Mohammed, A. M., & Hansen, J. M. (2018). Industry characteristics, stages of E-commerce communications, and entrepreneurs and SMEs revenue growth. *Technological Forecasting and Social Change*, *128*(1), 56–66. doi:10.1016/j.techfore.2017.10.017

Shahadat, M. M. H., Nekmahmud, M., Ebrahimi, P., & Fekete-Farkas, M. (2023). Digital Technology Adoption in SMEs: What Technological, Environmental and Organizational Factors Influence in Emerging Countries? *Global Business Review*, *09721509221137199*. doi:10.1177/09721509221137199

Stevens, J. (1996). *Applied multivariate statistics for the social sciences*. Lawrence Erlbaum.

Stjepić, A.-M., Pejić Bach, M., & Bosilj Vukšić, V. (2021). Exploring risks in the adoption of business intelligence in SMEs using the TOE framework. *JRFM, 14*(2), 58. doi:10.3390/jrfm14020058

Sun, S., Hall, D. J., & Cegielski, C. G. (2020). Organizational intention to adopt big data in the B2B context: An integrated view. *Industrial Marketing Management*, *86*, 109–121. doi:10.1016/j.indmarman.2019.09.003

Suryono, P., & Pitoyo, A. J. (2013). Kesesuaian Tingkat Pendidikan dan Jenis Pekerjaan Pekerja di Pulau Jawa: Analisis Data Sakernas Tahun 2010. *Jurnal Bumi Indonesia*, *2*(1), 59–68.

Tornatzky, L. G., & Fleischer, M. (1990). *The processes of technological innovation*. Lexington Books.

Tripopsakul, S. (2018). Social media adoption as a business platform: an integrated TAM-TOE framework. *PJMS, 18*(2), 350-362. doi:10.17512/pjms.2018.18.2.28

Yang, T., Xun, J., & Chong, W. K. (2022). Complementary resources and SME firm performance: The role of external readiness and E-commerce functionality. *Industrial Management & Data Systems*, *122*(4), 1128–1151. doi:10.1108/IMDS-01-2022-0045

Yeng, S. K., Osman, A., Haji, O. Y., & Safizal, M. (2015). E-Commerce adoption among Small and Medium Enterprises (SMEs) in Northern State of Malaysia. *Mediterranean Journal of Social Sciences*, *6*(5), 37–43. doi:10.5901/mjss.2015.v6n5p37

Zamani, S. Z. (2022). Small and Medium Enterprises (SMEs) facing an evolving technological era: A systematic literature review on the adoption of technologies in SMEs. *European Journal of Innovation Management*, *25*(6), 735–757. doi:10.1108/EJIM-07-2021-0360

Zhang, L., Li, D., Cao, C., & Huang, S. (2018). The influence of greenwashing perception on green purchasing intentions: The mediating role of green word-of-mouth and moderating role of green concern. *Journal of Cleaner Production*, *187*, 740–750. doi:10.1016/j.jclepro.2018.03.201

Chapter 8
Analyzing Inter–Firm Manufacturing for a Circular Economy and Green Supply Chain Management

Balaji Gopalan

iD https://orcid.org/0000-0002-1082-5597

CMS Business School, Bangalore, India

Rupesh Kumar Sinha

CMS Business School, Bangalore, India

V. Vinoth Kumar

iD https://orcid.org/0000-0002-8282-6740

CMS Business School, Bangalore, India

ABSTRACT

There has been a paradigm shift in how businesses manufacture products. Inter-firm manufacturing is a relatively new paradigm. This paper examines inter-firm manufacturing and presents an analytical framework in the light of a circular economy and green supply chain management. In developed countries, industry leadership is associated with manufacturing. Industry leaders are taking measures to encourage and prioritize manufacturing and establish new economies and business ecosystems across various industry sectors. This may be in the area of Information and communication technologies, pharma industries, 3D printing, food industries, housing, energy and utilities, businesses and financial services, and media. Today, various industries are shifting towards eco-friendly and sustainable businesses that align with circular economies and green supply chain management. For that purpose, a different analysis, one that associates performance metrics with an exergy analysis of industries in alignment with a circular economy and green supply chain management is necessary.

DOI: 10.4018/979-8-3693-2865-1.ch008

INTRODUCTION

Manufacturing around the world depends on the optimization of costs and profits, logistics and supply chain management, product portfolio management and standardization. Manufacturing is a way to improve economic growth rates for countries. Making of products and services in the internet economy is going through phenomenal transformations. Technology has the capacity to significantly transform the designing and manufacturing of products. It also has the capacity to transform various service sectors. The business ecosystem of product accessories and product portfolio management are also supported by numerous small and medium industries. Many research publications have been written on the technology transformation of products and services e.g., transformative, frugal and reverse engineering (Wooldridge, 2010; Christensen, 1997; Raynor and Christensen 2003; Immelt et al., 2009).

Technologies and inventions have resulted in the creation of new products, upgrades, new processes and services that add economic value or good. New material sciences for additive manufacturing (AM), new AM methods and sensor integration into products are also recent advancements. Advanced composites in material science with enhanced performance are now being used in weight-sensitive applications in the aerospace industries, automobile industries and sports equipment (Spowart et al., 2018). Brands like Nike have involved customers on NikeID, an online shopping portal that lets customers customize shoe designs before purchase. Nike also encourages customers to generate ideas on product improvements and customization of Nike products. iPod sports kits and sensors have been used in Nike shoes for workout-based voice feedback and songs to motivate runners. Lego toys is another example of how value co-creation has facilitated and sourced customer's independent creativity and fanbase for co-creativity and mass customization of Lego products on its websites. It has even encouraged youngsters in the age group of 4-12 year olds to engage in the customization and personalization of products for manufacturing of their co-designs (Roser et al., 2009). In the challenge of the product design process, production teams successfully resolved (1) identification and selection of the raw materials, (2) selection of technologies, (3) prototype production, (4) testing, (5) preparation of quality management procedures and documentation, (6) design of the production technology, (7) supply chain and logistics systems management, (8) making of the transport and storage equipment, and (9) outsourcing (HARTVÁNYI et al., 2023).

In recent years, wearable sports and healthcare devices that monitor vital signs and health have been the focus of research. Monitoring of bioelectrical signals, biophysical signals, and biochemical signals, are critical for athletic training, including the diagnosis and prevention of medical conditions, and rehabilitation. Monitoring of signals in health management (e.g. disease prediction) is now possible thanks to advanced manufacturing, new electronics, Internet of Things (IOT), and artificial intelligence algorithms (Sun et al., 2022). What distinguishes technologies from inventions and creative ideas is that it facilitates economic growth. For example, technologies such as analog film cameras have evolved into advanced digital cameras, digital single lens reflex, mirrorless cameras and smartphone cameras. Sensor technologies, micro/opto/nano industries, battery technologies, memory cards and telecommunications have transformed the assembly and manufacturing of cameras and the experience for the photographer. The camera industry has supported advertising, entertainment, publicity, archiving, sciences, photography, hobbies and various professions for more than a century.

BMW's M Division has facilitated improved product designs with the collaboration of customers and BMW engineers. Ducati, a two wheeler manufacturer used a Virtual Customer Environment called Tech Cafe for product conceptualization. Eli Lilly, a healthcare services firm, uses an Internet portal to integrate its services with pharma customers who consist of patients, clinicians, healthcare providers, doctors and researchers. IKEA, a Swedish furniture manufacturer, facilitates customers to co-design kitchen plans on their kitchen planner web portal before a store visit. Proctor and Gamble (P & G), a leader in consumer goods, has created an advisor program where customers provide feedback regarding their products and where 30% of ideas sourced in their R & D units are from external participants. A few other firms such as Samsung, Starbucks and Unilever have applied value co-creation by integrating new customer experiences with their brands in terms of new concepts, designs, packaging and advertising. The development of the Boeing 787 in terms of value co-creation involved concept to production of its aircraft between Boeing and its partners. This depended on knowledge management, integration of business processes and co-design.

In open and dynamic markets, only technology can give a firm a greater market share and economic growth (Dringoli, 2009). Extant research demonstrates that e-Government initiatives often fall short of achieving efficiency and governance due to a techno-centric focus resulting in minor improvements in service delivery (Feller et. al., 2011) such as with a network of municipalities in Sweden. Technology plays a significant role in transforming public administration with the creation, exploitation and advancement of transformational technologies in terms of value creation and service delivery for its citizens. Research from a variety of perspectives has argued that technology creation or service design no longer takes place within a single organization, but rather is distributed across multiple stakeholders in a value network (Bogers et. al., 2012; Ghezzi et. al., 2021). The aim is to explore how inter-firm manufacturing can implement co-creation by actively collaborating with businesses in a circular economy and integrating green supply chain management. The circular economy (CE) is about a system-level change towards sustainability of industries, and the objective is optimization of raw material utilization for products, components, and materials and value at all times, covering both technical and biological cycles of the end product (Husgafvel and Sakaguchi 2022).

RESEARCH REVIEW AND BACKGROUND

This section is on the review of publications and a background on how firms and brands have leveraged transformational technologies for inter-firm manufacturing and economic growth. Manufacturing of technologies add value to various businesses and services (von Hippel, 2009; Huston and Sakkab, 2006; Chesbrough, 2009). For example, Polaroid cameras leveraged its technology teams from project management, manufacturing and production, tool and mould design to prepare the designs for cameras (Fearis 1995). Polaroid's project planning involved detailing work plans, lead time management, deliverables and costing. An integrated production team along with suppliers were mobilized based on the quality of manufacturing, on time deliveries, production capacity and the use of computer aided design (CAD) software. Polaroid faced numerous challenges in the selection and design of tools for new camera production.

Firms are moving beyond their portfolio of products towards inter-firm manufacturing (see Figure 1). The industrial practice of research and development (R & D) is giving way to decentralized R&D seen more frequently in the case of multinational firms. An advantage of inter-firm manufacturing is that the design and production teams can leverage the product portfolio resources from a network of firms. The quality and quantity of identifying good ideas are increased in terms of economies of scale. For example, Inter-firm manufacturing has supported industry portfolios such as biotechnology, micro/nano/opto electronics manufacturers, new material sciences and chemistry, aviation and aerospace, health and medical sciences, energy related technologies and environments, information and communications technologies, manufacturing and engineering. The objective of the business ecosystem is to facilitate employment, standardization, inter-firm manufacturing, project management and financing for new products and services. At the same time, an exergy analysis is required for assessing the environmental impact of industries. An exergy analysis mapping the energy consumption, fuel consumption and waste generation across industries is required. It enables the determination of the location, types and magnitudes of wastes (contained exergy) and losses (exergy irreversibly lost) for industries. For example, most packaging employs plastic materials (e.g., pesticide containers; consumer goods packaging; sacks for fertilizer; etc.).

Inter-firm Manufacturing, Circular Economy and Green Supply Chain Management

There are several reasons that have led to inter-firm manufacturing. This is due to the growing availability of highly skilled professionals for networked projects in inter-firm manufacturing, private venture capital, inter-firm resource management and new technologies that enable new ways of manufacturing and also service operations management. Today, various industries are shifting towards a circular economy and green supply chain management that are environment friendly and sustainable. This has resulted in a lean production philosophy for manufacturing and reconfigured production line processes that are eco friendly and sustainable and conform to a circular economy (Hazen et al. 2021). Promotion of products that meet the requirements of product composition, labeling and stewardship and adhere to the principles of reduce, reuse and recycle are being encouraged. Product stewardship is associated with commitments to health, safety, environment protection and obligations towards society (Pinto 2023). Green supplier networks who work with manufacturers are evaluated and audited based on identification and assessment of their commitments towards environmental protection. Also, green packaging options that are biodegradable are becoming popular with businesses. Reverse logistics is also becoming common with manufacturing firms that are producing goods that are easily recyclable, reusable, reprocessed or remanufactured. The performance and reputation of manufacturing firms is found to improve with the incorporation of green purchasing practices in the distribution, logistics and supply chain management network. Improved product value, customer satisfaction, increased sales, improved market share and eco-friendliness are some of the gains of a circular economy and green supply chain management of manufacturing firms, small and medium industries. Ala-Harja and Helo (2015) presented decision making scenarios that resulted in consequences for food supply chains in both operational efficiency and environmental pollution: (i) centralization or decentralization, capacity utilization etc., (ii) transportation types and packaging, (iii) routing and scheduling. A supply chain management system for a circular economy requires economic efficiency, minimized environmental footprint and improved human health and well-being (Wognum et al. 2010; Beske et al. 2014; Tsolakis et al. 2014; Yakavenka et al. 2020).

Chesbrough (2003) proposes a concept where inter-firm projects may harness internal and external ideas and multiply their research and development (R&D) portfolio beyond the capacities of the firm. This inter-firm manufacturing creates enormous new opportunities for enhancing the economic value of the firm and facilitates creation of business ecosystems. A manufacturing firm can integrate and leverage the production knowledge of external firms to create additional value for its manufacturing by mobilizing and licensing of R&D portfolio or channel a technology team for spin-offs (see Figure 1).

Figure 1. Inter-firm Manufacturing
(Source: Researching a New Paradigm. Oxford University Press, UK, 2006. p3.)

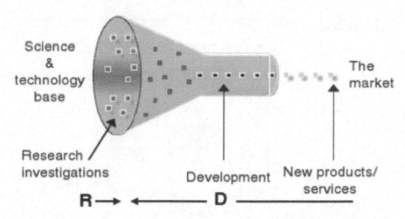

The current paradigm: a Closed Innovation model

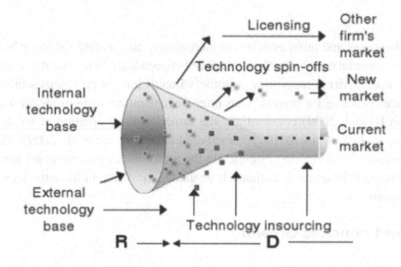

An Open Innovation paradigm

Inter-firm manufacturing is not to be confused with outsourcing of R&D. A manufacturing firm may outsource R&D work to external firms. But in inter-firm manufacturing, product or service ideas from other firms are evaluated and channeled towards its own R&D department through shared agreements between firms. Manufacturing projects based on a firm's internal R&D may mobilize the product design capabilities or product portfolios of external firms and vice versa (Kogut and Almeida, 1999; Chesbrough, 2003; Porter and Kramer, 2011; Choi and Valikangas, 2001; Christopherson et al., 2008; Chesbrough, 2009; Steinle and Scheile, 2008). Conversely, a firm's product or service portfolio may find additional opportunities for commercialization from inter-firm manufacturing R&D (see Figure 2). A related concept that has gained momentum across management disciplines is the co-creation of value (Prahalad and Ramaswamy 2004). Its similarity to inter-firm manufacturing needs to be comprehended. It involves integrating firms and customers towards customized products.

Figure 2. The Co-creation Matrix for Inter-firm Manufacturing and Services
(Source: Roser et al., 2009)

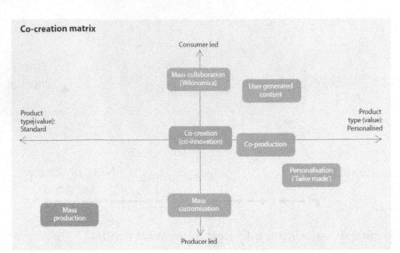

Customers, businesses and other entities are increasingly co-creating value for brands across social networks and in the internet economy. The difference between inter-firm manufacturing and co-creation is that the latter focuses on firms integrating customers directly into the customization and personalization of products, services or value for brands. Thus inter-firm manufacturing or ideation involving customers and firms (von Hippel, 2009) is essentially the same as the co-creation of value (Bell and Loane, 2010; Ramaswamy and Gouillart, 2010; Agarwal et al., 2008; Roser et al., 2009). This paper makes a contribution to research by evaluating empirically the performance indicators for various industries. A distinguishing feature of the analysis is that it is evaluated for different industry sectors and avoids the one-size-fits-all approach.

Businesses for Economic Growth

Various examples of implementing value co-creation practices across industries are discussed. Business types range from closed factory based R & D units for manufacturing products and services to inter-firm units and are broadly classified as (1) Factory based, (2) Cooperative, (3) Collaborative, and (4) Co-creative (see Figure 3). Factory based manufacturing is the most basic form of business. Co-operative businesses involve profit sharing, inter-firm R & D, subscriptions and memberships. Collaborative businesses involve cross licensing, copyrights, leasing, franchises, co-design, integrated markets and online shopping. Co-creative businesses focus more on co-branding, spin-offs, alliances, inter-firm investments for product and service customization and personalization and also focus on integrating customers.

Figure 3. Businesses for Economic Growth
(Source: Spiral Diagram developed by 100% Open, an Open Innovation Consultancy)

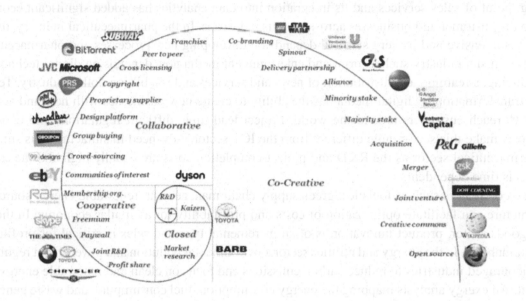

Inter-firm manufacturing may not be suited for any business, although most firms have a tendency to explore its opportunities in inter-firm manufacturing projects and this is not an imperative for every business, technology leader or entrepreneur (Gassman, 2006). Toyota integrates processes associated with R & D units, supplier-networks, manufacturing and production (Wilhem and Kohlbacher, 2011). This method has been mastered by Toyota manufacturing that facilitates continuous improvements in business processes and product design integrating knowledge management routines between the carmaker and its supplier-networks. Automakers in Japan practice *keiretsu* or a corporate governance system to encourage a competitive supplier network rather than compete with other firms in the market. Inter-firm product and service design between IBM, AT&T Bell Laboratories and Cisco, Intel Corporation and Microsoft have transformed businesses globally. This involved complementary R&D portfolio management, licensing and spin-offs.

Inter-Firm Manufacturing

Research has confirmed that in logistics firms, the employee efficacy, experience and proficiency with finance, materials management and production planning adds to the innovativeness and economic growth of firms (Gray et al., 2011; Grover and Kohli 2012; Rai et al. 2012). Technology support for businesses, market share, economic growth, resource management, R&D units, product or service portfolio and the internet economy are all facilitators of inter-firm product and service management (Chesbrough et al., 2006; Grover and Kohli, 2012; Rai et al., 2012; Messinger et al., 2009; Shang et al., 2011; Wagner and Majchrzak, 2007; Riedel et al., 2013). Table 4 summarizes the status of products and services and performance indicators across various sectors.

A study done at the Big Innovation Centre in the U.K. (Golightly et al., 2012) identified key drivers that affect the degree of open innovation in each sector. For instance, the Information and Communications Technology (ICT) sector is characterized by rapidly growing demand, transformational technologies, and a short life cycle of technologies where scaling up quickly is possible. Technologies such as mobile banking, point of sales services and its integration into data analytics has added significant economic value to the customer and businesses across various industries. In the pharmaceutical industry, the role of R&D is intensive and its very survival depends on developing new processes and pharmaceuticals. The entire media industry such as print and entertainment media now depends on digital technologies for producing, streaming and distribution of news and services and is a billion dollar industry. Technological transformation in digital media has the ability to create new businesses with new and archived content to reach customers around the world. Project lead time, difficult regulations and enormous R&D costs make this sector quite different from the ICT sector. Advanced manufacturing is similar to the pharmaceutical sector as the R&D and project completion costs are equally high and the sales of products is time dependent.

Value co-creators such as logistics, green supply chain management, renewable energy sources, IT infrastructure can facilitate optimization of costs and profitability for a circular economy. In the consumer goods sector, product innovation is of an incremental type and sales is critical for profitability and sustainability. In the energy and utilities sector, environmental pollution and government regulations have encouraged industries to reduce carbon emissions and focus on clean and renewable energy management. An exergy analysis mapping the energy consumption, fuel consumption and waste generation across industries is required (Banasik et al. 2017).

For example, agri-food wastes, such as grain byproducts, residual pulp, vegetable and fruit waste and food waste are generated annually in huge quantities. The practices of a circular economy encourage the recycling of these wastes for use as building blocks in bioplastics manufacturing or biofillers that are mixed with other bioplastics (Visco et al., 2022). Some of the examples of biodegradable plastics are polylactic acid, polybutylene succinate, poly caprolactone, polybutylene adipate terephthalate, polyhydroxyalkanoate, and bio-polyethylene. These biodegradable polymers may be used as biocompatible products.

The objectives of the circular economy also referred to as a bioeconomy aim at radical changes in manufacturing and production waste management, reduced water and energy consumption and for the attainment of zero waste production and enhanced environment management (Beghetto et al. 2021). Labeling and standardization of these biodegradable products such as plastic bottles, shopping bags, packaging, coffee cups and disposable items in alignment with a circular economy is required for recycling the waste or composting. Packaging material in huge quantities is frequently used in food catering businesses, online shopping deliveries, pharmaceutical sectors, textiles and fabrics, electronics, coatings and adhesives, consumer goods containers, automotive industries, construction industries, agriculture and horticulture. Biopolymers as a raw material in terms of production for industrial use is stated to reach 2.87 metric tonnes in the European Union (EU) by 2025 while the market demand is expected to be 360 Mt (European Bioplastics 2022). Studies have recommended even cultivation of biopolymer based crops to meet this demand. Some of the successful projects include nutraceutics and cosmetics, biopolymer based biogas production, tanning and processing using environment friendly methods and the recycling of vegetable and fruit waste.

In the textile industry, it is observed that the recycling of textile waste by shredding and reusing generated economic gains of US$11,798,662 and reduced the raw material consumption to about 31,335,767,040 kg (de oliveira Neto et al., 2022). The environmental pollution amounts to biotic, abiotic, water, air and erosion. The circular economy associated with the textile business involves materials, packaging, facilities, garments and programs for recycling discarded items. Even the recycling of food waste to produce natural fiber is recommended. The use of acetates in transforming cellulose waste present in cardboard, paper and cotton facilitates the making of new cellulose textile fiber in a more environment friendly way.

The process of enzymatic hydrolysis suggests using a method of grinding fabric waste into short fibers to obtain the desired textile structure and then a chemical pretreatment process using an alkaline solution is recommended for industrial use in the recycling of mixed fabrics including polyester and cotton (Piribauer et al. 2021). The life cycle assessment for this bio recycling method to study the stages of pretreatment, melt-spinning and enzymatic hydrolysis and its environmental consequences has shown promising results. Pretreatment has reduced environmental impact to 60% while the impact from melt spinning and enzymatic hydrolysis on the ecosystem and human health accounted for 30%.

Denim fabric when recycled was able to extract 53% of cotton in comparison to the recycling of 100% cotton fabric waste. The heat and energy plant utilization for recycling fabric waste as raw material was able to optimize the costs at around 30 to 45% for each meter of fabric. An additional energy cost of 8% was incurred in transforming the raw material into yarn or thread (Fidan et al. 2021). For the textile industry, the opportunities of moving towards a circular economy in terms of recycling is 99.69% taking into account the cost of mechanical recycling, electrical energy consumed and the use of lubricants in the recycling process. Shown in table 1 is a simulation of maximizing apparel manufacturing profitability after adoption of a circular economy. For a factory manufacturing apparels such as shirts, shorts, pants, skirts and jackets, with a variable cost reduction of $10 due to recycled raw material usage, the factory production can generate a maximum profitability of $1,52,200.

Table 1. Simulation of Apparel Manufacturing Profits After Adoption of Circular Economy

	Shirts	Shorts	Pants	Skirts	Jackets
Labor hours/unit	2	1	6	4	8
Recycled Cloth (sq. yd.)/unit	3	2.5	4	4.5	5.5
Selling price/unit	$35	$40	$65	$70	$110
Variable cost/unit	$5	$5	$15	$15	$25
Fixed cost for equipment	$1,500	$1,200	$1,600	$1,500	$1,600
Production plan, constraints on capacity					
	Shirts	Shorts	Pants	Skirts	Jackets
Rent Equipment	0	1	0	0	1
Units produced	0	2000	0	0	1000
Logical upper limit (Units). Constraints	0	4200	0	0	1250
Constraints on resources					
	Resource used	Available			
Labor hours	10000	10000			
Recycled Cloth (unit)	10500	10500			
Monetary Inputs					
Revenue	$1,90,000				
Variable Cost	$35,000				
Fixed Cost of Equipment	$2,800				
Profit	$1,52,200				

(Source: Albright and Winston 2013)

In the automotive industry, circular economies are moving more towards clean energy fuels, additive manufacturing to reduce raw material waste, cost effective LED lightings, renewable energy, factory water recycling, effluent waste control, recycling waste, recyclable packaging and material handling, energy efficient layout planning (Aguilar Esteva et al. 2020). Firms now focus on freight fuel economy, freight sharing, environment friendly transportation and freight carrier networks. Service networks in the automobile sectors are focusing on maintenance and remanufacturing using recyclable parts and components that provide the same performance and reliability as factory products. Even the shredding of material such as ferrous and non ferrous scrap has produced 10 million tonnes of raw material ready (Jody et al. 2011).

Exergy analysis is a method applied in industries to assess the environmental pollution of firms in the chemical sector, environmental engineering and also in the food industry (Zisopoulos et al. 2015; Cortez et al. 1997; Morris 1991; Apaiah et al. 2006). In the Netherlands, approximately 30% of total bread production accounted for 330 thousand tons of bread waste annually. Preserving the quality of perishable products and products having limited shelf life such as food necessitates the utilization of refrigeration systems throughout logistics and supply chain management resulting in additional energy consumption. This has led to 15% of the world's fossil fuel being spent on food transport refrigeration (Yakavenka et al. 2020; Adekomaya et al. 2016; Cortez et al. 1997) adding to the total greenhouse gas emissions produced by Food Supply Chain businesses. It is estimated that this is nearly 25% of the total amount generated worldwide (Vermeulen et al. 2012).

Exergy analysis is a scientific method and uses basic concepts in thermodynamics and studies the environmental consequences in terms of measuring the energy consumption and environmental costs as thermodynamic units also referred to in MegaJoules (MJ) and is applicable to any industry (Apaiah et al. 2005, 2006; Wall 2010). Products at the end of their life if not reusable become waste, and then its exergetic value is considered as a loss. Exergy losses for an industry may be measured based on the cause of a significant environmental consequence in terms of the production process, transportation and waste generated. The concept of exergy analysis brings efficiency into waste management with options that may be considered such as disposal, prevention and recycling of waste. For example, most packaging employs plastic materials (e.g., pesticide containers; consumer goods packaging; sacks for fertilizer; etc.). These materials need to be decontaminated, before the waste is recycled, in the framework of a circular economy.

An analysis matrix (Gobbo Junior 2007) identifies priorities for the industry in terms of decision making and analyzes various factors that improve inter-firm manufacturing across business network projects. The matrix in Table 2 tries to identify the decisions taken across different business networks and helps in reconfiguring the inter-firm networks. This helps focus on the following competitive priorities: innovation, cost, reliability, quality, speed and flexibility.

Table 2. Analysis Matrix of Competitive Priorities and Business Network Projects in Manufacturing

Decision Areas		Competitive Priorities					
		Cost	Quality	Speed	Flexibility	Innovation	Reliability
Business Network Project	**Vertical Integration**						
	Direction - "Virtual" integration and Lean Management	Customers or businesses inventory reduction; parts procurement at lower cost	Higher quality specification	On time delivery of goods	Increase in product mix; flexible quantities		Higher raw material control
	Supplier relationship - Decision to form strategic partnerships	Low cost financing for parts to maintain production capacity.	Customized raw material or finished goods	Logistics support availability for clients and parts		Material Science for improved raw material structure	Improved capacity planning
	Optimizing - Material Management and reducing waste	Reduce transported waste for recycling		Faster service requests			
	Balance - Decision to increase capacity	Growing business in terms of economies of scale			Flexible quantity of supplies		Scaling the equipment for factory
	Facilities - Localization Decision to locate facilities inside existing factory infrastructure	Low cost labor workforce; logistics infrastructure	Obsolete product cost reduction		A larger product mix based on required specification	Access to tacit Industry information	
	Size Decision to increase inter-firm co-operation	Production scale increase			Improved flexibility; new service access		Access to Financing; market evaluation
	Specialization/Focus Decision to increase vertical focus	Efficiency improvement	Increased Customer requirement focus				

(Source: Vinoth and Muthuvelayutham)

Analyzing Value Co-creation in Inter-Firm Manufacturing

The evaluation of Inter-firm manufacturing needs to be seen in various aspects. Let us identify some of the performance indicators that can be used to evaluate the performance of co-creation. If we need to start from zero, the basic evaluation metrics will be based on the value generated from co-creation. The question here is, does value co-creation facilitate economic growth and economies of scale and does it multiply the intensity of firms towards production in business ecosystems to create an economy? Hence brands initially during the process of value co-creation need to focus on new product design, patents, production management and portfolio management. This is explained in Figure 4.

Figure 4. Co-creation Performance Indicator (KPIs).
(Source: Roser et al., 2009)

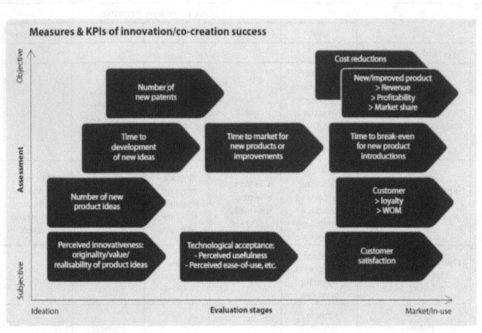

The sector-specific performance indicators of firms in the manufacturing of products or service industries is summarized in Table 4. It suggests and forms the basis for an analysis to explain the status of economic growth, performance indicators and sector characteristics in the manufacturing and service industries.

An empirical equation to study growing industries investment wise can be specified as:

$$Y = a+b_1X_1+b_2X_2+b_3X_3+\text{-------}+b_iX_i+\text{----} \quad i=1,2,3\ldots,n$$

Y = intensity or level of inter-firm innovativeness and production. It signifies the monetary value or profitability of co-creation projects.

This is measured by the investments in inter-firm manufacturing projects or services. It is the sum total of the project * amount invested in each project. The independent variables X_i i=1,2,3,....n, for each sector are derived from the performance indicators given in Table 4. If it is hypothesized that increases in Xi will lead to Y, i.e intensity in inter-firm production and monetary value or profitability of co-creation projects, then this implies that the slope coefficient bi in the multiple regression model is positive/negative. For example, if we hypothesize that increases in the level of competition in the manufacturing sector is likely to increase the level of inter-firm manufacturing, then, for empirical testing purposes, it is equivalent to the hypothesis that the slope coefficient associated with a densely distributed market share is negative.

In terms of exergy analysis and the alignment with a circular economy, the circularity index as a ratio of the combined environmental pollution factors that may be abiotic, biotic, water, air or erosion before and after an industry decides to invest in recycling waste may be calculated. This takes into consideration the reduction in environmental pollution from manufacturing on the reuse of production waste, optimization of energy consumption and reduction in the use of machinery lubricant oils in the recycling process. This is demonstrated in Table 3.

Table 3. Environmental Assessment of Textile Industries in the Circular Economy

Components	Annual Consumption (kg/kWh)	Compartiments/Unit (kg/kWh)					MIT-Mass Intensity Total
		Abiotic	Biotic	Air	Water	Erosion	
"Before" the Adoption of Circular Economy							
Cotton fiber		8.6	2.9	6.814	2.74	5.01	31,432,950,000.00
	4,600,000	39,560,000.00	13,340,000.00	31,344,400,000.00	12,604,000.00	23,046,000.00	
MIC-Mass intensity per compartment-Cotton fiber		39,560,000.00	13,340,000.00	31,344,400,000.00	12,604,000.00	23,046,000.00	31,432,950,000.00
"After" the Implementation of Circular Economy							
Fabric Fiber Recovery							
Reduction from the reuse (cotton shredding)		8.6	2.9	6.814	2.74	5.01	36,979,941,204.61
	5,411,764.71	46,541,176.51	15,694,117.66	36,875,764,733.94	14,828,235.31	27,112,941.20	
Waste discarding (cotton shredding)		8.6	2.9	6.814	2.74	5.01	5,546,991,204.61
	811,764.71	6,981,176.51	2,354,117.66	5,531,364,733.94	2,224,235.31	4,066,941.20	
MIC-Mass intensity per compartment-fiber recovery		39,560,000.00	13,340,000.00	31,344,400,000.00	12,604,000.00	23,046,000.00	31,432,950,000.00

(**Source:** de Oliveira Neto et al. 2022)

Table 4. Multiple Regression Models for Intensity of Inter-Firm Activity Across Industries for New Products and Services (Source: Gopalan and Natarajan 2014)

Sector	Status of Economic Growth	Performance & Sector Characteristics	Performance Indicators	Null Hypotheses
Advanced and Other Manufacturing Industries	Opportunities in circular economy and green supply chain management.	R&D management. Cost management. Product portfolio management. Project lead times. Growth opportunities for small and medium industries. Competitive.	$X1$ = R & D investments *(average)* $X2$ = Budget $X3$ = Intensity of industrial production and market leadership $X4$ = Circular economy and Green Supply Chain Management. *(Including exergy analysis)*	$b1 > 0$ $b2 > 0$ $b3 > 0$ $b4 > 0$
Consumer Goods	Mature market defined by incremental growth and quality management	Competitive. Economic growth based on demand for products and expansion of product portfolios. High growth industry and dynamic market. Production and service growth opportunities.	$X1$ = Intensity of production in the industry $X2$ = Shelf life of Products. *(average)* $X3$ = Circular economy and Green Supply Chain Management. *(Including exergy analysis)*	$b1 < 0$ $b2 < 0$ $b3 > 0$
Pharmaceutical	New processes and products, technological integration for the pharmaceutical sector takes time due to project lead time.	R&D is intensive. Growth is slow due to difficult regulations, pressures to manufacture and deliver quality products. Cost optimization for economies of scale. Product and process development takes more time	$X1$ = Regulations slowing industry growth *(past 5 years)* $X2$ = Medicines introduced *(Average for the last 5 years)* $X3$ = Investment and Economies of Scale *(average for the last 5 years)*	$b1 > 0$ $b2 > 0$ $b3 > 0$
Information and Communication Technologies	Mature market. Active Production line and growth of business processes	Rapid Growth of Startups, Transformational, Variety of Business Types, Mobile and Internet Economy growth. Sales of technologies, services, subscriptions and memberships. Technology creation by small and medium industries and Startups.	$X1$ = Growth rate of startups $X2$ = Successful new technologies and projects $X3$ = Mobile or Internet subscriptions $X4$ = Circular economy and Green Supply Chain Management. *(Including exergy analysis)*	$b1 > 0$ $b2 > 0$ $b3 > 0$ $b4 < 0$
Business and Financial Services	Opportunities for new businesses and process management and technology dependent	Growing customer membership and subscription in the mobile and internet economy. Traditional businesses. Technology dependent. Focus on secure transactions and information management.	$X1$ = New mobile technologies *(Products and services)* $X2$ = Growing market of customers	$b1 > 0$ $b2 > 0$
Media	Print media to digital media. New businesses for content and streaming. Growing market share.	Subscription and membership dependent on network connectivity, affordability and payment conveniences. Growth segment. Well established and opportunities for growth with global subscriptions.	$X1$ = Subscriptions/Membership to markets via the Internet Economy $X2$ = New businesses and market shares *(measured by Herfindahl-Hirschman Index)* $X3$ = Number of new business types in markets	$b1 > 0$ $b2 > 0$ $b3 > 0$
Energy and Utilities	Mature market. R&D management is intensive. Investments and demand. Renewable energy products. Exergy analysis for optimizing costs, waste reduction and adding value to industries	Challenges with making renewable energy products and investments required in the services sector. Inter-firm manufacturing, R & D intensive and standardization dependent. Consequences for green supply chain management and circular economies.	$X1$ = Energy Demand $X2$ = Carbon emission related regulations $X3$ = Number of new energy technologies $X4$ = MegaJoule or KiloWatt of energy used *(including renewable and sustainable sources)* $X5$ = Circular economy and Green Supply Chain Management. *(Including exergy analysis)*	$b1 > 0$ $b2 > 0$ $b3 > 0$ $b4 > 0$ $b5 > 0$

This analysis is useful across industry sectors for comprehending the level of inter-firm manufacturing and services. It can be applied in any industry by considering the business type, market share, investments in R&D, and intensity of business activity in industries. The aim of sustainable manufacturing defined by the National Institute of Standards and Technology (NIST) depends on five elements, namely, (1) demonstrated reduced negative environmental consequence, (2) improved energy and resource efficiency of technologies, (3) reduced waste production, (4) operational efficiency and (5) improved personnel health while incorporating quality processes for quality products (Hapuwatte and Jawahir 2021). In terms of the environmental consequences of material use and efficiency in manufacturing, the prioritization of optimizing material utilization, recycled material ratio in the product and recyclable material utilization are relevant. In terms of energy use and efficiency in manufacturing, the prioritization of utilizing renewable energy sources, energy efficiency of production lines, and energy efficiency of the product becomes relevant. In terms of other resources used and efficiency in manufacturing, water conservation, conservation of other critical resources and reduction of greenhouse gasses, hazardous emissions and solid waste emissions become relevant.

Other recommendations for a circular economy are (1) Government or private fund allocation for waste management, (2) training programs on circular economies, (3) economic penalties on non-compliant industries, (4) Life cycle assessment of the entire product, (5) promotion of environment friendly products, (6) designing recyclable products, components and materials, (7) responsible use of energy production, (8) data management and monitoring, (9) market for recycled products and (10) material banks.

MANAGERIAL IMPLICATIONS

Manufacturing depends on the optimization of costs and profits, logistics and supply chain management, product portfolio management and standardization. Manufacturing improves economic growth rates for countries. At the same time, an exergy analysis is required for assessing the environmental impact of industries. The circular economy (CE) is about a system-level change towards sustainability of industries, and the objective is optimization of raw material utilization for products, components, and materials and value at all times, covering both technical and biological cycles of the end product. Environment friendly inventory and raw material management for the industry has recommended promotion of products that meet the requirements of product composition, labeling and stewardship and adhere to the principles of reduce, reuse and recycle. Product stewardship is associated with the business philosophy of commitments to health, safety, environment protection and obligations towards society. Green supplier networks who work with manufacturers need to be evaluated and audited based on identification and assessment of their commitments towards environmental protection. Green packaging options that are biodegradable are being enforced in many countries that facilitate its reuse, recycling and disposal. Many industries that have a significant environmental impact need to focus on incorporating reverse logistics in manufacturing firms to produce goods that are easily recyclable, reusable, reprocessed or re-manufactured. The performance and reputation of manufacturing firms have improved when green purchasing practices are incorporated into the distribution, logistics and supply chain management of manufacturing networks of industries. In food processing industries, the decision making scenarios that resulted in consequences for food supply chains in both operational efficiency and environmental pollution were identified as: (i) centralization or decentralization, capacity utilization etc., (ii) transportation types and packaging, (iii) routing and scheduling. Green supply chain management for a circular economy aims to improve economic efficiency, minimized environmental footprint, human health and well-being. The environmental pollution amounts to biotic, abiotic, water, air and erosion. The objectives of a circular economy also referred to as a bioeconomy aim at radical changes in manufacturing and production waste management, reduced water and energy consumption and for the attainment of zero waste production and enhanced environment management.

FUTURE RESEARCH DIRECTION

In terms of exergy analysis and the alignment with a circular economy, the circularity index as a ratio of the combined environmental pollution factors that may be abiotic, biotic, water, air or erosion before and after an industry decides to invest in environmental compliance such as recycling of waste may be calculated. This may be used for the formulation of government policies for regulations, competitiveness and environmental compliance. Product portfolio planning requires an assessment of the product range profitability and exergy analysis in terms of the environmental consequences. Also, the aim of sustainable manufacturing defined by the National Institute of Standards and Technology (NIST) depends on five elements, namely, (1) demonstrated reduced negative environmental consequence, (2) improved energy and resource efficiency of technologies, (3) reduced waste production, (4) operational efficiency and (5) improved personnel health while incorporating quality processes for quality products. A circular economy towards environmental compliance in industries requires (1) government or private fund allocation for waste management, (2) training programs on circular economies, (3) economic penalties on non-compliant industries, (4) life cycle assessment of the entire product, (5) promotion of environment friendly products, (6) designing recyclable products, components and materials, (7) responsible use of energy production, (8) data management and monitoring, (9) market for recycled products and (10) material banks.

CONCLUSIONS

Research studies of inter-firm manufacturing, services and value co-creation have been mainly descriptive in nature in terms of how they are associated with the circular economy and green supply chain management. This paper provides an analysis that associates economic growth of industries with inter-firm manufacturing, services and performance indicators. The performance of industries can be empirically tested. It should be noted that these models do not explain the benefits of exergy analysis and other factors that may accrue to the firm that engages in inter-firm manufacturing and services that are aligned with a circular economy and green supply chain management. For that purpose, a different analysis, one that associates not just the performance metrics of industries but also the exergy analysis across industries is necessary. An exergy analysis mapping the energy consumption, fuel consumption and waste generation across industries is required. Exergy analysis as an indicator of environmental performance for an industry is demonstrated by comparing the environmental consequences to other commonly used indicators of environmental performance. It enables the determination of the location, types and magnitudes of wastes and losses for industries. Exergy losses for an industry may be measured based on the cause of significant environmental consequences in terms of the production process, transportation and waste generated. The concept of exergy analysis brings efficiency into waste management with options that may be considered such as disposal, prevention and recycling of waste.

Table 5. Data availability statement

Availability of data	Data availability statement	Policy
Data openly available in a public repository that does not issue DOIs	The data that support the findings of this study are openly available on Google Sheet at [https://docs.google.com/spreadsheets/d/1trA5DbRc2ns3WUUdTwsO86SEVYC4hNyETBJH-z0AhXg/edit?usp=sharing] <u>Click this link to access the Data and Simulation</u>	All

REFERENCES

Adekomaya, O., Jamiru, T., Sadiku, R., & Huan, Z. (2016). Sustaining the shelf life of fresh food in cold chain—A burden on the environment. *Alexandria Engineering Journal*, *55*(2), 1359–1365. https://doi.org/. doi:10.1016/j.aej.2016.03.024

Agarwal, R., Gupta, A.K. & Kraut, R. (2008). The interplay between digital and social networks. *Information Systems Research. 19*(3), 243-252.

Aguilar Esteva, L. C., Kasliwal, A., Kinzler, M. S., Kim, H. C., & Keoleian, G. A. (2021). Circular economy framework for automobiles: Closing energy and material loops. *Journal of Industrial Ecology*, *25*(4), 877–889. doi:10.1111/jiec.13088

Ala-Harja, H., & Helo, P. (2015). Green supply chain decisions—Case-based performance analysis from the food industry. *Transportation Research Part E: Logistics and Transportation Review*, *74*, 11–21. . doi:10.1016/j.tre.2014.12.005

Albright, S. C., Winston W. L. (2013). *Business Analytics - Data Analysis and Decision Making*. Cengage Learning.

Apaiah, R. K., Hendrix, E. M. T., Meerdink, G., & Linnemann, A. R. (2005). Qualitative methodology for efficient food chain design. *Trends in Food Science and Technology*, *16*, 204–214.

Apaiah, R. K., Linnemann, A. R., & Van Der Kooi, H. J. (2006). Exergy analysis: A tool to study the sustainability of food supply chains. *Food Research International*, *39*, 1–11.

Banasik, A., Kanellopoulos, A., Claassen, G., Bloemhof-Ruwaard, J., & Vorst, J. (2017). Assessing alternative production options for eco-efficient food supply chains using multi-objective optimization. *Annals of Operations Research, 250*(2), 341–362. doi:10.1007/s10479-016-2199-z

Beghetto, V., Bardella, N., Samiolo, R., Gatto, V., Conca, S.; Sole, R., Molin, G., Gattolin, A., Ongaro, N. (2021). By-products from mechanical recycling of polyolefins improve hot mix asphalt performance. *Journal of Cleaner Production*, *318*, 128627.

Beghetto, V., Sole, R., Buranello, C., Al-Abkal, M., & Facchin, M. (2021). Recent advancements in plastic packaging recycling: A mini-review. *Materials*, *14*, 4782.

Bell, J. and Loane, S., (2010). New-wave global firms: Web 2.0 and SME internationalization. *Journal of Marketing Management, 26*(3), 213-229.

Beske, P., Land, A., & Seuring, S. (2014). Sustainable supply chain management practices and dynamic capabilities in the food industry: A critical analysis of the literature. *International Journal of Production Economics, 152,* 131–143. doi:10.1016/j.ijpe.2013.12.026

Bogers, M. & West, J. (2012). Managing Distributed Innovation: Strategic Utilization of Open and User Innovation. *Types of Organizations & Organizational Behavior E-Journal.*

Chesbrough, H.W., (2003). The Era of Open Innovation. *MIT Sloan Management Review, 44.*

Chesbrough, H.W. (2009). *Open Innovation: The New Imperative for Creating and Profiting from Technology.* Harvard Business School Press.

Choi, D. & Valikangas, L. (2001). Patterns of strategy innovation. *European Management Journal.* Elsevier.

Christensen, C. M. (1997). *The Innovator's Dilemma.* Harvard Business School Press.

Christopherson, S., Kitson, M., & Michie, J. (2008, July). Christopherson,S., Kitson,M., Michie,J. (2008). Innovation, networks and knowledge exchange. *Cambridge Journal of Regions, Economy and Society, 1*(2), 165–173. doi:10.1093/cjres/rsn015

Cortez, L. A. B., Larson, D. L., & Da Silva, A. (1997). Energy and exergy evaluation of ice production by absorption refrigeration. *Transactions of the American Society of Agricultural Engineers, 40,* 395–403.

de Oliveira Neto, G. C., Teixeira, M. M., Souza, G. L. V., Arns, V. D., Tucci, H. N. P., & Amorim, M. (2022). Assessment of the Eco-Efficiency of the Circular Economy in the Recovery of Cellulose from the Shredding of Textile Waste. *Polymers (20734360), 14*(7), 1317. doi:10.3390/polym14071317

Dringoli, A. (2009). *Creating Value Through Innovation.* Edward Elgar Publishing.

Elia, G., Petruzzelli, A.M., & Urbinati, A. (2020). Implementing Open Innovation Through Virtual Brand Communities: A Case Study Analysis in The Semiconductor Industry. *Technological Forecasting and Social Change.*

Fearis, P. (1995). *The polaroid experience: Countdown to market.* WCDM, World Class Design to Manufacture. https://www.proquest.com/scholarly-journals/polaroid-experience-countdown-market/docview/207943859/se-2

Feller, J., Finnegan, P., and Nilsson, O. (2011). Open Innovation and Public Administration: Transformational Typologies and Business Model Impacts. *European Journal of Information Systems.*

Fidan, F. Ş., Aydoğan, E. K., & Uzal, N. (2021). Fidan, F.,S., Aydoˇgan, E.K., and Uzal, N (2021). An integrated life cycle assessment approach for denim fabric production using recycled cotton fibers and combined heat and power plant. *Journal of Cleaner Production, 287,* 125439. doi:10.1016/j.jclepro.2020.125439

Gassman, O. (2006) Opening up the innovation process towards an agenda. *R&D Management 36*(3), 223-228.

Ghezzi, A., Cavallo, A., Sanasi, S., Rangone, A. (2021). Opening Up to Startup Collaborations: Open Business Models and Value Co-creation in SMEs. *Competitiveness Review: An International Business Journal.*

Gobbo Junior, J. A(2007). Inter-firm manufacturing strategy. *Congresso Brasileiro de Engenharia de Fabricação.*

Golightly, J., Ford, C., Sureka, P., and Reid, B. (2012). *Realising the Value of Open Innovation.* BIG Innovation Centre. The Work Foundation, Lancaster University.

Gopalan, B. and Natarajan, R. (2014). Analytical models for Open Innovation and Value Co-creation. *Proceedings of the Decision Sciences Institute (DSI) Conference* in Tampa, Florida (USA).

Gray, P. H., Parise, S. & Iyer, B., (2011). Innovation impacts of using social bookmarking systems. *MIS Quarterly* (35:3), pp. 629-643.

Grover, V. & Kohli, R. (2012). Cocreating IT Value: New Capabilities and Measures for Multifirm Environments. *MIS Quarterly, 36*(1), 225-232.

Hapuwatte, B. M., & Jawahir, I. S. (2021). Closed-loop sustainable product design for circular economy. *Journal of Industrial Ecology, 25*(6), 1430–1446. doi:10.1111/jiec.13154

Hartványi, T., Huszár, V., & Palásthy, I. (2023). Pilot Research & Development of a Multifunctional and Multi-Purpose Sports Equipment - Automotive Technologies for the Olympics. *Acta Technica Corviniensis - Bulletin of Engineering, 16*(1), 1–5.

Hazen, B. T., Russo, I., Confente, I., & Pellathy, D. (2021). Supply chain management for circular economy: Conceptual framework and research agenda. *International Journal of Logistics Management, 32*(2), 510-537. doi:10.1108/IJLM-12-2019-0332

Husgafvel, R., & Sakaguchi, D. (2022). Circular Economy Development in the Construction Sector in Japan. *World (2673-4060), 3*(1), 1–26. doi:10.3390/world3010001

Immelt, J. R., Govindarajan, V., & Trimble, C. (2009). How GE is disrupting itself. *Harvard Business Review, 87*(10), 56–65.

Jody, B. J., Daniels, E. J., Duranceau, C. M., Pomykala, J. A., & Spangenberger, J. S. (2011). *End-of-life vehicle recycling: State of the art of resource recovery from shredder residue.* https://doi.org/doi:10.2172/1010492

Kogut B. and Almeida P. (1999). Localization of knowledge and the mobility of engineers in regional networks. *Management Science, 45*, 905-917.

Messinger, P. R., Stroulia, E., Lyons, K., Bone, M., Niu, R. H., Smirnov, K. & Perelgut, S. (2009). Virtual worlds - past, present, and future: New directions in social computing. *Decision Support Systems, 47*(3), 204-228.

Morris, D. R. (1991). Exergy analysis and cumulative exergy consumption of complex chemical processes:The industrial chlor-alkali processes. *Chemical Engineering Science, 46*, 459–465.

Pinto, L. (2023, February 15). performance. *Journal of Industrial Engineering and Management, 16*(1), 78–101. doi:10.3926/jiem.3686

Pinto, L. (2023). *Investigating the relationship between green supply chain purchasing practices and firms'.*

Piribauer, B., Bartl, A., & Ipsmiller, W. (2021). Piribauer, B.; Bartl, A.; Ipsmiller, W. Enzymatic textile recycling—Best practices and outlook. [PubMed]. *Waste Management & Research, 39*(10), 1277–1290. doi:10.1177/0734242X211029167

Porter, M.E. & Kramer, M.R. (2011). Creating shared value. *Harvard Business Review.*

Prahalad, C. K. and Ramaswamy, V. (2004). Co-creation experiences: The next practice in value creation. *Journal of Interactive Marketing, 18*(3), 5-14.

Rai, A., Pavlou, P., Im, G. and Du, S., 2012. Interfirm IT capability profiles and communications for cocreating relational value: Evidence from the logistics industry. *MIS Quarterly, 36*(1), 233-262.

Ramaswamy, V. & Gouillart, F. (2010). Building the Co-Creative Enterprise. *Harvard Business Review, 88*(10), 100-109.

Raynor, M. E., & Christensen, C. M. (2003). Innovating for growth: Now IS the time. *Ivey Business Journal, 68*(1), 1–9.

Riedel, C., Blohm, I., Leimeister, J.M. and Krcmar, H., (2013). The Effect of Rating Scales on Decision Quality and User Attitudes in Online Innovation Communities. *International Journal of Electronic Commerce, 17*(3), 7-36.

Roser, T., Samson A., Humphreys, P. and Cruz-Valdivieso, E. (2009). Co-creation: new pathways to value: An overview. *Promise Corporation.*

Shang, S. S. C., Li, E. Y., Wu, Y. & Hou, O. C. L. (2011). Understanding Web 2.0 service models: A knowledge-creating perspective. *Information & Management, 48*(5), 178-184.

Spowart, J. E., Gupta, N., & Lehmhus, D. (2018). Additive Manufacturing of Composites and Complex Materials. *JOM: The Journal of The Minerals, Metals & Materials Society* (TMS), *70*(3), 272–274. doi:10.1007/s11837-018-2742-2

Steinle, C., & Schiele, H. (2008). Limits to global sourcing? Strategic consequences of dependency on international suppliers: Cluster theory, resource-based view and case studies. *Journal of Purchasing & Supply Management, 14*, 3-14. doi:10.1016/j.pursup.2008.01.001

Sun, W., Guo, Z., Yang, Z., Wu, Y., Lan, W., Liao, Y., Wu, X., & Liu, Y. (2022). A Review of Recent Advances in Vital Signals Monitoring of Sports and Health via Flexible Wearable Sensors. *Sensors (14248220), 22*(20), N.PAG. doi:10.3390/s22207784

Tsolakis, N. K., Keramydas, C. A., Toka, A. K., Aidonis, D. A., & Iakovou, E. T. (2014). Agrifood supply chain management: A comprehensive hierarchical decision-making framework and a critical taxonomy. *Biosystems Engineering, 120*, 47–64. https://doi.org/ stems eng.2013.10.014. doi:10.1016/j.biosy

Vermeulen, S. J., Campbell, B. M., & Ingram, J. S. I. (2012). Climate change and food systems. *Annual Review of Environment and Resources, 37*(1), 195–222. . doi:10.1146/annurev-environ-020411-130608

Vinoth, V. K. & Muthuvelayutham, C. (2020). "Study on Sustainable Supply chain Implementation in Business Organisations". *International Journal of Research Culture Society, 16*, 192-196.

Visco, A., Scolaro, C., Facchin, M., Brahimi, S., Belhamdi, H., Gatto, V., & Beghetto, V. (2022). Agri-Food Wastes for Bioplastics: European Prospective on Possible Applications in Their Second Life for a Circular Economy. *Polymers (20734360), 14*(13), 2752–N.PAG. https://doi.org/ doi:10.3390/polym14132752

Wagner, C. and Majchrzak, A. (2007). Enabling customer-centricity using wikis and the wiki way. *Journal of Management Information Systems, 23*(3), 17-43.

Wall, G. (2010). On exergy and sustainable development in environmental engineering. *The Open Environmental Engineering Journal, 3*, 21–32.

Wilhelm, M. and Kohlbacher, F. (2011). Co-opetition and knowledge co-creation in Japanese supplier-networks: The case of Toyota. *Asian Business & Management, 10*(1), 66-86.

Wognum, P. M. N., Bremmers, H., Trienekens, J. H., Van Der Vorst, J. G. A. J., & Bloemhof, J. M. (2010). *Advanced engineering informatics systems for sustainability and transparency of food supply chains—Current status.*

Wooldridge, A. (2010). The World Turned Upside Down. London: *The Economist.*

Yakavenka, V., Mallidis, I., Vlachos, D., Lakavou, E. and Eleni, Z. (2020). Development of a multi-objective model for the design of sustainable supply chains: the case of perishable food products. *Annals of Operations Research, 294*, 593–621. doi:10.1007/s10479-019-03434-5

Zisopoulos, F. K., Moejes, S. N., Rossier-Miranda, F. J., Van Der Goot, A. J.,& Boom, R.M. (2015). Exergetic comparison of food waste valorization in industrial bread production. *Energy, 82*, 640–649.

KEY TERMS AND DEFINITIONS

Capacity: The maximum capability to produce.

Channels: The number of parallel servers.

Circular Economy: It is a change to the model in which resources are mined, made into products, and then become waste. A circular economy reduces material use, redesigns materials and products to be less resource intensive, and recaptures "waste" as a resource to manufacture new materials and products. (United States Environmental Protection Agency)

Decision Analysis: A set of quantitative decision-making techniques to aid the decision maker in dealing with decision situations in which uncertainty exists.

Eco-Labeling: A seal of approval for environmentally safe products

Efficiency: how well a machine or worker performs compared to a standard output level.

Goods: Tangible objects that can be created and sold at a later date.

Green Supply Chain Management (GSCM): "GSCM encompasses a set of environmental practices that encourage improvements to the environmental practices of two or more organizations within the same supply chain". Green supply chain management (GSCM) involves sustainable environmental processes built into conventional supply chains — from manufacturing to operations to end-of-life management — incorporating the principle of reduce, reuse, recycle, reclaim and degradable.

Infrastructure: The physical support structures in a community, including roads, water and sewage systems, and utilities.

Inventory Insurance: Against supply chain uncertainty held between supply chain stages.

Key Performance Indicators: A set of measures that help managers evaluate performance in critical areas.

Lean Production: An adaptation of mass production that prizes quality and flexibility.

Logistics: The transportation and distribution of goods and services.

Maintainability: The ease with which a product is maintained or repaired

Matrix Organization: An organizational structure of project teams that includes members from various functional areas in the company.

Operations Management: The design and operation of productive systems.

Operations: A function or system that transforms inputs into outputs of greater value.

Outsourcing: Purchasing goods and services that were originally produced in-house from an outside supplier.

Process: A group of related tasks with specific inputs and outputs.

Procurement: Purchasing goods and services from suppliers.

Product Lifecycle Management: Managing the entire lifecycle of a product

Production Design: The phase of product design concerned with how the product will be produced

Productivity: The ratio of output to input.

Project: A unique, one-time operation or effort.

Project: The one-of-a-kind production of a product to customer order that requires a long time to complete and a large investment of funds and resources.

Rapid Prototyping: Quickly testing and revising a preliminary design model.

Reliability: The probability that a given part or product will perform its intended function for a specified period of time under normal conditions of use.

Reverse Engineering: Carefully dismantling and inspecting a competitor's product to look for design features that can be incorporated into your own product.

Services: Acts, deeds or performances that provide value to the customer.

Standardization: Using commonly available parts that are interchangeable among products

Supply Chain Management: Managing the flow of information, products, and services across a network of customers, enterprises, and supply chain partners.

Sustainability: The ability to meet present needs without jeopardizing the needs of future generations.

Value Co-Creation: Co-Creating and customizing products with branded firms.

Value: The creation of value for the customer is an important aspect of supply chain management.

Section 3
Digital Transformation

Chapter 9
The Singularity Is Near?
Unraveling Artificial Intelligence, Ethos, and Human Rights in the Era of Emerging Digital Transform

Rigoberto García-Contreras

National School of Higher Education, National Autonomous University of Mexico, Mexico

David Valle-Cruz

ⓘD https://orcid.org/0000-0002-5204-8095

National Autonomous University of Mexico, Mexico

Rodrigo Sandoval-Almazán

ⓘD https://orcid.org/0000-0002-7864-6464

National Autonomous University of Mexico, Mexico

ABSTRACT

Artificial intelligence is growing exponentially, revolutionizing society, and approaching a virtual point called the "Singularity." This chapter explores the complex relationship between artificial intelligence, human rights, and their impact on social behavior and ethos. By proposing a framework and analyzing international cases, the authors provide examples of the challenges and opportunities arising from this interaction. Artificial intelligence presents enormous opportunities and potential benefits, but it also raises serious concerns about the risks associated with it. This research reveals the dual nature of artificial intelligence, which acts as a double-edged sword in societal impact. Like any emerging and exponential technology, it takes time and conscious thought to understand and manage the potential impact of artificial intelligence on society and human rights. This chapter highlights the need for an informed approach to the implementation of artificial intelligence to ensure the protection of human rights while harnessing the potential of artificial intelligence for social progress.

DOI: 10.4018/979-8-3693-2865-1.ch009

INTRODUCTION

Artificial intelligence has emerged as a transformative force of the 21st century, driving the Fourth Industrial Revolution and profoundly impacting human society (Moll, 2022). Its far-reaching impact is in simplifying daily tasks, advancing healthcare, automating social interactions, and improving decision-making processes in organizations and governments. Despite significant advancements in the artificial intelligence field, there remains a lack of clear understanding and a solid framework for addressing the impact of these technologies on human rights. The ethical and legal issues that arise with the use of artificial intelligence are complex and multifaceted and require an interdisciplinary approach to be adequately addressed (Kieslich et al., 2022). Furthermore, there are growing concerns about how artificial intelligence may perpetuate discrimination and inequality, as well as threaten privacy and individual freedom (Fjeld et al., 2020).

The development and implementation of artificial intelligence is a double-edged sword. On one hand, it offers significant benefits for humanity, such as improving medical care and automating tedious tasks. On the other hand, there are concerns about its potential negative consequences, such as the violation of human rights and the potential for misuse by those in power. The absence of regulation and governance in the field of artificial intelligence is a major concern, as it may result in the violation of certain human rights through the use and manipulation of personal data and information. Moreover, the gap between its use and lack of control may lead to the control of human behaviors, raising concerns about the ethical implications of artificial intelligence. It is crucial that a comprehensive ethical and legal framework be developed to address these issues and ensure that the benefits of artificial intelligence are distributed equitably, and its negative impacts are mitigated (Cheatham et al., 2019; Etzioni & Etzioni, 2017).

While emerging technologies have the potential to greatly improve people's quality of life, they also have negative consequences, coming from the technological singularity (Valle-Cruz et al., 2023). The technological singularity, which refers to the point in the future when machines will achieve intelligence and cognitive abilities that surpass those of humans, or their capabilities can be turned against other humans. These scenarios pose a significant threat to human rights. As this event approaches, it is crucial to anticipate and address the potential risks it could present.

The development and implementation of artificial intelligence brings great benefits, but we cannot ignore concerns about potential human rights abuses and violations by those in power (Huang et al., 2022). Lack of proper regulation and governance in the artificial intelligence field has raised concerns about the misuse and manipulation of personal data, which poses a serious threat to human rights. Moreover, the potential for artificial intelligence to control human behavior and its ethical implications reinforce the need for comprehensive ethical and legal frameworks. It is paramount to equitably distribute the benefits of artificial intelligence and mitigate its negative impacts through proper regulation. For instance, in terms of economic rights, one of the likely risks is the loss of jobs, as machines could replace workforce massively. This could lead to economic and social inequality, as certain individuals and groups become marginalized. Likewise, the increasing use of artificial intelligence in various aspects of life, from health care to criminal justice, also raises concerns about the possibility of artificial intelligence being used in ways that violate human rights.

To deal with these kinds of risks, it is needed to take proactive measures. Privacy, discrimination, and economic rights are concerns given that artificial intelligence could perpetuate inequalities, displace jobs, and violate human rights in many areas; as well as the instruments of fundamental human rights and freedoms (e.g., Universal Declarations of Human rights, International Covenants and Letters of Human rights). This paper seeks to explore the multifaceted connections between artificial intelligence and human rights and their effects on human life and social conduct. Subsequently, a framework is proposed to consider the ethical and legal implications of artificial intelligence in human rights, which is then tested in several scenarios. A discussion follows, leading to the conclusion and potential future research.

ARTIFICIAL INTELLIGENCE, HUMAN RIGHTS, AND ETHOS

Artificial intelligence has been recognized by the United Nations (UN) as an emerging technology with the potential to impact human rights. The organization actively participates in discussions and efforts to ensure the responsible and ethical use of artificial intelligence. The Universal Declaration of human rights and international conventions provide the basis for promoting and protecting human rights in the context of artificial intelligence. In this regard, this section analyzes the consequences of artificial intelligence in Economic, Social and Cultural Rights

Results Against Economic, Social, and Cultural Rights

Human rights include collective rights enshrined in the Universal Declaration of Human Rights (UDHR) and the International Covenants on Civil, Political, Economic, Social and Cultural Rights (ICCPR and ICESCR). These inherent rights, enjoyed from birth, require strong protection by governments, businesses and society (Version, 2018). Economic personnel standards include the right to work, equal pay, union formation, fair wages, decent housing, safe working conditions, access to education and vocational training, basic services, property rights and access to employment. Freedom included. Social human rights include rights to housing, work, education, social security, healthy environment, gender equality, adequate nutrition, health, culture, and sustainable development. Cultural human rights include the right to education, freedom of thought and expression, freedom of association and assembly, participation in cultural life, protection of artistic and intellectual works, access to information, gender equality, non-discrimination, It includes cultural diversity (Chakraborty, 2023).

Consequences on Emerging Technologies and Ethos

In recent decades, the significant advancement of emerging technologies, driven by societal needs and technological possibilities, has resulted in an increasingly close and dynamic relationship between technology producers and users (Lundvall, 2009). This relationship has led to rising user demands, pushing producers to create products and services that maintain market share by generating new needs and increasing dependence on their offerings (Yildirim & Correia, 2015). Consequently, human affairs have been reconfigured, with artificial intelligence and other technologies playing a pivotal role in shaping economic, social, and cultural aspects of society (Orlikowski, 2001).

The integration of emerging technologies has transformed traditional economic phenomena through the digital economy, incorporating artificial intelligence devices into various objects (Internet of Things), advanced technological devices (mobiles, smartphones, tablets, laptops), digital models (cloud platforms and digital services), the diversity, speed, and accuracy of data (Big Data, data analytics, and algorithmic decisions), and artificial intelligence systems for labor automation (Boenig-Liptsin et al., 2022; Jobin et al., 2019). While artificial intelligence provides opportunities for trade exchanges between producers and buyers, it has also led companies to commercialize our interactions (data and information) (Heeks, 2017), resulting in significant impacts on processes, policies, systems, and economic sectors (Criado et al., 2021; Valle-Cruz et al., 2020), and altering behaviors, needs, and modes of commercial exchange (e.g., e-commerce, e-business, and digital services). Social interaction technologies and collaborative software are having a major impact on interpersonal relationships (Dolata, 2017). Direct relationships between artificial intelligence and individuals occur through social media. The social web has changed social patterns and relationships between people, with millions of users accessing social networks every day (Kim et al., 2010). The desire to stay online has become obsessive, leading to significant consequences such as a lack of belonging, depression, anxiety and addiction (Fan et al., 2017; Sieber, 2019). This highlights the growing reliance on artificial intelligence tools for social interaction and the resulting changes in interpersonal relationships. This raises ethical and legal concerns that can lead to potential human rights violations in some economic, social, and cultural factors. We organize all these elements on Table 1 in order to describe the interactions that artificial intelligence performs on an integrated perspective.

Table 1. Economic, social, and cultural rights (ESCR)

Economic, Social and Cultural Rights (ESCR)		
Economic	**Social**	**Cultural**
Education		
Work		Cultural diversity
Housing		Discrimination
Basic services		Freedom of thought
Employment		Peaceful assembly
		Literary and artistic work
	Gender equality	
Trade unions	Health	
Fair remuneration	Sustainable development	
Rest		

Source: Authors' own elaboration

Negative Consequences of Artificial Intelligence in Human Rights

The possibility to create intelligent technologies formed a perfect ideology for science fiction literature. From those early ideas to our current era, fiction and science have converged in the search to improve human conditions. Since the first industrial revolution, economic, social, and cultural changes have moved through the machine age to the age of knowledge, innovation, and intelligent machines (Fourth Industrial Revolution). In other words, new knowledge and inventions periodically remake human societies (Drucker, 1993; Pan, 2016).

As technological progress continues to accelerate, it is becoming increasingly important to consider the implications of these advancements on human rights. The fields of human activity such as economic, social, and cultural changes have led to changes in human rights, as we described on Table 1, and while there are international treaties that establish universal rights, it is essential to re-evaluate the validity and vulnerability of these rights considering exponential technological advances. Some examples of these consequences include misuse of personal data by artificial intelligence algorithms, infringement of privacy rights, and potential discrimination in decision-making processes (Valle-Cruz et al., 2023). Additionally, the lack of transparency and accountability in artificial intelligence systems can lead to a lack of accountability for any negative impacts on human rights. It is crucial to consider and address these potential consequences in the development and deployment of artificial intelligence technology to ensure its responsible and ethical use. Some of these are mentioned below.

Privacy Violations

The collection and use of personal data by companies and government could threaten the privacy of individuals in five ways (The-Royal-Society, 2018):

- **Data collection:** some companies and applications collect and use users' personal data without their consent, which may violate their privacy.
- **Data analysis:** artificial intelligence algorithms can analyze people's personal data to generate detailed profiles, which may violate their privacy.
- **Facial recognition:** the use of facial recognition systems may allow companies and the government to track and monitor individuals, which may violate their privacy.
- **Marketing:** Some companies use personal data to personalize and enhance their advertising and marketing, which may violate users' privacy.
- **Advertising:** Some companies use personal data to create user profiles and display personalized advertisements, which may violate users' privacy.

It is important that steps are taken to ensure that personal data is handled ethically, and that individuals' privacy rights are respected. This includes implementing laws and regulations to protect privacy, as well as transparency and accountability

Workforce Replacement

The development of artificial intelligence could replace human jobs, which could increase unemployment and economic inequality, five examples are mentioned below (Organisation-for-Economic-Co-operation-and-Development, 2019):

- **Automotive** industry: production automation and robotics have replaced many workers in the automotive industry.
- **Banking and finance:** automated transaction processing systems and robotics are replacing many workers in the financial sector.
- **Retail:** automated customer service and order processing are replacing many workers in retail.
- **Public services:** automated systems and robots are replacing many workers in public services such as transportation, cleaning, and security.
- **Professional services:** automation of administrative tasks and robotics are replacing many workers in professional services such as accounting, law, and medicine.

It is important to consider the social and economic implications of workforce replacement, as it may have an impact on employment and economic inequality. Proper planning and regulation are needed to mitigate negative impacts and take full advantage of the opportunities of artificial intelligence.

Massive Control

The use of artificial intelligence in traffic control, public safety and crime detection could lead to increased surveillance and control by the state, which could limit individual freedom. Five such cases are presented below (Zuboff, 2019):

- **Traffic control:** the use of automated traffic control systems can allow authorities to monitor and control the movements of people in cities, which can limit individual freedom.
- **Citizen security:** the use of surveillance cameras with artificial intelligence can enable authorities to monitor and control people in public places, which can limit individual freedom.
- **Crime detection**: the use of automated crime detection systems may allow authorities to monitor and control people in public places, which may limit individual freedom.
- **Migration control:** the use of automated systems to control migration may allow authorities to monitor and control people at the border, which may limit individual freedom.
- **Access control:** the use of automated facial recognition systems to control access to buildings, facilities and events may allow authorities to monitor and control people, which may limit individual freedom.

It is important that steps are taken to ensure that artificial intelligence systems are used in an ethical and responsible manner and respect human rights, including privacy and individual freedom. This includes the implementation of laws and regulations to protect human rights, as well as transparency and accountability on the part of authorities and companies as to how artificial intelligence systems are used.

Responsibility and Dependence

If an artificial intelligence system makes a decision that harms someone, it may be difficult to determine who is responsible for that decision (Smith, 2021). Five examples of this are presented below.

- **Automated decision-making systems:** automated decision-making systems can make decisions based on data and algorithms, which can make it difficult to identify who is responsible for a particular decision.
- **Facial recognition systems:** automated facial recognition systems can make decisions based on data and algorithms, which can make it difficult to identify who is responsible for a particular decision.
- **Crime detection systems:** automated crime detection systems can make decisions based on data and algorithms, which can make it difficult to identify who is responsible for a particular decision.
- **Personnel selection systems:** automated personnel selection systems may make decisions based on data and algorithms, which may make it difficult to identify who is responsible for a particular decision.

- **Migration control systems:** automated migration control systems can make decisions based on data and algorithms, which can make it difficult to identify who is responsible for a particular decision.

It is important to establish appropriate accountability mechanisms and regulations to ensure that decisions made by artificial intelligence systems are ethical and legal, and that the appropriate individuals or institutions can be identified and held accountable in case of problems or errors.

Discrimination

The use of artificial intelligence algorithms to make automated decisions, such as selecting candidates for a job or accessing financial services, could perpetuate existing discrimination in society (Zuiderveen Borgesius, 2020). Four examples are presented below.

- **Credit systems:** some studies have found that automated credit systems can perpetuate racial and gender discrimination because they are based on historical data that reflect existing inequalities in society.
- **Human resources:** automated personnel selection systems may discriminate against certain candidates based on their gender, age, or race.
- **Crime detection systems:** Automated crime detection systems may discriminate against certain communities or ethnic groups because they are based on historical data that reflect existing inequalities in society.
- **Health systems:** Automated health systems may perpetuate racial and gender discrimination, as they are based on historical data that reflect existing inequalities in society.

It is important to conduct an ethical and diversity impact assessment during the development and implementation of artificial intelligence to minimize the potential negative consequences to human rights and ensure that the technology is used in a fair and equitable manner. Table 2 summarizes our analysis of the negative consequences to human rights from the use of artificial intelligence. Such an assessment would help identify and address any biases or issues that may arise and ensure that the technology is developed and implemented with the well-being of all individuals in mind. This is particularly important given the far-reaching and rapidly advancing nature of artificial intelligence, and its potential to affect many aspects of society. Conducting an ethical and diversity impact assessment is essential for responsible and responsible use of artificial intelligence.

Table 2. Negative consequences of the implementation of artificial intelligence in human rights

Negative consequences to human rights from the use of artificial intelligence in...				
Privacy violations	**Workforce replacement**	**Massive control**	**Responsibility and dependence**	**Discrimination**
Data collection	Automotive industry	Traffic control	Automated decision-making	Credit systems
Data analysis	Banking and finance	Citizen security	Facial recognition systems	Human resources
Facial recognition	Retail		Crime detection systems	
Marketing	Public services	Migration control	Personnel selection systems	Health systems
Advertising	Professional services	Access control	Migration control systems	

Source: Authors' own elaboration

TOWARDS A FRAMEWORK FOR ARTIFICIAL INTELLIGENCE NEGATIVE CONSEQUENCES IN THE HUMAN RIGHTS

This section delves into the relationship between artificial intelligence and human rights consequences, specifically examining how economic, social, and cultural factors interact with the adoption and use of artificial intelligence. The first part of the analysis provides an overview of economic, social, and cultural rights and how they are relevant to the discussion of artificial intelligence. The following three sections then examine the specific economic, social, and cultural negative consequences of artificial intelligence on these human rights, providing a comprehensive understanding of how this technology impacts the framework of human rights.

Economic, Social, and Cultural Rights

Artificial intelligence has embedded in a great part of human life: automating, optimizing, and facilitating their activities (Javaid et al., 2022; Mathew et al., 2023). The speed with which specialists in the discipline progress and develop new technologies has delayed the attention on ethical, human, and legal aspects. In this regard, Bostrom and Yudkowsky (2018) illustrate the following example: a bank uses a machine learning algorithm to suggest mortgage applications. One of the rejected applicants makes a complaint against the bank arguing that the algorithm racially discriminates against interested parties. Despite the bank's denial that the algorithm works unfairly, statistics show a tendency to approve applications from people with certain racial characteristics, regardless of whether they are equally qualified as other applicants. Hence, two questions arise: What is wrong? and why is the algorithm judging applicants according to their race?

Like the example above, which could be interpreted as a discrimination in credit systems, there are other unintended consequences of direct and indirect use of artificial intelligence. These consequences may be implicit in the coding of evaluative algorithms or in the premeditated use of artificial intelligence to exploit information and circumstances (Sieber, 2019). Despite technological advances in artificial intelligence, work continues a human-technical approach that ensures respect for human rights and ethical principles. However, for many experts, this is still inexact and under development (Bostrom & Yudkowsky, 2018; Cheatham et al., 2019). Therefore, a multidisciplinary framework addressing artificial intelligence governance considering economic, social, and cultural aspects is required (Etzioni & Etzioni, 2017; Specker Sullivan & Reiner, 2021).

A key factor for the human-social progress in artificial intelligence is the fostering of values, ethics, and safeguards. Hence, international human rights instruments (Fjeld et al., 2020) that guarantee safety and full confidence in artificial intelligence systems must be manifestly considered. Similarly, artificial intelligence systems and the humans behind them should aim to achieve total safety in their use to limit the presence of inadvertent consequences on social, economic, and cultural aspects (Commission, 2019).

Responding to this, legal norms and standards have begun to develop that analyze and regulate the use of artificial intelligence. For example: 1) Montreal declaration on artificial intelligence; 2) Asilomar artificial intelligence principles; 3) artificial intelligence4People principles; 4) UN report on artificial intelligence; 5) European Ethical Charter on the use of artificial intelligence, and 6) UNESCO Recommendation on the Ethics of artificial intelligence; 7) National Artificial Intelligence Initiative Act of 2020; 8) Artificial intelligence Bill of Rights. Although the interest in the normativity and ethical uses of artificial intelligence is remarkable, there is a lag in terms of human rights (Kriebitz & Lütge, 2020).

The existing discussion addresses the following. First, the possibility that one day artificial intelligence will function as an autonomous actor (still distant) and make decisions that violate human rights. Second, the responsibility of companies and governments that use it in a premeditated way against human rights and ethical principles (Kriebitz & Lütge, 2020). Clear examples are the apparition of new terms that are a consequence of the overuse and misuse of artificial intelligence by providers and consumers, for instance, "Digital Wellnes-Wellbeing", "Cybersecurity", "Nomophobia", "Snapchat dysmorphia", "Algorithmic bias", "Algorithmic opacity", and "Explainable artificial intelligence". Besides, the mainstream leads to the misuse of these current disruptive technologies, capable of persuading and controlling users to have them spend more time online and sometimes to rely on virtual interactions, in a strict sense of human dominance with technology in the middle.

Artificial Intelligence Consequences and Economic Rights

Nowadays, many people are connected to the Internet and use social media for diverse daily activities (e.g., Netflix, Spotify, Amazon, E-Bay, and Google). This is an opportunity for companies and business to adapt digital commerce models and reach almost anyone in the world. However, powerful companies, financial institutions, and even governments, self-provide privacy and non-disclosure agreements; while individuals become open sources of information through their online interactions that are recorded in Big Data (Rubel, 2016), because they explicitly accept a long list of "terms and conditions" that put at risk the privacy of their data; or, through cookies is possible to identify what we buy, what we read, where we are, and what we search (Rubel, 2016).

Therefore, artificial intelligence makes it possible for companies and ill-intentioned actors to collect, gather and analyze a large quantity of data (big data) in a sense of: "knowledge is power" and "if the service is free, the service is you"; meanwhile, companies protect information on actions and uses of artificial intelligence; which makes it an asymmetric and unrestricted relationship between both actors. In addition, as technology advances, the pressures of the big data market are greater and violate human dignity, transforming them into quantifiable, marketable, and manipulable subjects (Buettner, 2017). In this regard, the consequences can be interpreted as the violation of privacy in the data collection and analysis for marketing purposes and asymmetry in the control of data and information (de Nobrega, 2022).

Moreover, the underlying idea that machines are more accurate, efficient, effective and make decisions with greater objectivity in specific activities with creativity, overcoming routine activities persists (Jennings, 2010). Therefore, in the labor order, the current trend towards automation raises the possibility that one day artificial intelligence and related technologies could jeopardize workers' jobs and displace them from certain industries, altering labor rights and guarantees (Cheatham et al., 2019; Etzioni & Etzioni, 2017). Consequently, the possibility of human substitution will affect economic rights, and may also impact responsibility and dependence by underlying labor force decision-making and other economic decisions related to labor force replacement, including employment discrimination.

Artificial Intelligence Consequences and Social Rights

With artificial intelligence technologies entering on several areas of human life, much of the decisions that society makes are influenced by the interaction with and through artificial intelligence technologies, by assuming assertive decision making with the support of artificial intelligence. Based on this premise, it is necessary to consider personal autonomy to determine that the risks of its use do not outweigh the benefits and to balance the relationship between. In other words, it is evident that a large part of the social aspects is supported by a growing dependence on decision-making and a situation of control (Ashok et al., 2022).

Overall, artificial intelligence aims for collective well-being and personal and social balance (Specker Sullivan & Reiner, 2021). Nevertheless, there are several applications that use artificial intelligence to condition behavior and persuade people. The consequences of this are reflected in compulsive behaviors and the incremental dependence on technological applications; even transgressing human-social guarantees (Boyd, 2012). For example: The Internet has become an indispensable source of information and communication through search engines, email, and social networks (Dolata, 2017). On the other hand, emotions and feelings are indispensable for human well-being. One of the ways to satisfy emotional needs is through social interaction. For example, the use of digital social networks has replaced conventional social interaction, even expressions and forms of corporal language have been substituted by computer-mediated communication, for example, emoticons (Thelwall, 2014). Additionally, digital social relationships have a high impact on emotions and social behaviors. It is thus, today a "like" has an important impact on individuals and the absence of this sort of recognition can lead to emotional instability and mental disorders such as depression and anxiety based on an emotional dependence and control.

Artificial Intelligence Consequences and Cultural Rights

There is currently not a single field that is not being transformed by artificial intelligence. Right now, it is changing countries, industries, families, and individuals; in other words, the core of many human actions today is on the Internet, on technological tools, algorithms, and digital applications (Boyd, 2012; Stahl et al., 2022). Also, many decisions are supported by artificial intelligence results and predictions. For example: when using a search engine to find an object or topic of our interest, it will activate artificial intelligence functions to provide us with a wide number of options that will lead us to make an optimal decision based mainly on artificial intelligence (Ashraf, 2022; Rajendra et al., 2022). This has represented a change in consumption and commercial exchange patterns (Jordan, 2019; Pan, 2016).

The incorporation of technologies is transforming production and professional functions, with automation and the introduction of "artificial intelligence partners" into a variety of roles. This evolution will render certain methods of working obsolete and necessitate the acquisition of new knowledge and job skills (Drucker, 1993; Rubel, 2016); speeding up the possibility and acceptance of human replacement and new forms of workforce.

Likewise, technology society have drawn a digital division between those who have technological possibilities and those who do not, which inhibits full knowledge about innovations and technological advances in artificial intelligence (Schwab, 2017). Moreover, this represses the acquisition of cognitive faculties necessary for the technological era.

A sociotechnical framework for bringing artificial intelligence into the organization is proposed by STS theory, which highlights the links between technical systems, consisting of technology and processes, and social systems, consisting of people and relationships such as economy, culture, and society (Makarius et al., 2020). This framework emphasizes the importance of considering the social and organizational context in which artificial intelligence is implemented, as well as the technical aspects of the system. Socio-technical research also highlights the need for ethical considerations in the development and deployment of artificial intelligence systems. Krakowski et al (2022) propose an integration of ethics and artificial intelligence through sociotechnical, problem-based learning is proposed to address the societal impacts of artificial intelligence systems. As artificial intelligence systems are integrated into high stakes social domains, researchers now examine how to design and operate them in a safe and ethical manner (Dobbe et al., 2021).

In addition, sociotechnical research highlights the potential for artificial intelligence to exacerbate existing inequalities and the need for human control over artificial intelligence systems. A sociotechnical perspective for the future of artificial intelligence emphasizes the importance of narratives in shaping the development and deployment of artificial intelligence systems and calls for a diverse approach within the artificial intelligence community. By examining the social and technical aspects of artificial intelligence systems, the sociotechnical research can contribute to the development of artificial intelligence systems that are safe, ethical, and equitable, changing the narrative of future developments (Sartori & Theodorou, 2022).

Finally, the need to stay updated, connected and socializing within the digital world has led to overlook the risks involved in giving explicit consent on the use of our data; allowing those who manage artificial intelligence tools to monitor, use and manipulate users without restrictions. As a result of our analysis, we propose Figure 1 shows the framework of artificial intelligence in the economic, social, and cultural rights. In the next section we present the concluding comments of the study.

TESTING THE FRAMEWORK WITH SOME CASES OF ARTIFICIAL INTELLIGENCE AND HUMAN RIGHTS

This section analyzes the negative human rights impacts of artificial intelligence adoption. The aim is to gain a holistic view of the complex relationship between artificial intelligence and human rights and uncover potential problem areas for further investigation. Although the cases discussed cover economic, social, and cultural aspects, we classified them according to his three human rights categories considered in this study.

Artificial Intelligence and Economic Rights

Case 1. Netherlands Algorithm Devised to Predict the Probability of a Citizen Committing Tax Fraud

Figure 1. Framework of artificial intelligence and economic, social, and cultural rights

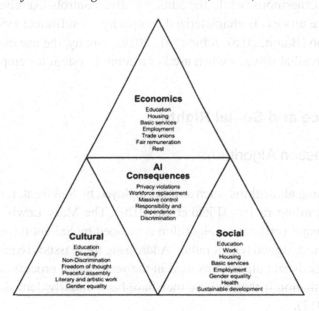

SyRI (System Risk Indication), an algorithm developed by the Dutch government to detect potential state fraud, has come into question due to its widespread impact on business human rights SyRI (System Risk Indication), an algorithm developed by the Dutch government to detect potential state fraud, has come into question due to its widespread impact on business human rights (Rubel, 2016). Although this algorithm was developed with good intentions, it poses serious ethical and legal dilemmas. The collection and use of sensitive personal data violates data protection rights and calls into question the protection of fundamental personal liberties. The lack of transparency regarding SyRI raises suspicions of data misuse and possible discrimination, exacerbating human rights violations (Jobin et al., 2019)

A disturbing aspect is the automation of the decision-making process inherent in these algorithms. Not only does this automation take away jobs, it also reduces responsibility, undermines social trust, and has negative economic impacts (Cheatham et al., 2019; Etzioni & Etzioni, 2017). Furthermore, the SyRI algorithm exercises excessive control, violating privacy, due process, and proportionality (Weber, 2010). These human rights violations go beyond mere economic consequences and perpetuate discrimination (Fjeld et al., 2020).

Case 2. Robo-Firing in the Workplace

Uber's use of real-time facial recognition software and location tracking for driver authentication and user security has led to a disturbing phenomenon known as "robofiring". In a notable incident in 2021, six drivers were fired following the discovery of detection software that allegedly exposed fraud and account sharing. However, the affected drivers contested the dismissal, claiming unfair dismissal due to algorithm error. The decision to terminate her employment lacked sufficient evidence to justify such action. This artificial intelligence-based incident in the workplace will have profound implications for workers' economic human rights. Above all, it violates the fundamental right to fair work and rights at work and undermines the principle of fair employment. Biased decision-making is evident as recruiters relied heavily on algorithm-generated results to carry out these headcount reductions (Cheatham et al., 2019; Jordan, 2019). Furthermore, while the administrative controls exercised over these algorithms remain hidden, the entire process is characterized by opacity, as sufficient evidence was not presented to support its termination (Baum, 2020; Jobin et al., 2019). Finally, the use of tracking and recognition technology violates individual privacy when used as a control system for employees or others (Weber, 2010).

Artificial Intelligence and Social Rights

Case 3. Tenant Selection Algorithms

The use of tenant screening algorithms, such as that employed by SafeRent, raises serious human rights concerns, especially regarding racism (Fjeld et al., 2020). The Mary Lewis case illustrates the challenges that can arise when a verification algorithm developed by Sailent results in an apartment rental being denied based on the assigned tenant rating. Addressing these issues requires landlords and tenants to be aware of the standards and algorithms used in the verification process so that they can appeal or provide additional information if they believe they have been unfairly denied. is important (Cheatham et al., 2019; Schwab, 2017).

Additionally, the use of algorithms for tenant verification raises privacy concerns such as the collection and use of personal data, lack of transparency and control over that data, and potential for discriminatory behavior (Fjeld et al., 2020). Landlords may rely on algorithms and their developers to make rental decisions, which may lead to liability and dependence on third parties. Additionally, algorithms can rely on biased, incomplete, or inaccurate data, which can lead to flawed decision-making processes.

Landlords are responsible for ensuring that the algorithms used are fair, transparent, and compliant with all applicable laws and regulations. Training algorithms on data that reflects past discrimination can unfairly influence minorities and perpetuate systemic discrimination. It is the landlord's duty to ensure that the algorithms used are fair and comply with all legal requirements related to ensuring human dignity and a decent standard of living.

Case 4. The Use of Clearview Artificial Intelligence's Facial Recognition Technology During War to Recognize Ukrainians

The use of facial recognition technology in war zones raises serious human rights concerns. This violates an individual's right to privacy by collecting and processing personal data without the individual's consent. In addition, violations of the right to freedom of expression can occur, as individuals can be prosecuted and imprisoned for expressing their views and political affiliation (Chakraborty, 2023). Discrimination and profiling of specific groups based on ethnicity, race, or nationality can also occur (Fjeld et al., 2020).

The use of facial recognition technology in war zones could further undermine the right to a fair trial. Algorithmic predictions should not serve as evidence of guilt, but could be used as the basis for investigations against citizens, potentially leading to arbitrary arrests and lack of due process (Baum, 2020). The use of facial recognition technology in combat zones facilitates the identification and targeting of individuals, which may lead to further human rights violations, including extrajudicial killings and enforced disappearances (Chakraborty, 2023).

Artificial Intelligence and Cultural Rights

Case 5. The Use of Artificial Intelligence Trained by 4Chan

The use of artificial intelligence trained on content disseminated by platforms such as 4Chan and other sources that disseminate hate speech has significant implications for cultural human rights. One of the main concerns is the prevalence of hate speech and discrimination against minorities (Aral & Eckles, 2019). This not only fosters an environment of prejudice but undermines principles of equality and respect for cultural diversity.

Moreover, the use of such artificial intelligence models carries risks to the right to privacy and freedom of expression. Individuals who express their opinions and affiliations may be subject to persecution and punishment as their activities are monitored and judged by her artificial intelligence. This can have a chilling effect on cultural expression and impede the free exchange of ideas.

The use of artificial intelligence trained on hate speech content also challenges the right to a fair trial (Chakraborty, 2023). Artificial intelligence predictions can be treated as evidence without proper scrutiny, leading to arbitrary arrests and lack of due process. This undermines the principles of justice, fairness, and presumption of innocence.

Additionally, the use of trained artificial intelligence based on hateful content increases the risk of extrajudicial killings and enforced disappearances. artificial intelligence's ability to identify and target people based on their beliefs and affiliations could lead to serious human rights violations, as people may be subject to persecution and violence based on their cultural background and beliefs. I have.

DISCUSSION

The rapid development of artificial intelligence contains both opportunities and risks that, if misused or used maliciously, can cause great damage. There are concerns about human rights abuses associated with the use of tenant screening algorithms, especially racism that can hinder access to basic human needs, housing. The lack of transparency and control over personal data in these algorithms raises privacy concerns and can lead to discriminatory practices. Moreover, reliance on these algorithms raises issues of liability and dependence on third parties, while flawed decision-making processes based on biased or inaccurate data unfairly influence minority groups. and may violate the rights of citizens.

Artificial intelligence has far-reaching implications for economic, social, and cultural rights. In the economic sector, data breaches and restrictions on freedom of expression can occur, excluding certain sectors. In conflict areas, the use of facial recognition technology can lead to serious human rights abuses such as invasion of privacy, restrictions on freedom of expression, and extrajudicial measures. Culturally, artificial intelligence trained on hateful content can perpetuate hate speech and discrimination, thereby exacerbating social problems.

Addressing these concerns requires the adoption of fair and transparent algorithms that adhere to legal and ethical standards that protect human dignity and ensure a decent standard of living. Oversight and regulation are essential to prevent discriminatory practices in the use of these algorithms. Improving the transparency of data usage and decision-making processes leads to better understanding and promotes accountability. Educational efforts are essential to promote responsible and ethical use of artificial intelligence algorithms. Further investigation and assessment will play an important role in identifying and preventing human rights violations, especially with the widespread use of generative artificial intelligence.

Although artificial intelligence has great benefits, it is important to be aware of the risks that come with it, especially in vulnerable countries, sectors, and professions. Politicians should prioritize the development of legal and ethical frameworks that protect people's living standards, job security, educational opportunities, fairness, equity, justice, freedom, autonomy, and privacy. Integrating transparency and accountability into complex artificial intelligence systems is necessary to create trust in their functioning and results. To prevent violations of basic human rights and ensure a positive impact on the economy, it is important to think about the potential impacts and unintended consequences of artificial intelligence.

CONCLUSION AND FUTURE DIRECTIONS

The framework proposed in this article aims to analyze the impact of artificial intelligence on economic, social, and cultural dimensions, gaining insight into the changes and behavioral changes that society is experiencing. Our proposal includes the sociotechnical perspective that integrates the several human activities into the frame of artificial intelligence negative risks. While this analysis shows that artificial intelligence has the potential to generate significant benefits through intelligent mass automation, it also reveals gaps and unforeseen consequences in various areas.

Artificial intelligence can be seen as a double-edged tool with both positive and negative effects. On the positive side, it has a demonstrated ability to simplify and improve many aspects of human life, evident from a technical and commercial point of view. However, our understanding of artificial intelligence is still in its early stages, leading to many open questions and unforeseen consequences. Data breaches, discrimination, and manipulation of systems and data are proving undesirable consequences, highlighting the ethical and legal challenges posed by artificial intelligence advancements beyond our understanding in the social sciences and humanities. has become

Harnessing the potential of artificial intelligence effectively while ensuring its responsible and beneficial use will require significant human and social progress. Strengthening social and legal regulation enforcement is key to regulating the use, application, and scope of artificial intelligence systems. A focus on human, moral, and social values support Asimov's vision of developing and using intelligent machines for the benefit of humanity.

The notion that artificial intelligence gains autonomy and poses a potential threat to humanity may seem extreme, but it is not the case that artificial intelligence can become invasive and persuasive with personal, economic, social, and cultural behavior. Specific features have been identified that allow to have and interact with them. It is therefore essential to prioritize the development and use of artificial intelligence systems based on fundamental human rights and an unwavering commitment to ethical principles such as justice, liberty, autonomy, charity, fairness, and transparency.

Future work should focus on maximizing the explanatory power of the proposed framework in specific contexts and promoting a deeper understanding of artificial intelligence's impact on psyche and human rights. Empirical studies play an important role in validating and refining the framework, accounting for all overlooked factors, and ensuring the robustness of the framework. Furthermore, with the aim of gaining a comprehensive understanding of the impact of artificial intelligence, additional research should be conducted to identify the potential impact of artificial intelligence on human rights.

REFERENCES

Aral, S., & Eckles, D. (2019). Protecting elections from social media manipulation. *Science*, *365*(6456), 858–861. doi:10.1126/science.aaw8243 PMID:31467206

Ashok, M., Madan, R., Joha, A., & Sivarajah, U. (2022). Ethical framework for Artificial Intelligence and Digital technologies. *International Journal of Information Management*, *62*, 102433. doi:10.1016/j. ijinfomgt.2021.102433

Ashraf, C. (2022). Exploring the impacts of artificial intelligence on freedom of religion or belief online. *International Journal of Human Rights*, *26*(5), 757–791. doi:10.1080/13642987.2021.1968376

Baum, S. D. (2020). Social choice ethics in artificial intelligence. *AI \& SOCIETY*, *35*(1), 165–176.

Boenig-Liptsin, M., Tanweer, A., & Edmundson, A. (2022). Data Science Ethos Lifecycle: Interplay of ethical thinking and data science practice. *Journal of Statistics and Data Science Education : An Official Journal of the of the American Statistical Association*, *30*(3), 228–240. doi:10.1080/2693916 9.2022.2089411

Bostrom, N., & Yudkowsky, E. (2018). The ethics of artificial intelligence. In *Artificial intelligence safety and security* (pp. 57–69). Chapman and Hall/CRC. doi:10.1201/9781351251389-4

Boyd, D. (2012). 6. Participating in the Always-On Lifestyle. In *The social media reader* (pp. 71–76). New York University Press. doi:10.18574/nyu/9780814764077.003.0010

Buettner, R. (2017). Predicting user behavior in electronic markets based on personality-mining in large online social networks: A personality-based product recommender framework. *Electronic Markets*, *27*(3), 247–265. doi:10.1007/s12525-016-0228-z

Chakraborty, S. (2023). Human Rights and Artificial Intelligence: Issues and Challenges. *Dynamics of Dialogue, Cultural Development, and Peace in the Metaverse*, 1–14.

Cheatham, B., Javanmardian, K., & Samandari, H. (2019). Confronting the risks of artificial intelligence. *The McKinsey Quarterly*, 1–9.

Commission, E. (2019). *AI: Ethics Guidelines for Trustworthy AI*. High-Level Expert Group on AI.

Criado, J. I., Sandoval-Almazan, R., Valle-Cruz, D., & Ruvalcaba-Gómez, E. A. (2021). Chief information officers' perceptions about artificial intelligence: A comparative study of implications and challenges for the public sector. *First Monday*.

de Nobrega, V. M. (2022). A Diverse (AI) World: How to Make Sure That the Digital World Reflects the Richness and Diversity of Our World. In Impact of Women's Empowerment on SDGs in the Digital Era (pp. 180–204). IGI Global.

Dobbe, R., Gilbert, T. K., & Mintz, Y. (2021). Hard choices in artificial intelligence. *Artificial Intelligence, 300,* 103555. doi:10.1016/j.artint.2021.103555

Dolata, U. (2017). *Apple, Amazon, Google, Facebook, Microsoft: market concentration-competition-innovation strategies.*

Drucker, P. F. (1993). The rise of the knowledge society. *The Wilson Quarterly, 17*(2), 52–72.

Etzioni, A., & Etzioni, O. (2017). Incorporating ethics into artificial intelligence. *The Journal of Ethics, 21*(4), 403–418. doi:10.1007/s10892-017-9252-2

Fan, L., Liu, X., Wang, B., & Wang, L. (2017). Interactivity, engagement, and technology dependence: understanding users' technology utilisation behaviour. *Behaviour \& Information Technology, 36*(2), 113–124.

Fjeld, J., Achten, N., Hilligoss, H., Nagy, A., & Srikumar, M. (2020). Principled artificial intelligence: Mapping consensus in ethical and rights-based approaches to principles for AI. *Berkman Klein Center Research Publication, 2020–1.*

Heeks, R. (2017). *Information and communication technology for development (ICT4D).* Routledge. doi:10.4324/9781315652603

Huang, C., Zhang, Z., Mao, B., & Yao, X. (2022). An overview of artificial intelligence ethics. *IEEE Transactions on Artificial Intelligence, 4*(4), 799–819. doi:10.1109/TAI.2022.3194503

Javaid, M., Haleem, A., Singh, R. P., & Suman, R. (2022). Artificial intelligence applications for industry 4.0: A literature-based study. *Journal of Industrial Integration and Management, 7*(01), 83–111. doi:10.1142/S2424862221300040

Jennings, K. E. (2010). Developing creativity: Artificial barriers in artificial intelligence. *Minds and Machines, 20*(4), 489–501. doi:10.1007/s11023-010-9206-y

Jobin, A., Ienca, M., & Vayena, E. (2019). The global landscape of AI ethics guidelines. *Nature Machine Intelligence, 1*(9), 389–399. doi:10.1038/s42256-019-0088-2

Jordan, M. I. (2019). Artificial intelligence—The revolution hasn't happened yet. *Harvard Data Science Review, 1*(1).

Kieslich, K., Keller, B., & Starke, C. (2022). Artificial intelligence ethics by design. Evaluating public perception on the importance of ethical design principles of artificial intelligence. *Big Data & Society, 9*(1), 20539517221092956. doi:10.1177/20539517221092956

Kim, W., Jeong, O.-R., & Lee, S.-W. (2010). On social Web sites. *Information Systems, 35*(2), 215–236. doi:10.1016/j.is.2009.08.003

Krakowski, A., Greenwald, E., Hurt, T., Nonnecke, B., & Cannady, M. (2022). Authentic Integration of Ethics and AI through Sociotechnical, Problem-Based Learning. *Proceedings of the AAAI Conference on Artificial Intelligence*, *36*(11), 12774–12782. doi:10.1609/aaai.v36i11.21556

Krieblitz, A., & Lütge, C. (2020). Artificial intelligence and human rights: A business ethical assessment. *Business and Human Rights Journal*, *5*(1), 84–104. doi:10.1017/bhj.2019.28

Lundvall, B.-A. (2009). Innovation as an interactive process: user-producer interaction to the national system of innovation. *African Journal of Science, Technology, Innovation and Development, 1*(2_3), 10–34.

Makarius, E. E., Mukherjee, D., Fox, J. D., & Fox, A. K. (2020). Rising with the machines: A sociotechnical framework for bringing artificial intelligence into the organization. *Journal of Business Research*, *120*, 262–273. doi:10.1016/j.jbusres.2020.07.045

Mathew, D., Brintha, N. C., & Jappes, J. T. W. (2023). Artificial intelligence powered automation for industry 4.0. In *New Horizons for Industry 4.0 in Modern Business* (pp. 1–28). Springer. doi:10.1007/978-3-031-20443-2_1

Moll, I. (2022). The fourth industrial revolution: A new ideology. *TripleC: Communication, Capitalism & Critique. Open Access Journal for a Global Sustainable Information Society*, *20*(1), 45–61.

Organisation-for-Economic-Co-operation-and-Development. (2019). *The impact of artificial intelligence on the future of work*. OECD.

Orlikowski, W. (2001). *The Duality of Technology. The Contemporary Giddens, Social Theory in a Globalizing Age. CGA Bryant and D. Jary*. Palgrave.

Pan, Y. (2016). Heading toward Artificial Intelligence 2.0. *Engineering (Beijing)*, *2*(4), 409–413. doi:10.1016/J.ENG.2016.04.018

Rajendra, P., Kumari, M., Rani, S., Dogra, N., Boadh, R., Kumar, A., & Dahiya, M. (2022). Impact of artificial intelligence on civilization: Future perspectives. *Materials Today: Proceedings*, *56*, 252–256. doi:10.1016/j.matpr.2022.01.113

Rubel, A. (2016). The Black Box Society: The Secret Algorithms that Control Money and Information, by Frank Pasquale. Cambridge: Harvard University Press, 2015. 320 pp. ISBN 978–0674368279. *Business Ethics Quarterly*, *26*(4), 568–571. doi:10.1017/beq.2016.50

Sartori, L., & Theodorou, A. (2022). A sociotechnical perspective for the future of AI: Narratives, inequalities, and human control. *Ethics and Information Technology*, *24*(1), 4. doi:10.1007/s10676-022-09624-3

Schwab, K. (2017). *The fourth industrial revolution*. Currency.

Sieber, A. (2019). Does facebook violate its users' basic human rights? *NanoEthics*, *13*(2), 139–145. doi:10.1007/s11569-019-00345-4

Smith, H. (2021). Clinical AI: opacity, accountability, responsibility and liability. *AI \& SOCIETY*, *36*(2), 535–545.

Specker Sullivan, L., & Reiner, P. (2021). Digital wellness and persuasive technologies. *Philosophy \& Technology, 34*, 413–424.

Stahl, B. C., Rodrigues, R., Santiago, N., & Macnish, K. (2022). A European Agency for Artificial Intelligence: Protecting fundamental rights and ethical values. *Computer Law \& Security Review, 45*, 105661.

The-Royal-Society. (2018). *The future of privacy: A review of the ethical and legal challenges*. The Royal Society.

Thelwall, M. (2014). Heart and soul: Sentiment strength detection in the social web with sentistrength, 2017. *Cyberemotions: Collective Emotions in Cyberspace*.

Valle-Cruz, D., Criado, J. I., Sandoval-Almazán, R., & Ruvalcaba-Gomez, E. A. (2020). Assessing the public policy-cycle framework in the age of artificial intelligence: From agenda-setting to policy evaluation. *Government Information Quarterly, 37*(4), 101509. doi:10.1016/j.giq.2020.101509

Valle-Cruz, D., García-Contreras, R., & Gil-Garcia, J. R. (2023). Exploring the negative impacts of artificial intelligence in government: The dark side of intelligent algorithms and cognitive machines. *International Review of Administrative Sciences*, 00208523231187051.

Version, P. (2018). *Artificial Intelligence & Human Rights : O PPORTUNITIES & R ISKS*.

Weber, R. H. (2010). Internet of Things--New security and privacy challenges. *Computer Law \& Security Review, 26*(1), 23–30.

Yildirim, C., & Correia, A.-P. (2015). Exploring the dimensions of nomophobia: Development and validation of a self-reported questionnaire. *Computers in Human Behavior, 49*, 130–137. doi:10.1016/j.chb.2015.02.059

Zuboff, S. (2019). *The age of surveillance capitalism: The fight for a human future at the new frontier of power: Barack Obama's books of 2019*. Profile books.

Zuiderveen Borgesius, F. J. (2020). Strengthening legal protection against discrimination by algorithms and artificial intelligence. *International Journal of Human Rights, 24*(10), 1572–1593. doi:10.1080/13 642987.2020.1743976

Chapter 10
Digital Transformation on Organizational Performance:
A Literature Review Analysis

Zuraihan Masri

Universiti Brunei Darussalam, Brunei

Mohammad Nabil Almunawar

iD https://orcid.org/0000-0001-5296-2576

Universiti Brunei Darussalam, Brunei

Muhammad Anshari

iD https://orcid.org/0000-0002-8160-6682

Universiti Brunei Darussalam, Brunei

Fairul Rizal Rashid

Universiti Brunei Darussalam, Brunei

ABSTRACT

The massive development of digital technology accelerated the pace of disruption in almost every industry, creating immense ambiguity and continuing to accelerate uncertainty in the business environment. The essentiality for an organization to adapt to rapid digital transformation led businesses to remain competitive and relevant in the industry. With the rise of the pandemic Covid 19, creating more challenges for organizations in the effort to improve digital maturity. This study focuses on digital transformation and its impact on an organization's performance while narrowing down the research to the telecommunication industry in the Brunei Darussalam context. The contribution of this study is expected to fill the gap in the literature regarding antecedents of a successful digital transformation.

DOI: 10.4018/979-8-3693-2865-1.ch010

INTRODUCTION

Digital development is imposing corporations to rethink their administrative models. Some companies display a better ability to exploit digital technologies to obtain a competitive advantage over the market in several industries. Traditional companies, with their closed, centralized, hierarchical, top-down organizational structures, are incapable to change and develop at the speed needed by digital distraction (Imran et al., 2018). To endure, traditional corporations must question their administrative models, learn from digital disruptors, and shift their organizational models and attitude (Imran et al., 2018).

Humans are transitioning towards a digital economy and social interactions and behavior. Though already underway for approximately half a century, the pace of change has quickened with the additional deployment of digital infrastructure, the propagation of smartphones that permit ubiquitous computing, and the generation of massive volumes of all types of data. These evolutions have turned data into a significant strategic resource (Hinings et al., 2018). At present many of them made a comparison between the former industrial transformations driven by general-purpose technologies like electricity or steam and digital transformation. Whether it is the Second Machine Age (Baptista et al., 2020), the Third Wave (Prester, Julian, Dubravka Cecez-Kecmanovic, Daniel Schlagwein, 2020), or Industry 4.0 (Bodrow, 2017), important shifts are in progress in society and the economy more generally. With this transformation, come erratic chances to improve well-being and express persistent social problems from health care to education and the environment (Mubarak, M.F. et al., 2018; Vial, 2019; Hess et al., 2016). Yet, such advantages arise with new challenges as digital transformation changes the structure and nature of markets and companies, increases concerns around occupations and skills, security, privacy, economic and social interaction (Ebert, 2019), the creation and composition of societies, and concepts of equity and inclusion in the present-day of industry 4.0. Researchers have recognized the important positive impacts of the digital transformation of industries on efficiency and performance on a macro level (Schwertner, 2017; Heavin & Power, 2018).

Against the framework of digitalization, globalization, changes in demography, and lack of resources, it is important for corporations to understand the effects and impacts associated with these megatrends and to prepare themselves for the upcoming. The world is becoming more and more digitized and crystal clear for all stakeholders because of innovative technologies, interconnectedness, algorithms, and big data storage. It is no longer only about a marketing policy to affect consumers, company branding to sustain workers, or to find methods to improve methods or systematize the manufacturing. At the present not only the integration and usage of state-of-the-art technologies and commercial models matter, but it is also significant to identify the interdependencies and influences on the basics of organizational behavior, such as the interaction among the two determining factor; skill and individuals. Hence, and due to the actuality of the topics, the effects of digitalization on management, and employees were reviewed and examined to proactively manage the required change to make sure the sustainability of the company and to sustain or extend their position in the market.

Information, communication, and connectivity technologies have enhanced greatly during the past period producing new functionalities (Anshari & Almunawar, 2021). These new digital technologies additionally empower the manufacturing, storage, and management of information, and enable interaction between electronic systems and human beings (Bodrow, 2017). Companies like Netflix, Amazon, Google, and Apple have effectively adapted these innovative digital technologies and have increased to excessive heights whereas others who did not adapt have not and became outdated. At present several organizations feel pressured to change to encounter client demands and competitive pressure through digital technologies (Vial, 2019). These changes are known as digital transformation. Though numerous consultancy-related studies express the significance and potential advantage of digital transformation there is a very little truly academic past study available on the idea of digital transformation (Almunawar et al., 2023). Some express that the fundamental technologies are social, analytics, portable, and cloud (Ebert, 2019; Anshari et al., 2022) but most deliver holistic nondeterministic definitions. Though there are studies that define the organizational impacts of the social, analytics, portable, and cloud technologies in isolation, there are few studies that define the impacts from a digital transformation perception i.e. a mixture of those technologies (Anshari et al., 2023).

The constant transformation that the making things digital are bringing along is having a most important influence on the employees at several levels like knowledge, rationalization, efficiency, performance, skill set, and so on (Rumaizi et al., 2023). The internal education of the company is improved by digital learning platforms through hosting personalized training and developmental programs for workers and leaders, in which they can join the training in arrangement with their work schedules, coordinated with their self-pacing and selection of theme (Sait & Anshari, 2021). These new training techniques support the acquisition of skills depending on the policies the administrations follow, and which instructive systems fail to address. Though, this, on the conflicting, demands the workers can uninterruptedly learn to retain with the developments of technology and avoid rationalization in the long run.

Recently, new digital technologies and their advantages were explored by conducting numerous inventiveness to all the workers (Omar & Anshari, 2023). This often includes transformations of key business processes and affects products and processes, as well as organizational ideas and organizational structures. Firms require to develop organizational practices to administrate these multifaceted transformations. A significant method is to express a digital transformation policy that acts as a fundamental idea to incorporate the whole prioritization, coordination, and execution of digital transformations within an organization. The manipulation and incorporation of digital techniques frequently distress huge parts of corporations and even exceed their borders, by affecting products, sales channels, commercial processes, and logistics. Potential advantages of digitization are manifold and include rises in efficiency or sales, modernizations in value creation, and also innovative methods of interaction with clients, among others. As a result, whole business models can be replaced or reshaped (Chanias, 2017). Because of this extensive scope and the far-reaching consequences, digital transformation plans aim to organize and order the several self-determining threads of digital transformation. To account for their company-spanning features, digital transformation policies cut across other commercial policies and should be associated with them. While there are several ideas of IT policies, these mostly describe the present and the upcoming operational events, the essential application systems and substructures, and the suitable organizational and fiscal framework to provide IT to perform commercial processes within a business. Therefore, IT policies generally concentrate on the organization of the IT infrastructure within a firm, with rather inadequate influence on driving inventions in commercial development. To some degree, this limits the customer-centric and product-centric chances that rise from innovative digital technologies, which frequently cross borders of firms. Additionally, IT policies present system-centric road maps to the upcoming usages of technologies in organizations, but they do not consider the transformation of products, methods, and mechanical characteristics that concur with the incorporation of technologies. Digital transformation policies take on a dissimilar perception and pursue dissimilar targets. According to a business-centric perception, these policies concentrate on the transformation of products, methods, and mechanical characteristics because of innovative techniques. Their scope is more broadly intended and obviously contains digital events at the interface with or completely on the side of clients, like digital techniques as part of customer products. This establishes a clear variance to process computerization and optimization, since digital transformation policies exceed the process paradigm, and comprise changes to and consequences for services, products, and commercial models. Digital business policies frequently deliberate the possibilities and the impacts of digital technologies for organizations.

DIGITAL TRANSFORMATION

Digital transformation is approximately adopting disruptive techniques to enhance effectiveness, social welfare, and value creation. Several multilateral organizations, national governments, and industry associations have produced strategic-foresight studies to ground their long-term strategies (Almunawar & Anshari, 2020). By recommending the implementation of public strategies regarding digital transformation, such groups assume to attain the goals. Digital transformation is expected to grow rapidly each year. Digitization has a proven effect on decreasing joblessness, raising quality of life, and increasing citizens' access to public services. Finally, digitization permits governments to work with greater efficiency and transparency.(Altenmüller et al., 2017; Shukla, 2016; JW Creswell, 2017). But some obstacles are reducing its dissemination, like insufficient or overly heterogeneous structures of company or philosophies, the absence of ROI (return on investment) visibility and digital transformation policies, and even the insight of cannibalization of current industries. External obstacles also occur, like the absence of recognition of in what way digital transformation will support all of the cultures, a lack of skills and a skilled worker, absent or insufficient regulation and customer safety, absent or inadequate infrastructure, and poor access to funding, mostly for medium and small-scale businesses.

Digital transformation was a basis of constant private enterprise and commercial dynamism, mainly in technology-intensive businesses. These firms have modernized themselves to function simultaneously in two different methods. The standard method retains traditional businesses and processes running, whereas a disruptive method pursues extra chances to exploit new marketplaces and revolutionize technologies, developments, services, or products. The market leaders are ahead of their competitors because they establish and commercialize new technologies to address clients' upcoming performance requirements. Though, these firms don't want to disassemble their current cash cows. So, they're not often at the forefront of commercializing innovative technologies that don't initially encounter the requirements of mainstream clients and that appeal to only small-scale or developing markets. So, disruptive firms discover the occupation gaps left by the market leaders. This is a source of invention and market change, which Clayton Christensen demonstrated by utilizing price and efficiency data from the hard-disk drive industry (Nwankpa & and Roumani, 2016). Organization for Economic Co-operation and Development studies has identified that 3D printing, robots, and associated devices have interrupted efficiency in their particular markets (Sarstedt et al., 2017; Homburg et al., 2019; Shahbaz et al., 2018). Similarly, some of the software technologies were disruptive, but this is because of their strategic significance, leading to their dispersion, implementation, and perceived value in different market segments through the initial markets. Some of the software technologies can't be deemed disruptive because they haven't found value recognition outside their preliminary markets.

Digital Transformation in Manufacturing Companies

Digital transformation mostly includes production methods in most sectors. This is most typical for industrial corporations. Decreasing expenses by digitizing the methods of developing, testing, and making innovative products is of paramount importance. Mobile applications are more significant to improve the production processes and internal communications of workers than to interact with clients who are mostly not end-users. Huge databases and information processing are more concentrated on production (Staab et al., 2016). The digitization of production processes creates several chances to enlarge the business and for its globalization/internationalization. However, the digitization of production processes creates several chances for the growth of business and its internationalization in traditional economic sectors. The industry's traditional value chain of original equipment manufacturers (OEMs), vendors, providers, and the aftermarket has been interrupted by innovative, digitally astute entrants in both the current and extended value chain. Innovative techniques contain propelled occupational model inventions that have confronted and prolonged the typical value chain in providing innovative facilities and products to the customer (Schildt, 2017). The digital trends result in the increasing relevance of innovative entrants in traditional segments and the formation of innovative segments (Almunawar et al., 2020). The regulatory practices, ecological trends, the expansion of innovative commercial models, changes in consumer behavior, and advances in connectivity technology rules the speed of this transformation. The effect was perceived typically in the after-sales phase of the value-added chain. Though, digital has an important transformational effect on R&D, assembly, procurement, promotion, and sales. In the parts segment, by the year 2025 through online 10% to 15% of all worldwide revenue will be created, and for service and parts Fretailing, China will be the most gorgeous marketplace for revenue development in digitization. Companies in the manufacturing process must also reply to fundamental expectations of consumers around privacy in data and security. The capability to manage and secure customer information is a challenge confronted by most industries in this more and more digital world. Digital transformation needs an in-depth evaluation of the present condition of commercial models and business methods in the organization. The analysis precedes the growth of a digital transformation policy. The analysis should respond to queries gathered into several areas like Digital Transformation Attitude: Managing Support for Digital Business Strategy; The degree of usage of digital techniques in the work of staff; The degree of usage of digital communication channels; Digital infrastructure; Digital tools that encounter client requirements and internal methods; Investments in digital solutions - what resources can be allocated to methods of digital transformation. The analysis should emphasize several key areas like suppliers, users, and partners, stockholders, organizational leadership, and organizational staff. The analysis should demonstrate in what way an organization's digitization will produce more value for customers, in what way it will help investor relations, in what way it will improve interaction with partners, in what way it will change corporate culture, and in what way efficiently the change in organization and process to digital transformation (Wessel et al., 2021). Digital transformation also comprises the provision of facilities of similar high quality through all access channels at any time utilizing mobile applications and cloud services.

Technology Aspects of Digital Business Transformation

Cloud Computing

Cloud computing is a model that allows a user or organisation to access a shared pool of configurable computing resources like servers, networks, applications, storage, and services through the Internet. These can be quickly supplied and discharged with minimal interaction among service providers or organization effort. These types of cloud models endorse availability and are comprised of

- four deployment models like Hybrid Cloud, Public Cloud, Community Cloud, and Private Cloud.
- three service models like Cloud IaaS (Infrastructure as a Service), Cloud PaaS (Platform as a Service), and Cloud SaaS (Software as a Service).
- five important features like Measured Service, Fast elasticity, Resource pooling, Broad network access, On-demand self-service.

The most important enabling techniques contain:

- fast WAN ie wide-area networks,
- powerful, cheap server computers, and
- high-performance virtualization for commodity hardware (Al-Ruithe et al., 2018).

Cloud computing is an innovative technology for enterprises. Firms in all vertical markets and sizes of the company will increasingly depend on public cloud services. Though, some variances will apply. Huge enterprises (around 250 workers), who already signify more than 80% of present cloud spending, will continue investing more than SMEs (small and middle enterprises). Between SMEs, larger ones (with 100 to 249 workers) are probable to rise spending quicker than smaller ones. The adoption of the cloud in the EU resulted in tangible financial benefits between enterprises. The most significant advantages of cloud computing are a reduction of expenditures, technical employees, and hard work. Commercial benefits from cloud computing are (Saini et al., 2019)

- Reduced total cost - advantages of cloud services resulted from economies of scale that an access provider can attain.
- Expectable costs – generally cloud services are paid each and every month or depending on the usage with small or no upfront costs. This implies that rather than creating a considerable preliminary capital investment, services or technology are bought by present functioning expenses.
- Access to the top technology - cloud services allow administrations to profit from the best technologies, without making any preliminary expenses.
- Charging in usage - administrations pay for actual instead of maximum usage in the model of cloud services. Even now the implementation of the cloud is common and still rising in the EU in both the public and private sectors.
- For customers that have used cloud, the attraction for additional adoption associate with effectiveness, flexibility, and agility – for those that were not yet introduced minimum expenses and adaptability are the most important attractions.

- Commercial benefits encompassed higher efficiency (41%), more efficient mobile working (46%), more usage of standard processes (35%), improved capability to enter innovative business areas (33%), and the capability to initiate in new places (32%). Over the past few years, cloud techniques were emerging extremely fast, and predictions express that this trend will endure as they offer a device for optimum resource efficiency. The emphasis will endure on the management of security and service. The IoT (Internet of things) is the internetworking of physical devices, automobiles (also called "smart devices" and "connected devices"), constructions, and other substances - embedded with a software package, electronics, actuators, sensors, and network connectivity that permit such objects to accumulate and exchange data. The IoT is defined in 2013 by the IoTGSI (Global Standards Initiative on the Internet of Things) as "the substructure of the information society." The IoT permits objects to be controlled or sensed remotely across current network infrastructure, producing chances for more direct incorporation of the natural environment into computerized systems and resultant in enhanced effectiveness, precision, and financial benefit along with decreased human interference (Clohessy et al., 2017; Itten et al., 2020; Borangiu et al., 2019; Camarinha-Matos et al., 2019; Heilig et al., 2017).

Mobile Computing

Cloud IoT service is a portion of several effective business information systems. Mobile Technology is a significant part of digital transformation techniques.

- Mobile technologies realize the aim of digital transformation and offer consistent collaboration with the client at all touchpoints with business.
- The development of a mobile digital business platform based on tablets or smartphones.
- Business converting society and the worldwide economy is work flexibility and digital relationship.
- The advantages of mobile techniques consist of greater efficiency, 26% more profitable in comparison to normal. The usage of mobile techniques in commercial and the present level of incorporation among techniques are completely triggered by the requirements of the company and concentrated on optimum business processes management (Abolhassan, F., 2017).

Big Data and Data Analysis

The volume of commercial information (terabytes and progressively petabytes of information) recommends why handling and examining it is a challenge. It's no longer effective for data warehouses to achieve single, standardized loads. In a cloud model, pooling data resources permits superior flexibility and quicker invention for dynamic business requirements. Cloud computing has altered the factors that have imposed the outdated relational database limitations because it delivers virtualization, dynamic resource allocation, and considerable economies of scale to manage huge quantities of data (On-Piu Chan, 2020).

DEFINITION OF THE DIGITAL TRANSFORMATION

Digitization

Based on the context, there are numerous dissimilar definitions of "digitization" which vary. One of the most widespread associations with the term digitization is the conversion to digital from analog. Investigators across dissimilar areas would describe digitization as the conversion of some kind of physical or analog artifact into a digital artifact. One (simple) instance of this would be taking a picture and converting it into a digital image. One (more multifaceted) instance would be a synthesizer. A sound is created by synthesizers through "constant variables like altering voltages" instead of binary 0s and 1s (Schallmo & and Williams, 2018). The first description can be well-thought-out a more transformation-oriented definition. The next description could be perceived as a process-oriented definition. Firms should not merely convert analog things into digital objects just to follow the existing trends. Bendor-Samuel, Peter (2017) argue that any material with two distinguished states can store and interconnect digitized signals. "This has inspired numerous scholars to express the "immaterial" (Jarlbrink & Snickars, 2017). quality of information produced through digitization while deemphasizing the quantifiable systems (transistors) on which that information is retained" (Milosevic et al., 2018). This meaning of digitization highlights the advanced method of mediation among immaterial (i.e. business methods) and material (i.e. sensors). Moreover, some manufacturing authorities were also produced extra definitions of digitization. For instance, Cisco has well-defined digitization as "the collaboration of people, method[s], information and things to offer intelligence and actionable perceptions that enable commercial consequences" (Khin & Ho, 2019). This definition focuses on the significance of data and methods but also emphasizes the newly acquired knowledge which is the most important variance among digitization and Business Process Reengineering (BPR). Another specialist, Garnter, describes digitization by indicating, "the goal is to generate and offer innovative value to clients, not just enhance what is already being offered or completed" (Forni, 2016). Moreover, digitization is defined as digitally empowering physical or analog things to implement artifacts into business methods with the ultimate purpose of obtaining newly formed facts and producing innovative value for the shareholders.

Digitalization

Digitalization is well-defined as fundamental variations made to commercial models and commercial operations based on newly attained facts gained through value-added digitization inventiveness. In 1971, the first usage of the term "digitalization" can be found. Robert Machal said about the "digitalization of society" regarding the limitations and possibilities for computer-based research. A digital consulting business, I-SCOOP (2016), provides a brief definition of digitalization. "Digitalization implies the usage of digital techniques and data (natively digital and digitized) to produce income, enhance business, transform/replace business methods (not just digitizing them) and produce a situation for digital business, whereby digital information is at the fundamental" (Lombardi, 2019; Shah, 2018).

Digital Transformation

The digital transformation is otherwise known as "digitalization". At present, it is described infrequently in the past study. Digital transformation is described as a societal phenomenon. Certainly, it is supposed as an important evolution of society, obsessed by generations is known as "digital" for which digital techniques are extremely deep-rooted in their principles and day-to-day practices. In this context, corporations can adapt themselves by developing a new one or altering their business models. Though, the digital transformation of corporations was considered a business model appears arguable and partial because it can impact other components of an organization like working environment, organizational structure, principles, and even beliefs. Moreover, digital transformation is described as "a troublesome or incremental alteration method. It begins with the implementation and usage of digital techniques, then developing into an implicit complete alteration of an organization, or intentioned to follow supply chain". (Butt, Javaid., 2020)

STRATEGIC IMPERATIVES OF DIGITAL TRANSFORMATION OR PRINCIPLES OF DIGITAL INFORMATION

Standard, set up organizations have arrived at an advanced tipping point. Following quite a while of misusing data innovations to improve the productivity of their activities and intensify their correspondences, they should now move their concentration to advanced to convey more noteworthy client esteem. Pioneers face an obvious decision: change carefully in the interest of clients, or danger of being deserted by them for carefully empowered contenders, problematic market contestants, or new advanced business developments.

Computerized change requires dire and basic change. Achievement relies upon raising items and administrations into carefully empowered arrangements and client communications into connecting with, client-driven encounters. The organizations that have done so are receiving the benefits. A new report by the Massachusetts Institute of Technology and Accenture reports that organizations who arrive at a more elevated level of advanced development are 26% more beneficial, become 9% quicker and accomplish 12% higher market valuations than their industry peers. But leaders are struggling to chart a clear digital transformation path and execute it effectively (Ross, Jeanne W et al., 2017). Most report that their digital investments have disappointed the bottom line. Sure, they note some successes—a great app here that attracts new users or better data that helps to customize products. But the kind of digital transformation that unleashes new value for the customer? That's not common.

There are a lot of reasons why administrations discover moving historical computerized listing points to release client esteem is moderate and troublesome. For single, numerous organizations start by appointing such a large number of choices to computerized offices that might be extraordinary at innovation however need client knowledge. Then once more they work with the executive's consultancies whose broad industry aptitude can daze them to advancement development openings in the interest of clients. Repeatedly, the quest for advanced change isn't vital as specialists, intellectuals and organizations act like world-renowned children in a sweets store, pursuing the following computerized craze without a perspective on what clients need most.

While digitization has been reworking the principles for development for quite a long time, representatives load up, and investors are currently provoking pioneers to outline next-level procedures. Set up organizations have more in danger, however, those that accomplish this change consolidate current qualities with computerized aptitude and can accomplish unprecedented development.

ORGANIZATIONAL PERFORMANCE

Organizational performances are the definitive dependent variable of interest for investigators anxious with just around any extent of management. Marketplace competition for clients, capital, and inputs make organizational performance important to the endurance and accomplishment of the contemporary business. As a significance, this concept has attained a fundamental role as the considered aim of contemporary manufacturing activity. Promotion, human resources (HR), processes, and policy are all eventually judged by their influence on organizational performance. Measurement is important in permitting investigators and executives to estimate the specific activities of companies and administrators, in which organizations stand vis-à-vis their competitors, and in what way companies develop and accomplish over time. Its significance as the ultimate appraising standard is reflected in its pervasive usage as a dependent variable. In comparison to the leading part that organizational performance performs in the organizational area is the restricted consideration paid by investigators to what performance is and in what way it is measured. The definition of organizational performance is an unexpectedly open query with few articles utilizing constant definitions and events (Lombardi, 2019). Performance is so widespread in organization research that its structure and definition are not often obviously justified; instead, its correctness, no matter what method, is incontestably presumed (Iqbal et al., 2019).

Organizational Efficiency Versus Organizational Performance

The main variance between organizational efficiency and organizational performance is that the person can use it efficiently to assess just about every process that makes your business run. Though, efficiency is always about the financial prices and the results of doing something. Efficiency is particularly significant when it comes to evaluate the return-on-investment of marketing and sales (Lombardi, R. 2019).

Organizational efficiency is a wider concept that encapsulates organizational performance, but with a foundation in legislative philosophy that fascinate alternative performance goals (George et al., 2019). Generally, strategic management research and management research more definitely, has taken a more limited experimental view, highlighting the fundamental part of the stock market, financial, and accounting consequences. Organizational performance includes three detailed regions of company consequences:

(a)   stockholder return (over-all stockholder return, financial value-added, etc.);
(b)   product market performance (market share, sales, etc.); and
(c)   financial performance (return on investment, return on resources, incomes, etc.).

Organizational efficiency is wider and fascinates organizational performance and also the plethora of internal performance results normally related to more effective or efficient operations and other external events that associate with deliberations that are wider than those simply related to financial evaluation (either by stockholders, clients, or managers), like CSR (corporate social responsibility).

RELATIONSHIP BETWEEN DIGITAL TRANSFORMATION AND ORGANIZATIONAL PERFORMANCE

The development ensures that a class endures the fluctuating environments in the world. Correspondingly, digital development makes sure that a business can navigate through all technical changes that happen across the world. Nonstop invention and growth aid to enhance business outcomes. All incompetencies were eliminated by digital business transformation and even leads to more possibilities for growth.

Digital transformation is an initial transformation in what way an organization transports value to its clients. Digital transformation is altering the way business is performed and, in several situations, generating new modules of businesses. Businesses are taking a step back with digital transformation, and reentering everything they do, from interior systems to client communications both in-person and online. Digital transformation offers a valuable chance for fundamental business purposes, like HR and finance, to transfer from manual processes and systematize key areas such as payroll, permitting leaders to concentrate on extensive business chances.

Digital transformations bring complex advantages to a work. Several factors result in digital transformations like competition, regulatory rules, developing economy, market environments, customer performance, and much more. The important elements for an effective digital transformation can be an attractive site, an authoritative logo design, and much more. Additionally, there are data storage, updated in process, etc. that are also a portion of a digital transformation. Digital transformation leads to an exceptional chance to provide a remodel to the business developments. These techniques are produced over the period and frequently have events that are time-consuming and redundant. Such responsibilities can be cut down with digitalization. Business developments like communication, analytics, and data storage can become more cooperative and flexible with the usage of new technical improvements. This leads to exploiting the revenues and create tasks swift. The occupation can interchange at a rapid pace and pool the remaining resources towards additional development and improvement. Clients are the soul and heart of a business and create the driving force for it. Consequently, client experience is energetic for the accomplishment of a business. The digital business has an improved client experience to provide in comparison to an outdated business. As information, communication, and analytics all become solid and cooperative, the flow of information is rapid, and therefore more appropriate and pleasing products can be produced for the clients.

Old structures and methods must be reconsidered, and new technologies can be implemented for commerce to stay inexpensive within their manufacturing. Businesses are confronted with several challenges as they direct their method with the help of digital transformation. This hurdle can vary from limited funds for innovative technology to the nonexistence of the know-how or expertise essential to level innovative digital inventiveness. Then the one challenge that is vital to overwhelm is making an efficient digital strategy (Wertz, Jia 2018).

Strategy is what gives industries the outline they want to efficiently exploit the digital tools. And short of it, funds and efforts can go wasted. As an illustration, a company with millions or thousands of social media supporters that don't involve with them successfully to change those supporters is a seamless example of jumping on the digital transformation trend but not having a strategy in place to exploit on the chance (Wertz, Jia 2018). Numerous organizations and devices have positively influenced the business, for example, a logo creator, a web designer, and so forth since they could perceive the need and potential for such items. Computerized change likewise assists organizations with stretching out and offer more highlights to their current clients and subsequently expanding the profits.

With the advanced change, the progression of data gets quick. Divisions cannot just store client data, for example, past purchasing history and inclinations yet additionally make these subtleties accessible with the client relationship offices. Outfitted with this knowledge, the agents can make redid benefits just as help keep up enduring associations with the clients. The computerized change of business forestalls the bottleneck of information and data. As there is a brisk progression between the departmental progression of data and the end of excess undertakings, the effectiveness of the business increments. This can help lessen certain working expenses related to complex and tedious work processes. In a data-driven environment, the board knows about all the potential roads for development and development. Also, with a solid client base, client relations, a quick progression of data, and mechanized work processes, associations think that it is simpler to develop and extend.

For example, an association with a solid site can look forward towards improved logo thoughts. With the computerized change, the best way to look is ahead. As firms join the advanced upset, they think that it is simpler to make more formative chances that advantage the labor force, income just as the clients. As this trifecta becomes content, the business is viewed as an inside and out progress.

To empower computerized change and modernization of firms, progressed human resources are required. Each region and branch of a business ought to be available to be affected by such innovative makeover. Industry 4.0 can be characterized as an umbrella term, signifying an assortment of late ideas, just as various connected orders inside the business change the business tasks (Nwankpa & and Roumani, 2016). The variables of advanced change taken in this investigation incorporate big data, CPS, IoT, and interoperability (Pousttchi et al., 2019). Such innovations can possibly empower a change in perspective towards business settings (Nadeem et al., 2018; Wang et al., 2020), and the very marvel can be additionally explained as an innovation push.

PREVIOUS EMPIRICAL STUDIES FROM

Considerate in what way digitalization is distressing and altering leadership practices in administrations is important because nowadays digitization is implemented in almost all segments of the financial and HR in a very deep manner and at an extremely quick pace. From production, big data is utilized in sectors like logistics, trade, farming, well-being, financial services, and client service. And also new techniques and solutions to determine their commercial forward and to continue to be in the extremely inexpensive marketplace. This suggests fluctuations in the work system and financial system, it also suggests fluctuations in thinking, leadership management, and acting. This digital transformation can be supported when the company requirements to change from their outdated, ordered form to a flexible, reorganized organization with a project/team-oriented leadership to retain pace with the multifaceted and quickly altering environment (digital-centric business) and the growing client needs (customer-led market). Moreover, the generation alters to the digital natives (Generation Y and Z) from the baby boomer, which have exclusive features and abilities when compared to historical generations, will need innovative leadership and working structures. Leadership 4.0, innovative leadership, or digital leadership suggest the utilization of the new digital media for communication and teamwork, but it also needs the conversion of leadership policies and approaches to digital realism. The upcoming leader can use innovative techniques and resolutions, adjust himself fast to variations and succeed them to have a developer spirit and can absorb rapidly. They should also be appropriate, reliable, and passionately intellectual, and should result democratically, share responsibilities, be in control, critical and supportive, and endorse networks, belief in and stimulate workers, and provide them consistent feedback (Foerster-Metz et al., 2018). From the perspective of an author, the so-called VOPA (networking, openness, participation, agility) leadership model intended by Tay et al (2017), integrates all those features and can be utilized as the fundamental model for digital management by encompassing each and every fundamental element for an effective commercial and organizational culture in the digital age and reflecting also the requirements from the innovative generations. The fundamental of digital leadership constructed on belief is not innovative because in human relationships "hope" is one of the important emotions. The leader requires hope in the organization and the workers require hope in the leader and conversely, then only the correct conclusions can be made and the essential activities can be engaged within the period of growing insecurity, complexity, and speediness. All the additional four facts are supportive of the formation and maintenance of hope. Uncertainty and fear can be avoided through honesty and transparency and provide a vibrant opinion and can understand easily. Contribution and participation provide the opportunity to vigorously involve, adjust and undertake accountability. Agility permits us to react earlier and framework-based and networking allows and supports the distribution, cooperation, and improvement. Leaders require to have a personal and direct meeting with all workers, specifically, to the innovative capacities from the succeeding generations since they are the developer of change in the digital environment (Hodkiewicz et al., 2020).

The innovative digital techniques and resolutions are not just inspiring the requirement for change, they also allow and support the alteration itself. Some instances are big data in mixture with learning algorithms that allow leaders and organizations to better forecast and regulate their methods and applications, permit them to improve the work like flows of material, aimed marketing events, and assessing worker's tasks or performance. Similarly, the incorporation of interactive media can support the engagement with many more workers in dispersed administrations as it was probably earlier with ordinary conference structures. Here the information can be shared by leaders who can also provide consistent updates, foster comprehension, and generate belief in the spread labor force simultaneously. Additionally, the convention of data-enabled TMS ie talent-management systems (according to mathematic data analysis) can increase the number of expressively estimated workers against their information and capabilities, rise the accuracy of these assessments and free up the management to focus on the personal connection (Foerster-Metz et al., 2018). But it should keep in mind that the way techniques interferes or takes over in some of the decision-making events also accepts the hazard of reducing the imaginative adaption to a problematic issue and the damage of the past background and the administrations will be progressively reliant on the workers of these new techniques as they most probably lack internal incomes with the ability to program and route this system. Therefore, the leaders and managers are required to examine their occupational and marketplace condition initially, then choose about the accurate structure and policy and include their workers in the digital transformation.

DIGITAL TRANSFORMATION IN DEVELOPING COUNTRIES

In the time of the Fourth Industrial Revolution, Digital Transformation, and Artificial Intelligence, a significant worry for the two business analysts and policymakers were the effects of these significant changes in transit the economy capacities. Especially such progressions are required to influence, between others, the pace of advancement of the work rate, finance, and work efficiency. Advanced change can easily matters for a few while creating natural life tougher for other people. It very well may be a motor for accelerating the development of the financial system and simultaneously, it very well may be a capacity in upsetting this development if the proper structure for its consolidation doesn't occur. The effects are yet dubious and will rely upon a few unique elements including the degree of advancement, the steady degree of joblessness, the nature of the actual and human investment, and the size of the populace.

This section aims to examine the connection between financial development, digital transformation, efficiency, and service for a set of developed and developing nations. The nations were chosen subsequent the international organizations of developed and developing countries of UNCTAD (2019), UNDP (2019), and UN (2019), (Musakwa & Odhiambo, 2019) with possible comprehensive LMS ie least squares method. The article is concerned with probing the influences of digital transformation upon the example of developing nations and therefore arise with appropriate and exciting inference for such nations. Another influence is utilizing a single complex directory for advanced change that is equivalent across the selected set of developed and evolving nations, rather than utilizing single lists each seizing a dissimilar component of computerized change. The pre-owned list is DEI (digital evolution index) which replicates the complete position of computerized change within the nation and contemplates both the market interest sides of computerized change.

Digital Transformation Lists and Macro-Economic Variable

A few establishments, studies, and ventures have demonstrated wide revenue in figuring files that measure the position of computerized change across the various nations. In the accompanying segments, the goal is to break down the regular records in the past examination and look at their connections to GNI per capita, work efficiency, and business. Consequently, in the wake of investigating the distinctive records, the paper will continue in the examination by picking a specific file of advanced change and study its relationship to the chose macroeconomic factors utilizing econometric models.

One of the regular proportions of computerized change is the Digital Adoption Index (DAI); it is an overall record that quantifies nations' advanced selection across three components of the economy: individuals, government, and business, and it stresses more the "supply-side" of computerized reception. The generally DAI is determined as a straightforward normal of the three sub-files. Each sub-record incorporates the mechanical prerequisites important for advancing computerized improvement, upgrading efficiency, and encouraging business wide-based development (Group, 2016).

In 2018, Euler Hermes distributed the new version of the Enabling Digitalization Index (EDI) with usage in 115 nations to gauge their abilities in controlling advanced organizations and in supporting customary organizations. The list assesses nations as far as their help to digitalization and henceforth positions them as per computerized agreeable guideline with its diverse institutional, calculated, and specialized perspectives (Sven Cravotta, 2019). It, consequently, centers around the hierarchical and empowering climate of advanced change inside the country and on the help that the administration coordinates towards empowering mechanical development.

Likewise, The Digital Economy and Society Index (DESI), is a composite record created by Cámara and is being distributed each year by the European Commission since 2014. It centers around EU nations specifically to gauge the means and systems embraced by those nations towards advancing the computerized economy and society. It is developed of significant markers on Europe's present computerized approaches. The DESI includes five head strategies: network, human resources, utilization of web access, incorporation of computerized innovation, and advanced public administrations (Mazzucato, 2018).

Another list is DiGiX which is a composite record of 18 sub-pointers determined for 99 nations around the globe. It means to quantify the level of digitalization in those nations through get-together and grouping data identified with three sides: supply conditions (framework and expenses), request conditions (specialized cultural and legislative appropriation), and institutional climate (guidelines and coordinations) (Aly, 2020).

In a comparable setting, the DEI is an information-driven general assessment of the advancement of the computerized economy across 60 nations, accumulating more than 100 distinct markers across four key drivers: supply conditions, request conditions, institutional climate, and development, and change. The list, hence, reflects both the current circumstance of advanced change inside the country, and proportionately the advancement rate at which the nation is improving. This has the capability of distinguishing and giving applicable ramifications to venture and advancement. This is accomplished because of the communication among four drivers:

1. the country's advanced framework;
2. the interest for innovation;
3. the institutional climate; and
4. innovation and advancement.

It also gives features on the developing dangers and difficulties related to the consistent reliance on computerized innovation (Zuti, 2018).

Because of information accessibility and importance to the target of the examination, it was picked to investigate three advanced change records that catch various elements of computerized change and are simultaneously accessible for the non-industrial nations. Those records are the DEI, the EDI, and the DAI. It is accepted that utilizing a solitary composite record that covers those various elements of advanced change and is simultaneously normalized across the various nations has the capability of indicating pertinent and sound outcomes. The relationship to the diverse macroeconomic factors is investigated in the coming area.

DIGITAL TRANSFORMATION IN DEVELOPED COUNTRIES

Advanced change as another and present-day term in business and mechanical writing is normally characterized as the mix of computerized innovation into the business that outcomes in, once in a while basic, changes in business activity and conveyance of significant worth to clients. It is influencing operational work as well as impacts working society, human relations, and speed of progress, on microeconomic just as macroeconomics level. The world is seeing development difficulties and consistent political stuns which some of the time cause tough situations for nations' legislatures in managing regular issues just as improvement issues. That is constraining nations to search for strategies that will animate development and make new openings – make their economies more grounded. Advanced change is a mix of computerized innovation into a business that brings about central changes in the manner the world works together conveys and creates on a public and worldwide level. There is an expansion in innovative public going through which is associated with an increment in the requirement for cutting edge just as the significance and advantages that it brings to the advancement of the economy. This purported advanced or innovative area is one of the essential areas in the main world economies, beginning from the European Union and the US. EU remembered it in the essential record "Europe 2020" which considers this to be a critical factor in keen development dependent on tech information and advancement. Europe, particularly western and northern Europe, is attempting to keep its intensity in the worldwide tech field with the USA and quick developing nations, for example, India and China just as Asian tech monsters such are Singapore, South Korea, and Japan. There is an expansion in the European country's interest in computerized change through private and public ICT area advancement which as a rule emphatically affects monetary development just as key markers such are GDP, profitability, and work.

These days the subject of computerized business change is generally talked about both in scholarly and business networks. This change can be characterized as a change at various degrees of business associations that fuses both the broad use of computerized advances to improve existing business cycles and rehearses and the investigation of computerized development to change the general plan of action. The noticed conversation on the need for the mechanical and business parts of advanced change confirms the need for an arrangement among IT and business, explicitly in the joining of IT-technique and business procedure to accomplish characterized objectives (Lezina et al., 2016; Kane et al., 2015; Urbach et al., 2017). This conversation additionally audits the fundamental comprehension of the significance of this pattern, however, there is as yet a requirement for an explanation of the separate difficulties and impacts (Bley et al., 2016). From a scholarly perspective, the part of IT in associations has changed over the long run from "IT as a help work" to "IT as a driver for business advancement" (Kiesling et al., 2010). It addresses the developing significance of IT for associations and their capacity to confront more technique situated difficulties. In like manner, the situation of the IT-director or CIO has changed generally in evolved nations in the course of the most recent couple of years. Also, an organization's capacity to change progressively relies on its capacity to change its IT or purported "IT deftness" (Nissen & Von Rennenkampff, 2015). High IT readiness can add to expanded business deftness and accordingly make an upper hand.

Within this exploration, the attention is on organizations' present perspectives concerning its part just as the arrangement of IT rehearses with the plan of action and targets. The exploration is by and large in accordance with existing investigations for created nations in the writing. In the United States, a progression of studies longitudinally investigated the job and errands of IT just as attributes of the CIO. Following a comparable methodology, the examination (Nissen & Termer, 2014) researched business as usual in Germany. The outcomes show a specific similitude, as could be normal with both, the US and Germany as completely developed nations.

As opposed to this, the current investigations on Russian experience and practice with IT executives center generally around restricted viewpoints, for example, the capacity to withstand and rapidly recuperate from troublesome occurrences including impromptu personal time and potential information misfortunes (Ivanova et al., 2015). In outline, there isn't a lot of information on how the changing job and circles of the obligation of IT are examined in the writing for created nations are acknowledged and executed by IT the board in Russia. One of the primary more extensive endeavors to survey the job and elements of IT offices in Russian organizations was embraced in (Lezina et al., 2016). The creators infer that today the job of IT at numerous Russian organizations is, best case scenario, an empowering influence, frequently an instrument to build effectiveness, and in a sizeable number of cases, it still just is a helpful work. Specifically, there is a stamped absence of review IT as a driver of development. The current commitment fabricates and develops these underlying outcomes.

FRAMEWORK

From the review of previous literature, the conceptual framework for the study will be framed as given below.

Figure 1. Conceptual framework

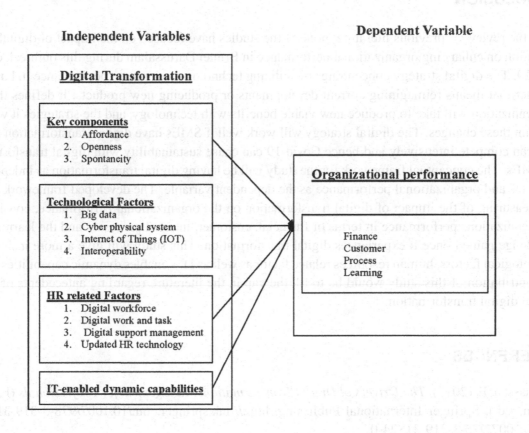

Previous researchers have noted that digital transformation has resulted positive significant impact on businesses performance and productivity on a macro level. Several studies in the past have focused on impact of digital transformation on organization performance. Also, empirical studies have indicated that dynamic capabilities enhances the organizational performance when implementing new technology. Several factors of digital transformation such as IoT, big data, cyber physical systems (CPS) and interoperability have the potential to enable a paradigm shift in the direction of business settings. Despite the discussion on digital technology and its adverse effects, in the current scenario it offers an valuable solution.

The conceptual framework builds for this research aim to illustrate and consolidate the measures into an omnibus assessment of the impact of digital transformation on organizational performance in Brunei Darussalam perspective. It defines relevant variable and maps out how it relates between dependent and independent variables. Considering digital transformation as independent variables and having few factors such as key component: affordance, openness, spontaneity, HR related factors, technological factors and IT-enable dynamic is expected to show changes and how it affects the dependent variables. Organizational performance act as the dependent variables in this conceptual framework will enable this research to relate digital transformation and further analyze its impact in financial, customer, processes, and the learnings within the organization.

CONCLUSION

From the review of previous literature, none of the studies have focused on the impact of digital transformation on enhancing organizational performance in Brunei Darussalam during this outbreak of CO-VID-19. The digital strategy concentrates on utilizing technology to increase performance in business, whether that means reimagining current developments or producing new products. It defines the way an organization will take to produce new viable benefits with technology, and the strategies it will use to attain these changes. The digital strategy will work well if SMEs have digital transformation so that they can compete intensively and hence Covid-19 can cause sustainability with digital transformation for SMEs. The conceptual framework for the study will be having digital transformation as independent variables and organizational performance as the dependent variable. The developed framework allows the measuring of the impact of digital transformation on the organizational performance, considering the organizations performance in terms of financial, customer, internal processes and the learning and knowledge gained once it experiences digital transformation. This study will give a more insight into technological factors, human resources related factor as well as IT – enables dynamic capabilities. Thus, the contribution of this study would be to fill the gap in the literature regarding antecedents of a successful digital transformation.

REFERENCES

Abolhassan, F. (2017). *The Drivers of Digital Transformation. Management for Professionals* (F. Abolhassan, Ed.). Springer International Publishing. http://link.springer.com/10.1007/978-3-319-31824-0 doi:10.1007/978-3-319-31824-0

Al-Ruithe, M., Benkhelifa, E., & Hameed, K. (2018). Key Issues for Embracing the Cloud Computing to Adopt a Digital Transformation: A study of Saudi Public Sector. *Procedia Computer Science*. https://linkinghub.elsevier.com/retrieve/pii/S1877050918305076

Almunawar, M. N., & Anshari, M. (2020). Multi-sided networks of digital platform ecosystem: The case of ride-hailing in Indonesia. *Asia Pacific Journal of Information Systems*, *30*(4), 808–831. doi:10.14329/apjis.2020.30.4.808

Almunawar, M. N., de Pablos, P. O., & Anshari, M. (Eds.). (2023). *Digital Transformation for Business and Society: Contemporary Issues and Applications in Asia*. Taylor & Francis. doi:10.4324/9781003441298

Altenmüller, T., Bauernhansl, T., Kyek, A., & Waschneck, B. (2017). Production Scheduling in Complex Job Shops from an Industrie 4.0 Perspective: A Review and Challenges in the Semiconductor Industry. *CEUR Workshop Proceedings*. CEUR. https://ceur-ws.org/Vol-1793/paper3.pdf

Aly, H. (2020). Digital transformation, development and productivity in developing countries: is artificial intelligence a curse or a blessing? *Review of Economics and Political Science*. Emerald. https://www.emerald.com/insight/content/doi/10.1108/REPS-11-2019-0145/full/html

Anshari, M., & Almunawar, M. N. (2021). Adopting open innovation for SMEs and industrial revolution 4.0. *Journal of Science and Technology Policy Management*, *13*(2), 405–427. doi:10.1108/JSTPM-03-2020-0061

Anshari, M., Hamdan, M., Ahmad, N., Ali, E., & Haidi, H. (2023). New knowledge creation and loss during COVID-19: Sustainable knowledge management's perspective. *International Journal of Learning and Intellectual Capital*, *20*(6), 587–611. doi:10.1504/IJLIC.2023.134898

Anshari, M., Syafrudin, M., & Fitriyani, N. L. (2022). Fourth industrial revolution between knowledge management and digital humanities. *Information (Basel)*, *13*(6), 292. doi:10.3390/info13060292

Baptista, J., Stein, M.-K., Klein, S., Watson-Manheim, M. B., & Lee, J. (2020). Digital work and organisational transformation: Emergent Digital/Human work configurations in modern organisations. *The Journal of Strategic Information Systems*, *29*(2). https://linkinghub.elsevier.com/retrieve/pii/S0963868720300263

Bendor-Samuel, P. (2017). The power of digital transformation in a data-driven world. *Forbes*. https://www.forbes.com/sites/peterbendorsamuel/2017/07/21/the-power-of-digital-transformation-in-a-data-driven-world/?sh=cc5e2523f2c3

Blair, R. A., Morse, B. S., & Tsai, L. L. (2017). Public health and public trust: Survey evidence from the Ebola Virus Disease epidemic in Liberia. *Social Science & Medicine*, *172*, 89–97. doi:10.1016/j.socscimed.2016.11.016 PMID:27914936

Bley, K., Leyh, C., & Schaffer, T. (2016). *Digitization of German Enterprises in the Production Sector-Do they know how digitized they are?* AISEL. https://aisel.aisnet.org/amcis2016/EntSys/Presentations/9/

Bodrow, W. (2017). Impact of Industry 4.0 in service oriented firm. *Advances in Manufacturing*, *5*(4), 394–400. http://link.springer.com/10.1007/s40436-017-0196-3

Borangiu, T., Trentesaux, D., Thomas, A., Leitão, P., & Barata, J. (2019). Digital transformation of manufacturing through cloud services and resource virtualization. *Computers in Industry*. Elsevier. https://linkinghub.elsevier.com/retrieve/pii/S0166361519300107

BughinJ. R.KretschmerT.van ZeebroeckN. (2019). Experimentation, learning and stress: The role of digital technologies in strategy change. *Available at* SSRN 3328421. doi:10.2139/ssrn.3328421

Butt, J. (2020). A Conceptual Framework to Support Digital Transformation in Manufacturing Using an Integrated Business Process Management Approach. *Designs 4.3*, *17*.

Camarinha-Matos, L. M., Fornasiero, R., Ramezani, J., & Ferrada, F. (2019). Collaborative Networks: A Pillar of Digital Transformation. *Applied Sciences*. MDPI. https://www.mdpi.com/2076-3417/9/24/5431

Chanias, S. (2017). *Mastering digital transformation: The path of a financial services provider towards a digital transformation strategy*. AISnet. https://aisel.aisnet.org/ecis2017_rp/2/

Chen, Y.-Y. K., Jaw, Y.-L., & Wu, B.-L. (2016). Effect of digital transformation on organisational performance of SMEs. *Internet Research, 26*(1). 186–212. https://www.emerald.com/insight/content/doi/10.1108/IntR-12-2013-0265/full/html

Cillo, V., Petruzzelli, A. M., Ardito, L., & Del Giudice, M. (2019). Understanding sustainable innovation: A systematic literature review. *Corporate Social Responsibility and Environmental Management, 26*(5), 1012–1025. doi:10.1002/csr.1783

Clohessy, T., Acton, T., & Morgan, L. (2017). The Impact of Cloud-Based Digital Transformation on IT Service Providers. *International Journal of Cloud Applications and Computing, 7*(4). http://services.igi-global.com/resolvedoi/resolve.aspx?doi=10.4018/IJCAC.2017100101

Creswell, J. W. J.C. (2017). *Research design: Qualitative, quantitative, and mixed methods approaches.* Amazon. https://www.amazon.in/Research-Design-Qualitative-Quantitative-Approaches/dp/1452226105

Di Vaio, A., Syriopoulos, T., Alvino, F., & Palladino, R. (2020). *"Integrated thinking and reporting" towards sustainable business models: A concise bibliometric analysis.* Meditari Account. Res.

Ebert, C. (2019). Digital transformation. *IEEE Softw.* IEEE. https://www.chcduarte.com/dx2018.pdf

Foerster-Metz, U. S., Marquardt, K., Golowko, N., Kompalla, A., & Hell, C. (2018). Digital Transformation and its Implications on Organizational Behavior. *Journal of EU Research in Business.* https://ibimapublishing.com/articles/JEURB/2018/340873/

Forni, A. (2016). *Gartner reveals top predictions for IT organizations and users in 2017 and beyond.*

George, B., Walker, R. M., & Monster, J. (2019). Does Strategic Planning Improve Organizational Performance? A Meta-Analysis. *Public Administration Review, 79*(6), 810–819. https://onlinelibrary.wiley.com/doi/abs/10.1111/puar.13104

Group, W. B. (2016). World Development Report 2016: Digital Dividends. *World Bank Group flagship report.* World Bank Publications. https://books.google.co.in/books?id=dAl-CwAAQBAJ

Haidt, J. & Allen, N. (2020). *Scrutinizing the effects of digital technology on mental health.*

Heavin, C., & Power, D. J. (2018). Challenges for digital transformation – towards a conceptual decision support guide for managers. *Journal of Decision Systems, 27.* https://www.tandfonline.com/doi/full/10.1080/12460125.2018.1468697

Heilig, L., Schwarze, S., & Vos, S. (2017). *An analysis of digital transformation in the history and future of modern ports.* AISNET. https://aisel.aisnet.org/hicss-50/da/decision_support_for_scm/2/

Hess, T., Matt, C., Benlian, A., & Wiesböck, F. (2016). Options for formulating a digital transformation strategy. *MIS Quarterly Executive.* http://search.ebscohost.com/login.aspx?direct=true&profile=ehost&scope=site&authtype=crawler&jrnl=15401960&AN=115879199&h=QyVwVRj0ZlOg7sMRTNzRQApgAyeYo204HYsgFcdVL6%2FJdayO%2BXl7oLQDQO3IHOPYd%2BopvZ8Kw8unktp8OPzeHA%3D%3D&crl=c

Hinings, B., Gegenhuber, T., & Greenwood, R. (2018). Digital innovation and transformation: An institutional perspective. *Information and Organization, 28*(1), 52–61. https://linkinghub.elsevier.com/retrieve/pii/S1471772718300265

Hodkiewicz, M., Klüwer, J. W., Woods, C., Smoker, T., & French, T. (2020). Digitalization and reasoning over engineering textual data stored in spreadsheet tables. *IFAC-PapersOnLine, 53*(3), 239–244. https://linkinghub.elsevier.com/retrieve/pii/S2405896320301853

Homburg, C., Wielgos, D., & Kühnl, C. (2019). *Digital business capability and its effect on firm performance.* MaDoc. https://madoc.bib.uni-mannheim.de/48903/?rs=true&

Hussain, A., Shahzad, A., & Hassan, R. (2020). Organizational and Environmental Factors with the Mediating Role of E-Commerce and SME Performance. *Journal of Open Innovation, 6*(4), 196. doi:10.3390/joitmc6040196

Imran, M., & Hameed, W. (2018). Influence of Industry 4.0 on the Production and Service Sectors in Pakistan: Evidence from Textile and Logistics Industries. *Social Sciences, 7*(12), 246. https://www.mdpi.com/2076-0760/7/12/246

Iqbal, A., Latif, F., Marimon, F., Sahibzada, U. F., & Hussain, S. (2019). From knowledge management to organizational performance. *Journal of Enterprise Information Management, 32*(1), 36–59. https://www.emerald.com/insight/content/doi/10.1108/JEIM-04-2018-0083/full/html

Itten, R., Hischier, R., Andrae, A. S. G., Bieser, J. C. T., Cabernard, L., Falke, A., Ferreboeuf, H., Hilty, L. M., Keller, R. L., Lees-Perasso, E., Preist, C., & Stucki, M. (2020). Digital transformation—life cycle assessment of digital services, multifunctional devices and cloud computing. *The International Journal of Life Cycle Assessment, 25*(10). 2093–2098. http://link.springer.com/10.1007/s11367-020-01801-0

Ivanova, V. V., Kazakova, E., Lezina, T. A., Martyanova, V. N., Saltan, A. A., Anette, S., & Dirk, S. (2015). *Comparing bachelor studies in business informatics at universities in Russia and Germany.* Cyberleninka. https://cyberleninka.ru/article/n/16415853

Jarlbrink, J., & Snickars, P. (2017). Cultural heritage as digital noise: nineteenth century newspapers in the digital archive. *Journal of Documentation, 73*(6), 1228–1243. https://www.emerald.com/insight/content/doi/10.1108/JD-09-2016-0106/full/html

Kane, G. C., Palmer, D., Philips Nguyen, A., Kiron, D., & Buckley, N. (2015). Strategy, Not Technology, Drives Digital Transformation. *MIT Sloan Management Review.* Deloitte. https://sloanreview.mit.edu/projects/strategy-drives-digital-transformation/

Khin, S., & Ho, T. C. (2019). Digital technology, digital capability and organizational performance. *International Journal of Innovation Science, 11*(2), 177–195. https://www.emeraldinsight.com/doi/10.1108/IJIS-08-2018-0083

Kiesling, M., Wilke, H., & Kolbe, L. M. (2010). *Overcoming challenges for managing IT innovations in non-IT companies.* AMCIS. https://core.ac.uk/download/pdf/301344818.pdf

Kim, G., Shin, B., & Kwon, O. (2012). Investigating the value of sociomaterialism in conceptualizing IT capability of a firm. *Journal of Management Information Systems*, *29*(3), 327–362. doi:10.2753/MIS0742-1222290310

Lasi, H., Fettke, P., Kemper, H.-G., Feld, T., & Hoffmann, M. (2014). Industry 4.0. *Business & Information Systems Engineering*, *6*(4), 239–242. doi:10.1007/s12599-014-0334-4

Lezina, T., Nissen, V., Reimer, K., & Saltan, A. (2016). The Role and Tasks of IT in Russian Companies A Survey of the Status Quo. In: *GSOM Emerging Markets Conference 2016*. PurePortal. https://pureportal.spbu.ru/en/publications/the-role-and-tasks-of-it-in-russian-companies-a-surveyof-the-stat

Lombardi, R. (2019). Knowledge transfer and organizational performance and business process: past, present and future researches. *Business Process Management Journal*, *25*(1), 2–9. https://www.emerald.com/insight/content/doi/10.1108/BPMJ-02-2019-368/full/html

Makin, S. (2018). *Searching for digital technology's effects on well-being*. Outlook.

Marczewska, M., & Kostrzewski, M. (2020). Sustainable Business Models: A Bibliometric Performance Analysis. *Energies*, *13*(22), 6062. doi:10.3390/en13226062

Mazzucato, M. (2018). Mission-oriented research & innovation in the European Union. *European Commission*. https://www.obzor2020.hr/userfiles/Mazzucato Report Missions_2018.pdf

Mikalef, P., & Pateli, A. (2017). Information technology-enabled dynamic capabilities and their indirect effect on competitive performance: Findings from PLS-SEM and fsQCA. *Journal of Business Research*, *70*, 1–16. doi:10.1016/j.jbusres.2016.09.004

Milosevic, N., Dobrota, M., & Barjaktarovic Rakocevic, S. (2018). *Digital economy in Europe: Evaluation of countries' performances*, *36*(2), 861–880. https://hrcak.srce.hr/index.php?show=clanak&id_clanak_jezik=312156

Mubarak, M. F., Shaikh, F. A., Mubarik, M., Samo, K. A., & Mastoi, S. (2019). The Impact of Digital Transformation on Business Performance. *Engineering, Technology &. Applied Scientific Research*, *9*(6), 5056–5061.

Mubarak, M. F., Yusoff, W. F. W., Mubarik, M., Tiwari, S., & Kaya, K. A. (2018). Nurturing Entrepreneurship Ecosystem in a Developing Economy: Myths and Realities. *Journal of Technology Management and Business*, *6*(1). https://publisher.uthm.edu.my/ojs/index.php/jtmb/article/view/4251

Mugge, P., & Gudergan, G. (2017). The Gap Between the Practice and Theory of Digital Transformation, Whitepaper. *The 50th Hawaiian International Conference of System Science*. IEEE.

Musakwa, M. T., & Odhiambo, N. M. (2019). THE impact of remittance inflows on poverty in Botswana: an ARDL approach. *Journal of Economic Structures*, *8*(1), 42. https://journalofeconomicstructures.springeropen.com/articles/10.1186/s40008-019-0175-x

Nadeem, A., Abedin, B., Cerpa, N., & Chew, E. (2018). Editorial: Digital Transformation & Digital Business Strategy in Electronic Commerce - The Role of Organizational Capabilities. *Journal of theoretical and applied electronic commerce research*, *13*(2). https://www.scielo.cl/scielo.php?script=sci_arttext&pid=S0718-18762018000200101&lng=en&nrm=iso&tlng=en

Nissen, V., & Termer, F. (2014). Business IT-Alignment Ergebnisse einer Befragung von IT-Fuhrungsk-raften in Deutschland. *HMD Praxis der Wirtschaftsinformatik*, *51*(5), 549–560. https://link.springer.com/article/10.1365/s40702-014-0060-x

Nissen, V., & Von Rennenkampff, A. (2015). *Measuring and managing IT agility as a strategic resource-examining the IT application systems landscape*, 6(60). https://cyberleninka.ru/article/n/17214559

Nwankpa, J. K., & Roumani, Y. (2016). *IT Capability and Digital Transformation: A Firm Performance Perspective*. AISEL. https://aisel.aisnet.org/icis2016/ISStrategy/Presentations/4/

Omar, A. M., & Anshari, M. (2023). Super Smart Society 5.0: Innovation in Public Policy Post-Industry 4.0. In Digital Transformation for Business and Society (pp. 91-110). Routledge.

On-Piu Chan, J. (2020). Digital Transformation in the Era of Big Data and Cloud Computing. *International Journal of Intelligent Information Systems*, *9*(3). http://www.sciencepublishinggroup.com/journal/paperinfo?journalid=135&doi=10.11648/j.ijiis.20200903.11

Pousttchi, K., Gleiss, A., Buzzi, B., & Kohlhagen, M. (2019). Technology Impact Types for Digital Transformation. In: *2019 IEEE 21st Conference on Business Informatics (CBI)*. IEEE. https://ieeexplore.ieee.org/document/8807798/

Prester, J. (2020). *Emerging Leaders in Digital Work: Toward a Theory of Attentional Leadership*. AISEL. https://aisel.aisnet.org/icis2020/is_workplace_fow/is_workplace_fow/12/

Ross, J. (2017). How to develop a great digital strategy. *MIT Sloan Management Review, 58*(2).

Rumaizi, I. H., Anshari, M., Almunawar, M. N., & Masri, M. (2023). Maslow's Hierarchy of Needs and Digital Wallet Usage Among Youth. In *Digital Psychology's Impact on Business and Society* (pp. 179–202). IGI Global. doi:10.4018/978-1-6684-6108-2.ch008

Saini, H., Upadhyaya, A., & Khandelwal, M. K. (2019). *Benefits of cloud computing for business enterprises: A review. Proceedings of International Conference on Advancements in Computing & Management (ICACM)*. IEEE. 10.2139/ssrn.3463631

Sait, M. A., & Anshari, M. (2021). Industrial Revolution 4.0: A New Challenge to Brunei Darussalam's Unemployment Issue. [IJABIM]. *International Journal of Asian Business and Information Management*, *12*(4), 33–44. doi:10.4018/IJABIM.20211001.oa3

Sarstedt, M., Ringle, C. M., & Hair, J. F. (2017). Treating Unobserved Heterogeneity in PLS-SEM: A Multi-method Approach. In *Partial Least Squares Path Modeling*. (pp. 197–217). Springer International Publishing. http://link.springer.com/10.1007/978-3-319-64069-3_9 doi:10.1007/978-3-319-64069-3_9

Schallmo, D. R. A., & Williams, C. A. (2018). *Digital Transformation Now*. Springer. https://www.springer.com/gp/book/9783319728438

Schildt, H. (2017). Big data and organizational design – the brave new world of algorithmic management and computer augmented transparency. *Innovation*, *19*(1), 23–30. https://www.tandfonline.com/doi/full/10.1080/14479338.2016.1252043

Schwertner, K. (2017). Digital transformation of business. *Trakia Journal of Science, 15* (Suppl.1), 388–393. http://tru.uni-sz.bg/tsj/TJS_Suppl.1_Vol.15_2017/65.pdf

Shah, B. B. P. (2018). *Assessing digital transformation capabilities.* MIT. https://dspace.mit.edu/handle/1721.1/121798

Shahbaz, M. S., Chandio, A. F., Oad, M., Ahmed, A., & Ullah, R. (2018). No Title. *International Journal of Sustainable Construction Engineering and Technology, 9*(2). https://publisher.uthm.edu.my/ojs/index.php/IJSCET/article/view/3579

Shahbaz, M. S., Sohu, S., Khaskhelly, F. Z., Bano, A., & Soomro, M. A. (2019a). A Novel Classification of Supply Chain Risks. *Engineering, Technology &. Applied Scientific Research, 9*(3), 4301–4305.

Shahbaz, M. S., Soomro, M. A., Bhatti, N. U. K., Soomro, Z., & Jamali, M. Z. (2019b). The impact of supply chain capabilities on logistic efficiency for the construction projects. *Civil Engineering Journal, 5*(6), 1249–1256. doi:10.28991/cej-2019-03091329

Shukla, R. K. (2016). *Coordination Practices in Supply Chain Management, 16*(1), 44–54. https://web.a.ebscohost.com/abstract?direct=true&profile=ehost&scope=site&authtype=crawler&jrnl=097 25814&asa=Y&AN=117524981&h=kdg%2B0rzQUfc2d7vKDCs%2FmxcD12t%2BaXWAqe4UX3q KO2VUkHxdd75I%2B7tf6dzUuzwnNxen6CiEB7G6SQLKfUzuMA%3D%3D&crl=c&resultNs=Admi nWebAuth&resultLocal=ErrCrlNotAuth&crlhashurl=login.aspx%3Fdirect%3Dtrue%26profile%3Dehost %26scope%3Dsite%26authtype%3Dcrawler%26jrnl%3D09725814%26asa%3DY%26AN%3D117524981

Staab, N. (2016). *P. and & Oliver.* Digitalisierung der Dienstleistungsarbeit. https://edoc.unibas.ch/57929/

Sven Cravotta, M. G. (2019). Digitalization in German family firms – some preliminary insights. *Revistes, 4*(1). https://revistes.ub.edu/index.php/JESB/article/view/j051

Tay, H. L., & Low, S. W. K. (2017). Digitalization of learning resources in a HEI – a lean management perspective. *International Journal of Productivity and Performance Management, 66*(5), 680–694. https://www.emerald.com/insight/content/doi/10.1108/IJPPM-09-2016-0193/full/html

Urbach, N., Drews, P., & Ross, J. (2017). Digital business transformation and the changing role of the IT function. *MIS Quarterly Executive, 16* (2), 1–4. https://www.researchgate.net/profile/Nils_Urbach/publication/318113029_Digital_Business_Transformation_and_the_Changing_Role_of_the_IT_Function/links/595bb148458515117741b2a0/Digital-Business-Transformation-and-the-Changing-Role-of-the-IT-Function.pdf

Vial, G. (2019). Understanding digital transformation: A review and a research agenda. *The Journal of Strategic Information Systems, 28*(2), 118–144. https://linkinghub.elsevier.com/retrieve/pii/S0963868717302196

Wamba, S. F., Gunasekaran, A., Akter, S., Ren, S. J., Dubey, R., & Childe, S. J. (2017). Big data analytics and firm performance: Effects of dynamic capabilities. *Journal of Business Research, 70*, 356–365. doi:10.1016/j.jbusres.2016.08.009

Wang, H., Feng, J., Zhang, H., & Li, X. (2020). The effect of digital transformation strategy on performance. *International Journal of Conflict Management*, *31*(3), 441–462. https://www.emerald.com/insight/content/doi/10.1108/IJCMA-09-2019-0166/full/html

Wang, Y., McKee, M., Torbica, A., & Stuckler, D. (2019). Systematic literature review on the spread of health-related misinformation on social media. *Social Science & Medicine*, *240*, 112552. doi:10.1016/j.socscimed.2019.112552 PMID:31561111

Webster, F., Rice, K., & Sud, A. (2020). A critical content analysis of media reporting on opioids: The social construction of an epidemic. *Social Science & Medicine*, *244*, 112642. doi:10.1016/j.socscimed.2019.112642 PMID:31731136

Wertz, J. (2018). *Digital Transformation Is Critical For Business Development*.

Wessel, L., Baiyere, A., Ologeanu-Taddei, R., Cha, J., & Blegind Jensen, T. (2021). Unpacking the Difference Between Digital Transformation and IT-Enabled Organizational Transformation. *Journal of the Association for Information Systems*, *22*(1), 102–129. https://aisel.aisnet.org/jais/vol22/iss1/6/

Wong, J., Koh, W. C., Alikhan, M. F., Abdul Aziz, A. B. Z., & Naing, L. (2020). Responding to COVID-19 in Brunei Darussalam: Lessons for small countries. *Journal of Global Health*, *10*(1), 010363. doi:10.7189/jogh.10.010363 PMID:32566154

Yahya, A. (2020). *Effects of COVID-19 outbreak on Brunei's economy*.

Zuti, B. (2018). *Digitalization, regional competitiveness and the governments of the future*. Sznet Istvan University. http://publicatio.bibl.u-szeged.hu/13581/7/13581.pdf

Chapter 11
Examining the Impact of Gender Differences, Sustainable Urbanism, and Digital Transformation on Online Consumer Buying Behavior:
A Perspective Towards SDG Alignment

Ahmad Huzaimi Johari
Universiti Brunei Darussalam, Brunei

Annie Dayani Ahad
Universiti Brunei Darussalam, Brunei

Muhammad Anshari
iD https://orcid.org/0000-0002-8160-6682
Universiti Brunei Darussalam, Brunei

ABSTRACT

The COVID-19 pandemic has triggered a significant surge in online shopping across various contexts, influencing the buying behaviors of consumers, particularly those engaged in online and social media-based transactions. This study aims to investigate the impact of gender disparities, customer location, sustainable development goals (SDG) alignment, and digital transformation on consumers' online buying behaviors. The research adopts qualitative methods, employing online interviews to collect primary data. The findings highlight that contemporary consumers exhibit the ability to assess choices and make informed decisions. Notably, factors influencing online shopping behavior encompass influences from close social circles, predominantly family members and friends, as well as virtual social constructs like social network friends. The study emphasizes the crucial role of SDGs and digital transformation in shaping and understanding these evolving consumer behaviors.

DOI: 10.4018/979-8-3693-2865-1.ch011

INTRODUCTION

Smart mobile devise has impacted our lifestyles rapidly, it keeps on changing and not only has become more global, but it also has become more complex and uncertain due to its fast-paced (Iqbal, Melhem & Kokash, 2012; Rudhumbu et al., 2016). According to Karima and Tjokrosoekarto (2020); Musa and Nurhaidah (2015) stated that not only our lifestyles has changed due to globalisation but also our economy, technology and communication has changed and has become more digitalised. As a result, we are now living in the era of digital.

One of the major proofs that we are now currently living in a digital era is the usage of social media that has become an important aspect in our today's life (Ahad & Anshari, 2017). Society nowadays can be seen to rely more on social medias as medium in receiving and sharing information and to connect with people for networking, business, knowledge and even entertainment purposes (Gibson, 2018).

A report made by ISEAS (2018) shows that about 55 percent of the population in the Southeast Asia region shown to be avid social media users. At which, by the year 2018 the social media penetration specifically in Brunei Darussalam is 95 percent, 83 percent in Singapore and Malaysia came in third with 75 percent – the social media penetration within the Southeast Asia region shows no sign of slowing down.

With the increase of social media penetration (Gibson, 2018), more businesses specifically those in the Micro, Small and Medium Entrepreneurship (MSME) industry must restructure their organisational action plan especially those involving business marketing activities. In fact, nowadays according to Karima and Tjokrosoekarto (2020); Stephen (2016) stated that almost every business uses and implement their business marketing campaigns via social media (Ahad et al., 2017).

However, in November 2019 one major problem has emerged and still ongoing to this year is the COVID-19 pandemic – according to Page, Hinshaw and McKay (2021), the COVID-19 disease firstly detected in Wuhan, China; it is an infectious disease caused by a new coronavirus strand. With the spread of this disease, it has led many governments around the world to take actions such as implementing travel and specific activities restrictions; and lockdown (Syaifullah et al., 2021; Kuckertz et al., 2020; Anshari et al., 2022).

With the implementation of strict restrictions and lockdown in most countries, it has impacted the country's economic activities and become a major problem for start-up business owners and MSME (Syaifullah et al., 2021; Kuckertz et al., 2020). Thus, this is where social media now become major mediums for MSMEs in diverting and diversifying their marketing and sale channels.

Not only the pandemic has affected business owners in terms of their sales, but it also impacted consumers' buying behaviours. According to Ali Taha et al. (2021) stated that since the society are now in in the period of doing self-isolation it has changed the way consumers behave – at which consumers are now taking advantages on the presence of social medias as medium to shop online. Yet again, due to the presence of strict restriction and lockdown in most countries, it has affected consumers' demand towards all types of businesses though there are some businesses seen to experience an increase in demand (Syaifullah et al., 2021; Kuckertz et al., 2020).

As results on the increase in the numbers of MSMEs that have changed their organisational action plan by focusing and using social media as medium to do business and marketing – indeed it not only helps in creating convenience but also ease to use for the business consumers (Rafiq & Javeid, 2018). With the presence and increase of online shopping (or the usage of social media as medium of doing online business), consumers will be able to look at the abundance of similar products that are available.

The only things that the consumers should do is to compare and make choice wisely on the products that they need or want such as comparing in terms of quality, designs, features, price, discounts and many more (Rafiq & Javeid, 2018; Razzaq et al. 2018). According to Rafiq and Javeid (2018) stated that as consumers can now choose desired favourable products easily via online, more people from different age prefer doing shopping online especially students.

Now, Rafiq and Javeid (2018); and Lamb et al. (2013) suggested that most businesses especially those within MSMEs do their market segmentation focusing only on demographics of their consumers – this enables most entrepreneurs to understand better on their consumers' buying behaviours, their consuming and buying pattern. Although there are many advantages can be seen when doing online shopping, yet again, online shopping also leads to many risks and disadvantages involved that may affect consumers' buying behaviours (Rafiq & Javeid, 2018).

Furthermore, according to Rafiq and Javeid (2018); and Audrain-Pontevia and Vanhuele (2016) stated that based on their study, gender differences also play major role towards consumers' online buying behaviours. This can be look upon the difference in shopping style, consuming, and buying pattern and perception towards one product. Meanwhile, according to Ren and Kwan (2009) other factor such as place of residence also affected consumers' online buying behaviours. At which those with greater accessibility of internet are likely to do shopping online (Anshari et al., 2021).

Therefore, it is very interesting to look at the impact of gender differences and place of residence towards consumers' online buying behaviours as there is little to none research being made in the country specifically focusing on Instagram as the main medium. The purpose of this study is to analyse and to understand better on how gender differences and place of residence affects consumers' online buying behaviours.

LITERATURE REVIEWS

Štefko and Steffek (2018) stated that our virtual world kept on changing rapidly at which those that are relevant and current for today may be out-of-date tomorrow. Social media especially are one of the examples, according to Appel et al. (2020) stated that social media nowadays is different than a year ago as it kept on developing at a rapid and at fundamental pace. Štefko and Steffek (2018) also stated that most of entrepreneurs tend to find it quite challenging in making sure that the business is using and keeping up with new technologies especially those related with virtual reality, Internet of Things (IoT), Artificial Intelligence (AI) – at which these listed technologies are seen to shape today's picture (Anshari et al., 2021a). Therefore, there is no doubt on the importance and power of social media as a medium in doing online business. Thus, for entrepreneurs it is important to understand how to use it effectively.

During the COVID-19 pandemic outbreak, social media is seen to play an important role; it has impacted our daily activities especially in terms of work, education, shopping, and entertainment (Almunawar & Anshari, 2024; Anshari et al., 2023). With the presence of social distancing and lockdown, many individuals have used social medias to communicate with one other, to seek for support and help, and even for self-entertainment (Nabity-Grover, Cheung & Bennett Thatcher, 2020). During the pandemic, according to Nabity- Grover, Cheung, and Bennett Thatcher (2020) assumed that it has made individual to be more conscious of how they want to show themselves and they disclose on social media during the pandemic especially those involving with personal health, impact on behaviour and perceptions on others health.

Social Commerce via Social Media Platform

Nowadays, most businesses especially those within the Micro, Small and Medium Entrepreneurship (MSMEs) tend to use digital marketing as part of their strategy. Instagram, Facebook and websites are amongst the most used social media platforms in selling products. Furthermore, social media plays an important role in building and maintaining brand of a business especially by having an interaction with consumers.

From the eye of Joo and Teng (2016) suggested that social media helps in providing variety of information for businesses to various groups either directly or indirectly. Whereby, Constantinides (2010) believes that social media is now regarded as a more trustworthy platform in establishing brand credibility in the consumers' eyes.

Karima & Tjokrosoekarto (2020) believed that there three types of social medias that exist in today's world, these are; (1) Blogs – a place to devote writing and sharing opinions; can be used as personal or even use by company and shared to multiple people; (2) Online Communities – social media usually seen to be affiliated with community at which it acts as a platform to post comments, reviews and discussions between users; and lastly (3) Social Networks – usually helps in providing entrepreneurs benefits as it helps in connecting one user with other.

Social Media Marketing

While, social media marketing can be defined as the process of promoting a brand, increasing sales, understanding consumer preferences, and retaining consumers using a digital technology as medium (Karima & Tjokrosoekarto, 2020; Kannan & Li, 2017). Karima and Tjokrosoekarto (2020) also stated that many entrepreneurs has already benefited from the usage of social medias.

From there it can be said that social media can easily be accessed especially in creating business brand, creation of word of mouth amongst consumers, crowd sourcing and even buzz marketing (Karima & Tjokrosoekarto, 2020). Other researchers like Eid and El-Gohary (2011) also stated that the presence of social media also helps in increasing the business efficiency especially in developing marketing strategies.

Furthermore, the reason why digital marketing is recommended; according to digital media theory found in Karima & Tjokrosoekarto (2020) and Percy (2018) stated that digital marketing helps in reaching more potential consumers especially during the pandemic outbreak. Thus, entrepreneurs should improve their marketing strategy by using social media especially Instagram, Facebook and many more. As pandemic has affected individual especially on their buying behaviours, it is important for entrepreneurs to determine a more clearer target market (Karima & Tjokrosoekarto, 2020).

Background of Study

According to an article published by Borneo Bulletin (2020); about 60 percent of the world's population is now already online. Whereby, about 4.5 billion people around the world has connectivity with the internet at which social media users have also surpassed the 3.8 billion marks. Looking from the given trends, an estimation of more than half of the world's population will use social media soon. Although it being stated there will be an increase on the usage of internet and social media, there are still some challenges faced and works need to be done to ensure everyone around world has fair and equal access to digital connectivity. In Brunei Darussalam, the nation penetration rate was ranked in fourth placed globally with 410,000 users (94 percent). Meanwhile, the nation is seen to be the second highest for social media usage with 410,000 users (94 percent). The nation is also known to be in third rank for Instagram usage globally in terms of population ratio. At which the rate of growth of Instagram usage was about 2.4 percent in the year 2020. For Facebook usage, the nation rank in 10th place globally with 310,000 users (about 89 percent). Moving forward to February 2022, the nation has recorded about 116.5 percent of the nation's population are active social media users (statista.com). From this, the nation can see an increase in social media penetration from 2020 to 2022. The COVID-19 outbreak began in China in November 2019 and in December 2019; since then, has spread worldwide including Brunei Darussalam. To stop the spread of the COVID-19 transmission, the World Health Organization (WHO) has classified COVID-19 as pandemic and has advised that every country that is affected by the virus to implement physical distancing strategy since March 2020. In Brunei Darussalam as cases spiked in March 2020, the nation's government took a great major action which is to ban its residents to leave the country and the foreigners from entering the country. Not forgetting return citizens were also placed in quarantine centres. Most importantly, the government carried out lockdown (Australian Institute of International Affairs, 2021). From these actions, the nation managed to report no local COVID-19 cases infection for one whole year, though the nation sees a second wave of COVID-19 in September 2021.

With lockdown and partial lockdown being reinstated, many has turn themselves on using online and social media as to maintain social distancing amongst family and friends. Not only that it also has helped the community in enabling them to work and study at home. Not forgetting, seeking entertainment, and buying goods can also be done using social media (Ho, 2021) in ensuring that the community abide the rules and regulations set up by the nation's government.

According to study made by Ali Taha et al. (2021); Criteo (2020) stated that there are increase in number of consumers downloading social media for online shopping during lockdown in Italy and Slovakia. From the study also there are about 70 percent of participants stated that they used (visited) social media several times a day.

Another study made by Indonesian researchers Parahiyanti and Prasasti (2021); Jayani (2020) stated the average Indonesians spend on using social media are about 3 hours and 26 minutes every day (especially during the pandemic outbreak). At which, Whatsapp ranked to be the top accessed social media with 84 percent, while Facebook and Instagram with 82 percent and 79 percent respectively.

Figure 1. The study framework model

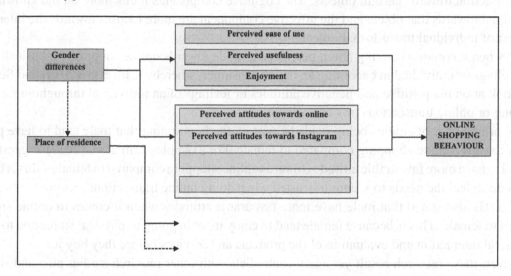

Looking from the given Figure 1 shown above is the whole study framework model at which it consisted of the gender and place of residence as the main study focuses. Whereby, each of these focuses is further broken down based on several different factors. There are also possibilities that gender differences may also have be affected towards the place of residence focuses as well in terms of online buying behaviours, thus, the line connected was in dotted styles.

For gender differences, there are 7 factors to be studied at which three of these factors were related with the Technology Acceptance Model (TAM) found in Davis (1989) study. The three factors were in coloured in the green boxes. And the other possible factors also include in understanding the perceived attitudes towards online shopping, Instagram advertisements, subjective norms and trusts and risk factors; that might be different between male and female genders towards online shopping.

Meanwhile, the place of residence (geographical factors) only focuses more on the internet connectivity of the users; whether their place of residence affect their internet connectivity at which the connectivity also may also affect the users' online buying behaviours. Lastly, we also decided to add on the possibilities of delivery services and charges as factors influencing users' online buying behaviours when it comes to geographical factors focus.

The Model

Looking from the given study framework model, there are 8 main questions to be answered for this study. This information can be found below.

Perceive Attitude Towards Online Shopping

According to Lim et al. (2019) and; Fishbein and Ajzen (1975) stated that the words attitude in this case can be defined as a multi-dimensional that made up by different components at which these components can be look at as either behavioural, cognitive and even affective components. The behavioural component in within the attitude's context can be look at those related with behavioural intention; the feelings or action towards certain objects. The cognitive components focus more on the knowledge of an individual towards that object and the affective component are more focuses towards the interest and disinterest of individual towards that object.

Now, when it comes to talking about perceived attitude towards online shopping; it basically looks on the feelings of individual in becoming an online consumer; whereby; Lim et al. (2019) and Schlosser (2003) look at on the positive and negative attitudes or feelings of an individual throughout the online purchasing or online transactions process being made.

There are number of studies being made by past researchers stating that male tend to have positive attitudes towards online shopping compared to female. For examples Lim et al. (2019) suggested that male tend to have more favourable attitudes towards online shopping compared to female – this is because female tend to feel the needs to secure or trusted when doing online transactions.

Wu (2003) also stated that male have more favourable attitudes when it comes to online shopping compared to female. This is because female tend to enjoy more in going to physical stores and to be able to a physical interaction and evaluation of the products and services before they buy it.

However, these research result yet again contradicts with other research studies also and some research studies also suggested that female tend to have more favourable attitudes towards online shopping compared to male. The reasons behind these are because there is presence of compact and variety of products information that are available for them to look upon before buying the products (Xia Liu et al., 2008), while male tend to prefer going out and just went straight to physical store in buying the products (Amin et al., 2010).

However, as there is presence of website and other social media advancement attributes has led to another research study being made. At which the research study made by Miao Zhao et al. (2009) resulted in both genders to have favourable attitudes towards online shopping. Thus, this discussion has led us to the following question:

Q$_1$: *Does both genders showcase favourable attitudes towards online shopping?*

Perceived Ease of Use and Perceived Usefulness

Under this subsection readers will see that there are two different questions being developed.

Firstly, the perceived ease of use and perceived usefulness according to Lim et al. (2019), Akhlaq & Ahmed (2016); and Davis (1989) suggested that both factors are parts of the Technology Acceptance Model (TAM) at which this model basically helps in determining the usage if information system that helps in understanding user acceptance towards technology.

Perceived ease of use focuses more on how an individual see that using system are easy to be use and learn; and not forgetting how it is free to be learnt by individual (Lim et al., 2019). Now within this scenario, the presence of perceived ease of use may affected on the usage of computer (Davis, 1989) or social media (Lim et al, 2019).

When talking about gender differences, most study suggested that male tend to have higher knowledge and higher adaptability on the usage of technology (Lim et al., 2019) as such male gender is seen to have higher skills in those related with computer or technology such as systems, database and many more (Kay, 2006). In 2001, a study made by Teo suggested that female tend to take more time to be familiar with new technology such as applications and systems. However, since this study made 21 years ago, there is still possibility on the change of statistics that suggest female tend to have lower self-efficacy towards technology. As a result, from this, it has led the us to the following question:

Q_2: *Does male tend to have greater ease of use when doing online shopping compared to* *female?*

Meanwhile, perceived usefulness focuses more on how using the technology system may enhance online buying experience (Lim et al., 2019; and Davis, 1989). As this being stated, with the advancement of technology systems and the capability in using the technology, Lim et al. (2019)

stated that male tend to have perceive a greater usefulness when it comes to shopping online compared to female since male gender is known to have greater self-efficacy towards technology and less time carried out compared to female (Teo, 2001). Thus, question can be stipulated that:

Q_3: *Does male perceive a greater usefulness when doing online shopping compared to female?*

Perceived Attitude Towards Social Media Advertising

Boudreau and Watson (2006) stated that advertising is one of the most important factors that can helps in building and creating brand awareness of one business. As a result, many businesses from micro to large companies tend to invest more money in doing marketing especially nowadays with the advancement of technology has allow the businesses to market their business online via social media application (Lim et al., 2019).

However, the advertisements factors such as pictures aesthetic, usage of colours, usage of words and many more affected both male and female gender towards advertising especially in this case Instagram advertising. Many research studies agreed that male tend to have more favourable attitude towards online advertising compared to female such as Lim et al. (2019) stated that male tend to be attracted by the state-of-the-art website designs or even the presence of catchy advertisement information and content; male prefer the online interactivity and also the pictorial features provided by the business (Ray, Sormunen and Harris; 1999).

From this result, Lim et al. (2019) suggested that it is important for business owner to create design that would suit the taste of the business target market, in this case focuses more gender differences. Nevertheless, based from the research studies discussion shown above, it was decided that the question would be:

Q_4: *Does male tend to perceive a much favourable attitude towards Instagram advertisement?*

Enjoyment

Enjoyment or perceived enjoyment is also part of the Technology Acceptance Model (Akhlaq & Ahmed, 2016); and Davis, 1989). Whereby according to Davis (1989), enjoyment within the context of online shopping is the process of using computer or mobile phone is seen to be enjoyable or pleasant.

According to past study made by different researchers (Lim et al., 2019) stated that female tend to enjoy more in doing online shopping compared to male – at which this can be look upon on the processes that most female do when it comes in doing online shopping such as surveying or browsing products at their own leisure times (unlimited shopping times), endless product choices, to some extent most products are fast delivered which makes female to enjoy more in online shopping.

James (2013) also stated that it is much less time taken and less hassle when it comes to doing online shopping which made female to have a pleasant experience while doing online shopping.

James (2013) also explained that male tend to shop with an objective mind. To put it simply, they shop for what they want specifically (purposeful activity). Thus, this led the question to be written:

Q_5: *Does male perceived less enjoyment compared to female when doing online shopping?*

Subjective Norms

Subjective norms can be defined as a behaviour that were performed by an individual that were basically influenced by other people that the individual close with such as family or friends (Lim et al., 2019; and Fishbein & Ajzen, 1975). For this factor, according to Garbarino & Strahilevitz (2004); and Taylor & Todd (1995) suggested that female tends to be influenced by subjective norms compared to male. At which based from their findings stated that with the presence of recommendation or influence from friends, female tend to increase their willingness in purchasing products online. As a result, from this, the question is written as:

Q₆: *Does male are less likely to be influenced by subjective norms compared to female when doing online shopping?*

Trust and Risk Factors

When doing online shopping, the most common problems faced by online consumers would be lack of trust or presence of risk. At which female often have higher insecurities when buying online compared to male (Lim et al., 2019; and Cao et al., 2015). This is because female tend to be more concerned about their privacy which resulted them to have much lesser time in shopping online. Thus, this question formulated as:

Q₇: *Does male tend to perceive lower risk compared to female when it comes to online shopping?*

Place of Residence (Geolocation Factors)

Another study to look upon on what might have affected consumer's online buying behaviours would be on place of residence or in other words geographical areas of each of the consumers. Two things that might be affected consumers' online buying behaviours when it impacted by place of residence, they are: **(1) due to lack of shopping places and opportunities in the physical world (distribution of shopping malls)** and **(2) due to accessibility of internet connection in one place.**

According to Ren and Kwan (2008) stated that consumers' online buying behaviours shaped by the geographic dispersion of shopping opportunities within consumers' area. As a result, consumers that are more likely within an area that are having spatial distribution of shopping malls tend to prefer doing physical shopping compared to those consumers that have fewer or poorer access to shopping opportunities.

In other words, those consumers that have a fewer or poorer access to shopping opportunities tend to shop more via online – as according to Ren and Kwan (2008); and Anderson et al., (2002) stated that it is easier and more convenient for such consumers to shop online, and it will take less time for them to travel to carry out shopping tasks physically.

There are still little to no information or study being made in relation towards one place of residence's accessibility of internet affected consumers' online buying behaviours. However, based form study made by Ren and Kwan (2008) stated that government plays major role in this case as only government has the right to implement policy measures and facilitate internet accessibility in one place especially for those living in the poor accessibility of shopping opportunities areas. Therefore, the question can be summarised as:

Q₈: *Does those living outside the Brunei-Muara District tend to have poor internet accessibility that affect online shopping behaviours?*

METHODOLOGY

The research deployed qualitative methods to gather respondent's point of views, opinions and understanding of the topic. The given interview questions that were prepared were all in open-ended questions to ensure that the respondents to feel more less threatening in answering the interview questions. With such questions being asked it also enabled interviewees to give unrestrained and free responses. Furthermore, the listed questions were not specifically asked in exact manner and some interviewees would also be asked with a question in ensuring that the answer was consistent for the study.

Once the interview list of questions checked and approved, the interview was conducted via online by doing either: (1) usage of Zoom meeting, Microsoft teams or any video conference application or (2) by face-to-face interaction.

The participants of the interviews were those living in different districts (related with place of residence) specifically in the age range that are eligible in using social media and those have the ability in buying or consuming products and services online. Before asking questions to the interviewees, paper was given to the interviewees for consent proof. However, their names remain anonymous when doing the collection of data.

There are four sections of interviews. The first section focuses more on getting basic information of the interviewees; this is more looking onto the demographics of the study. Second section focuses more social media usage; this is to understand better on interviewees' social media usage such as which application that they tend use more and this result can be compared with other interviewees answers as well.

Third section focuses more on understanding interviewees' online buying behaviours. This was enabling us to compare the habit of male and female interviewees during their buying processes. Finally, the fourth section focuses more on place of residence (geographic factors); under this section, we have decided to focus more in studying the accessibility of internet and how it has affected some of the interviewees buying processes.

Ethical Considerations

To carry out this survey questionnaire, we also looked upon the ethical considerations that needs to be taken into an account. The considerations are Confidentiality: participants that would participate in the survey questionnaire would be ensured that their information was kept confidential. Voluntary participation: we believed that the participants have the rights to opt in or out from the survey questionnaire at any point of time. Anonymity: participants were aware that the study did not know the identities of each of the participants. Consent: we provided explanation on the purpose, benefits or risks on the survey questionnaire being carried out to the participants before the agree or decline to join. Potential of harm: all types of harm (physical, social, and many more) should be kept at minimum.

Analysis

The interview or data collection for this study were carried for three whole weeks at which the interviews started on the 22nd of August 2022 and successfully ended on the 8th of September 2022. The interviews were carried out in two different methods depending on the availability of the interviewees; they are based on Zoom meeting (video conference application) and interviews done by physical method (face-to-face interaction).

During the data collection process, it was able to exceed the targeted population that were explained on subsection *Study Population* – whereby, the study managed to obtain 24 interviewees which consists of 12 males' and 12 females' interviewees. Out of these 24 interviews, 7 interview sessions (5 males' and 2 females' interviewees) were carried out by face-to-face interaction. While, the rest were done via Zoom meeting.

Both genders population, majority of them lived in CBD. Majority of the male interviewees are working under private sectors (5 interviewees). While, 3 interviewees are still studying and for apprenticeship and unemployment recorded 2 interviewees each. No male interviewees were recorded working under government sectors.

Regarding income, majority of the male interviewees have made income around $501 to $1000 (5 interviewees), 4 male interviewees have made income $500 and below, and only 3 male interviewees have made income above $1000. For female interviewees, most of them have made income of $500 and below (8 interviewees), the other 4 female interviewees have made income around $501 to $1000; and no female interviewees have made income above $1000. Meanwhile **Table 1** on the next page showcases the summarisation of interviewees' social media usage.

Table 1. Summarisation of interviewees' social media usage

GENDER	MOST GO-TO SOCIAL MEDIA APPLICATIONS (TOP 3)	AVERAGE HOURS WHEN USING INSTAGRAM
MALE	1. Instagram 2. Facebook 3. WhatsApp	Majority answered **3 to 4** hours spent on Instagram application
FEMALE	1. Instagram 2. TikTok & WhatsApp 3. Facebook	Varies some stated they spent **12 hours** on average (with breaks), some stated **8 hours** in a day.

Looking from the above **Table 1**, both genders use Instagram as their most go-to social media application. When asked why Instagram as their most go-to social media, most of the interviewees answered that most of their family and friends have an account so it is easier for them to follow and keep up-to-date with their life and some stated most businesses especially small businesses operated their businesses through Instagram.

Meanwhile the average hours spend by most male interviewees on Instagram application is between 3 to 4 hours in a day and some also stated they only spend minimum of 30 minutes in a day. While most female interviewees stated that Instagram is now becoming part of their daily routine, as a result some stated that they spend up to 12 hours average in a day with breaks in every activity. Also, few numbers of female interviewees stated that due to their work and study most of the time, they spend minimum of 30 minutes in a day.

Q1: Does both genders showcase favourable attitudes towards online shopping?

For the first question, looking back from the overall results of the interview session with male and female genders, the study has found that majority of both genders actually does not showcase favourable attitudes towards online shopping. Instead, one of the studies made by past researchers, Miao Zhao et al. (2009); indeed, contradicted with this study. Furthermore, other studies made by different number of researchers such as Lim et al. (2019), Amin P.D. et al. (2010), Xia Liu et al. (2008) and Wu (2003) that suggested only one gender showcased favourable attitudes towards online shopping were also seen to contradict with this study.

This is because the overall results from the interview showcased that both genders showcased favourable attitudes towards physical shopping due to **1) craving or the need to have physical interaction** includes in the need to ask further information about certain products and **2) the need to evaluate and trying on the products physically**; same statement as stated by Wu (2003). Lastly, **3) convenience** that allows people to just go straight away to the physical shop and buy products immediately; same statement as stated by Amin et al. (2010).

However, when being asked about the current situation faced by societies worldwide, the COVID-19 Pandemic; majority of the interviewees stated that it does affect their view towards online shopping which is positive. Most of the answers given by both genders, they nowadays tend to opt for both actions (physical and online shopping) based upon situations and type of products and services that they look for. Furthermore, another reason that most interviewees started to opt for online shopping is due to the needs to abide with the rules and regulations set by the nation's government during the pandemic situations (consistent with statement made by Ho, 2021).

Affected by Situations

Like it has been stated before, the situations can be look upon with the current environment faced by today's societies for example COVID-19 Pandemic – at which has led the nation's government to keep up-to-date in changing the rules and regulations for its people to abide. Thus, this also showcased that both genders started to opt for either physical; when restrictions such as lockdown being lifted, or online shopping; when lockdown or other strict restrictions being implemented or re-implemented by the government.

Other situations can also be based on the attitudes of using social media in this case Instagram; looking back from the overall results made from the interview, it shows that some of the interviewees, male and female tend to use Instagram as a medium to window shopping only; once they have met the products that they want, they just went to the physical shop and do the transactions physically.

Affected by Types of Products or Services

Now, when talking about why both genders decided to either opt for physical or online shopping is also due to the types of products and services that they seek in the first place. For example, products like clothing, accessories, and shoes; both genders stated that it is better for them to go to physical stores as they have greater chance to do physical evaluation, whether it fits or even whether it suitable to their body as well.

In terms of products that both genders tend to do online shopping is mostly food and beverages, and services such as event planning services. The reasons behind this are because nowadays, there are more numbers of small business that sell food and beverages via online. Both genders also stated that it is easier for them to compare prices for the products.

Q2: Does male tend to have greater ease of use when doing online shopping compared to female?

Firstly, considering that this study focuses more on Instagram as medium to do online shopping, it can be said that by looking upon the overall results of the interview sessions from both genders, that both genders are now equal in having a greater ease of use when doing online shopping.

There are few factors that can contributed to this finding; **1) Instagram is easy to use and understand and 2) female gender nowadays also have increased on their knowledge related with computer and technology**.

When asked about what makes Instagram easier to use as medium for online shopping, both genders (majority) stated that with the presence of search buttons, presence of algorithms that remembers their interests, presence of different features that can be used such as Instagram Story, Instagram Reels and many more have allowed both genders to be able to view products and services easily and considering it is also easy to understand how the application works.

Q3: Does male perceived a greater usefulness when doing online shopping compared to female?

Q4: Does male tend to perceived a much favourable attitude towards Instagram advertisement?

Meanwhile for this question, the study sees that male do tend to perceive favourable attitude towards Instagram advertisement. There are different factors that affect the interest of interviewees towards Instagram advertising such as the picture aesthetic, usage of colours and words (Lim et al., 2019).

Such factors have shown that both genders tend to be attracted by it. However, for male the reason why they perceived favourable attitudes compared to female is because most of the advertisements tend to be straight-forward; the presence of pictorial features (Ray, sormunen and Harris; 1999) whereby, the products are shown as the main focus in the post together with the price of the products as well. For female although they tend to get attracted by it, they focus more on the aesthetic of the pictures and the theme used throughout the business account profile. Yet again, most of them tend to only stop on the account and just view the account profile without the intention of buying it.

Q5: Does male perceived less enjoyment compared to female when doing online shopping?

From the overall interview; although, majority of the male interviewees tend to said that they enjoy doing shopping online, however there are 2 factors that can be look upon that male tend to perceived less enjoyment when doing shopping online, they are based from **1) the tone** that they enjoy online shopping tend to be answered in sort of "sarcastic" tone and **2) observation made during physical interview**, they somehow answered the question in insincere manner or just for the sake of answering. This can be because male gender tends to shop either physically or via online when they only need the products; purposeful activity. From there male gender tends to shop with an objective mind based from study made by James (2013).

In regards, to female gender they do show enjoyment when shopping online as a result from, the presence of variety of products, the ability for them to browse the products at their own time and most importantly, the fast delivery services being provided (same statement stated by Lim et al., 2019). The enjoyment amongst female interviewees towards online shopping might change to a hassle is due to the process in searching and surveying good quality products (based from *4.4 Q3: Does male perceive a greater usefulness when doing online shopping compared to female?*).

Q6: Does male are less likely to be influenced by subjective norms compared to female when doing online shopping?

From the overall interview sessions, it can be said that male also tend to be influenced by subjective norms as well; this contradicted with the study made by Garbarino & Strahilevitz (2004); and Taylor & Todd (1995). When asked who are the most influential people that affect both genders interest towards online shopping, majority of the interviewees stated that family especially siblings and cousins play major role in influencing the willingness to shop online especially based on their point of views and opinions.

Friends also influenced interviewees in buying products online especially based from their personal experience buying products on certain Instagram accounts. Not forgetting, interviewees also affected from friends when their friends wear, use or consume certain products that led them to have positive outcomes. Other factors such as trends also influenced interviewees as well. However, some interviewees stated that they might have to observed and study more on the trends whether it fits them, interest them or not.

Q7: Does male tend to perceive lower risk compared to female when it comes to online shopping?

When talking about trust and risk factors when doing online shopping especially when using Instagram application; based from the overall interview sessions, indeed, that male also tend to have higher insecurities when buying online which equally the same as female (contradicted with Lim et al., 2019 and Cao et al., 2015 studies).

When being asked questions like what makes these interviewees have that sense of security when approaching online business account on Instagram application, most of them stated that they looked upon the presence of high number of followers, presence of Instagram Highlights at which the business owner showcased past customers' reviews and feedbacks of the business, and the activeness of the business to upload new update post on their accounts. Not forgetting, other people's (subjective norms) opinions as well like friends and family.

In regard to question like if the interviewees had faced scam or fraud; majority of them stated that they have never experienced once before although only few stated that they experienced one before for example one interviewee stated that the perfume that interviewee bought from particular Instagram account tend to be knock-off when the business itself stated that it is an original products.

However, aside from scam and fraud, most interviewees stated that they have encountered bad customer services such as late reply on messages, tone usage on messages tend to be rude, and some got blocked by the business account instantly without knowing the reasons why. This factors also have led some of the interviewees to think twice in buying online especially on Instagram application.

Q8: Does those living outside CBD tend to have poor Internet accessibility that affect online shopping behaviours?

Firstly, when asked about the online shopping activities towards the interviewees; those who live within areas that can access numbers of shopping malls and department stores tend to prefer doing physical shopping compared to those who live within areas that are much more rural. For example, interviewees living within the Tutong District showcases great interest towards online shopping rather than going to the physical shop, this can be seen to concur with study made by Ren and Kwan (2008).

Next, when the interviewees were asked whether their internet connectivity is good or bad; majority stated that they have sort of a good internet connectivity. However, the connectivity sometimes might be affected by; 1) the size of the family members living in one house; whereby this can be affected when large family member uses Wi-Fi at the same time which causes the connectivity to lag; and 2) some residence only uses limited Wi-Fi quota; at which Wi-Fi quota will be finished either mid of the month or at the end of the month which causes the internet connectivity to lag.

The 2 factors are the most common problems faced by the interviewees, therefore; they tend to 1) uses mobile data as a substitute; most female interviewees tend to solve this matter by using mobile data when they need to buy things online immediately; 2) avoid online shopping when it is mid of the month and end of the month; at which most interviewees try to avoid online shopping on this particular time, some might opt for physical shopping.

Looking from the above results, it can be said that those living in Tutong District are also have a good internet accessibility. In fact, other factor that affect online shopping behaviour that related with place of residence includes; delivery services and charges. Delivery services and charges become one of the main problems made by interviewees, at which, nowadays the delivery charges tend to be quite expensive even for those delivery services that are nearer to their place of residence, thus, this caused them to think twice when buying online as most interviewees try to not overspent on products that they bought in the first place. Average delivery charges that most interviewees agreed to pay for (especially business within the same areas or district) $4 to $5; while, those delivery services that are outside from their district would be $7 to $8.

However, some interviewees also stated that rather than paying extra money for delivery services, it is better for themselves to pick-up the products or meet-up the business owners at certain places. This can also be due to some interviewees' residence addresses are hard to follow due to some living in non-urban or non-city areas.

CONCLUSION

This study basically focuses on understanding impact of gender differences and place of residence towards online buying behaviours, at which Instagram application is used in this study as the medium for online shopping. As proposed questions were set, the study carried out interviews to ensure if the set questions were answered or not. Therefore, from these results, the study revealed that male tend to perceive greater usefulness when buying online especially within Instagram application. They also reacted positively with the presence of Instagram advertisement compared to female; however, doing online shopping, male tend to feel that it is less enjoyable as they do shop only as purposeful activity. There were several results that contradicted with other past researchers' works for example nowadays, male and female gender somehow prefer to do physical shopping compared to online shopping; this can be might due to several factors such as types of products. Not forgetting, with the advancements of technology and systems, female nowadays also tend to have equal self-efficacy towards technology; male also tend to showcase equal insecurities and trust feelings towards some online businesses. As a result, from this, it could be concluded that consumers have good decision-making skills before making purchases. Influences from other people especially family members and friends are the majority factors that affected online buying behaviours as well. This no longer only affected towards female gender according to some studies, but instead, it also now affected towards male gender as well. Furthermore, place of residence also affected online buying behaviours, study in regards to Wi-Fi connectivity and accessibility. However, when doing this study, the study revealed that other factors also affecting interviewees online buying behaviours regarding place of residence factors; it was also affected by delivery services and charges. Finally, the study can recognise on the variety of factors affecting online shopping of a person; especially regarding gender differences and place of residence.

REFERENCES

Ahad, A. D., & Anshari, M. (2017). Smartphone habits among youth: Uses and gratification theory. [IJCBPL]. *International Journal of Cyber Behavior, Psychology and Learning*, 7(1), 65–75. doi:10.4018/IJCBPL.2017010105

Ahad, A. D., Anshari, M., & Razzaq, A. (2017). Domestication of smartphones among adolescents in Brunei darussalam. [IJCBPL]. *International Journal of Cyber Behavior, Psychology and Learning*, 7(4), 26–39. doi:10.4018/IJCBPL.2017100103

Akhlaq, A. and Ahmed, E., 2016. Gender Differences Among Online Shopping Factors in Pakistan. *Organizations and Markets in Emerging Economies*, 7(13), 76-78.

Ali Taha, V., Pencarelli, T., Škerháková, V., Fedorko, R., & Košíková, M. (2021). The Use of Social Media and Its Impact on Shopping Behavior of Slovak and Italian Consumers during COVID-19 Pandemic. *Sustainability (Basel)*, 13(4), 1710. doi:10.3390/su13041710

Almunawar, M. N., & Anshari, M. (2024). Customer acceptance of online delivery platform during the COVID-19 pandemic: The case of Brunei Darussalam. *Journal of Science and Technology Policy Management*, 15(2), 288–310. doi:10.1108/JSTPM-04-2022-0073

Amin, P.D., & Amin, B. (2010). A Critical Review of Gender Difference in Online Shopping. *Indian journal of marketing*, 40(11), 43-52.

Anderson, W. P., Chatterjee, L., & Lakshmanan, T. R. (2002). *E-commerce, transportation and economic geography.* STELLA Focus Group 1 Kick-off Meeting: Globalization, E-commerce and Trade, Siena, Italy.

Anshari, M., Alas, Y., Razzaq, A., Shahrill, M., & Lim, S. A. (2021). Millennials consumers' behaviors between trends and experiments. In Research Anthology on E-Commerce Adoption, Models, and Applications for Modern Business (pp. 1492-1508). IGI global.

Anshari, M., Almunawar, M. N., & Masri, M. (2022). Digital twin: Financial technology's next frontier of robo-advisor. *Journal of Risk and Financial Management*, 15(4), 163. doi:10.3390/jrfm15040163

Anshari, M., Almunawar, M. N., Masri, M., Hamdan, M., Fithriyah, M., & Fitri, A. (2021a). Digital wallet in supporting green FinTech sustainability. In *2021 Third International Sustainability and Resilience Conference: Climate Change* (pp. 352-357). IEEE. 10.1109/IEEECONF53624.2021.9667957

Anshari, M., Hamdan, M., Ahmad, N., Ali, E., & Haidi, H. (2023). COVID-19, artificial intelligence, ethical challenges and policy implications. *AI & Society*, 38(2), 707–720. doi:10.1007/s00146-022-01471-6

Appel, G., Grewal, L., Hadi, R., & Stephen, A. (2020). The future of social media in marketing. *Journal of the Academy of Marketing Science*, 48(1), 79–95. doi:10.1007/s11747-019-00695-1

Audrain-Pontevia, A. (2016). Where do customer loyalties really lie, and why? Gender differences in store loyalty. *International Journal of Retail & Distribution Management*, 44(8). . doi:10.1108/IJRDM-01-2016-0002

Boudreau, M. C., & Watson, R. T. (2006). Internet advertising strategy alignment. *Internet Research*, 16(1), 23–37. doi:10.1108/10662240610642523

Brunei: social media penetration 2022 (2022). Statista. https://www.statista.com/statistics/883777/brunei-social-media-penetration/

Bruneians rank high in social media usage. (2020). Borneo Bulletin Online. https://borneobulletin.com.bn/bruneians-rank-high-social-media-usage/

Cao, Y., Lu, Y., Gupta, S., & Yang, S. (2015). The effects of differences between ecommerce and m-commerce on the consumers' usage transfer from online to mobile channel. *International Journal of Mobile Communications*, *13*(1), 51. doi:10.1504/IJMC.2015.065890

Constatinades, E., Romero, C. L., & Gomez, M. A. (2010). *Effects of web experience on consumer choice: a multicultural approach.*

Criteo. (2020). *Comportamento Degli Utenti di Appnel 2020: Italia (Report).* Criteo. https://www.criteo.com/it/wpcontent/uploads/sites/9/2020/07/Deck-GlobalAppSurvey- IT.pdf

Davis, F. D. (1989). Perceived usefulness, perceived ease of use, and user acceptance of information technology. *Management Information Systems Quarterly*, *13*(3), 319. doi:10.2307/249008

Eid, R., & El-Gohary, H. (2011). The impact of emarketing use on small business enterprises' marketing success. *Service Industries Journal.*

Fishbein, M., & Ajzen, I. (1975). *Belief, attitude, intention and behavior: An introduction to theory and research.*

Garbarino, E., & Strahilevitz, M. (2004). Gender differences in the perceived risk of buying online and the effects of receiving a site recommendation. *Journal of Business Research*, *57*(7), 768–775. doi:10.1016/S0148-2963(02)00363-6

Gibson, N. (2018). *An Analysis of the Impact of Social Media Marketing on Individuals' An Individuals' Attitudes and Perceptions at NOVA Community A Community College.*

Ho, H. (2021). COVID-19 in Brunei Darussalam: How Does the Small Nation Cope? | *Heinrich Böll Foundation | Southeast Asia Regional Office.*

Hou, F., Bi, F., Jiao, R., Luo, D., & Song, K. (2020). Gender differences of depression and anxiety among social media users during the COVID-19 outbreak in China: A cross-sectional study. *BMC Public Health*, *20*(1), 1648. doi:10.1186/s12889-020-09738-7

Iqbal, A., Melhem, Y., & Kokash, H. (2012). Readiness of the university students towards entrepreneurship in Saudi private university: An exploratory study. *European Scientific Journal.*

James, R. (2013). *Student Feature Male and Female Attitudes to Online Shopping.* Women in Society.

Jayani, D. H. (2020). *Orang Indonesia Habiskan Hampir 8 Jam untuk Berinternet.* Katadata. https://databoks.katadata.co.id/datapublish/2020/02/26/indonesia-habiskan- hampir-8-jam-untuk-berinternet

Joo, T. M., & Teng, C. E. (2016). use of Social Media in PR: A Change of Trend. World Academy of Science, Engineering and Technology. *International Journal of Humanities and Social Sciences.*

Kannan, P. K., & Li, H. (2017). Digital marketing: A framework, review and research agenda. *International Journal of Research in Marketing*, *34*(1), 22–45. doi:10.1016/j.ijresmar.2016.11.006

Kay, R. (2006). Addressing gender differences in computer ability, attitudes and use: The laptop effect. *Journal of Educational Computing Research*, *34*(2), 187–211. doi:10.2190/9BLQ-883Y-XQMA-FCAH

Korenkova, M., Maros, M., Levicky, M., & Fila, M. (2020). Consumer Perception of Modern and Traditional Forms of Advertising. *Sustainability (Basel)*, *12*(23), 9996. doi:10.3390/su12239996

Krasnova, A., Veltri, N., Eling, N., & Buxmann, P. (2017). Why men and women continue to use social networking sites: The role of gender differences. *The Journal of Strategic Information Systems*, *26*(4), 261–284. doi:10.1016/j.jsis.2017.01.004

Kuckertz, A., Brändle, L., Gaudig, A., Hinderer, S., Morales Reyes, C. A., Prochotta, A., Steinbrink, K. M., & Berger, E. S. C. (2020). Startups in times of crisis – A rapid response to the COVID-19 pandemic. *Journal of Business Venturing Insights*, *13*(April), e00169. Advance online publication. doi:10.1016/j.jbvi.2020.e00169

Lim, Y., Cheng, B., Cham, T., Ng, C., & Tan, J. (2019). Gender Differences in Perceptions and Attitudes Toward Online Shopping: A Study of Malaysian Consumers. [JMAP]. *Journal of Marketing Advances and Practices*, *1*(2), 12–15.

Liu, X., He, M., Gao, F., & Xie, P. (2008). An empirical study of online shopping customer satisfaction in China: A holistic perspective. *International Journal of Retail & Distribution Management*, *36*(11), 919–940. doi:10.1108/09590550810911683

Musa, M. I., Nurhaidah (2015). Dampak pengaruh globalisasi bagi kehidupan bangsa indonesia. *Jurnal Pesona Dasar*, *3*(3)

Nabity-Grover, T., Cheung, C., & Bennett Thatcher, J. (2020). Inside out and outside in: How the COVID-19 pandemic affects self-disclosure on social media. *International Journal of Information Management*, *55*, 102188. doi:10.1016/j.ijinfomgt.2020.102188

Page, J., Hinshaw, D., & McKay, B. (2021). What We Know About the Origins of Covid-19. *Wall Street Journal*. https://www.wsj.com/articles/what-we-know-about-the-origins-of-covid-19-11624699801

Percy, L. (2018). *Strategic integrated marketing communications. (2018).* Taylor & Francis Group. doi:10.4324/9781315164342

Rafiq M. Y., & Javeid H. M. U. (2018). *Impact of Gender Differences on Online Shopping Attitude of University Students*, 1-9.

Ray, C. M., Sormunen, C., & Harris, T. M. (1999). Men's and women's attitudes toward computer technology: A comparison. *Office Systems Research Journal*.

Razzaq, A., Samiha, Y. T., & Anshari, M. (2018). Smartphone habits and behaviors in supporting students self-efficacy. *International Journal of Emerging Technologies in Learning*, *13*(2), 94. doi:10.3991/ijet.v13i02.7685

Ren, F., & Kwan, M. (2009, April). (2008). The Impact of Geographic Context on E-shopping Behavior. *Environment and Planning. B, Planning & Design*, *36*(2), 262–278. doi:10.1068/b34014t

Rudhumbu, N., Svotwa, D., Munyanyiwa, T., & Mutsau, M. (2016). *Attitudes of Students towards Entrepreneurship Education at Two Selected Higher Education Institutions in Botswana: A Critical Analysis and Reflection.* Academic Journal Of Interdisciplinary Studies., doi:10.5901/ajis.2016.v5n2p83

Schlosser, A. E. (2003). Experiencing Products in the Virtual World: The role of goal and imagery in influencing attitudes versus purchase intentions. *The Journal of Consumer Research*, *30*(2), 184–198. doi:10.1086/376807

Štefko, R., & Steffek, V. (2018). Key Issues in Slow Fashion: Current Challenges and Future Perspectives. *Sustainability (Basel)*, *10*(7), 2270. doi:10.3390/su10072270

Stephen, A. T. (2016). The role of digital and social media marketing in consumer behavior. *Current Opinion in Psychology*, *10*, 17–21. doi:10.1016/j.copsyc.2015.10.016

Syaifullah, J., & Syaifullah, M., Sukendar, Mu, & Junaedi, J. (2021). Social Media Marketing and Business Performance of MSMEs During the COVID-19 Pandemic. *The Journal of Asian Finance. Economics and Business*, *8*(2), 523–531. doi:10.13106/JAFEB.2021.VOL8.NO2.0523

Taylor, S., & Todd, P. A. (1995). Understanding information technology usage: A test of competing models. *Information Systems Research*, *6*(2), 144–176. doi:10.1287/isre.6.2.144

Teo, T. S. (2001). Demographic and motivation variables associated with Internet usage activities. *Internet Research*, *11*(2), 125–137. doi:10.1108/10662240110695089

Zhao, M., & Dholakia, R. R. (2009). A multi-attribute model of web site interactivity and customer satisfaction: An application of the Kano model. *Managing Service Quality*, *19*(3), 286–307. doi:10.1108/09604520910955311

Chapter 12

Organisational Change
and Knowledge Sharing

Section 4

Business, Management, and Digital Transformation

Chapter 12
Organisational Change and Knowledge–Sharing Strategies in Managing Risks

Naizatul Hakimah Abdullmalek
Universiti Brunei Darussalam, Brunei

Thuraya Farhana Said
(iD) https://orcid.org/0000-0002-0571-7460
Universiti Brunei Darussalam, Brunei

Muhammad Anshari
(iD) https://orcid.org/0000-0002-8160-6682
Universiti Brunei Darussalam, Brunei

ABSTRACT

The study is a case-based analysis of a merging Telco organisation that created uncertainties for many stakeholders. A qualitative research method was deployed in order to examine whether knowledge sharing could be used to ease and reduce uncertainties in facilitation in ensuring employee readiness, where objectives such as finding out factors to influence communication in ensuring change readiness and finding out the role of knowledge sharing as a potential platform for effective communication in times of organisational change and uncertainties were examined. In addition, the study also employed bibliographic analysis of the published articles on knowledge transfer and organisational change to track the trends of the topic and determine its recency. This paper is expected to give insights on the role of knowledge sharing and its significance in the context of organisational change especially from developing country's perspective.

DOI: 10.4018/979-8-3693-2865-1.ch012

INTRODUCTION

Change is a prevalent aspect that happens over time in an organisation to keep up with the ever-changing times purpose of efficiency and effectiveness. However, the idea of change creates uncertainties, a recognised outcome of organisational change which could affect employees in the organisation (Allen, Jimmieson, Bordia & Irmer, 2007). For instance, employees might not be able to cope with the changes that could lead to the inability to execute assigned tasks properly or reach expected responsibilities effectively. As a result, the employees within the organisation would not be able to support the organisational goals. This is also supported by Bordia, Hobman, Jones and Gallois (2004), who argued that uncertainty could create a psychological tension that may affect promotion opportunities, training and coaching processes or stress levels in the employees. Thus, rectifying any potential issues that may come from organisational change is important. For one, practicing effective communication is recommended to combat such issues. Smooth facilitation of communication is not only essential, but also allows discussion with employees that surrounds the level of acceptance and issues that may arrive from the change (Husain, 2013; Landaeta, Mun, Rabadi & Levin, 2008). In the present study, the Lewin's Change Management model (1947) was used to assess the role of communication in making employees ready during the change processes.

Knowledge sharing is identified as an important catalyst for change processes from the unfreezing stage to the moving stage (Hussain et al. 2018; Anshari et al., 2016). Understanding and capitalising knowledge and it's sharing process between employees is not only able to help organisations achieve success, but would also help achieve a holistic comprehension of knowledge sharing in the organisation (Ipe, 2003; Ordoñez de Pablos, 2023). The aim of the current research is to investigate whether knowledge sharing could be used as a platform in easing channeling for effective communication among employees in terms of their readiness to changes. Following the research aim, the objectives of the research are to find out what factors influence employees' communication that could ensure readiness during change, and to find out the role of knowledge sharing as a potential platform in communication in facilitating organisational change.

LITERATURE REVIEW

Communication in Organisational Change

According to Greenan (2003), organisational changes occur when there are changes within the administration of decision-making power and skills or communication structures for organisational change. Organisations comprise of individuals that are firstly managed in the event of changes being imposed, then followed by the management of the organisational structure, processes and practices (Branson, 2008). The change in the organisation can be stimulated or triggered by external and/or internal factors. External factors include political, economic, social, technological, environmental and legal factors (Craig & Campbell, 2012; Anshari & Lim, 2017). The internal factors refer to the structural changes in the size of the organisation, the shift of organisational control from having an inexistent organisational structure to a more demonstrated structure, and changes of managerial figures (Barnett & Carroll, 1995). Similarly, Ziaee Bigdeli et al. (2017) noted that effectiveness in an organisation is influenced by external and also internal conditions. Thus, it is important for organisations to quickly respond for survival in the turbulent environment. Most importantly, external factors are not only impacting the structural dimensions of the organisation, but the organisational culture and the communication process in the organisation.

Communication during change is essential during transitions, where efforts are needed to encourage the effectiveness of communication that would result in employees to be ready in the occurrence of organisational change (Anshari et al., 2019). The importance of effective communication in the context of change management can influence the readiness of employees in influencing a high level of acceptance (Husain, 2013). Based on a study by Husain (2013), the significance of effective communication during change can be attributed to the different factors that influence effective communication into organisational change (Ordóñez de Pablos, 2024). This is supported by Nelissen and van Selm (2008), where communication in the management is substantial in creating a positive outcome on the response towards organisational change (Sait & Anshari, 2021). In relations to change management, effective communication is important to adopt as it leads to the effectiveness in attaining organisational goals accordingly (John, 2018).

Figure 1. Change management model

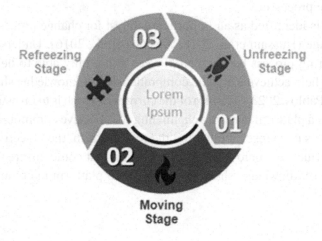

Lewin's Change Management model, as analysed by Hussain et al. (2018), was adopted in this present study to assess the correlation between communication and employee readiness in the context of change facilitation. The Lewin's Change Management model highlights the three important stages of change: (1) the unfreezing stage, (2) the moving stage, and (3) the refreezing stage (see Figure 1). As stated by Lewin (1947), the unfreezing stage is deemed as the introduction to change facilitation in an organisation, where any outcome from an employee's level of acceptance towards the change implemented is imminent. Subsequently, the moving process illustrates how the facilitation of change occurs with different change processes involved, where knowledge sharing is focused on in the current study, as it is noted to be an important catalyst to the unfreezing stage and the moving stage of the change process (Hussain et al., 2018). Then, the refreezing stage takes place whereby simulation and implementation of organisational change takes place (Lewin, 1947). The analysis done by Hussain et al. (2018) also identified employee involvement in change and the leadership that helps facilitate change in reaching completion of change facilitation and implementation (Jaman & Anshari, 2021). The catalytic role of knowledge sharing is supported by Van den Hooff and de Ridder (2004) where communication and the climate surrounding it are one of the key variables to demonstrate knowledge sharing and make it into a platform to ensure effective communication.

Employee Readiness during Change

To ensure a successful organisational change, the readiness of employees for changes need to be addressed, which is discussed in the following section. Failure to ensure employees' readiness for change may result in managers and employees having to spend more time and energy in rectifying potential issues and resistance impacted from the implemented change (Smith, 2005). The contributing factors that allow resistance to occur when facing the uncertainties of organisational change include inexperience, trust and job security (Bateh, Castenada & Farah, 2013). Thus, it is evident that the importance of change readiness is advocated and encouraged in order to facilitate the changes to the employees and to meet the urgency of the changes imposed (Bateh, Castenada & Farah, 2013; Anshari & Hamdan, 2022).

The two categorised factors in influencing communication for employee readiness are identified as organisational culture and the manager-subordinate relationship in the organisation. Literatures from various papers are discussed to support the factors that contribute to the effectiveness of communication and how it leads to ensuring employees to be ready.

Factors influencing Communication for Employee Readiness during change

Organisational Culture

According to Rashid, Sambasivan and Rahman (2004), the effect of organisational culture is evident when an organisation has undergone a changing process, primarily on the level of acceptance in relations to the attitudes of individuals towards the changes in an organisation.

Organisational commitment is identified by Griffin, Phillips and Gully (2014) as one of the key employee work-related attitudes, aside from job satisfaction and organisational fairness. According to Maxwell and Steele (2003), the outcomes of organisational commitment align with various literatures where employee's commitment plays a role in the ability to adapt and adopt to the organisational goals and culture; the inspiration that organisations advocate for; and the acceptance of additional responsibilities for the managers and additional tasks for the subordinates.

Organisational Commitment

Organisational culture becomes affected when an organisation goes through changes, which can be seen in the work-related attitude, organisational commitment (Rashid, Sambasivan & Rahman, 2004). As reported by Iverson (1996), organisational commitment, a work-related attitude, is a factor to the level of acceptance in organisational change. Variables such as the extent of affiliation of the individual towards the organisation is found to be significant in how accepting they are of changes in an organisation. This is supported by a study conducted by Baruch and Cohen (2007), where employees with a certain extent of affiliation resist the need for change in the organisation due to perceptions like the inability to adjust to changes because of lack of resources.

Organisational Structure

According to Barnett and Carol (1995), organisational structure is one of the factors to influence or trigger organisational change. Stare (2011) further added that the existence of managers in the setting of an organisation impacts the likelihood of great performance in executing tasks.

Based on a study by Krupa and Ostrowska (2012), differences in decision-making can be seen in a hierarchical or flat structure, where objectives of flat structures focus on particular problems that are concerned with effectiveness of problem-solving strategies, whereas in hierarchical structures, decision-making is done in lieu of the significance that can be derived from flat decisions. The importance of organisational structure lies in whether restructuring collaborative functions would be conducive in creating an efficient output, which is found to impede ineffectiveness due to the possibility of conflicts arising from forcing organisational functions that are of different missions and visions (Le Meunier-Fitzhugh and Piercy, 2008).

Manager-Subordinate Relationship

The importance in studying manager-subordinate relationships in the context of change can be related back to what is involved in fostering a positive relationship between employees and managers, which is supported by a study conducted by Pandita, Singh and Choudhary (2019). A study conducted by Samarayanake and Takemura (2017) states the positive and significant correlation between having organisational commitment and employee readiness. Having a strong commitment over the organisation and having trust between employees are the two factors identified that influence the readiness in employees during the course of organisational change. Effective communication is highlighted as one of the key activities to foster trust between employees into the most ideal state as well as to induce strong commitment from the organisational employees during the change (Samaranayake and Takemura, 2017). The notion of trust is also supported by Shah, Irani and Sharif (2017) where it is identified as one of the variables to ensure readiness in employees during organisational change. Moreover, the openness to constructive feedback and the ability to distinguish different channels of communication also influence effective communication (John, 2018). Several literatures have pointed that leadership and level of acceptance are two distinct factors in ensuring a smooth facilitation of communication in ensuring employee readiness during change (Anshari & Hamdan, 2023).

Leadership

Leadership is identified as one of the variables to ensuring employee readiness (Shah, Irani and Sharif, 2017). According to Furst and Cable (2008), to facilitate an effective organisational change, it is crucial to have a better understanding on why and how resistance occurs within the organisation. Employees' resistance to change may not only reflect the method of how managers lead the subordinates, but also indicates the manager-employee relations and its nature. This is supported by Johannsdottir, Olafsson and Davidsdottir (2015) who stated that the role of leadership is shown to be significant in organisational change in terms of how employees can accept and show positive attitudes towards the change initiatives according to the sustainability strategies. The analysis done by Hussain et al. (2018) also identified employee involvement in change and the leadership that helps facilitate change for reaching completion of change facilitation and implementation.

Level of Acceptance

Level of acceptance towards changes is identified as a crucial determinant to manager-subordinate relationship in communicating changes to ensure employee readiness. This is supported by Cai, Loon and Wong (2018), where level of acceptance is noted to be impacted when trust is fostered in the organisation, which ultimately reduces resistance to change. However, individuals may resort to resistance to the changes. Some identified factors are inability to foresee what the future holds, more commonly known as myopia, the overwhelming stress individuals would face from drastic environmental changes resulting from the lack of preparation, barriers in communication between employees, and cynicism that arrives from the belief of unable to achieve the new objectives set up from the organisational change (Landaeta, Mun, Rabadi & Levin, 2008).

Knowledge Sharing as a Platform for Communication

In order to further understand how effective communication can be facilitated in change, knowledge sharing is assessed as a platform in ensuring communication effectiveness. According to the Lewin's Change Management model (1947), knowledge sharing is perceived to be the platform to ease change facilitation, where Van den Hooff and de Ridder (2004) further elaborated that communication is an important key variable to optimise knowledge sharing, which catalyses the change facilitation process. The focus placed on knowledge sharing creates the ease of effective change facilitation into an organisation as well, with the implementation of knowledge sharing to not only create a base for recognising the advantages, but to also reduce resistance and build trust in the organisation towards the management (Muqadas et al., 2017; Anshari et al., 2022). This is also supported by de Bem Machado et al. (2019), where knowledge sharing as a platform for communication is noted to create a push towards innovation in the organisational change.

It is vital to be able to identify communication barriers as a whole in order to be able to foster effective communication in a workplace (Belmejdoub, 2017). Rani (2016) distinguished that there are five different barriers to communication, which are attitudinal barriers, behavioural barriers, cultural barriers, language barriers and environment (noise) barriers. It is also noted how differences in attitudes, value and perception amongst employees may lead to behavioural issues such as abuse of power & discrimination. Cultural barriers in communication would lead to misunderstanding where differences in cultures would result in heightened anxiety and uncertainty, norms and roles established in the organisation, where cross-cultural issues often lead to violations of expectations, non-alignment of beliefs and values of employees, stereotyping of different cultures, and the issues arising from ethnocentrism (Jenifer & Raman, 2015; Anshari et al., 2023).

Behaviours that may arise from poor practice of knowledge sharing may lead to knowledge hiding, where this is defined as the "intentional attempt by an individual to withhold or conceal knowledge that has been requested by another person" (Connelly, Zweig, Webster & Trougakos, 2012). Knowledge hiding behaviours such as playing stupid, evasive hiding and rationalized hiding, are noted to be the common manifestation of the behaviours, which these commonly result from the distrust of individual that engage in the knowledge sharing process (Connelly, Zweig, Webster & Trougakos, 2012). Psychological ownership of the knowledge, whether it is knowledge-based or organisational-based, controls such as age factors and the time span being in the organisation and territoriality in employees may also contribute to knowledge hiding (Peng, 2013).

It is important to familiarise oneself with the communication process, where different elements of the process would include the sender, the channel of communication, the encoding and decoding of the message, the receiver, the feedback and the noise that may interfere with the quality of the message communicated. This is because according to Keyton (2014), any problems that may arise from any part of the communication process may hinder the effectiveness of the communication process (as cited in Lunenburg, 2010). Communication barriers are not possible to abolish, but rather minimise the negative impacts, as they are regarded as one of the diagnostic tools to identify necessary steps that overcome issues stemming from these barriers. Few general guidelines include conducting face-to-face communications whenever possible, familiarise self with different barriers possible and the solutions to them, being empathetic towards one another, practicing direct and ambiguous communication, and repetition of message deliver to ensure accuracy of the message (Truter, 2006). Belmejdoub (2017) explains that aspects like organisational culture assessment, troubleshooting cultural errors and communication skills are essential in minimising communication barriers.

CONCEPTUAL FRAMEWORK

Figure 2. Proposed conceptual framework of the study from various literatures

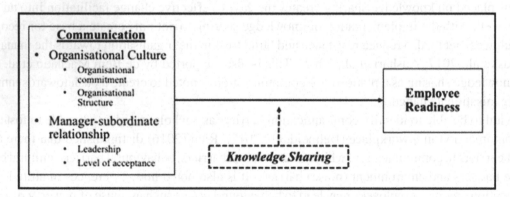

To ensure effective communication in employee readiness, different factors are identified to find out what influence the communication process in facilitating change. Knowledge sharing is then assessed as a potential platform in delivering communication to reach employee readiness. Two main categories that influence communication include organisational culture and manager-subordinate relationship. Under organisational culture, organisational commitment and organisational structure are distinct in what are affected during change. Leadership and level of acceptance of employees are also prominent in evaluating manager-subordinate relationship in the context of how to cope with the organisational change (Figure 2).

METHODOLOGY

The research employed bibliographic analysis of previously published works on knowledge transfer and organisational transformation in order to follow the trends of the topic and establish how recently it had been discussed. This topic first appeared in the Scopus database in 1959, according to the search results for articles published since this topic's initial publication. Furthermore, the study deployed case-based analysis on the change of Telco's organisation and how knowledge transfer strategies were analysed and investigated in this study. The study was conducted based on the recent consolidation of Telco organisations, where the organisation took over the telecommunications structure. There was a transfer of assets between three major telco companies. The three existing telecommunications service providers are now primarily focused on retail operations, with equal access to the main Telco Provider's (TP) network infrastructure. The vision of TP is to be the pioneering digital platform, a trusted partner driving growth and innovation for all industries, supporting a skilled and unique smart nation that is competitive and collaborating globally, and with a mission to unify the national networks and create a modern and cost-efficient digital platform connecting the entire country.

Research Design

The research mainly focused on the ability to be able to gauge the readiness of employees by considering the role of communication in the organisation when dealing with radical change that has occurred within the organisation. In order to meet the research objectives, qualitative research was adopted by garnering information in the form of interviews. According to Bryant (2006), qualitative analysis allows the narrative of the respondents to be explored and response of employees to be understood, such as the different reasonings to which voices are used and how management perceive these voices.

The interview questions were derived from the literature that has been reviewed. Different questions surround the topics of acceptance or resistance towards change and what influences employee readiness and the role of communication in the process. Open-ended interviews were done for all participants which included relevant topics to the research conducted (Hoffmann, 2007). By conducting general questions such as what the participants' last thoughts on the interview, this would allow the responses to have increased saliency in expressing greater interest in the individual's concerns rather than when provided with specific questions (McFarland, 1981). The interview consisted of twelve questions with three main topics, which are the 'Introduction'; 'Work-related attitudes, Employee readiness and change'; and 'Effective communication and Knowledge Sharing'.

Data Collection Method

The data collection process was initiated by approaching the intended organisation by submitting paper and electronic versions of the permission letter to conduct the research interview. E-mail was used as the primary communication means for both the interviewer and the Communications and PR Manager, the focal person of contact from the organisation. The list of respondents comprise of different domains in the organisation of about 10-12 participants, which then was filtered according to six core domains, which are under Operation, Corporate, Finance, DCIT, HR

Figure 3. Qualitative design based participant selection for study
(Source: Author's Compilation, 2022)

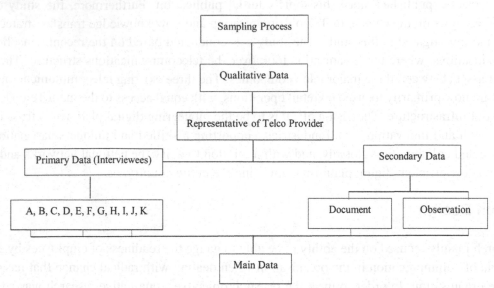

and Network Factory. Scheduling and appointments for the interview sessions were made according to the availability of both the interviewer and the interviewees, and they were briefed on the expected questions to be discussed. Prior to starting the interviews, the interviewees were asked to sign a consent letter as an acknowledgement to the agreement of the research participation. The interviews conducted were based on a focus group basis according to the participants' respective domains (Figure 3). This is because focus groups allow different perspectives of information to be gathered, along with highlighting differences that can be seen from comparing information gathered (Rabiee, 2004). The duration taken for the interview session lasted between 30 minutes to 1 hour 30 minutes depending on the size of the interview group.

Sampling: Type and Target

Purposive sampling was used for the current research, as it is known for its practicality and efficient nature of the method in the selection of participants (Tongco, 2007). This is supported by Etikan, Musa and Alkassim (2016) where purposive sampling places a focus on the ability to get saturated and comprehensible data in order to be able to draw up conclusions. Therefore, the target audience that is found to be best fitting to conduct the study are managers and employees of the TP. Nominees of the different domains of the organisation were quantified into eleven participants in total, which were then divided according to the relevance as a core domain: two participants under Operations, one participant under Corporate, one participant under Finance, two participants under DCIT, one participant under HR and four participants under Network Factory.

Data Analysis Method

The data gathered from the interviews were collected by thorough transcription to strengthen the validation of the responses. All data collected were then compiled into a spreadsheet for the ease of coding according to topics and questions discussed, which were further categorised according to which domain the interviewees belong to. Subsequently, the responses were analysed and assessed via thematic analysis. After completion of analysis, the findings were further analysed and compared to published literatures, whether they support or contradict the statements of the literatures. From the thorough analysis, a conclusion was made from the data gathered.

Data Analysis Process

A focus group interview was conducted to investigate the factors that influences communication in ensuring employees' readiness and the significance of knowledge sharing in delivering effective communication in organisational change. From the interviews, there were six focus groups consisting of eleven participants in total, where the categorisation of participants varies from one to four participants according to their relevance as a core department. The focus groups are categorised into: Operations, Finance, Corporate, DCIT, HR and Network Factory. Prior to the questions that touch on the research objectives, the interviewees were asked about their job description and role in the telecommunication industry.

Table 1. Description of interviewees who participated in the data collection

Domain	Interviewee(s)	Job Description	Extent of Affiliation
Operations	Interviewee A	Manager	More than 10 years
	Interviewee B	Manager	Less than 10 years
Finance	Interviewee C	Employee	More than 1 year
Corporate	Interviewee D	Manager	More than 10 years
DCIT	Interviewee E	Employee	More than 20 years
	Interviewee F	Employee	Less than 1 year
HR	Interviewee G	Employee	Less than 1 year
Network Factory	Interviewee H	Employee	Less than 10 years
	Interviewee I	Employee	More than 20 years
	Interviewee J	Manager	More than 30 years
	Interviewee K	Manager	More than 30 years

ANALYSIS

Using the search keyword "organization change AND knowledge transfer, there were 3856 articles published from 1959–2022 in the Scopus indexed database. Figure 4 shows how the number of publications has changed over time since the first discussion topics were added to the Scopus database in 1959.

This time period goes from 1959 to 2022. There was an increasing number of publications on this topic from 2001 to 2019.

Figure 4. Documents by year on knowledge transfer and organisational change
(Source: Scopus, 1959 -2022)

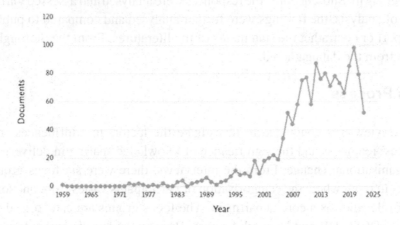

The discussion of Knowledge Transfer and Organizational Change is widely discussed in Social Science, Business Management, Medicine, Engineering, and Computer Science (See Figure 5).

Figure 5. Documents by subject area
(Source: Scopus, 1959 -2022)

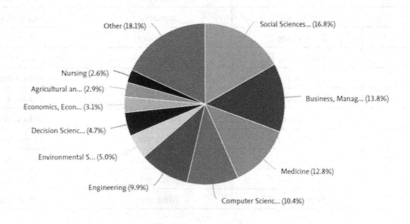

The largest contributors to this research are still developed countries such as the US, UK, Canada, Australia, Germany, and the Netherlands. While research from developing countries is very lacking, the results of this research can be a scientific contribution, especially lessons learned from developing countries (See Figure 6).

Figure 6. Documents by country
(Source: Scopus, 1959 -2022)

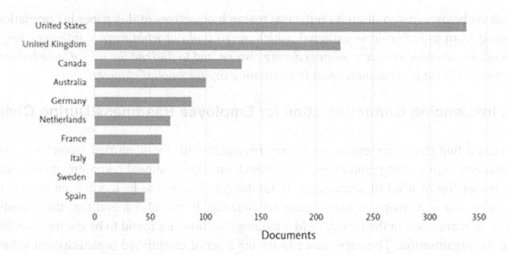

From the results of the bibliographic analysis in Figure 7, it is found that there are three large clusters in the domain of this research which are separated by different colors. The first cluster is research trends with the colour green discussing a lot in the fields of public healthcare delivery, health service research, organisational innovation, and organisational culture. The red cluster is a research domain that discusses trends about organisational learning, sustainable development and government technology. And the blue cluster also discusses a lot in the healthcare domain but focuses more on human centric such as patient care, healthcare personnel, and attitude to health.

Figure 7. Bibliographic analysis on knowledge transfer and organisational change

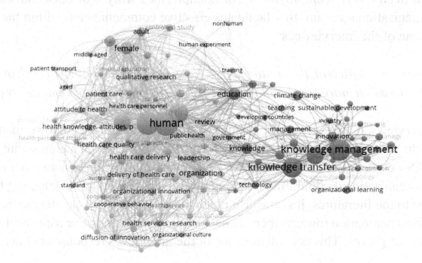

FINDINGS AND DISCUSSION

The discussion below aims to discuss on the two research objectives of this paper in correlation to the data gathered from the interviews gathered, which are to *find out what factors influence employees' communication that could ensure readiness during change*, and to *find out the role of knowledge sharing as a potential platform in communication in facilitating organisational change.*

Factors Influencing Communication for Employee Readiness During Change

It was revealed that the interviewees' responses resonated with the identified factors that influence the communication in making employees ready, which are organisational commitment, organisational structure, leadership & level of acceptance. In the bigger picture, the factors fall under two themes: organisational culture & manager-subordinate relationship. It was also found that the organisational core values, as mentioned in the Research Methodology section, are found to be the basis on how they operate in the organisation. The importance of having a set of established organisational values lie in the efforts to nurture the organisational culture & manager-subordinate relationships in order to align employees to the organisation's identity, thus easing change facilitation. This is supported by Sullivan, Sullivan and Buffton (2001).

Conducive Organisational Culture

Organisational culture is one of the factors that demonstrates the influence of communication in making sure employees are ready during change. The impact on organisational culture in organisational change is supported by Rashid, Sambasivan and Rahman (2004), where the authors found that there is an association between culture and attitudinal tendencies when change occurs. When asked about the communication system in the organisation, culture plays a significant role in effectively communicating with one another in all levels of employment. For example, the ability to be open and accountable seems to be part of organisational culture that facilitates effective communication within the organisation as highlighted by one of the interviewees:

I think communication is efficient, the culture here is that people are very open to each other. What makes it easier and what makes it more acceptable is that I see a belief in taking accountability (Interviewee D).

From the interviews, it also seems that having the culture of employee empowerment greatly affects employees' productivity in executing their tasks and responsibilities, which aligns with a study done by Meyerson and Dewettinck (2012). Consequently, the effect of having an empowering culture results in the heightened organisational commitment in employees (Janssen, 2004). Comparing the responses of the interviewees to the literatures, it seems that the organisation fosters a positive culture that strengthens the employees' perception towards them, hence the advocacy of positive aspects of the organisation towards their working lives. This is evident in one of the interview's responses below:

They don't leave you to figure things out by yourself. It's easy to mingle with everyone. Even with all the training, the managers and teams also help out with whatever training that we need & help guide us. They also say to not be afraid of mistakes because it's understandable that newbies are afraid to do this and that. (Interviewee F)

A good manager should be empowering, but also align with the mission and vision of the company (Interviewee G).

Not only that, Interviewee D noted "the inspiring desire to contribute to TP" as what made the interviewee ready, which reflects on the employee's strong organisational commitment towards the organisation. This is consistent with the study done by Janssen (2004).

Culture also seems to play a distinct role in the form of organisational structure. According to Maduenyi, Oke, Fadeyi and Ajagbe (2015), there is a significant impact in how an organisation performs in accordance to their structure. A study by Holtzhausen (2002) states that an organisation with structural changes is found to have improved information flow and communication process. This is suggested in the context of TP, where employees from different telecommunications company's experiences are seen to remark on the improvement of communication, which they attributed this to the efforts of 'trying to be a flat structure', as noted by one of the interviewees:

For top to bottom communication, there aren't many constraints as we are trying to be flat (Interviewee G).

To dissect the responses of interviewees further in comparison to the literatures, variables of organisational culture, which are organisational commitment & organisational structure, are further analysed in order to evaluate the influence of organisational culture has on communication that will lead to employee readiness.

Organisational Commitment

It appears that organisational commitment is one of the determining factors to what influences communication in organisational change, as the importance of strong organisational commitment in making employees ready is supported by Samaranayake and Takemura (2017). Employees' organisational commitment can be assessed in terms of their extent of affiliation (Iverson, 1996). This is further elaborated by Baruch and Cohen (2007), where a certain extent may affect how they perceive the changes imposed to the organisation. The impact of extent of affiliation towards communication processes in the organisation is supported by De Nobile (2016) where high level of affiliation results from the positive communication practices of an organisation, thus strengthening the employees' organisational commitment. It was found at the time of interview that five of the interviewees have an extent of affiliation of more than 10 years in the telecommunications industry, meanwhile six of the respondents have an extent of affiliation for less than 10 years, if not none (refer to Table 1).

It is found that the interviewees have a mixed response when asked about the effect of change that is impacted to the organisational culture. Through their extent of affiliation towards the telecommunication industry, some found that their prior experience in the telecommunication industry did not affect their adaptability towards the change. The response of the interviewee seems to not be affected by the changing culture as they are not as familiar to their previous organisation's culture, which can be seen in the response below:

Honestly, the transformation [in the telecommunication industry] did not really affect me. I was only for 8 months, so I am unsure of the culture that they have there. However, I can say that TP has a dynamic and performance-oriented culture (Interviewee G).

However, some saw differences coming into the current organisation in comparison to their previous organisation. This is shown to be evident in the clash of organisational culture when processing work, as quoted by one of the interviewees below:

The previous organisation I was in was the only telecommunications company that was fully absorbed into TP. Before we definitely had less people working in the organisation. So, it was only later on when we were working to consolidate the assets that the team discovered that maybe we need a cultural change as we confronted this change. So we decided to develop new processes and policies to have a unified view on how things should work, which is really important to standardise the quality of work that we put in because it was really messy in the beginning when we try to track certain things, there was just no in-depth communication that escalated to a legal dispute, and I had no way to backtracking documents, but now we have new policies new standards that we introduce really quickly. With this, it wasn't as if people were thinking about what to put in or how to record it (Interviewee D).

From the quotation above, it suggests that employees' organisational commitment, in the form of extent of affiliation, plays a significant role when change happens. Prior experiences in the telecommunications industry can aid in effectively communicating the change between the employees. The response also shows to be consistent with the study done by De Nobile (2016).

Organisational Structure

It is found that organisational structure appears to be a determinant to influence communicating organisational changes, which is supported by Barnett and Carroll (1995). Communication was found to be present when the consolidation project of TP, an infrastructural change, was communicated to the employees of the telecommunications industry from the board members involved in the project. According to Avgerou (2000), a flattened organisational structure helps facilitate improved communication in the context of structural changes (as cited by Doherty, Champion & Wang, 2010). This is found to be evident in TP's efforts to create a flat structure, as mentioned by one of the interviewees:

Every organisation has their own culture, as for TP I guess the biggest difference for me would be the organisational chart, because where I was from we have a lot of hierarchy, whereas TP is quite flat. I feel like everything is open and it's easier to talk to anyone and then from that I feel like everything is more efficient as well in terms of our work and relationships with the colleagues (Interviewee C).

For top to bottom communication, there aren't many constraints as we are trying to be flat (Interviewee G).

From the responses gathered, it is found that flat organisational structure encourages more openness in communication between individuals during change, especially with decision-making. The openness in the communication can be seen in cases such as team-building, as mentioned by a few of the responses from the interviewees:

Teamwork is emphasised, which aligns with TPP's core values, so exercises were initiated to do activities like coming up with a framework & to develop departmental mission & vision, FAQs, Q&A sessions, forums. (Interviewee A)

The current board of directors are very understanding of how employees feel and deal with the change. Team building fosters togetherness and it's a value because it's not a manager's initiative. (Interviewee E).

The senior management team sees the importance of having team building activities not because of the danger of people rTPing out, but people actually need to speak to one another. This kind of opportunity we have the opportunity to put work aside and unwind, that's how we get to improve in culture and get to know other people [cross-functions] (Interviewee F).

Continuous improvement is seen as a practice that is constantly advocated in the organisation by the top management of TP, with supportive efforts to communicate this 'best practice' thoroughly regardless of levels. The concept of continuous improvement not only aligns with a few of the organisation's core values, "Explore possibilities" and "Go beyond", but it is also a practice that when adopted may help smoothly facilitate organisational change. This aligns with a study by Irani and Sharp (1997). The promotion of continuous improvement can be seen to be facilitated in the flat structure, as discussed by the interviewees:

TP's management is a very supportive management, and it is very non-discriminatory. The management practices openness as well. (Interviewee B).

There's definitely a cultural gap, however, in TP, we don't want that to happen so we try to adopt the best practice. We also value continuous improvement. So whatever best practice previous employees from other telecommunications companies have, please share with us. (Interviewee G)

Having flatter structure and open communication, it seems able to create trust in the workplace whereby effective communication is fostered and this is similar to the study by Samaranayake and Takemura (2017).

Positive and strong Manager-Subordinate Relationship

There is a significance in having a strong manager-subordinate relationship when ensuring effective communication in an organisation. This is supported by John (2018) where he stated that the existence of trust is important between employees in an organisation. Shah, Irani and Sharif (2017) further supports trust between employees and the management in the organisation as to influencing readiness. In the Bruneian context, the role of managers is expected to be assumed by an individual with a trustworthy characteristic and lead by example, where communication and employee empowerment is sought for in order to gain organisational commitment from the employees (Md Zain, Ali Yusob & Ang, 2012). Two factors have been identified to fall under this theme; leadership and level of acceptance.

Leadership

Besides having a conducive organisational culture for effective communication, having positive manager-subordinate relationships is seen to be essential and that it is the role of the leadership that is present in the organisation to influence the level of acceptance from managers and employees when change is communicated. As seen in the quotation from one manager and one employee below:

TP's management is a very supportive management, and it is very non-discriminatory. The management practices openness as well. (Interviewee B).

Managers in TP are transparent in communicating changes to the employees, because when the change is not communicated, people will experience culture shock from it. Through this transparency as well, people would be more accepting of the change (Interviewee G).

The view that supportive management and leadership is shared amongst all interviewees regardless of their position and length of service. Indeed, this is similar to Johannsdottir, Olaffson and Davidsdottir (2015) who have stated that the role of leadership has a major significance in change facilitation. Nelissen and van Selm (2008) also argued the importance of communication style from the top management of the organisation to employees in order to achieve positive results is crucial in change facilitation. This can be seen in the responses stated below:

The top management takes change facilitation seriously which was a surprise to me because where I came from, organisational change wasn't like a priority. For example, they had an SMT meeting to discuss broad topics with the line managers. We also have change management as part of their agenda, to really change the mindsets of these people (Interviewee C).

From the interview, having the right group of people as a focal point in ensuring change facilitation is especially important in ensuring readiness in employees. The expectation from introducing change management as a department in the organisation is to help facilitate change and its repercussion to the employees, where it is deemed to be effective in making sure employees are ready. Without a proper understanding of the significance of change, organisations will not be able to achieve their expected goals, as supported by Nastase, Giuclea and Bold (2012).

How we deal with mindset is to have quarterly meetings. Change Management department is also introduced in efforts to facilitate changes in the organisation (Interviewee A).

I am a part of the Change Management team as well where I lead the team to help realign the mindsets of the employees here to go TP way, not their previous organisation's way (Interviewee B).

Change Management [team] and the change ambassadors, one of the ways to support mindset, to help create 'that' mindset (Interviewee C).

We also have the change management as part of the SMT meeting agenda, because I'm in corporate sector of the board meeting so I see them raise this to the board to really change the mindsets of these people (Interviewee D).

With a strong foundation to manager-subordinate relationships, change facilitation is seen to be eased. This is supported by a study by Pandita, Singh and Choudhary (2019).

Level of Acceptance

Level of acceptance of employees towards changes is identified as a crucial determinant to manager-subordinate relationship in communicating changes to ensure employee readiness. This is supported by Cai, Loon and Wong (2018), where level of acceptance is noted to be impacted when trust is fostered in the organisation, which ultimately reduces resistance to change. However, from the interviews conducted, it was shown that mindset plays a role in how changes are accepted in the context of change facilitation.

The mentality towards cautiousness is involved. The 'territorial' behaviour can be seen initially because these people come from different backgrounds, they tend to be cautious. This cautiousness can be due to competency gap and fear of negligence (Interviewee A).

Frequent meetings to realign different mindsets of the salesco representatives. So every 8AM, we have a daily system to ensure that daily goals are reached and everything is executed hands-on (Interviewee B).

When you recruit three different companies into one, cultural barriers can be an issue because a lot of people have their set of mindsets (Interviewee G).

From the interviews, mindset is prevalent as a factor in making sure employees are ready as perception of how change is accepted can shape how employees behave in the event of change. This aligns with a study done by Cai, Loon and Wong (2018). Resistance to change can be seen in the earlier stages of change facilitation of the consolidation, which can be seen when some individuals exhibit behaviours such as cynicism towards changing cultural practices. Communication process, in this case, is crucial to be looked at to remedy issues leading to ineffectiveness, as supported by Keyton (2011).

Knowledge Sharing as a Platform for Communication

From the data gathered during the interview, the role of knowledge sharing as a potential platform in communication is revealed to be prevalent in the context of preparing employees in making them ready. This is aligned with the studies conducted by Hussain et al. (2018), where he discussed how knowledge sharing is deemed to be one of the processes during change, and also identified as the catalyst in facilitating change. Responses from the interviewees are as follows:

I believe that knowledge sharing is essential for a company towards achieving success, because it firstly makes the organization's best problem-solving experiences reusable, enabling better and faster decision making. Knowledge sharing also stimulates innovation and growth. Not only that, knowledge sharing improves communication and collaboration within a company, thus making employees feel valued (Interviewee A).

I think knowledge is really important, because when we know what each other does it makes our jobs more efficient, it makes their job more efficient (Interviewee D).

With knowledge sharing in place, at least in the case of absence of the focal person in the server or network, I'll be able to back them up (Interviewee F).

From the responses gathered, it seems that knowledge sharing allows ease in communication in terms of change facilitation, thus enabling knowledge sharing to be a catalytic platform in order to communicate the change to the employees. This is shown to be reflected when compared to the Lewin's Change Management model (1947) as well as a study conducted by Van den Hooff and de Ridder (2004). With knowledge sharing being practiced in the organisation, it can also be remarked to provide a safe space in order for employees to be able to develop their skill sets. For example, one of the interviewees discussed on the existence of a department that focuses on learning and development:

In TP, I'm actually in the Learning and Development [department], it's the one that provides training to employees here. Yes, what we do here is onboarding training, to teach the company's policies and what to do. We also provide training to improve in one area that the employees lack skills in, to upskill themselves, regardless if they are skilful or not (Interviewee G).

The concept of knowledge sharing has also been proven to be prevalent to the organisation, as knowledge development is noted to be one of the factors to perform the key objective to reach industry transformation in the telecommunications industry. This can be seen to be practiced in TP due to the establishment of the Knowledge Management department, as evident in one of the interviewees' responses:

I am a Knowledge Manager, where my team looks after the governance of a knowledge base. I focus on implementing a Knowledge Management framework and cultivating a Knowledge Sharing Culture in the organisation. My team also focuses on implementing knowledge sharing tools and environment in the organisation, and helps assist elicit knowledge by facilitating brainstorming and workshops (Interviewee A).

However, the management of knowledge is considerably a new concept being integrated into the current telecommunications industry. With the right focal points to encourage the concept of knowledge management, different tools and platforms are introduced into the organisation in hopes to have the culture of knowledge sharing being integrated into the working lives of the employees in TP.

The goal is to make knowledge management more appealing. With a knowledge portal available, this allows content regulation and helps knowledge retention. As knowledge sharing is also a new concept, a symposium is also introduced to share findings on how different departments analyse data (Interviewee A).

Fortunately, the efforts to integrate knowledge sharing into the organisational culture are to be of positive results, where it was found that information is actively transferred. This eases the knowledge sharing processes between employees in the organisation. A discussion by de Bem Machado et al. (2019) talks further on knowledge sharing as a communication platform and how it pushes the innovative initiatives in the context of organisational change. This is apparent in the heavy utilisation of these knowledge sharing tools and platforms provided to the employees.

The communication platform, SharePoint, is heavily used by the Finance team, with the different divisions in Finance, so whenever we need new information we can just go onto SharePoint and find the info that we need as it is frequently updated (Interviewee C).

A knowledge sharing platform called SharePoint is my holy grail because during COVID, we didn't go into the office for 6 months with the normal hours. I think Knowledge Sharing platforms are very critical that should be implemented even before COVID happen, so now if we'd want to search for a file we don't need to go through the hassle of contacting different people, we can just access it through one shared platform, and we have an organised system on how files are arranged (Interviewee D).

In HR, we will meet and have this knowledge sharing session called impulse session. How it works is that if you have something that you want to share, you prepare a PowerPoint based on it and present that time. It's a weekly basis session. If that knowledge is perhaps good, then we can take that knowledge to implement it (Interviewee G).

However, some of these platforms are still underutilised and have low usage. Understandably, these underutilised tools are fairly new to the employees and still are yet adapting to the knowledge sharing culture.

Usage of the knowledge sharing tools and platforms has been low as we have only introduced some of the tools last year and introduced a knowledge sharing culture (Interviewee A).

Yammer is very new for a lot of us, a combo of FB & IG & Blogging, it is underutilised because we have yet to find the identity or the proposition to say to utilise it as often (Interviewee C).

Evidence of knowledge sharing platforms not only is evident in the daily working lives of the employees in the organisation, it also dates back to when the consolidation project was announced. All of the interviewees agreed that the town hall act as an important platform in sharing any form of knowledge, be it about organisational changes or not. This can be seen in one of the interviewees' response and how the interviewee perceives the significance of town hall is:

Quarterly cascades of town halls can be done in order to align employees, which can be done by divisions at first then a townhall at a bigger scale (Interviewee A).

We need to be more transparent, how we can do this is via townhalls, from there when we speak out about what issues need to be raised and what solutions can be proposed (Interviewee G).

According to Belmejdoub (2017), in order to ensure that communication is fostered effectively, identifying communication barriers in the organisation is crucial. Through the interviews, it was found that some find attitudinal, cultural and environmental barriers to what affects communication in the organisation. It is also found that the existence of communication barriers impacts knowledge sharing in an organisation.

Some employees do still have the 'mind my own business' mindset, and having to practice the knowledge sharing culture will take time because some don't really see the value in knowledge yet (Interviewee B).

Over here at the headquarters, we are segregated into domains. The closed-up area is HR, these glass panels weren't here before, they just installed these, whereas those out there are corporate and the vacant rooms being for audits, and I feel that this is not effective in how we perceive our colleagues. The physical walls make it hard for us to break down our barriers, though it's slowly improving because there are some traditions that HR have that we were just recently invited to (Interviewee D).

For me, we were in K-Hub at that time, I thought that my team consists of 6 people only, but it turns out that we are more than 20 people but you'd need to go out of the rooms. After moving to the Telehouse in Bandar, that's when I know more on who my teammates are. Just the walls that separates us creates a barrier in talking for us (Interviewee F).

I was a bit affected by the lessening interaction between people when the pandemic outbreak started. Another barrier is that in terms of projects, you need to know who the stakeholders are, which is what we call stakeholder management. By identifying the correct stakeholders in place, there wouldn't be barriers in communication taking place (Interviewee G).

Based on the responses from above, it can be inferred that despite having some barriers being present in the organisation, the knowledge sharing culture that is continuously advocated in the organisation has helped in managing the negative impacts that comes from the barriers. This is aligned with a study done by Truter (2006). The interviews have also revealed that there are not any concerns that have been associated with knowledge hiding, where the advocacy of knowledge sharing and knowledge development & the practice of open communication can be attributed to the absence of knowledge hiding in the organisation. This aligns with studies done by Dyer and Nobeoka (2000) and Garon (2012).

To me there's not really any knowledge hiding as it is not significant at all. There is a strong willingness to learn because there are a lot of young engineers who are hungry to learn, and that they have the drive to the right direction, especially with experienced employees (Interviewee B).

It really is down to the culture. Knowledge sharing comes down to the practice of open communication here. Fundamentally you need to be on the same boat when it comes to the core values. I think that it's good that the corporate communication department is giving us articles to do regarding the core values because this helps us understand truly the values being instilled in TP and incorporate that in our lives (Interviewee F).

CONCLUSION

In summary, the role of knowledge sharing is crucial in order for communication processes to be facilitated smoothly in the context of change. Not only knowledge sharing provides a platform to improve the culture of an organisation when undergoing changes, but it also fosters a positive relationship between managers and subordinates. With factors such as commitment, organisational structure, leadership and level of acceptance, employee readiness can be ensured with the assistance of knowledge sharing as a platform for communication. However, the likelihood of knowledge sharing to not be of existence occurs when the factors achieve a negative result, such as poor commitment and resistance to change. This may lead to a phenomenon known as knowledge hiding. Therefore, it is ideal to consider the importance of the factors that can influence communication in ensuring that employees are ready for changes that may potentially be imposed, as change is inevitable and happens over time to keep up with the ever-changing times.

REFERENCES

Allen, J., Jimmieson, N. L., Bordia, P., & Irmer, B. E. (2007). Uncertainty during organisational change: Managing perceptions through communication. *Journal of Change Management*, 7(2), 187–210. doi:10.1080/14697010701563379

Anshari, M., Alas, Y., & Guan, L. S. (2016). Developing online learning resources: Big data, social networks, and cloud computing to support pervasive knowledge. *Education and Information Technologies*, 21(6), 1663–1677. doi:10.1007/s10639-015-9407-3

Anshari, M., Almunawar, M. N., Lim, S. A., & Al-Mudimigh, A. (2019). Customer relationship management and big data enabled: Personalization & customization of services. *Applied Computing and Informatics*, 15(2), 94–101. doi:10.1016/j.aci.2018.05.004

Anshari, M., & Hamdan, M. (2022). Understanding knowledge management and upskilling in Fourth Industrial Revolution: Transformational shift and SECI model. *VINE Journal of Information and Knowledge Management Systems*, 52(3), 373–393. doi:10.1108/VJIKMS-09-2021-0203

Anshari, M., & Hamdan, M. (2023). Enhancing e-government with a digital twin for innovation management. *Journal of Science and Technology Policy Management*, 14(6), 1055–1065. doi:10.1108/JSTPM-11-2021-0176

Anshari, M., & Lim, S. A. (2017). E-government with big data enabled through smartphone for public services: Possibilities and challenges. *International Journal of Public Administration*, 40(13), 1143–1158. doi:10.1080/01900692.2016.1242619

Anshari, M., Syafrudin, M., & Fitriyani, N. L. (2022). Fourth industrial revolution between knowledge management and digital humanities. *Information (Basel)*, 13(6), 292. doi:10.3390/info13060292

Anshari, M., Syafrudin, M., Tan, A., Fitriyani, N. L., & Alas, Y. (2023). Optimisation of knowledge management (KM) with machine learning (ML) Enabled. *Information (Basel)*, 14(1), 35. doi:10.3390/info14010035

Barnett, W. P., & Carroll, G. R. (1995). Modeling internal organisational change. *Annual Review of Sociology*, *21*(1), 217–236. doi:10.1146/annurev.so.21.080195.001245

Baruch, Y., & Cohen, A. (2007). The dynamics between organisational commitment and professional identity formation at work. In *Identities at work* (pp. 241–260). Springer. doi:10.1007/978-1-4020-4989-7_9

Bateh, J., Castaneda, M. E., & Farah, J. E. (2013). Employee resistance to organisational change. [IJMIS]. *International Journal of Management & Information Systems*, *17*(2), 113–116.

Belmejdoub, A. (2017). *MANAGING ORGANISATIONAL COMMUNICATION: An Analysis of Communication Knowledge*. Stakeholder Requirements and Barriers to Effective Communication in the Workplace.

Bordia, P., Hunt, E., Paulsen, N., Tourish, D., & DiFonzo, N. (2004). Uncertainty during organisational change: Is it all about control? *European Journal of Work and Organizational Psychology*, *13*(3), 345–365. doi:10.1080/13594320444000128

Branson, C. M. (2008). Achieving organisational change through values alignment. *Journal of Educational Administration*, *46*(3), 376–395. doi:10.1108/09578230810869293

Bryant, M. (2006). Talking about change: Understanding employee responses through qualitative research. *Management Decision*, *44*(2), 246–258. doi:10.1108/00251740610650229

Cai, W. J., Loon, M., & Wong, P. H. K. (2018). Leadership, trust in management and acceptance of change in Hong Kong's Civil Service Bureau. *Journal of Organizational Change Management*, *31*(5), 1054–1070. doi:10.1108/JOCM-10-2016-0215

Connelly, C. E., Zweig, D., Webster, J., & Trougakos, J. P. (2012). Knowledge hiding in organizations. *Journal of Organizational Behavior*, *33*(1), 64–88. doi:10.1002/job.737

Craig, T., & Campbell, D. (2012). *Organisations and the business environment*. Routledge. doi:10.4324/9780080454603

de Bem Machado, A., Souza, M. J., & Catapan, A. H. (2019). Systematic Review: Intersection between Communication and Knowledge. *Journal of Information Systems Engineering & Management*, *4*(1), em0086.

De Nobile, J. (2016). Organisational communication and its relationships with job satisfaction and organisational commitment of primary school staff in Western Australia. *Educational Psychology*, *37*(3), 380–398. doi:10.1080/01443410.2016.1165797

Doherty, N. F., Champion, D., & Wang, L. (2010). An holistic approach to understanding the changing nature of organisational structure. *Information Technology & People*, *23*(2), 116–135. doi:10.1108/09593841011052138

Dyer, J. H., & Nobeoka, K. (2000). Creating and managing a high-performance knowledge-sharing network: The Toyota case. *Strategic Management Journal*, *21*(3), 345–367. doi:10.1002/(SICI)1097-0266(200003)21:3<345::AID-SMJ96>3.0.CO;2-N

Etikan, I., Musa, S. A., & Alkassim, R. S. (2016). Comparison of convenience sampling and pur-posive sampling. *American Journal of Theoretical and Applied Statistics*, *5*(1), 1–4. doi:10.11648/j.ajtas.20160501.11

Furst, S. A., & Cable, D. M. (2008). Employee resistance to organisational change: Managerial in-fluence tactics and leader-member exchange. *The Journal of Applied Psychology*, *93*(2), 453–462. doi:10.1037/0021-9010.93.2.453 PMID:18361644

Garon, M. (2012). Speaking up, being heard: Registered nurses' perceptions of workplace communication. *Journal of Nursing Management*, *20*(3), 361–371. doi:10.1111/j.1365-2834.2011.01296.x PMID:22519614

Greenan, N. (2003). Organisational change, technology, employment and skills: An empirical study of French manufacturing. *Cambridge Journal of Economics*, *27*(2), 287–316. doi:10.1093/cje/27.2.287

Griffin, R. W., Phillips, J. M., & Gully, S. M. (2014). *Organisational Behaviour: Managing People and Organisations* (12th ed.). Cengage.

Hoffmann, E. A. (2007). Open-ended interviews, power, and emotional labor. *Journal of Contemporary Ethnography*, *36*(3), 318–346. doi:10.1177/0891241606293134

Holtzhausen, D. (2002). The effects of a divisionalised and decentralised organisational structure on a formal internal communication function in a South African organisation. *Journal of Communication Management (London)*, *6*(4), 323–339. doi:10.1108/13632540210807152

Husain, Z. (2013). Effective communication brings successful organisational change. *The Business & Management Review*, *3*(2), 43.

Hussain, S. T., Lei, S., Akram, T., Haider, M. J., Hussain, S. H., & Ali, M. (2018). Kurt Lewin's change model: A critical review of the role of leadership and employee involvement in organisational change. *Journal of Innovation & Knowledge*, *3*(3), 123–127. doi:10.1016/j.jik.2016.07.002

Ipe, M. (2003). Knowledge sharing in organizations: A conceptual framework. *Human Resource Devel-opment Review*, *2*(4), 337–359. doi:10.1177/1534484303257985

Irani, Z., & Sharp, J. M. (1997). Integrating continuous improvement and innovation into a corporate culture: A case study. *Technovation*, *17*(4), 199–223. doi:10.1016/S0166-4972(96)00103-4

Iverson, R. D. (1996). Employee acceptance of organisational change: The role of organisational commitment. *International Journal of Human Resource Management*, *7*(1), 122–149. doi:10.1080/09585199600000121

Jaman, S. F. I., & Anshari, M. (2021). Facebook as marketing tools for organizations: Knowledge man-agement analysis. In *Research Anthology on Strategies for Using Social Media as a Service and Tool in Business* (pp. 117–131). IGI Global. doi:10.4018/978-1-7998-9020-1.ch007

Janssen, O. (2004). The barrier effect of conflict with superiors in the relationship between employee empowerment and organizational commitment. *Work and Stress*, *18*(1), 56–65. doi:10.1080/02678370410001690466

Jenifer, R. D., & Raman, G. P. (2015). Cross-cultural communication barriers in the workplace. *Inter-national Journal of Management*, *6*(1), 348–351.

Johannsdottir, L., Olafsson, S., & Davidsdottir, B. (2015). Leadership role and employee acceptance of change: Implementing environmental sustainability strategies within Nordic insurance companies. *Journal of Organizational Change Management, 28*(1), 72–96. doi:10.1108/JOCM-12-2013-0238

John, K. N. (2018). Importance of Communication to Stakeholders in all Organisations.

Krupa, T., & Ostrowska, T. (2012). Decision-making in flat and hierarchical decision problems. *foundations of management, 4*(2), 23-36.

Landaeta, R. E., Mun, J. H., Rabadi, G., & Levin, D. (2008). Identifying sources of resistance to change in healthcare. *International Journal of Healthcare Technology and Management, 9*(1), 74–96. doi:10.1504/IJHTM.2008.016849

Le Meunier-Fitzhugh, K., & Piercy, N. F. (2008). The Importance of Organisational Structure for Collaboration between Sales and Marketing. *Journal of General Management, 34*(1), 19–36. doi:10.1177/030630700803400102

Lewin, K. (1951). *Field theory in social science: selected theoretical papers* (D. Cartwright, Ed.).

Lunenburg, F. C. (2010). Communication: The process, barriers, and improving effectiveness. *Schooling, 1*(1), 1–10.

Maxwell, G., & Steele, G. (2003). Organisational commitment: A study of managers in hotels. *International Journal of Contemporary Hospitality Management, 15*(7), 362–369. doi:10.1108/09596110310496006

McFarland, S. G. (1981). Effects of question order on survey responses. *Public Opinion Quarterly, 45*(2), 208–215. doi:10.1086/268651

Meyerson, G., & Dewettinck, B. (2012). Effect of empowerment on employees performance. *Advanced Research in Economic and Management Sciences, 2*(1), 40–46.

Muqadas, F., Rehman, M., Aslam, U., & Ur-Rahman, U. (2017). Exploring the challenges, trends and issues for knowledge sharing. *VINE Journal of Information and Knowledge Management Systems, 47*(1), 2–15. doi:10.1108/VJIKMS-06-2016-0036

Nastase, M., Giuclea, M., & Bold, O. (2012). The impact of change management in organizations-a survey of methods and techniques for a successful change. *Revista De Management Comparat International, 13*(1), 5.

Nelissen, P., & van Selm, M. (2008). Surviving organisational change: How management communication helps balance mixed feelings. *Corporate Communications, 13*(3), 306–318. doi:10.1108/13563280810893670

Ordoñez de Pablos, P. (2023). Digital innovation and green economy for more resilient and inclusive societies: Understanding challenges ahead for the green growth. *Journal of Science and Technology Policy Management, 14*(3), 461–466. doi:10.1108/JSTPM-05-2023-193

Ordóñez de Pablos, P. (2024). Digital transformation, innovation and competitiveness: Some insights from Asia. *Journal of Science and Technology Policy Management, 15*(1), 1–5. doi:10.1108/JSTPM-01-2024-222

Pandita, D., Singh, M., & Choudhary, S. (2019). The Changing Dynamics of Manager-Subordinate Relationships in Organizations: An Empirical Study. *European Business Review, 00–00.* doi:10.1108/EBR-04-2017-0072

Peng, H. (2013). Why and when do people hide knowledge? *Journal of Knowledge Management, 17*(3), 398–415. doi:10.1108/JKM-12-2012-0380

Rabiee, F. (2004). Focus-group interview and data analysis. *The Proceedings of the Nutrition Society, 63*(4), 655–660. doi:10.1079/PNS2004399 PMID:15831139

Rani, K. U. (2016). Communication barriers. *Journal of English Language and Literature, 3*(2), 74–76.

Rashid, Z. A., Sambasivan, M., & Rahman, A. A. (2004). The influence of organisational culture on attitudes toward organisational change. *Leadership and Organization Development Journal.*

Sait, M. A., & Anshari, M. (2021). Industrial Revolution 4.0: A New Challenge to Brunei Darussalam's Unemployment Issue. [IJABIM]. *International Journal of Asian Business and Information Management, 12*(4), 33–44. doi:10.4018/IJABIM.20211001.oa3

Samaranayake, S. U., & Takemura, T. (2017). Employee readiness for organizational change: A case study in an export oriented manufacturing firm in Sri Lanka. *Eurasian Journal of Business and Economics, 10*(20), 1–16. doi:10.17015/ejbe.2017.020.01

Shah, N., Irani, Z., & Sharif, A. M. (2017). Big data in an HR context: Exploring organizational change readiness, employee attitudes and behaviors. *Journal of Business Research, 70,* 366–378. doi:10.1016/j.jbusres.2016.08.010

Smith, I. (2005). Achieving readiness for organisational change. *Library Management, 26*(6/7), 408–412. doi:10.1108/01435120510623764

Stare, A. (2011). The impact of the organisational structure and project organisational culture on project performance in Slovenian enterprises. *Management, 16*(2), 1–22.

Sullivan, W., Sullivan, R., & Buffton, B. (2001). Aligning individual and organisational values to support change. *Journal of Change Management, 2*(3), 247–254. doi:10.1080/738552750

Truter, I. (2006). Barriers to communication and how to overcome them: management. *South African Pharmaceutical Journal. Suid-Afrikaanse Tydskrif vir Apteekwese, 73*(7), 55–58.

Van den Hooff, B., & de Ridder, J. A. (2004). Knowledge sharing in context: The influence of organisational commitment, communication climate and CMC use on knowledge sharing. *Journal of Knowledge Management, 8*(6), 117–130. doi:10.1108/13673270410567675

Zain, M., Yusob, A., & Ang, S. (2012). The key principles of managing people: The Brunei perspective. *Educational Research, 3,* 594–602.

Ziaee Bigdeli, A., Baines, T., Bustinza, O. F., & Guang Shi, V. (2017). Organisational change towards servitization: A theoretical framework. *Competitiveness Review, 27*(1), 12–39. doi:10.1108/CR-03-2015-0015

Chapter 13
Comparing PLS–SEM Statistical Technologies for Educating the Importance of Linearity:
Attitude Theory Validation in Digital Marketplace

Dwi Kartikasari

https://orcid.org/0000-0002-3222-4426

Universiti Brunei Darussalam, Brunei

ABSTRACT

This study aims to reveal how well two PLS-SEM statistical technologies—WarpPLS and SmartPLS—work for testing attitude theory with different types of relationships: linear and nonlinear. Non-probability sampling collects 786 internet customers from the digital marketplace. In the linear relationships between the theory of reasoned action baseline (attitudes and subjective norms) and online buying intention, SmartPLS and WarpPLS deliver similar loadings, reliability, validity, and path coefficients. WarpPLS is more effective in validating the nonlinear relationship of consumer ethnocentrism to attitudes toward imports, but SmartPLS is more comprehensive in providing robustness and advanced features. Teachers should educate students on the importance of testing linearity in the required preliminary checks. This step helps them choose the suitable software algorithm and get more accurate results and reports. This study is limited to the default parameter and standard application; future works can explore more advanced settings and complex path models.

DOI: 10.4018/979-8-3693-2865-1.ch013

BACKGROUND

Over the years, statistical technologies have evolved and found their place in the education system, starting from high school where Excel and its statistical add-ins provide basic functions (Claxton, 2009). As the complexity of statistical cases increased in higher education, more advanced tools like SPSS and Eviews were introduced. For a significant period, SPSS reigned supreme in both the statistical technology world and education (Yin et al., 2021). However, as research studies became more intricate, researchers began to explore structural equation modeling (SEM) through various statistical applications: SmartPLS, WarpPLS, and R for partial least squares structural equation modeling (PLS-SEM) or Amos, Lisrel, and Mplus for Covariance Based (CB-SEM). These software, listed in descending order of popularity, have become the go-to tools for researchers (Sakaria et al., 2023).

In the early years, the use of CB-SEM was more prevalent, and PLS-SEM was relatively less familiar (Hsu et al., 2006). However, as students grappled with issues of normality, linearity, homoscedasticity, classical assumptions, and minimum sample size, PLS-SEM emerged as a viable alternative for explanatory and predictive analysis. PLS-SEM quickly gained traction, offering a practical solution to these challenges (Ghasemy et al., 2020). Since 2015, PLS-SEM has taken almost the most dominant role in analyzing complex interrelationships between variables, further solidifying its position (Hair et al., 2018).

Despite being the most popular statistical packages for PLS-SEM, WarpPLS and SmartPLS, there is a noticeable dearth of comparison studies between these two (Sakaria et al., 2023). This gap in research is particularly relevant for students who need guidance in making the optimal choice between these tools. Both WarpPLS and SmartPLS offer unique algorithms and features, and their suitability is contingent upon the users' specific conditions (Memon et al., 2021). This study aims to fill this gap by comparing the effectiveness of these PLS-SEM statistical technologies using a case study that validates attitude theory with different types of relationships, including linear and nonlinear.

This study is vital as it updates the comparison of both software with novel features, such as quadratic effects for SmartPLS and Djikstra for WarpPLS, that were not available in past studies (Memon et al., 2021). It can provide more empirical evidence to support the effectiveness and relevance of appropriate statistical tools, given the nature of nonlinear relationships in an extended context from tourism (Rasoolimanesh et al., 2018) into marketing and attitude theory. It sharpens past comparative studies with gap analysis and datasets representing linear and nonlinear relationships (Kumar & Purani, 2018). Educators of research methods can use this study to underline the importance of linearity checks to justify their students' selection of data analysis strategies.

LITERATURE REVIEW AND HYPOTHESES

PLS-SEM Among Multivariate Data Analysis

Multivariate analysis, a powerful tool, enables researchers to simultaneously use many (more than two) variables (multivariate) for explanation and prediction. This study, for instance, utilizes four variables. Many multivariate methods derived from univariate analysis (which examines the distribution of a single variable) and bivariate analysis (which studies two variables and employs correlation, simple regression, and analysis of variance). In multivariate analysis, researchers can choose to declare no dependent variables (e.g., factor and cluster analysis), relate variables to one dependent variable, also known as single equation form (e.g., multiple regression), or many dependent variables even where they are interrelated in the mediation model, also called multiple equation models (e.g., structural equation models/SEM). The researcher can confidently determine which independent variables predict each dependent variable by using theory, past knowledge, or other guidelines. This logical process ensures the scientific rigor of multivariate analysis (Hair et al., 2019). This study, for example, employs four variables with interrelated models. Hence, SEM is the appropriate approach for this study.

Structural Equation Modeling (SEM) is a statistical method that can be calculated using either common variance, which involves the covariance (CB-SEM), or total variance, which is often referred to as Variance Based/VB-SEM. The latter, known as component-based SEM or PLS-SEM, has gained significant traction in the past decade across various sectors of social sciences research, notably in business. It is favored over CB-SEM due to its superior ability to handle complex models and provide solutions that are otherwise unattainable because of non normal data distributions, non metric scales, small sample size, and other rigorous assumptions (Hair et al., 2019). However, PLS-SEM is still growing and some debate is still raging in some areas such as goodness-of-fit applicability (Hair et al., 2017) or linearity violations (Kock, 2022) where they are relatively already established in CB-SEM. This ongoing debate presents an exciting yet cautious opportunity for researchers to contribute to the academic discourse.

Consumer Ethnocentrism and Attitudes Toward Imported Products

Consumer ethnocentrism is a superior belief that consumers hold about their in-group of a nation, causing them to discriminate against products from foreign countries. It was initially introduced to predict attitudes toward foreign products (Shimp & Sharma, 1987). The social identity theory explains that ethnocentric consumers seek to benefit from national identity when they prefer home-country products and have unfavorable attitudes toward out-group goods (Kartikasari et al., 2023). Much research unearthed a negative connection between ethnocentrism and attitudes toward foreign products (Šapić et al., 2018; Xin & Seo, 2020), but few found negligible association (Long et al., 2022). Although past studies show the primarily negative one-tail direction from consumer ethnocentrism to attitudes toward import, this study hypothesizes a more neutral two-tail direction tone as it represents the default setting of both PLS-SEM applications. As such, Hypothesis 1 is offered:

H1: Consumer ethnocentrism significantly affects attitudes toward imported gear using SmartPLS and WarpPLS.

Attitudes and Subjective Norms and Online Buying Intention of Imported Gear

The digital marketplace establishes a commercial environment that facilitates efficient and convenient transactions between buyers and sellers. The rapid growth of e-commerce presents a significant challenge to traditional enterprises but makes online buying more vital in today's era (Almunawar et al., 2021). Imports are easily accessible via cross-border e-commerce (Kartikasari et al., 2023), and imported gear is among the most sold products on the e-trade, along with electronics and cosmetics (Canover & Kartikasari, 2021).

Theories of attitude include the theory of reasoned actions (TRA) (Fishbein & Ajzen, 1975). The latter pays tremendous attention to customers' intentions to execute an observed behavior, in our case, the e-consumption of imported gear. It proposes three distinct factors of intention that are not reliant on any other fundamentally. The first factor is the individual's attitude towards the activity, which pertains to the extent to which a consumer has a positive or negative assessment of the conduct being investigated. Another determinant is a social element known as the subjective norm, which pertains to the viewed social influence to either engage in or abstain from the action (Ajzen, 1991). Many studies have demonstrated that attitudes (Long et al., 2022; Šapić et al., 2018; Xin & Seo, 2020) and subjective norms (Park & Kitty, 2002) positively affect foreign purchase intention, some found negligible linkages between subjective norms and foreign purchase intention (Son et al., 2013; Xin & Seo, 2020). Although past studies show the mainly positive one-tail direction from ethnocentrism to attitudes and subjective norms toward import, this study hypothesizes a more neutral two-tail direction tone as it represents the default setting of both PLS-SEM applications. As such, Hypothesis 2 is offered:

H2a: Attitudes affect online buying intention of imported gear significantly using both SmartPLS and WarpPLS

H2b: Subjective norms affect the online buying intention of imported gear significantly using both SmartPLS and WarpPLS

Figure 1 describes all hypotheses in the framework.

Figure 1. The theoretical structural framework
Source: Author's Compilation (2024)

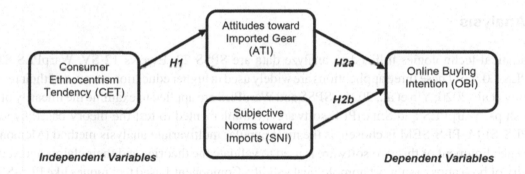

METHODOLOGY

Data Collection

A non-probability sampling strategy, including convenience, snowball, and quota, was applied to collect quantitative data via a web-based survey on social media sites, including TikTok, WhatsApp, and Instagram. The quota was monitored to get a balanced respondent profile by targeting a minimum of 100 samples for e-commerce providers like Shopee and Lazada and for gear product types like footwear, textiles, and bags. The questionnaire was translated and back-translated by language professionals to ensure precise and trustworthy translation. Following that, a group of scholars and colleagues reiterated the wording to identify respondents' issues when attempting to understand the statements (Elangovan & Sundaravel, 2021, p. 6). This study drew 786 valid internet customers from all over Indonesia, exceeding the required sample size by power analysis. The samples are typically students living in major cities, particularly in Java and Sumatra, the most populous islands in Indonesia, and females. Female respondents dominantly participating in fashion studies are consistent with a prior inquiry (Beaudoin et al., 2000; Zuliarni et al., 2023).

Model Specification and Measure

To avoid the risks of not being specific enough or too much, the model is set up to include three exogenous variables that represent the three types of relationships: non-linear, quasi-linear, and linear. The structural model, variables, and measures are constructed based on theories and past studies. To assure comparability and generalizability, an improved 3-item single-factor consumer ethnocentrism tendency scale was employed in this investigation (Lindquist et al., 2001). Three items for measuring online buying intention are adopted from past studies (Aljukhadar et al., 2021). Three assertions in each latent variable of the theory of reasoned action about attitudes and subjective norms toward imported gear were drawn from prior research (Maksan et al., 2019; Son et al., 2013). Three indicators were used to evaluate attitudes: pleasure, fun, and pleasant feelings, and subjective norms: approval from family and friends and alignment with influential people, as presented in Table 1. All constructs have three items totaling 12 statements in this survey. All items have 7-point Likert scale choices. Gap percentage was calculated as an absolute change divided by the minimum values between coefficients resulting from WarpPLS and SmartPLS.

Data Analysis

The statistical technologies utilized to analyze data are SPSS 22, Eviews 12 SV, WarpPLS 8.0, and SmartPLS 4.0.9.6. These three applications are widely used in higher education because of their relevance (Ghasemy et al., 2020; Yin et al., 2021). SPSS and WarpPLS are applied to examine the linearity of tested relationships. WarpPLS and SmartPLS software are implemented to test the theory-based hypotheses using PLS-SEM. PLS-SEM is chosen as the most popular multivariate analysis method (Memon et al., 2021). The alignment of this two software is used to validate the theories and their claims and verify the suitability of both apps to support nomological validity. Component-based techniques like PLS-SEM are appropriate for theory testing during the first phases of model development, mainly when the observed data are not distributed as a multivariate normal as covariance-based SEM requires (Hsu et al., 2006). After initial data processing, these two PLS-SEM programs' measurement and structural model outputs are further compared and evaluated.

RESULTS

Preliminary data analysis proves that the dataset does not satisfy the distributional assumptions of the normality test but is within an acceptable range of skewness and kurtosis; thus, PLS-SEM is justified for this dataset. Subsequent analysis on loading, reliability, validity, structural model, and goodness-of-fit is ready to commence. The step-by-step approach is essential to systematically educate students in solving a problem (Hair et al., 2018).

Loading Comparison

The first measurement model assessment is individual item reliability. Factor loadings signify convergent validity and are expected to surpass the minimum limit of 0.708 (Hair et al., 2017). Table 1 demonstrates that all reflective items meet this minimum requirement. However, both software offers slightly different outer loadings, as found by past studies (Kumar & Purani, 2018). The difference gap between these outcomes ranges from as small as 0.04% for SNI2 to 11.87% for CET3. These gaps are caused mainly by the difference in the precision level of decimal places. The limitations and future works section further discusses this variance of precision. The consumer ethnocentrism construct has the highest gap among other constructs; all its items show the top three gaps.

Table 1. Loading comparison between WarpPLS and SmartPLS output

Variable	Item	Dimension	Loading		
			Warp	**Smart**	**Gap**
Consumer ethnocentrism (CET)	CET1	Patriotism - un-Indonesian	0.902	0.955	5.92
	CET2	Employment impact – out of work	0.897	0.890	0.80
	CET3	Patriotism - A real citizen	0.854	0.763	11.87
Attitude toward Imported Gear (ATI)	ATI1	Pleasure	0.940	0.939	0.12
	ATI2	Positive emotions	0.953	0.954	0.15
	ATI3	Fun	0.926	0.927	0.07
Subjective Norms toward Imports (SNI)	SNI1	Friend's approval	0.923	0.922	0.11
	SNI2	Family's approval	0.946	0.946	0.04
	SNI3	Other important people's behavior	0.918	0.920	0.27
Online Buying Intention toward Imports (OBI)	OBI1	Likeliness	0.913	0.911	0.17
	OBI2	Prediction	0.948	0.950	0.18
	OBI3	Intention	0.935	0.936	0.06

Source: Author's Compilation (2024)

Construct Reliability and Validity Comparison

Cronbach's alpha and composite reliability within 0.70 – 0.95 imply tolerable internal consistency reliability (Hair et al., 2017). Table 2 reveals that all Alpha coefficients are identical, as found by past studies (Kumar & Purani, 2018). All Alpha values are within the threshold. Thus, construct reliability is verified. Because Alpha is considered conservative, composite reliability (Djikstra's rho_a) is the most suitable criterion for verifying the accurate factor model (Hair et al., 2018). Table 2 exposes that WarpPLS gives more acceptable outcomes as they are within the tolerable range. However, SmartPLS presents a 20.05% gap with WarpPLS value for the consumer ethnocentrism tendency construct to reach 1.135, surpassing the reasonable threshold of 1. Combining composite reliability and alpha findings, SmartPLS effectively establishes construct reliability for ATI, SNI, and OBI, except for CET. In contrast, WarpPLS successfully established construct reliability for all constructs. This finding completes the past study as it failed to present Djikstra's composite reliability for WarpPLS 5.0 because the software did not provide the feature during the period of the past study (Kumar & Purani, 2018).

Table 2. Construct reliability and validity comparison between WarpPLS and SmartPLS output

Criteria		Constructs			
		CET	ATI	SNI	OBI
Cronbach's alpha	WarpPLS	0.860	0.934	0.921	0.925
	SmartPLS	0.860	0.934	0.921	0.925
	Gap (%)	0.05	0.01	0.01	0.03
Composite reliability (Djikstra's rho_a)	WarpPLS	0.945	0.936	0.921	0.926
	SmartPLS	1.135	0.935	0.921	0.927
	Gap (%)	20.05	0.08	0.04	0.07
Average variance extracted (AVE)	WarpPLS	0.782	0.884	0.864	0.869
	SmartPLS	0.762	0.884	0.864	0.869
	Gap (%)	2.56	0.04	0.01	0.04

Note: CET = Consumer Ethnocentrism Tendency, ATI = Attitudes toward Imports, SNI = Subjective Norms toward Imports, OBI = Online Buying Intention
Source: Author's Compilation (2024)

Convergent validity is established by AVE more than 0.5, suggesting that the construct accounts for over 50% of the variation in its indicators (Hair et al., 2017). Table 2 discloses that all AVE values exceed this minimum limit. Thus, convergent validity is established. However, consumer ethnocentrism tendency AVEs from SmartPLS and WarpPLS diverge with a 2.56% difference. Although not presented in any table in this paper, discriminant validity is established using the HTMT (heterotrait-monotrait ratio of correlations) criterion as the state-of-the-art method to assess discriminant validity. SmartPLS and WarpPLS converge on their values and are excellent below the stricter threshold of 0.85 (Kock, 2022), consistent with past studies' findings (Kumar & Purani, 2018).

The Role of Linearity on Attitude Theory Testing and Model Quality

Once the outer model is established, the inner model is evaluated starting from the collinearity Variance inflation factor (VIF). Both statistical programs offer this service. However, VIFs from these two programs are different, as WarpPLS provides full collinearity and block VIF, while SmartPLS collinearity VIF (Kumar & Purani, 2018). Nonetheless, all full VIFs are below the threshold of 3.3, demonstrating common method bias does not exist in this model, and block VIFs are below 5, suggesting it is free from collinearity issues.

Subsequently, the structural model is assessed using three techniques: WarpPLS, SmartPLS without quadratic effect, and SmartPLS with quadratic effect (S-QE), as presented in three different columns in each hypothesis in Table 3. P-values should be less than 5% to accept a hypothesis. Hence, H2a and H2b derived from the theory of reasoned actions are accepted by WarpPLS and SmartPLS. However, the relationship of CET – ATI shows a more complicated interpretation than that of H2. WarpPLS provides a straightforward indication to accept H1. In contrast, SmartPLS delivers problematic outcomes. SmartPLS without quadratic effect rejects H1. When the quadratic effect comes into play, the p-values of QE (CET) – ATI is less than 5%. Conversely, the path coefficient is positive, showing the reverse direction from the consumer ethnocentrism model (Shimp & Sharma, 1987). Further, the CET ATI for the third technique is still 0.382, suggesting rejecting H1. In summary, WarpPLS accepts H1, but Smart-PLS rejects it. However, SmartPLS indicates the nonlinearity of the CET-ATI relationship by revealing the significance of QE (CET) – ATI at 0.006. This nonlinearity statement and its impact on accepting or rejecting a hypothesis will be further detailed in Table 4.

Table 3. Attitude theory hypotheses testing comparison between WarpPLS and SmartPLS output

Criteria	H1				H2a			H2b		
	W	S	S-QE		W	S	S-QE	W	S	S-QE
			CET - ATI	QE (CET) -ATI						
Beta/Path	-0.179	-0.037	-0.053	0.151	0.376	0.373	0.373	0.355	0.358	0.358
P values	<0.001	0.500	0.382	0.006	<0.001	0.000	0.000	<0.001	0.000	0.000
Effect Size	0.032	0.001	0.003	0.030	0.226	0.150	0.150	0.210	0.137	0.137
R-squared	0.032	0.001	0.031		0.436	0.435	0.435			
Adj. R-sq.	0.031	0.000	0.028		0.434	0.434	0.434			
Q-squared	0.037	-0.003	-0.001		0.436	0.292	0.298			
SRMR	0.041	0.211	0.204							

Note: CET = Consumer Ethnocentrism Tendency, ATI = Attitudes toward Imports, SNI = Subjective Norms toward Imports, OBI = Online Buying Intention, W = WarpPLS output, S = SmartPLS output, QE = Quadratic effects, SRMR = Standardized Root Mean Squared Residual, Adj = Adjusted, sq = square

Source: Author's Compilation (2024)

Path coefficients show a negative relationship between CET and ATI, as revealed by both statistical technologies under consideration. WarpPLS gives an absolute higher beta value (-0.179) than SmartPLS (-0.037) with a more than 95% confidence interval. The beta coefficients for H2a show a negligible difference with 0.376 and 0.373 and H2b with 0.355 and 0.358. As such, SmartPLS and WarpPLS provide accurate nomological validity to support the theory of reasoned actions. However, only WarpPLS supports the applicability of the consumer ethnocentrism tendency concept and its relationship with attitude toward imports. Figure 2 describes all results from Table 3 in the structural model.

Figure 2. The structural model comparison between WarpPLS and SmartPLS
Note: * statistically significant
Source: Author's Compilation (2024)

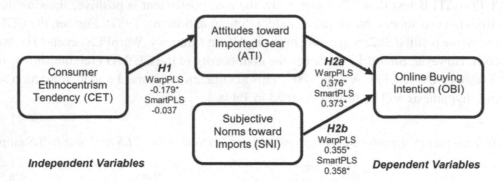

The effect size or f-square suggests Cohen's minimum limit of 0.02, 0.15, and 0.35 to determine the weak, moderate, and strong effects from a practical standpoint (Hair et al., 2017). WarpPLS tends to give more sizable effect sizes than SmartPLS. The effect size of H1 is small (0.032) according to WarpPLS but negligible (0.001) to SmartPLS. Likewise, the effect size of H2b is moderate (0.210) according to WarpPLS but small (0.137) to SmartPLS.

The R-squared is the primary metric to assess a model's efficacy, determining the level of prediction accuracy and variance explained, hence called coefficient determination. Adjusted R-sq provides a more suitable value of variance, which is explained by adjusting the complexity of the model. Stone Geisser's Q-square suggests predictive power or relevance with values greater than 0, signifying the predictive significance of a particular endogenous construct (Hair et al., 2017). These three measures are calculated for each dependent variable, in this case, ATI and OBI. WarpPLS and SmartPLS provide similar R-square values for H2a and H2b except for H1, as WarpPLS excels in this dataset. As such, R2 coefficients derived from WarpPLS validate this study's unbiased and precise model specification. This finding is supported by Q-square, where SmartPLS shows negligible predictive power on H1 as its Q-square is negative (-0.003). A previous study also found that the effect sizes and Q-square of WarpPLS were higher than SmartPLS's (Kumar & Purani, 2018).

SRMR assesses model fit, although the debate over goodness-of-fit applicability in PLS-SEM is still raging. SmartPLS and WarpPLS offer different SRMR coefficients. SmartPLS proposes two types of SRMR, estimated and saturated, while WarpPLS only uncovers one value for SRMR. SmartPLS reveals that the saturated model is 0.033, and the estimated model is 0.204 and 0.211, respectively. The advocated threshold is below 0.8 (Hair et al., 2017), which is satisfied by the saturated model but not the estimated model. It is noteworthy to note that the estimated model is more recommended than the saturated model. Meanwhile, WarpPLS divulges that its SRMR value of 0.041 meets the good-fit requirement.

The Importance of Linearity on Attitude Theory Validation

Some differences between SmartPLS and WarpPLS outputs in loadings, alpha, and AVE are minor because they do not point to any disparities in meeting the threshold. In contrast, the gaps in Djikstra composite reliability and structural model differ quite contrastingly, especially in interpreting H1. The elucidation for this occurrence resides in the characteristics of the association between CET and ATI.

Table 4 shows that the more linear-like or quasi-linear the relationship, the more likely both statistical technologies will converge on similar results.

Table 4. Linearity tests and hypotheses testing comparison between WarpPLS and SmartPLS output

Relationship	SPSS		Eviews	WarpPLS	Remarks
	Sig	Remark	F-statistic		
CET-ATI	0.000	Nonlinear	0.000	Warped	H1 was accepted by WarpPLS but rejected by SmartPLS. This gap is because of the nonlinear nature of the relationship
ATI-OBI	0.919	Linear	0.2015	Warped	Both accept H2a because of the arguably quasi-linearity nature of the relationship
SNI-OBI	0.130	Linear	0.7469	Linear	Both accept H2b because of the linearity nature of the relationship

Note: CET = Consumer Ethnocentrism Tendency, ATI = Attitudes toward Imports, SNI = Subjective Norms toward Imports, OBI = Online Buying Intention
Source: Author's Compilation (2024)

Table 4 presents the linearity test in SPSS, Eviews, and WarpPLS. To determine whether relationships are linear or nonlinear, this study conducted the SPSS linearity test and Eviews Ramsey Reset Tests on the scores for latent variables in the partial regressions of the path model. If a partial regression analysis yields statistically significant values (<5%), it signals the chance existence of a non-linear impact (Hair et al., 2018). Using SPSS and Eviews presented in Table 4, nonlinear effects undoubtedly exist in one path: CET-ATI. In contrast, SNI-OBI is linear. Nevertheless, ATI-OBI is ambiguous because SPSS and WarpPLS provide conflicting outcomes. As such, Figure 3, Figure 4, and Figure 5 present the plots for three relationships. The plots are to map the nature of interaction in the model (Hair et al., 2018). Figure 3 shows that CET-ATI is not linear. Figure 4 shows that the plot of ATI-OBI is slightly (quasi) linear. Figure 5 displays that the relationship of SNI-OBI is linear. This study provides actual data on three different natures of the relationship: linear (SNI-OBI), quasi-linear (ATI-OBI), and nonlinear (CET-OBI), to showcase the role of linearity in hypothesis testing.

Figure 3. The nonlinear plot between CET-ATI
Note: CET = Consumer Ethnocentrism Tendency, ATI = Attitudes toward Imports
Source: Author's Compilation (2024)

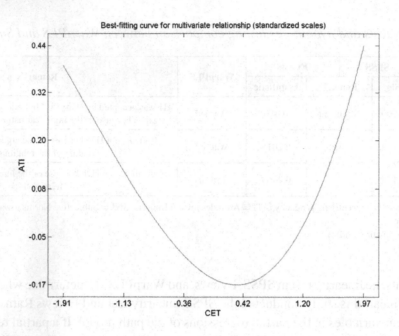

Figure 4. The quasi linear plot between ATI-OBI
Note: ATI = Attitudes toward Imports, OBI = Online Buying Intention
Source: Author's Compilation (2024)

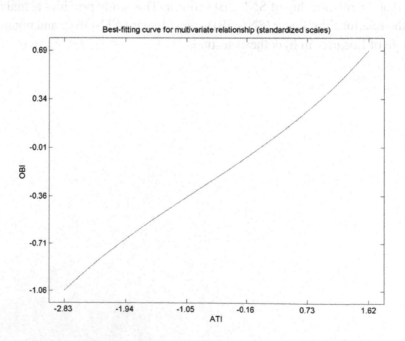

Figure 5. The linear plot between SNI-OBI
Note: SNI = Subjective Norms toward Imports, OBI = Online Buying Intention
Source: Author's Compilation (2024)

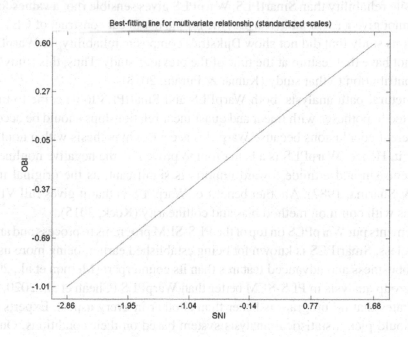

These differences in the types of relationships between CET-ATI, ATI-OBI, and SNI-OBI cause the convergent decision in accepting H2a and H2b yet divergent verdicts in interpreting the results for H1 (Kock, 2022). Even with the two-stage process when using the quadratic effect, the SmartPLS results for H1 still do not provide empirical support for the theory. Meanwhile, WarpPLS makes more theoretical sense because of its focus on nonlinear model specification, as found by past studies (Kumar & Purani, 2018).

DISCUSSIONS

The statistical structural equation modeling applications SmartPLS and WarpPLS provide slightly different outer loadings, primarily due to variations in decimal accuracy. Despite variations in output gaps, the loadings' interpretation still satisfies the minimal criterion, as discovered by previous research (Kumar & Purani, 2018). The nonlinear consumer ethnocentrism construct has a more significant disparity than linear constructs. When relationships are linear, WarpPLS and SmartPLS usually give identical results. Nevertheless, when relationships are not linear, they give different results. Because of this, worries about linearity should be taken very seriously when planning study methods.

The construct validity and reliability criteria are further checked to compare the structural equation modeling statistical tools even more. Similar to the above findings of factor loadings, both SmartPLS and WarpPLS effectively verify construct reliability via Cronbach's alpha, convergent validity via AVE, and discriminant validity via HTMT for all constructs, regardless of the nature of their relationship. The output gaps between SmartPLS and WarpPLS are almost negligible, and both results are acceptable within the recommended guidelines in these four criteria. The gap starts from zero for discriminant validity (HTMT) to 20 percent for composite reliability. However, WarpPLS has done a better job of proving Djikstra's composite reliability than SmartPLS. WarpPLS gives sensible rho_a values for all constructs, but SmartPLS cannot give a reasonable rho_a value for the nonlinear construct of CET. This paper fills the gap of a previous study that did not show Djikstra's composite reliability for WarpPLS 5.0 because the software did not have that feature at the time of the previous study. Thus, this study's original result is an empirical contribution to that study (Kumar & Purani, 2018).

Regarding structural path analysis, both WarpPLS and SmartPLS tools come to the same conclusion: attitude-related hypotheses with linear and quasilinear relationships should be accepted. However, they come to different conclusions because WarpPLS accepts a hypothesis with a nonlinear link while SmartPLS rejects it. Hence, WarpPLS is a better tool to prove that the negative nonlinear link between consumer ethnocentrism and attitude toward imports is significant, as the original inventor initially claimed (Shimp & Sharma, 1987). Another benefit of WarpPLS is that it gives full VIF values, which help find problems with common method bias and collinearity (Kock, 2015).

The latter statements put WarpPLS on top of the PLS-SEM programs to process and analyze nonlinear datasets. Nevertheless, SmartPLS is known for being established earlier, being more user-friendly, and providing more robustness and advanced features than its counterpart (Memon et al., 2021). SmartPLS can handle multigroup analysis in PLS-SEM better than WarpPLS (Cheah et al., 2020, 2023). As such, this manuscript states that no program is better than another in every aspect. Experts and researchers doing research should pick a statistical analysis system based on their conditions. Our goal with this piece is to provide empirical evidence to readers about how each app differs in processing the linearity characteristics so that readers can make the right choice.

In multivariate data analysis, some underlying statistical inference assumptions substantially affect the ability to represent multivariate relationships, such as normality and linearity. Linearity checks can be done in WarpPLS, SmartPLS, SPSS, and Eviews (Hair et al., 2018). Researchers can better use graphics provided by some programs to understand linear, quasi-linear, or nonlinear relationships and make the appropriate choice of statistical software.

Preceding a model estimate, the researchers must verify that conceptual and statistical assumptions are fulfilled (Hair et al., 2019, p. 33). In addition to the advice of linearity as one of the preliminary checks, linearity is a test included as a complementary method for assessing the results' robustness, where SmartPLS excels in this robustness aspect from WarpPLS. In WarpPLS, linearity consideration is assessed before the structural model evaluation. In SmartPLS, a linearity check is conducted after the structural model evaluation to detect potential nonlinear effects on the model (Hair et al., 2018).

According to these studies that underlie the importance of linearity checks, either before or after the evaluation, this study concludes that linearity checks are necessary. This manuscript encourages linearity checks as part of preliminary consideration on distributional assumptions besides normality tests, as advised by past studies (Hair et al., 2019), to ensure students implement the appropriate statistical technologies to process the dataset. An appropriate statistical tool that considers the linear or nonlinear pattern of relationships and provides an appropriate algorithm accordingly could increase the effectiveness of the proposed model (Rasoolimanesh et al., 2018).

Theoretical Implications

The theory of reason actions (TRA), consumer ethnocentrism, and social identity theory are among the most popular theories concerning attitudes toward imports. The theory of reason actions is expected to be generalizable and relevant across various contexts as an established theory. This study finds that the nature of the relationship of the theory of reason actions is somewhat linear. Thus, any statistical technologies will reveal identical measurement and structural model assessment results. Unsurprisingly, this manuscript delivers empirical evidence to the theory of reason actions, like the majority of findings, by supporting the connection between attitudes and foreign purchase intention (Long et al., 2022; Šapić et al., 2018; Xin & Seo, 2020) and the linkage between subjective norms and foreign purchase intention (Park & Kitty, 2002), rejecting other conflicting studies (Son et al., 2013; Xin & Seo, 2020). Future studies should consider using predictors from the theory of reason actions as they are verified as vital.

The findings of this study provide empirical evidence for a positive quasi-linear relationship between attitude and online buying intention for imported gear, which aligns with the theories of attitudes and the majority of previous research findings (Long et al., 2022; Xin & Seo, 2020). Attitude is described as an evaluative judgment, which can be either positive or negative, about consumer behavior in the context of shopping (Maksan et al., 2019). The more positive consumers' attitudes toward imports, the more likely they are to develop online buying intentions for the corresponding products. Internet marketing educators can use this finding to showcase the importance of understanding targeted consumers' attitudes in devising effective marketing plans.

Methodological Implications

The connection between ethnocentrism and attitudes toward foreign products is found nonlinear, resulting in conflicting findings between results from two statistical tools. WarpPLS can validate the applicability of the theories underlying attitudes and consumer ethnocentrism than SmartPLS because of its focus on nonlinear model specification (Kumar & Purani, 2018). Using WarpPLS, the negative connection between ethnocentrism and attitudes toward foreign products is validated as found by past studies (Šapić et al., 2018; Shimp & Sharma, 1987; Xin & Seo, 2020). It is worth reiterating that only one study, which utilized SmartPLS and did not report linearity, rejected this association (Long et al., 2022). This case from past study is significant as it provides an alternative perspective and underscores the importance of testing linearity. Our study, by proposing methodological implications and emphasizing the need to test linearity before making informed digital decisions, can potentially enhance the accuracy of future studies' findings when choosing statistical technologies for the ethnocentrism variable between Smart-PLS and WarpPLS. Future studies on consumer ethnocentrism should include linearity tests in their methodology. Research method teachers should educate students to test linearity before any estimation is attempted (Hair et al., 2019) to decide the appropriate algorithm and increase the effectiveness of the proposed model (Rasoolimanesh et al., 2018).

Educators and trainers in statistics and research methods should teach their students about the importance of testing linearity before conducting data analysis. This procedure helps their students decide which method and statistical technologies are appropriate for their dataset (Kumar & Purani, 2018). Linearity tests can be redone as complementary analyses for robustness tests after the model estimation. Linearity tests should be done as complementary with preliminary consideration.

Practical Implications

Advertisers of foreign brands should not be discouraged in ethnocentric markets, knowing that ethnocentrism has little impact on consumers' attitudes toward imports. Attitudes and subjective norms influence purchase intentions toward imports more significantly than consumer ethnocentrism tendency, meaning that promotion to the consumers' social circle will effectively shape consumers' attitudes and drive them to buy the marketers' products. This argument means that promotional activities such as social media, digital marketing, word of mouth, and other traditional marketing practices such as creating attractive events to promote the product merits or advertising the popularity of their products among consumer circles (Putri et al., 2023) or discounts, cashback, online services, expedited delivery, other incentives (Ramadanty & Kartikasari, 2020), and branding (Irianto & Kartikasari, 2020) can influence consumers' decisions as marketers surround their external environment with buzz and promotions (Ryu, 2011).

Instead, marketing managers selling foreign gear should take these findings as an opportunity to market their products to new countries, even when these countries are known as highly ethnocentric. Although the practical implication of the H1 finding is that firms can reasonably expect that the more ethnocentric consumers are, the more likely they are to develop more negative attitudes toward imports, the strength of H1 is small, -0.179 according to WarpPLS output. International marketers should focus on other potential predictors, such as cosmopolitanism or xenocentrism, with possible more significant effects to compensate for this disadvantage coming from ethnocentric tendencies. Cosmopolitanism refers to the cognitive inclination of individuals to venture beyond the confines of their culture, community, and society (Long et al., 2022). Xenocentrism is a belief that foreign things are superior to consumers' native lifestyles, products, or ideas (Diamantopoulos et al., 2019). This study provides guidelines for global business owners who wish to work in Indonesian settings to design a comprehensive business model that is more about attitudes and social circles compatible with Indonesia's updated culture.

Subjective norms' (SNI) significant effect sizes on online buying intention toward imports can be explained by the collectivistic vs. individualistic cultures. Collectivists, or those with an interdependent mindset, perceive themselves within the collective framework. They prioritize group objectives and rely on social norms and obligations to influence their actions. Individualistic persons, also known as independent individuals, typically perceive themselves as autonomous and apart from others. In other words, individuals with this characteristic tend to perceive themselves as distinct from people in their close relationships (Vabø & Hansen, 2016). Due to Indonesia, in particular, and Asia, in general, being a collectivist culture, subjective norms are dominant (Son et al., 2013). Management practitioners should take this generalization cautiously, as effective business practices in Indonesia might not be as effective in other countries in Asia, although they share similar collectivist cultures.

This study's sample profile can also explain the significant effect of subjective norms on online buying intention. Since students and young consumers dominate this survey, youths seek their circles' approval more than older adults, especially in fashion decision-making (Tulloch, 2010). However, researchers in the past found that subjective norms might not be seen as a vital social influence factor for in-group conformity. Thus, findings vary by region and demographic background (Son et al., 2013). As such, sellers in the digital marketplace should customize their marketing strategies according to the targeted culture and customer behavior, as no size fits all or no tactic fits all markets.

Limitations and Future Works

Default parameters are used in both software as implemented by past studies (Kumar & Purani, 2018). There are some parameters that researchers can set in each software so that both can offer identical outcomes (Kock, 2016), but that is not the focus of this study because this study aims for education purposes where students are assumed to be beginners. Moreover, minimum interference in setting the algorithm ensures the replicability of this study's findings. Future works can further explore the comparison toward parameter setting that results in similar outcomes to narrow the head-to-head comparison.

This study focuses on the standard application of both apps that most higher education use for diplomas and bachelor degrees, comprising reflective indicators and simple path analysis. Formative indicators, moderation, mediation, robustness, and multi-group analysis of more advanced analysis techniques are not discussed here, although they are extremely interesting for future works.

Criteria shown in the study, such as Djikstra and SRMR, are selected because both software provide their values. There are differences in how they name some criteria, such as Djikstra and rho_a. Although names can be different, as long as they refer to the same concept and are included as basic operations for inner and outer model assessment, they are included in this study. Criteria that do not meet this requirement are out of scope. Furthermore, gap analysis is limited by the accuracy level in three-digit numbers for WarpPLS. Future studies can expand the criteria for comparison and gap analysis, given that these statistical technologies are advancing in precision level and features.

This manuscript focuses exclusively on topics related to small data, a term referring to datasets that are manageable in size and complexity. Despite the broader range of approaches and measures available to tackle the analysis requirements of 'big data', researchers are presented with more exhaustive issues and exciting trends in the era of the prevalence of big data (Hair et al., 2019). This era allows for the assessment of consumer attitudes and the employment of PLS-SEM in ways that were previously unimaginable. For example, machine learning models have utilized attitude theories to recognize semantic sentiments expressed by social media users and clusters as the amount and variety of data grows (Wang et al., 2022). Instead of frequently feeling overwhelmed by technological advancement, it should inspire researchers to explore new frontiers in research design.

CONCLUSION

This study compares the result of loadings, construct reliability, validity, and path coefficients from two PLS-SEM statistical technologies, i.e., WarpPLS and SmartPLS, and finds that both provide similar results for the linear relationship of the theory of reasoned actions baseline, i.e., attitudes and subjective norms, to purchase intention. The gap starts from zero for discriminant validity (HTMT) to 20 percent for composite reliability. In structural path analysis, two software provide opposite findings as one accepts and another rejects a hypothesis. WarpPLS is more effective in validating the nonlinear relationship of consumer ethnocentrism to attitudes toward imports. Educators should highlight the importance of testing linearity as part of mandatory preliminary distributional assumption checks to justify the software algorithm selection for more accurate findings. Linearity robustness check complements this step, where SmartPLS has more advantages than its competitor. This study is limited in default parameter setting and standard application; future works can explore more advanced and complex path models.

ACKNOWLEDGEMENT

I want to express my deep gratitude to my research supervisors, Dr Mohammad Nabil Almunawar, Dr Muhammad Anshari Ali, and Dr Wardah Hakimah Binti Sumardi, for their patient guidance, enthusiastic encouragement, and useful critiques of this research work. I would also like to thank Dr. Nurul Amirah Ishak and Dr. Norulazidah Omar Ali for their advice and assistance in keeping my progress on schedule. Finally, I thank my parents, husband, and children for their support and encouragement throughout my study.

REFERENCES

Ajzen, I. (1991). The Theory of Planned Behavior. *Organizational Behavior and Human Decision Processes*, *50*(2), 179–211. doi:10.1016/0749-5978(91)90020-T

Aljukhadar, M., Boeuf, B., & Senecal, S. (2021). Does consumer ethnocentrism impact international shopping? A theory of social class divide. *Psychology and Marketing*, *38*(5), 735–744. doi:10.1002/mar.21461

Beaudoin, P., Moore, M. A., & Goldsmith, R. E. (2000). Fashion leaders' and followers' attitudes toward buying domestic and imported apparel. *Clothing & Textiles Research Journal*, *18*(1), 56–64. doi:10.1177/0887302X0001800106

Canover, R. S., & Kartikasari, D. (2021). Penetration of imported products on e-commerce platform in indonesia and strategies for improving local product competitiveness. [IJEBAR]. *International Journal of Economics, Business, and Accounting Research*, *5*(1), 23–33. doi:10.29040/ijebar.v5i1.1328

Cheah, J. H., Amaro, S., & Roldán, J. L. (2023). Multigroup analysis of more than two groups in PLS-SEM: A review, illustration, and recommendations. *Journal of Business Research, 156*. doi:10.1016/j.jbusres.2022.113539

Cheah, J. H., Thurasamy, R., Memon, M. A., Chuah, F., & Ting, H. (2020). Multigroup analysis using smartpls: Step-by-step guidelines for business research. *Asian Journal of Business Research*, *10*(3), I–XIX. doi:10.14707/ajbr.200087

Claxton, D. B. (2009). Data for Principals, Parents, and Other Stakeholders in Physical Education: Statistical Assessment Made Easy with Excel. *Strategies (Reston, VA)*, *22*(5), 20–24. doi:10.1080/08924562.2009.10590836

Diamantopoulos, A., Davydova, O., & Arslanagic-Kalajdzic, M. (2019). Modeling the role of consumer xenocentrism in impacting preferences for domestic and foreign brands: A mediation analysis. *Journal of Business Research, 104*, 587–596. doi:10.1016/j.jbusres.2018.12.007

Elangovan, N., & Sundaravel, E. (2021). Method of preparing a document for survey instrument validation by experts. *MethodsX*, *8*(April), 1–9. doi:10.1016/j.mex.2021.101326 PMID:34434840

Fishbein, M., & Ajzen, I. (1975). *Belief, Attitude, Intention, and Behavior: An Introduction to Theory and Research*. Addison-Wesley.

Ghasemy, M., Teeroovengadum, V., Becker, J. M., & Ringle, C. M. (2020). This fast car can move faster: A review of PLS-SEM application in higher education research. *Higher Education, 80*(6), 1121–1152. doi:10.1007/s10734-020-00534-1

Hair, H. G. T. M., Ringle, C. M., & Sarstedt, M. (2017). A Primer on Partial Least Squares Structural Equation Modeling (PLS-SEM) (2nd ed.). Sage Publications Ltd.

Hair, J. F., Black, W. C., Babin, B. J., & Anderson, R. E. (2019). *Multivariate Data Analysis* (8th ed.). Cengage., doi:10.1002/9781119409137.ch4

Hair, R. J. J., Sarstedt, M., & Ringle, C. M. (2018). When to use and how to report the results of PLS-SEM. *European Business Review, 31*(1), 2–24. https://doi.org/10.1108/EBR-11-2018-0203

Hsu, S. H., Chen, W. H., & Hsieh, M. J. (2006). Robustness testing of PLS, LISREL, EQS and ANN-based SEM for measuring customer satisfaction. *Total Quality Management & Business Excellence, 17*(3), 355–372. doi:10.1080/14783360500451465

Irianto, D., & Kartikasari, D. (2020). Fan Loyalty toward International Football Team : The Role of Brand Image. *International Journal of Applied Business Research, 2*(1), 58–72. doi:10.35313/ijabr.v2i01.95

Kartikasari, D., Almunawar, M. N., Anshari, M., & Sumardi, W. H. (2023). Foreign versus Domestic Products in Cross-border E-commerce: a Conceptual Framework. *Jurnal Bisnis Dan Manajemen (JBM), 19*(2), 44–59. https://doi.org/https://doi.org/10.23960/jbm.v19i2.91

Kock, N. (2015). Common method bias in PLS-SEM: A full collinearity assessment approach. *International Journal of e-Collaboration, 11*(4), 1–10. doi:10.4018/ijec.2015100101

Kock, N. (2016). Hypothesis Testing with Confidence Intervals and P Values in PLS-SEM. *International Journal of e-Collaboration, 12*(3), 1–6. doi:10.4018/IJeC.2016070101

Kock, N. (2022). WarpPLS User Manual : Version 8.0. In ScriptWarp Systems.

Kumar, D. S., & Purani, K. (2018). Model Specification Issues in PLS-SEM: Illustrating Linear and Non-linear Models in Hospitality Services Context. *Journal of Hospitality and Tourism Technology, 9*(3), 338–353. doi:10.1108/JHTT-09-2017-0105

Lindquist, J. D., Vida, I., Plank, R. E., & Fairhurst, A. (2001). The modified CETSCALE: Validity tests in the Czech Republic, Hungary, and Poland. *International Business Review, 10*(5), 505–516. doi:10.1016/S0969-5931(01)00030-0

Long, F., Bhuiyan, M. A., Aziz, N. A., & Rahman, M. K. (2022). Predicting young Chinese consumers' intentions to purchase Western brands: Structural model analysis. *PLoS ONE, 17*, 1–17. doi:10.1371/journal.pone.0267563

Maksan, M. T., Kovačić, D., & Cerjak, M. (2019). The influence of consumer ethnocentrism on purchase of domestic wine: Application of the extended theory of planned behaviour. *Appetite, 142*, 104393. doi:10.1016/j.appet.2019.104393

Memon, M. A., Ramayah, T., Cheah, J., Ting, H., Chuah, F., & Cham, T. H. (2021). PLS-SEM Statistical Programs: A Review. *Journal of Applied Structural Equation Modeling*, 5(1), i–xiv. doi:10.47263/JASEM.5(1)06

Park, H. J., & Kitty, G. D. (2002). Attitudes, Subjective Norms and Behavioral Intentions toward Purchasing Imported Casual Clothing. *Journal of the Korean Society of Clothing and Textiles*, 26(12), 1791–1803.

Putri, F. S., Purwosaputro, R., Putri, S. K. M., & Ananda, A. S. (2023). Analysis of the influence of perceived value on browsing behavior in C2C E-Commerce with depth of review as antecedent. *International Journal of Data and Network Science*, 7(4), 1613–1626. doi:10.5267/j.ijdns.2023.8.002

Ramadanty, M. L., & Kartikasari, D. (2020). Purchase Intention of e-Payment : The Substitute or Complementary Role of Purchase Intention of E-Payment : The Substitute or Complementary Role of Brand, Sales Promotions, and Information Quality. *2nd International Conference on Applied Economy and Social Science, October*, (pp. 298–308). ScitePress. 10.5220/0010355402980308

Rasoolimanesh, S. M., Ali, F., & Jaafar, M. (2018). Modeling residents' perceptions of tourism development: Linear versus non-linear models. *Journal of Destination Marketing & Management*, 10(May), 1–9. doi:10.1016/j.jdmm.2018.05.007

Ryu, J. S. (2011). Consumer attitudes and shopping intentions toward pop-up fashion stores. *Journal of Global Fashion Marketing*, 2(3), 139–147. doi:10.1080/20932685.2011.10593092

Sakaria, D., Maat, S. M., & Mohd Matore, M. E. E. (2023). Examining the Optimal Choice of SEM Statistical Software Packages for Sustainable Mathematics Education: A Systematic Review. *Sustainability (Basel)*, 15(4), 3209. doi:10.3390/su15043209

Šapić, S., Kocić, M., & Filipović, J. (2018). Brand and consumer characteristics as drivers of behaviour towards global and local brands. *Zbornik Radova Ekonomskog Fakulteta u Rijeci*, 36(2), 619–645. doi:10.18045/zbefri.2018.2.619

Shimp, T. A., & Sharma, S. (1987). Consumer Ethnocentrism: Construction and Validation of the CETSCALE. *JMR, Journal of Marketing Research*, XXIV(9), 280–289. doi:10.1177/002224378702400304

Son, J., Jin, B., & George, B. (2013). Consumers' purchase intention toward foreign brand goods. *Management Decision*, 51(2), 434–450. doi:10.1108/00251741311301902

Tulloch, C. (2010). Style-Fashion- Dress : From Black to Post-Black. *Fashion Theory*, 14(3), 273–304. doi:10.2752/175174110X12712411520179

Vabø, M., & Hansen, H. (2016). Purchase intentions for domestic food: A moderated TPB-explanation. *British Food Journal*, 118(10), 2372–2387. doi:10.1108/BFJ-01-2016-0044

Wang, J., Shu, T., Zhao, W., & Zhou, J. (2022). Research on Chinese Consumers' Attitudes Analysis of Big-Data Driven Price Discrimination Based on Machine Learning. *Frontiers in Psychology*, 12(February), 1–15. doi:10.3389/fpsyg.2021.803212 PMID:35178011

Xin, L., & Seo, S. (2020). The role of consumer ethnocentrism, country image, and subjective knowledge in predicting intention to purchase imported functional foods. *British Food Journal*, 122(2), 448–464. doi:10.1108/BFJ-05-2019-0326

Yin, L., Hassan, H., & Mokhtar, M. (2021). Application of SPSS Data Processing Technology in International Education in China. *Proceedings - 2021 2nd International Conference on Education, Knowledge and Information Management,* (pp. 570–573). IEEE. 10.1109/ICEKIM52309.2021.00130

Zuliarni, S., Kartikasari, D., Hendrawan, B., & Windrayati Siregar, S. S. (2023). The impact of buying intention of global fashion on local substitute: The role of product design and price. *Heliyon, 9*(11), e22160. doi:10.1016/j.heliyon.2023.e22160 PMID:38045170

ADDITIONAL READING

Castro, M., & Lizasoain, L. (2012). Statistical modeling techniques in educational research: Data mining, structural equation models and hierarchical linear models [Las técnicas de modelización estadística en la investigación educativa: Minería de datos, modelos de ecuaciones estructurales y modelos jerárquicos lineales]. *Revista Española de Pedagogía, 70*(251), 131–148.

Gagné, P., & Furlow, C. F. (2009). Automating multiple software packages in simulation research for structural equation modeling and hierarchical linear modeling. *Structural Equation Modeling, 16*(1), 179–185. doi:10.1080/10705510802561543

Graham, J. M. (2008). The general linear model as structural equation modeling. *Journal of Educational and Behavioral Statistics, 33*(4), 485–506. doi:10.3102/1076998607306151

Kira, I. A., Shuwiekh, H., & Laddis, A. (2023). The Linear and Non-Linear Association between Trauma, Dissociation, Complex PTSD, and Executive Function Deficits: A Longitudinal Structural Equation Modeling Study. *Journal of Loss and Trauma, 28*(3), 217–234. doi:10.1080/15325024.2022.2101734

Maydeu-Olivares, A., Shi, D., & Rosseel, Y. (2019). Instrumental Variables Two-Stage Least Squares (2SLS) vs. Maximum Likelihood Structural Equation Modeling of Causal Effects in Linear Regression Models. *Structural Equation Modeling, 26*(6), 876–892. doi:10.1080/10705511.2019.1607740

Mulaik, S. A. (2009). *Linear causal modeling with structural equations*. Linear Causal Modeling with Structural Equations. doi:10.1201/9781439800393

Nikhashemi, S. R., Jebarajakirthy, C., & Nusair, K. (2019). Uncovering the roles of retail brand experience and brand love in the apparel industry: Non-linear structural equation modelling approach. *Journal of Retailing and Consumer Services, 48*, 122–135. doi:10.1016/j.jretconser.2019.01.014

Raykov, T., & Penev, S. (1997). Structural equation modeling and the latent linearity hypothesis in social and behavioral research. *Quality & Quantity, 31*(10), 57–78. doi:10.1023/A:1004269215766

KEY TERMS AND DEFINITIONS

ATI (Attitude Toward Imports): A favorable or unfavorable feeling about a specific behavior or thing.

Attitude: Theories provide insight into how attitudes are formed and how they might lead to changes in behaviour and attitude. Multiple theories explain attitudes, such as the theory of reasoned action, dissonance theory, the theory of individual differences, persuasive theory, conformity theory, balance theory, attribution theory, personal space theory, and learning theory.

CET (Consumer Ethnocentrism): A biased tendency that consumers hold that makes them tend to judge home-country products favorably and foreign substitutes unfavorably.

Default parameters in software: This refers to the specific primitive values or objects that are assigned as their initial values.

Imports: Commodities or services that are of foreign origin and are brought into a country by importers.

Linearity: In statistics refers to the linear nature of relationships between variables. In these relationships, a modification in one variable precisely matches an alteration in another area of interest. A graph represents a linear relationship as a straight line connecting two points. The straighter the line, the more "linear" the relationship between the variables. An uncomplicated illustration of a linear relationship can be observed in the correlation between travel duration and the distance covered. The relationship between distance and time is linear when travelling at a constant speed; therefore, doubling the time will result in doubling the distance.

Loadings: Also known as factor or outer loadings, are computed as the correlations between a latent variable and its measurement variables. This definition differs from cross-loadings, calculated as correlations between a measurement variable and the other latent variables.

Non-Probability Sampling: An approach to sampling that involves selecting participants based on reasons other than randomness, such as convenience, purpose, judgment, or quota.

Path Coefficients: Also known as regression coefficients, serve as the underlying statistical mechanism in structural equation modeling and, consequently, in linear regression. The term "connection strengths" refers to the parameters of the model and the estimations of effective connectivity.

Path Models: These illustrate the causal relationships between variables of interest. To interpret path models, read them from left to right, where the independent variables on the left predict the outcome (primary interest) variable(s) on the right. There are explicit guidelines for creating path models. For instance, arrows can have a single head or be bidirectional, but two arrows with single heads cannot be employed to depict bidirectional relationships. Linear arrows represent cause-and-effect relationships, whereas curved bidirectional arrows indicate correlations. Path models delineate quantitative studies, including regressions or more intricate structural equation models. The beta, or standardized coefficient, is typically reported in both circumstances.

PLS-SEM (Partial Least Square Structural Equation Modeling): A component-based multivariate analysis for analyzing complex path modeling between observed and latent variables by estimating parameters similar to the principal component with a multiple regression approach.

Purchase Intention: This refers to the consumer's willingness to acquire a product or service. It is frequently chosen as the foundation for studying purchase behavior. Research indicates that intention is often the primary determinant of actual purchasing behavior.

Reliability vs. Validity: Reliability refers to the degree to which the findings may be replicated when the study is conducted again under the same circumstances. Validity refers to the degree to which the results accurately assess their intended assessment. Reliability is evaluated by examining the consistency of results across time, among various observers, and within different test sections. In contrast, the degree to which the findings concur with accepted theories and other measurements of the same subject is a validity test. The reliability of a measurement does not guarantee its validity; while the results may be reproducible, they may not be accurate. A valid measurement is typically reliable; if a test yields precise outcomes, it should be capable of being replicated.

Reliability: A statistical metric used to assess the consistency of a test, scale, or construct. It is referred to as construct reliability or composite reliability.

Robustness: This pertains to the resilience and durability of a statistical model, tests, and methods. If the prerequisites of a study are satisfied, the validity of the models can be confirmed by employing mathematical proofs. Several models rely on hypothetical scenarios not present in real-world data analysis. Consequently, these models can yield accurate outcomes even if the actual conditions are not precisely met. Robust statistics work well even when data comes from various probability distributions. Outliers or minor changes in the model assumptions in a given dataset do not significantly affect a robust model. A robust statistic is immune to errors in the results. Robustness is a characteristic frequently found in quantitative research.

SEM (Structural Equation Modeling): An advanced multivariate analysis used to simultaneously analyze a complicated path model. It consists of two mainstreams: covariance-based structural equation modeling (CB-SEM) and variance (component) based partial least squares (PLS-SEM).

SmartPLS: A statistical software with a graphical user interface well-known for its ability to model complex path models using PLS-SEM approaches and supplement them with comprehensive additional analyses.

SNI (Subjective Norms Toward Imports): Are values consumers hold from their social circles, like family, friends, and others.

TRA (The Theory of Reasoned Action): A principle that an intention stimulates a specific action, and attitudes and subjective norms stimulate that intention.

Validity: A statistical metric used to assess the accuracy of a test, scale, or construct. There is convergent, discriminant, and nomological validity.

WarpPLS: A statistical software with a graphical user interface that is well-known for its ability to model nonlinearity among variables in path models using SEM approaches.

Chapter 14
Investigating the Impact of Demographic Factors on Personal Innovativeness in Digital Wallet Usage:
An Exploratory Study

Muhammad Azmi Sait
https://orcid.org/0000-0002-5175-6436
Universiti Brunei Darussalam, Brunei

Mohammad Nabil Almunawar
https://orcid.org/0000-0001-5296-2576
Universiti Brunei Darussalam, Brunei

Muhammad Anshari
https://orcid.org/0000-0002-8160-6682
Universiti Brunei Darussalam, Brunei

Masairol Masri
Universiti Brunei Darussalam, Brunei

ABSTRACT

This study examines demographic factors and personal innovativeness to information technologies (PIIT) among Brunei Darussalam's digital wallet users. Analyzing data from 181 respondents, it explores the influence of gender, age, and adopter category on PIIT levels. Results show no significant correlation between gender and PIIT levels, challenging gender-based assumptions. Age groups also exhibit no significant association with PIIT levels, contrary to expectations. However, the adopter category demonstrates a significant relationship with PIIT levels, highlighting the impact of adoption behavior. Tailored marketing, product design, and policy interventions are needed for digital inclusion. Findings of this study have implications for academia, industry, and policymaking, providing insights into technology adoption behaviors in the digital wallet domain.

DOI: 10.4018/979-8-3693-2865-1.ch014

INTRODUCTION

Digital wallets, as a type of financial technology (fintech) payment tool, are increasingly gaining significance on a global scale. This trend is driven by a shift in preferences towards more convenient and rapid payment transactions (Gomber et al., 2017; Nabila et al., 2018). The escalating demand for cashless payment methods worldwide (Singh and Sinha, 2020), coupled with the widespread use of smartphones facilitating e-commerce activities in recent years (Alam et al., 2021), has further underscored the growing relevance of digital wallets in today's world.

In the Asia Pacific region, China stands out as the dominant force in the digital wallet market. It boasts the highest number of digital wallet users, with reports indicating a staggering 1.18 billion users, representing over 45 per cent of the country's population. This sizable user base accounts for 42.1 per cent of global digital wallet users (Boku, 2021). The surge in digital wallet adoption in China is attributed to the favorable technological landscape in the country, along with the population's readiness to embrace and integrate this technology into their daily payment transactions (Capgemini Research Institute, 2021; Charlotte, 2022).

In the case of Brunei Darussalam, a country with exceptionally high internet penetration of over 95 per cent of the total population (The World Bank Group, 2022a), as well as a significant number of mobile cellular subscriptions totaling up to 536,589 subscribers in 2020 (The World Bank Group, 2022b), the adoption of digital wallets remains relatively low (AITI, 2019). This disparity can be attributed to the recent introduction of digital wallet technologies in Brunei Darussalam, with the BruPay digital wallet being launched only in late 2018 (Sait et al., 2023). It is noteworthy that digital wallet usage in Brunei is still in its infancy compared to neighboring countries, where digital wallet markets have already reached a more mature stage of development (Boku, 2021).

Beyond the COVID-19 pandemic, the digital wallet industry in Brunei Darussalam has experienced significant growth, largely driven by the social restrictions imposed by the government to mitigate the spread of the virus. There has been a notable surge in cashless transactions, increasing by up to 116 per cent compared to previous years, alongside a reported decline in ATM cash withdrawals (Rasidah, 2020). These trends indicate a shift towards a digital economy in Brunei Darussalam, aligning with the government's initiative outlined in the Digital Economy Masterplan 2025 (Prime Minister's Office, 2021).

According to Rogers (1995), the innovation decision-making process involves two main categories of individuals: adopters and resistors. Additionally, Rogers (1995) suggests that adopters can be further classified as either early adopters or late adopters, with their levels of personal innovativeness differing from each other. Early adopters typically exhibit higher levels of personal innovativeness, while late adopters may display lower levels. This raises an intriguing question about whether adopters' demographic characteristics play a role in determining their level of personal innovativeness.

Therefore, given the widespread availability of digital wallet services in Brunei Darussalam accessible to all residents, the objective of this study is to investigate variations in personal innovativeness to information technology (PIIT) among respondents based on their demographic characteristics, including gender, age, and adopter categories. Considering the recent introduction of digital wallet technology in Brunei in 2018 (Sait et al., 2023), it is logical to target digital wallet users as respondents, as they are likely to exhibit a certain level of personal innovativeness towards information technologies.

The subsequent sections of this paper are structured as follows: The following section conducts a review of relevant literature, examining prior studies that have investigated the determinants of personal innovativeness. This is followed by the methodology section, which outlines the sampling procedure and the quantitative approach employed to achieve the study's objectives. Following this, the results and discussion section presents the study's findings, encompassing the demographic profiles of respondents and the associations found between demographic characteristics and personal innovativeness levels. Lastly, the conclusion section will summarize the study's outcomes and delineate its limitations, along with recommendations for future research.

LITERATURE REVIEW

As per Rogers (1995), personal innovativeness denotes the extent to which an individual or another unit of adoption embraces new ideas at an earlier stage compared to other members within a system. Agarwal and Prasad (1997) subsequently redefined personal innovativeness to enhance its relevance in the domain of information technology adoption. They introduced a new construct known as personal innovativeness to information technologies (PIIT), conceptualizing it as a trait not tied to a particular individual or environment configuration. PIIT is defined as individuals' willingness to experiment with new information technologies.

However, the extent of PIIT has been observed to vary depending on the demographic characteristics of individuals. For instance, in the context of gender, a study conducted by Lattu and Maulana (2023) revealed that men exhibit a greater inclination to adopt new brands of ride-hailing applications compared to women. This suggests that gender disparities influence individuals' readiness to experiment with and persist in using new technologies, such as those in the ride-hailing industry. However, contrary to previous findings, a recent study by Kotsev and Stoycheva (2024) discovered no significant difference in PIIT levels between genders. This contradicts the stereotype that one gender surpasses the other in terms of PIIT. Therefore, this study propose the hypothesis below:

H1: There is a significant association between gender and PIIT level among respondents

According to Gulamhuseinwala et al. (2015), young populations are more inclined to adopt new innovative technologies, particularly within the realm of fintech, due to their higher levels of PIIT. This notion is supported by the work of Anshari et al. (2021), which suggests that younger generations, having been born into the digital age, naturally exhibit greater PIIT compared to older age groups. Additionally, Kotsev and Stoycheva (2024) argue that as individuals age, their inclination to explore new technologies tends to diminish, although this trend is contingent upon individual characteristics and circumstances. However, given the increasing integration of technology into daily life, the influence of age on PIIT levels may differ in contemporary society. Consequently, this study posits the following hypothesis.

H2: There is a significant association between age category and PIIT level among respondents

According to Rogers (1995), personal innovativeness refers to the extent to which individuals or groups adopt new innovations, particularly in the early stages of their introduction. Furthermore, Rogers (1995) suggests that early adopters are more likely to exhibit higher levels ofPIIT, as they typically possess significant knowledge of preceding technologies or innovations. However, a knowledge gap exists regarding this common assumption, particularly in the context of financial technologies, which are considered novel globally. Consequently, there are individuals who adopt such new technologies upon their initial introduction and others who adopt them at a later stage (Agarwal and Prasad, 1997). Therefore, it is essential to investigate this phenomenon by proposing the hypothesis below.

H3: There is a significant association between adopter category and PIIT level among respondents

Given the scarcity of studies specifically investigating the antecedents of PIIT, this study seeks to address this gap in the literature by examining the relationships between gender, age groups, and adopter category (duration of technology usage) and their impact on PIIT levels.

METHODOLOGY

This exploratory study aims to explore the relationship between respondents' demographics and their level of PIIT. To achieve this goal, data were collected from 181 respondents using a simple random sampling method, comprising digital wallet users in Brunei Darussalam. Digital wallets are considered a recent technological introduction in the country, having been launched in 2018 (Sait et al., 2023).

An link of the online survey questionnaire was distributed through various social media platforms such as WhatsApp, Facebook, and Instagram to maximize outreach. Upon accessing the survey, respondents were presented with an information sheet outlining the survey's purpose and specifying that only digital wallet users were eligible to participate. Consent forms were required to be digitally signed by respondents to confirm their agreement to participate in the study.

The survey questionnaire gathered demographic information from respondents, including gender, age, duration of digital wallet usage, and their PIIT, measured on a 5-point Likert Scale (with 1 denoted for "Strongly Agree", 2 for "Agree", 3 for "Neutral", 4 for "Disagree" and 5 for "Strongly Disagree"). The measurement items for PIIT were adapted from Agarwal and Prasad (1997), and the construct's reliability was assessed using SPSS v. 24. The item descriptions and reliability tests for PIIT are summarized in Table 1 below. The reliability test yielded a Cronbach's alpha value of 0.824, indicating that the measurement items used for this construct are statistically reliable.

Table 1. Construct items and reliability test for personal innovativeness to information technology (PIIT)

Item	Description	Source	Cronbach Alpha
PIIT1	I am usually the first to try new technologies among my peers and friends	Agarwal and Prasad (1997)	0.824
PIIT2	I would usually look for ways to try out new technologies whenever I hear of it		
PIIT3	I know more about new technologies compared to others in my circle of friends and families		

Furthermore, to explore the relationship between respondents' demographic profiles and their levels of PIIT, the Chi-square (χ^2) test is employed. As noted by McHugh (2013), the Chi-square test serves as a statistical tool for determining significant associations between two categorical variables, without reliance on assumptions about data distribution. This non-parametric test is commonly utilized in research to investigate group differences among nominal or ordinal variables, offering insights into observed distinctions and identifying contributing categories. By analyzing the variance between observed and expected frequencies within a contingency table, the Chi-square test assesses the independence of the variables under examination.

Prior to conducting the Chi-square (χ^2) test, demographic data of respondents are prepared to ensure they meet the categorical requirement for this analysis (McHugh, 2013). For example, respondents' ages are grouped into "young" (below 27 years old) and "old" generations (above 27 years old). Similarly, adopter categories are classified as "early adopters" (using digital wallets for more than 2 years prior to the survey) and "late adopters" (using digital wallets for less than 2 years prior to the survey). Additionally, with regards to the PIIT, it was categorised into three classes: high, moderate and low, depending on the average score of the three items of the PIIT construct.

In gathering secondary data, comprehensive searches were conducted across various literature databases, including Google Scholar, Scopus, Science Direct, Emerald Insights, and ResearchGate. Boolean operators, revolving around relevant keywords such as "personal innovativeness," "age," "gender," and "adopter category," were employed to refine search results. Additionally, research papers focusing on these keywords were extensively reviewed to establish a foundational understanding of the topic at hand. Only articles and research papers available in Malay and English languages were considered for inclusion in this study.

RESULTS

Demographic Profile of Respondents

In this study, there were a total of 181 respondents, all of whom were digital wallet users in Brunei Darussalam. The majority of participants were female, comprising 71.3 per cent of the total respondents, while male respondents constituted 28.7 per cent. In terms of age groups, 51.9 per cent of respondents belonged to the younger generation (below 27 years old), with the remaining 48.1 per cent categorized as belonging to the older generation (above 27 years old). Regarding the duration of digital wallet usage, 61 per cent of respondents reported using digital wallets for over 2 years at the time of the survey (classified as early adopters), while 39 per cent indicated using digital wallets for less than 2 years (classified as late adopters). The table below summarises the demographic profiles of the respondents in this study.

Table 2. Demographic profile of respondents

	N	%
Gender		
Male	52	28.7%
Female	129	71.3%
Total	181	100%
Age Groups		
Young Age Group (i.e., less than 27 years old)	94	51.9%
Old Age Group (i.e., more than 27 years old)	87	48.1%
Total	181	100%
Adopter Category		
Early Adopter (i.e., used digital wallet more than 2 years)	109	61%
Late Adopter (i.e., used digital wallet less than 2 years)	72	39%
Total	181	100%

Descriptive Variable Analysis

The results of the descriptive variable analysis for PIIT indicate an average score of 2.60 across the three measurement items. Interestingly, the item with the lowest mean, PIIT2 (2.50), is perceived as the strongest indicator of personal innovativeness among respondents, followed by PIIT1 (2.60) and PIIT3 (2.70), which has the highest mean. This suggests that respondents are particularly inclined to seek out and try new technologies as soon as they hear about them, showcasing a strong inclination towards early adoption. Therefore, emphasizing the novelty and innovative aspects of digital wallet technologies may appeal to such individuals.

Table 3. Descriptive variable analysis of personal innovativeness to information technologies (PIIT)

Item	Description	Mean	Std Dev
PIIT1	I find myself being an early adopter of new technologies among my peers and friends.	2.60	1.13
PIIT2	I'm always seeking ways to try out new technologies as soon as I hear about them.	2.50	1.06
PIIT3	I find that I have more knowledge about new technologies compared to others in my circle of friends and family.	2.70	1.09
Average Personal Innovativeness to Information Technologies		2.60	1.1

Chi-Square Analysis

The primary objective of this study is to investigate the potential correlation between demographic attributes (specifically gender, age groups, and adopter category) and Personal Innovativeness to Information Technologies (PIIT). First, a chi-square test was conducted to assess the association between gender (male and female) and PIIT levels. Notably, the chi-square test met the prerequisite criterion as no expected cell frequencies were less than 5. The analysis revealed a lack of statistically significant relationship between gender and PIIT, as evidenced by (2) = 0.03, with a p-value of 0.999. Consequently, the initial hypothesis (H1) positing a difference in PIIT levels between genders is rejected. This outcome resonates with prior research, specifically the findings of Kotsev and Stoycheva (2024), who similarly reported no discernible variance in PIIT levels between male and female cohorts.

Subsequently, a chi-square test was employed to evaluate the relationship between age groups (young and old groups) and PIIT levels. It is noteworthy that the chi-square test adhered to the prerequisite criterion, with no expected cell frequencies falling below 5. The analysis yielded a non-significant relationship between age groups and PIIT levels, as evidenced by (2) = 5.288, with a p-value of 0.07. Consequently, the initial hypothesis (H2) suggesting a disparity in PIIT levels between age groups is rejected. This finding challenges prevailing beliefs articulated by Gulamhuseinwala et al. (2015) and Anshari et al. (2021), which assert that younger individuals exhibit higher levels of PIIT and are thus more inclined to adopt new technologies compared to their older counterparts. Furthermore, it contradicts the findings of Kotsev and Stoycheva (2024), who reported a significant association between personal innovativeness and age, indicating that younger individuals possess greater personal innovativeness than older individuals.

Finally, a chi-square test was utilized to examine the relationship between adopter category (i.e., early adopter and later adopter) and PIIT levels. It is noteworthy that the chi-square test met the prerequisite criterion, with no expected cell frequencies falling below 5. The analysis revealed a significant relationship between adopter category and PIIT levels, as evidenced by (2) = 7.318, with a p-value of 0.026. Consequently, the initial hypothesis (H3) proposing a disparity in PIIT levels between adopter categories is supported. This finding further validates the association between adoption behavior (i.e., being an early vs. late adopter) and PIIT levels, as posited by earlier studies such as that of Rogers (1995). According to Rogers, early adopters exhibit a higher inclination toward adopting new technologies due to their awareness and understanding of emerging technologies, which makes them more inclined to take risks in adopting novel technologies.

DISCUSSION

The demographic profile analysis of respondents in this study offers pertinent insights into the user landscape of digital wallets within the context of Brunei Darussalam. Noteworthy is the predominance of female respondents, constituting 71.3% of the total cohort, which suggests a significant gender representation within this technological domain. Furthermore, the distribution across age cohorts delineates a balanced demographic, albeit with a slight skew towards the younger segment, indicative of a diverse user base encompassing both younger and older generations. Moreover, the segmentation based on the duration of digital wallet usage underscores the presence of a substantial cohort classified as early adopters, denoting users with extensive experience spanning over 2 years.

Delving deeper into respondents' personal innovativeness towards information technologies (PIIT) through descriptive variable analysis reveals nuanced inclinations. Despite exhibiting a moderate overall inclination towards personal innovativeness, respondents manifest a conspicuous proclivity towards embracing novelty, as indicated by a robust inclination towards seeking and experimenting with emerging technologies upon their inception. This propensity underscores a predisposition towards early adoption, highlighting the significance of accentuating innovative attributes to resonate with such tech-savvy individuals.

Chi-square analysis, deployed to scrutinize potential correlations between demographic attributes and PIIT levels, yields intriguing insights. Contrary to conventional assumptions, no statistically significant relationship is discerned between gender and PIIT levels, debunking prevalent gender-related disparities in technological innovativeness. Similarly, the absence of a significant association between age cohorts and PIIT levels challenges conventional wisdom positing higher innovativeness among younger demographics.

However, a significant relationship emerges between adopter categories and PIIT levels, reaffirming extant literature underscoring the influence of adoption behavior on technological innovativeness. This finding corroborates the notion that early adopters, characterized by their cognizance and propensity for risk-taking, exhibit heightened personal innovativeness, thereby predisposing them towards embracing nascent technological advancements.

IMPLICATIONS OF STUDY

Theoeretical Implication

This study significantly contributes to the advancement of theory in the field of technology adoption by examining the intricate relationship between demographic characteristics and personal innovativeness to information technologies (PIIT). Through empirical evidence, the study enriches our understanding of how factors such as gender, age, and adopter category influence PIIT levels, shedding light on the complex interplay between individual traits and technology adoption behaviors.

Furthermore, the findings may lead to the refinement and development of theoretical constructs related to personal innovativeness and technology adoption. By delving into the multidimensionality of PIIT and its implications for predicting adoption behaviors across different demographic groups, researchers can enhance the explanatory power of existing theoretical frameworks.

Practical Implications

Practically, digital wallet providers can leverage the insights from this study to devise targeted marketing strategies tailored to different demographic segments. By aligning messaging and product features with the preferences and behaviors of specific demographic groups, companies can boost user engagement and adoption rates. Additionally, the study's insights can inform the design and development of digital wallet solutions that are more user-friendly and accessible to diverse populations. Prioritizing features that cater to the unique needs of older users or designing interfaces appealing to different gender preferences can enhance the overall user experience and drive adoption.

Policy Implications

Policymakers can utilize the findings to design interventions aimed at promoting digital inclusion and reducing barriers to technology adoption. Initiatives such as digital literacy programs or financial incentives targeted at underrepresented demographic groups may help bridge the digital divide and promote wider access to digital wallet technologies. Lastly, organizations can develop training and educational programs based on the study's insights to enhance digital literacy and promote technology adoption among diverse populations. By equipping individuals with the knowledge and skills needed to effectively use digital wallet technologies, organizations can empower them to participate more fully in the digital economy.

LIMITATIONS OF STUDY AND RECOMMENDATION FOR FUTURE STUDIES

The study has several limitations that may impact the robustness and generalizability of its findings. Firstly, the reliance on a simple random sampling method via social media platforms introduces potential sampling bias, as certain demographic groups may be underrepresented due to differential access or participation rates. Moreover, the cross-sectional design utilized in the study limits the ability to establish causal relationships between demographic characteristics and personal innovativeness, as it does not capture temporal changes or longitudinal trends. Additionally, the study's reliance on self-report measures for data collection, particularly regarding personal innovativeness, raises concerns about response bias and the accuracy of reported behaviors and attitudes. Furthermore, the study's focus solely on digital wallet users in Brunei Darussalam restricts the generalizability of findings to other populations or contexts, highlighting the need for caution in extrapolating results beyond the study sample. Lastly, while the study reported acceptable reliability for the measurement instrument used, the limited number of items may not fully capture the multidimensional nature of personal innovativeness, potentially compromising the validity of results.

To address these limitations and advance understanding in the field, future studies could consider several methodological enhancements. Firstly, adopting longitudinal research designs would allow for the tracking of changes in personal innovativeness over time, offering insights into the stability and evolution of technology adoption behaviors among different demographic groups. Secondly, incorporating mixed-methods approaches, such as qualitative interviews or focus groups, alongside quantitative analyses can provide deeper insights into the underlying motivations and barriers influencing personal innovativeness. Moreover, diversifying sampling strategies to include both online and offline methods could enhance the representativeness of the sample and mitigate potential biases associated with self-selection. Comparative studies across different countries or regions would also be valuable in elucidating cultural variations in personal innovativeness and technology adoption behaviors. Lastly, future research endeavors could focus on refining measurement tools to develop comprehensive instruments that capture the multifaceted nature of personal innovativeness, thereby enhancing the reliability and validity of findings in this area of inquiry.

CONCLUSION

In conclusion, the study unveils valuable insights into the demographic composition and personal innovativeness of digital wallet users in Brunei Darussalam. The findings highlight a diverse user base, with a notable prevalence of female respondents and a balanced representation across age cohorts. Despite exhibiting a moderate overall inclination towards personal innovativeness, users demonstrate a distinct proclivity towards embracing novelty, particularly evident among early adopters. Notably, while gender and age cohorts do not significantly influence personal innovativeness, adoption behavior emerges as a pivotal determinant, with early adopters exhibiting heightened innovativeness. These findings underscore the importance of targeted strategies focusing on innovative attributes to foster wider acceptance and utilization of digital wallet technologies within the Brunei Darussalam market.

REFERENCES

Agarwal, R., & Prasad, J. (1997). The role of innovation characteristics and perceived voluntariness in the acceptance of information technologies. *Decision Sciences*, *28*(3), 557–582.

AITI. (2019), *Brunei Darussalam Information Communications Technology (ICT) Business Report 2019*. AITI.

Alam, M. M., Awawdeh, A. E., & Muhamad, A. I. (2021). Using e-wallet for business process development: challenges and prospects in Malaysia. Business Process Management Journal. Emerald Publishing Limited.

Anshari, M., Arine, M. A., Nurhidayah, N., Aziyah, H., & Salleh, M. H. A. (2021). Factors influencing individual in adopting eWallet. *Journal of Financial Services Marketing, 26*(1), 10–23. doi:10.1057/s41264-020-00079-5

Gomber, P., Koch, J.-A., & Siering, M. (2017). Digital Finance and FinTech: Current research and future research directions. *Journal of Business Economics, 87*(5), 537–580. doi:10.1007/s11573-017-0852-x

Gulamhuseinwala, I., Bull, T. & Lewis, S. (2015). FinTech is gaining traction and young, high-income users are the early adopters. *Journal of Financial Perspectives, 3.*

Kotsev, E., & Stoycheva, B. (2024). AIP Conference Proceedings: Vol. 3063. *Antecedents of individual innovativeness: Exploring gender, age and job nature.* AIP Publishing.

Lattu, A. and Maulana, A. (2023). Determinant Factors of Personal Innovativeness in Information Technology of Ride-Hailing New Brand: The Role of Gender. *International Journal of Health Engineering and Technology (IJHET), 2.*

McHugh, M.L. (2013). The chi-square test of independence. *Biochemia Medica, Medicinska naklada, 23*(2), 143–149.

Nabila, M., Purwandari, B., Nazief, B. A. A., Chalid, D. A., Wibowo, S. S., & Solichah, I. (2018). Financial Technology Acceptance Factors of Electronic Wallet and Digital Cash in Indonesia. *2018 International Conference on Information Technology Systems and Innovation, ICITSI 2018 - Proceedings*, (pp. 284–289). IEEE. 10.1109/ICITSI.2018.8696091

Prime Minister's Office. (2021), *Brunei Darussalam Sustainable Development Goals Annual Report 2021.* Prime Minister's Office.

Rasidah, H.A.B. (2020). COVID-19 drives 116% growth in interbank fund transfers: AMBD. *The Scoop.*

Rogers, E. M. (1995). *Diffusion of innovations* (Vol. 12).

Sait, M. A., Almunawar, M. N., Anshari, M., & Masri, M. (2023). Digital Wallet Adoption in Supporting Financial Inclusion: A Conceptual Framework. *2023 International Conference on Sustainable Islamic Business and Finance (SIBF).* IEEE. 10.1109/SIBF60067.2023.10380043

Singh, N., & Sinha, N. (2020). How perceived trust mediates merchant's intention to use a mobile wallet technology. *Journal of Retailing and Consumer Services, 52,* 101894. doi:10.1016/j.jretconser.2019.101894

The World Bank Group. (2022a). *Individuals using the Internet (% of population) – Brunei Darussalam.* World Bank Group. https://data.worldbank.org/indicator/IT.NET.USER.ZS?locations=BN

The World Bank Group. (2022b). *Mobile cellular subscriptions – Brunei Darussalam.* The World Bank Group. https://data.worldbank.org/indicator/IT.CEL.SETS?end=2020&locations=BN&start=2010

Compilation of References

Abed, S. S. (2020). Social commerce adoption using TOE framework: An empirical investigation of Saudi Arabian SMEs. *International Journal of Information Management, 53*(1), 102118. doi:10.1016/j.ijinfomgt.2020.102118

Abolhassan, F. (2017). *The Drivers of Digital Transformation. Management for Professionals* (F. Abolhassan, Ed.). Springer International Publishing. http://link.springer.com/10.1007/978-3-319-31824-0 doi:10.1007/978-3-319-31824-0

Abot, M. D. 2020. Factors influencing adoption of artificial insemination by smallholder livestock farmers in dryland production systems of Kenya *(Doctoral dissertation, University of Nairobi)*.

Adekomaya, O., Jamiru, T., Sadiku, R., & Huan, Z. (2016). Sustaining the shelf life of fresh food in cold chain—A burden on the environment. *Alexandria Engineering Journal, 55*(2), 1359–1365. https://doi.org/. doi:10.1016/j.aej.2016.03.024

Agarwal, R., Gupta, A.K. & Kraut, R. (2008). The interplay between digital and social networks. *Information Systems Research. 19*(3), 243-252.

Agarwal, R., & Prasad, J. (1997). The role of innovation characteristics and perceived voluntariness in the acceptance of information technologies. *Decision Sciences, 28*(3), 557–582.

Aguilar Esteva, L. C., Kasliwal, A., Kinzler, M. S., Kim, H. C., & Keoleian, G. A. (2021). Circular economy framework for automobiles: Closing energy and material loops. *Journal of Industrial Ecology, 25*(4), 877–889. doi:10.1111/jiec.13088

Ahad, A. D., & Anshari, M. (2017). Smartphone habits among youth: Uses and gratification theory. [IJCBPL]. *International Journal of Cyber Behavior, Psychology and Learning, 7*(1), 65–75. doi:10.4018/IJCBPL.2017010105

Ahad, A. D., Anshari, M., & Razzaq, A. (2017). Domestication of smartphones among adolescents in Brunei darussalam. [IJCBPL]. *International Journal of Cyber Behavior, Psychology and Learning, 7*(4), 26–39. doi:10.4018/IJCBPL.2017100103

Ahmad, K., Maabreh, M., Ghaly, M., Khan, K., Qadir, J., & Al-Fuqaha, A. (2022). Developing future human-centered smart cities: Critical analysis of smart city security, Data management, and Ethical challenges. *Computer Science Review, 43*, 100452. doi:10.1016/j.cosrev.2021.100452

Ahmed, F., Al Kez, D., McLoone, S., Best, R. J., Cameron, C., & Foley, A. (2023). Dynamic grid stability in low carbon power systems with minimum inertia. *Renewable Energy, 210*, 486–506. doi:10.1016/j.renene.2023.03.082

Ahmed, S. A., Huang, Q., Zhang, Z., Li, J., Amin, W., Afzal, M., Hussain, J., & Hussain, F. (2024). Optimization of social welfare and mitigating privacy risks in P2P energy trading: Differential privacy for secure data reporting. *Applied Energy, 356*, 122403. doi:10.1016/j.apenergy.2023.122403

Aithal, P., & Rao, P. (2016). Green education concepts & strategies in higher education model. *International Journal of Scientific Research and Modern Education (IJSRME) ISSN (Online)*, 2455-2563.

AITI. (2019), *Brunei Darussalam Information Communications Technology (ICT) Business Report 2019*. AITI.

Ajzen, I. (1991). The Theory of Planned Behavior. *Organizational Behavior and Human Decision Processes*, *50*(2), 179–211. doi:10.1016/0749-5978(91)90020-T

Akhlaq, A. and Ahmed, E., 2016. Gender Differences Among Online Shopping Factors in Pakistan. *Organizations and Markets in Emerging Economies*, *7*(13), 76-78.

Ala-Harja, H., & Helo, P. (2015). Green supply chain decisions—Case-based performance analysis from the food industry. *Transportation Research Part E: Logistics and Transportation Review*, *74*, 11–21. . doi:10.1016/j.tre.2014.12.005

Alam, M. M., Awawdeh, A. E., & Muhamad, A. I. (2021). Using e-wallet for business process development: challenges and prospects in Malaysia. Business Process Management Journal. Emerald Publishing Limited.

Alas, Y., Anshari, M., Sabtu, N. I., & Yunus, N. (2016). Second-chance university admission, the theory of planned behaviour and student achievement. *International Review of Education*, *62*(3), 299–316. doi:10.1007/s11159-016-9558-5

Albright, S. C., Winston W. L. (2013). *Business Analytics - Data Analysis and Decision Making*. Cengage Learning.

Ali Taha, V., Pencarelli, T., Škerháková, V., Fedorko, R., & Košíková, M. (2021). The Use of Social Media and Its Impact on Shopping Behavior of Slovak and Italian Consumers during COVID-19 Pandemic. *Sustainability (Basel)*, *13*(4), 1710. doi:10.3390/su13041710

Ali, M., & Abdel-Haq, M. K. (2021). Bibliographical analysis of artificial intelligence learning in Higher Education: is the role of the human educator and educated a thing of the past? In *Fostering Communication and Learning With Underutilized Technologies in Higher Education* (pp. 36–52). IGI Global. doi:10.4018/978-1-7998-4846-2.ch003

Ali, O., Shrestha, A., Osmanaj, V., & Muhammed, S. (2020). Cloud computing technology adoption: An evaluation of key factors in local governments. *Information Technology & People*, *34*(2), 666–703. doi:10.1108/ITP-03-2019-0119

Aljukhadar, M., Boeuf, B., & Senecal, S. (2021). Does consumer ethnocentrism impact international shopping? A theory of social class divide. *Psychology and Marketing*, *38*(5), 735–744. doi:10.1002/mar.21461

Allen, J., Jimmieson, N. L., Bordia, P., & Irmer, B. E. (2007). Uncertainty during organisational change: Managing perceptions through communication. *Journal of Change Management*, *7*(2), 187–210. doi:10.1080/14697010701563379

Almunawar, M. N., & Anshari, M. (2020). Multi-sided networks of digital platform ecosystem: The case of ride-hailing in Indonesia. *Asia Pacific Journal of Information Systems*, *30*(4), 808–831. doi:10.14329/apjis.2020.30.4.808

Almunawar, M. N., & Anshari, M. (2024). Customer acceptance of online delivery platform during the COVID-19 pandemic: The case of Brunei Darussalam. *Journal of Science and Technology Policy Management*, *15*(2), 288–310. doi:10.1108/JSTPM-04-2022-0073

Almunawar, M. N., de Pablos, P. O., & Anshari, M. (Eds.). (2023). *Digital Transformation for Business and Society: Contemporary Issues and Applications in Asia*. Taylor & Francis. doi:10.4324/9781003441298

Almunawar, N., Ordóñez de Pablos, P., & Anshari, M. (2023). *Sustainable Development and the Digital Economy: Human-centricity, Sustainability and Resilience in Asia*. Routledge. doi:10.4324/9781003388753

Al-Ruithe, M., Benkhelifa, E., & Hameed, K. (2018). Key Issues for Embracing the Cloud Computing to Adopt a Digital Transformation: A study of Saudi Public Sector. *Procedia Computer Science*. https://linkinghub.elsevier.com/retrieve/pii/S1877050918305076

Al-Sharif, M. A. B. (2023). ETHICAL ISSUES WITH TECHNOLOGY IN HIGHER EDUCATION. *Integrating Technology Into Student Affairs (# 9 SAPPI Series)*, (9), 69.

Altenmüller, T., Bauernhansl, T., Kyek, A., & Waschneck, B. (2017). Production Scheduling in Complex Job Shops from an Industrie 4.0 Perspective: A Review and Challenges in the Semiconductor Industry. *CEUR Workshop Proceedings*. CEUR. https://ceur-ws.org/Vol-1793/paper3.pdf

Aly, H. (2020). Digital transformation, development and productivity in developing countries: is artificial intelligence a curse or a blessing? *Review of Economics and Political Science*. Emerald. https://www.emerald.com/insight/content/doi/10.1108/REPS-11-2019-0145/full/html

Amin, P.D., & Amin, B. (2010). A Critical Review of Gender Difference in Online Shopping. *Indian journal of marketing, 40*(11), 43-52.

Amin, W., Huang, Q., Umer, K., Zhang, Z., Afzal, M., Khan, A. A., & Ahmed, S. A. (2020). A motivational game-theoretic approach for peer-to-peer energy trading in islanded and grid-connected microgrid. *International Journal of Electrical Power & Energy Systems, 123*, 106307. doi:10.1016/j.ijepes.2020.106307

Anderson, W. P., Chatterjee, L., & Lakshmanan, T. R. (2002). *E-commerce, transportation and economic geography*. STELLA Focus Group 1 Kick-off Meeting: Globalization, E-commerce and Trade, Siena, Italy.

Andrew, F., & Julie, R. (2005). Sustainable development: Lost meaning and opportunity? *Journal of Business Ethics, 60*(1), 17–27. doi:10.1007/s10551-005-2927-9

Anh, N. V., & Cheng, A. Y. (2020). Supply Chain Optimization in the Digital Age: A Big Data Analytics Perspective on Resilience and Efficiency. *AI, IoT and the Fourth Industrial Revolution Review, 10*(2), 11–18. https://scicadence.com/index.php/AI-IoT-REVIEW/article/view/15

Anita, N. (2011). India′s progress toward achieving the Millennium development goal. *Indian Journal of Community Medicine, 36*(2), 85–92. doi:10.4103/0970-0218.84118 PMID:21976790

Anshari, M., Alas, Y., Razzaq, A., Shahrill, M., & Lim, S. A. (2021). Millennials consumers' behaviors between trends and experiments. In Research Anthology on E-Commerce Adoption, Models, and Applications for Modern Business (pp. 1492-1508). IGI global.

Anshari, M., Alas, Y., & Guan, L. S. (2016b). Developing online learning resources: Big data, social networks, and cloud computing to support pervasive knowledge. *Education and Information Technologies, 21*(6), 1663–1677. doi:10.1007/s10639-015-9407-3

Anshari, M., Alas, Y., & Guan, L. S. (2017). Pervasive knowledge, social networks, and cloud computing: E-learning 2.0. *Eurasia Journal of Mathematics, Science and Technology Education, 11*(5), 909–921. doi:10.12973/eurasia.2015.1360a

Anshari, M., Alas, Y., Sabtu, N. P. H., & Hamid, M. S. A. (2016a). Online Learning: Trends, issues and challenges in the Big Data Era. *Journal of E-learning and Knowledge Society, 12*(1).

Anshari, M., Alas, Y., Yunus, N., Sabtu, N. I., & Hamid, M. H. (2015). Social customer relationship management and student empowerment in online learning systems. *International Journal of Electronic Customer Relationship Management, 9*(2-3), 104–121. doi:10.1504/IJECRM.2015.071711

Anshari, M., & Almunawar, M. N. (2021). Adopting open innovation for SMEs and industrial revolution 4.0. *Journal of Science and Technology Policy Management, 13*(2), 405–427. doi:10.1108/JSTPM-03-2020-0061

Anshari, M., Almunawar, M. N., Lim, S. A., & Al-Mudimigh, A. (2019). Customer relationship management and big data enabled: Personalization & customization of services. *Applied Computing and Informatics, 15*(2), 94–101. doi:10.1016/j.aci.2018.05.004

Anshari, M., Almunawar, M. N., & Masri, M. (2022). Digital twin: Financial technology's next frontier of robo-advisor. *Journal of Risk and Financial Management*, *15*(4), 163. doi:10.3390/jrfm15040163

Anshari, M., Almunawar, M. N., Masri, M., Hamdan, M., Fithriyah, M., & Fitri, A. (2021a). Digital wallet in supporting green FinTech sustainability. In *2021 Third International Sustainability and Resilience Conference: Climate Change* (pp. 352-357). IEEE. 10.1109/IEEECONF53624.2021.9667957

Anshari, M., Almunawar, M. N., Masri, M., & Hrdy, M. (2021). Financial technology with AI-enabled and ethical challenges. *Society*, *58*(3), 189–195. doi:10.1007/s12115-021-00592-w

Anshari, M., Almunawar, M. N., & Razzaq, A. (2021). Developing talents vis-à-vis fourth industrial revolution. [IJABIM]. *International Journal of Asian Business and Information Management*, *12*(4), 20–32. doi:10.4018/IJABIM.20211001.oa2

Anshari, M., Arine, M. A., Nurhidayah, N., Aziyah, H., & Salleh, M. H. A. (2021). Factors influencing individual in adopting eWallet. *Journal of Financial Services Marketing*, *26*(1), 10–23. doi:10.1057/s41264-020-00079-5

Anshari, M., & Hamdan, M. (2022). Understanding knowledge management and upskilling in Fourth Industrial Revolution: Transformational shift and SECI model. *VINE Journal of Information and Knowledge Management Systems*, *52*(3), 373–393. doi:10.1108/VJIKMS-09-2021-0203

Anshari, M., & Hamdan, M. (2023). Enhancing e-government with a digital twin for innovation management. *Journal of Science and Technology Policy Management*, *14*(6), 1055–1065. doi:10.1108/JSTPM-11-2021-0176

Anshari, M., Hamdan, M., Ahmad, N., Ali, E., & Haidi, H. (2023). COVID-19, artificial intelligence, ethical challenges and policy implications. *AI & Society*, *38*(2), 707–720. doi:10.1007/s00146-022-01471-6

Anshari, M., Hamdan, M., Ahmad, N., Ali, E., & Haidi, H. (2023). New knowledge creation and loss during COVID-19: Sustainable knowledge management's perspective. *International Journal of Learning and Intellectual Capital*, *20*(6), 587–611. doi:10.1504/IJLIC.2023.134898

Anshari, M., & Lim, S. A. (2017). E-government with big data enabled through smartphone for public services: Possibilities and challenges. *International Journal of Public Administration*, *40*(13), 1143–1158. doi:10.1080/01900692.2016.1242619

Anshari, M., & Sumardi, W. H. (2020). Employing big data in business organisation and business ethics. *International Journal of Business Governance and Ethics*, *14*(2), 181–205. doi:10.1504/IJBGE.2020.106349

Anshari, M., Syafrudin, M., & Fitriyani, N. L. (2022). Fourth industrial revolution between knowledge management and digital humanities. *Information (Basel)*, *13*(6), 292. doi:10.3390/info13060292

Anshari, M., Syafrudin, M., Fitriyani, N. L., & Razzaq, A. (2022). Ethical responsibility and sustainability (ERS) development in a metaverse business model. *Sustainability (Basel)*, *14*(23), 15805. doi:10.3390/su142315805

Anshari, M., Syafrudin, M., Tan, A., Fitriyani, N. L., & Alas, Y. (2023). Optimisation of knowledge management (KM) with machine learning (ML) Enabled. *Information (Basel)*, *14*(1), 35. doi:10.3390/info14010035

Apaiah, R. K., Hendrix, E. M. T., Meerdink, G., & Linnemann, A. R. (2005). Qualitative methodology for efficient food chain design. *Trends in Food Science and Technology*, *16*, 204–214.

Apaiah, R. K., Linnemann, A. R., & Van Der Kooi, H. J. (2006). Exergy analysis: A tool to study the sustainability of food supply chains. *Food Research International*, *39*, 1–11.

Appel, G., Grewal, L., Hadi, R., & Stephen, A. (2020). The future of social media in marketing. *Journal of the Academy of Marketing Science*, *48*(1), 79–95. doi:10.1007/s11747-019-00695-1

Aral, S., & Eckles, D. (2019). Protecting elections from social media manipulation. *Science, 365*(6456), 858–861. doi:10.1126/science.aaw8243 PMID:31467206

Arnaud, D. (2019). Six key drivers for sustainable development. *International Journal of Environmental Sciences & Natural Resources, 18*(4), 555–994.

Ashok, M., Madan, R., Joha, A., & Sivarajah, U. (2022). Ethical framework for Artificial Intelligence and Digital technologies. *International Journal of Information Management, 62*, 102433. doi:10.1016/j.ijinfomgt.2021.102433

Ashraf, C. (2022). Exploring the impacts of artificial intelligence on freedom of religion or belief online. *International Journal of Human Rights, 26*(5), 757–791. doi:10.1080/13642987.2021.1968376

Attaran, M. (2020). Digital technology enablers and their implications for supply chain management. Supply Chain. *Forum Int. J., 21*, 158–172.

Audrain-Pontevia, A. (2016). Where do customer loyalties really lie, and why? Gender differences in store loyalty. *International Journal of Retail & Distribution Management, 44*(8). . doi:10.1108/IJRDM-01-2016-0002

Awa, H. O., & Ojiabo, O. U. (2016). A model of adoption determinants of ERP within T-O-E framework. *Information Technology & People, 29*(4), 901–930. doi:10.1108/ITP-03-2015-0068

Babatunde, O. M., Munda, J. L., & Hamam, Y. (2022). Off-grid hybrid photovoltaic–micro wind turbine renewable energy system with hydrogen and battery storage: Effects of sun tracking technologies. *Energy Conversion and Management, 255*, 115335. doi:10.1016/j.enconman.2022.115335

Bag, S., Yadav, G., Dhamija, P., & Kataria, K. K. (2021). Key resources for industry 4.0 adoption and its effect on sustainable production and circular economy: An empirical study. *Journal of Cleaner Production, 281*, 125233. doi:10.1016/j.jclepro.2020.125233

Balaji, K. (2024). The Nexus of Smart Contracts and Digital Twins Transforming Green Finance With Automated Transactions in Investment Agreements: Leveraging Smart Contracts for Green Investment Agreements and Automated Transactions. *Harnessing Blockchain Digital Twin Fusion for Sustainable Investments*. IGI Global.

Banasik, A., Kanellopoulos, A., Claassen, G., Bloemhof-Ruwaard, J., & Vorst, J. (2017). Assessing alternative production options for eco-efficient food supply chains using multi-objective optimization. *Annals of Operations Research, 250*(2), 341–362. doi:10.1007/s10479-016-2199-z

Baptista, J., Stein, M.-K., Klein, S., Watson-Manheim, M. B., & Lee, J. (2020). Digital work and organisational transformation: Emergent Digital/Human work configurations in modern organisations. *The Journal of Strategic Information Systems, 29*(2). https://linkinghub.elsevier.com/retrieve/pii/S0963868720300263

Barnett, W. P., & Carroll, G. R. (1995). Modeling internal organisational change. *Annual Review of Sociology, 21*(1), 217–236. doi:10.1146/annurev.so.21.080195.001245

Baruch, Y., & Cohen, A. (2007). The dynamics between organisational commitment and professional identity formation at work. In *Identities at work* (pp. 241–260). Springer. doi:10.1007/978-1-4020-4989-7_9

Barzman, M., Gerphagnon, M., Aubin-Houzelstein, G., Baron, G. L., Benard, A., Bouchet, F., & Mora, O. (2021). Exploring digital transformation in higher education and research via scenarios. *Journal of Futures Studies, 25*(3), 65–78.

Bateh, J., Castaneda, M. E., & Farah, J. E. (2013). Employee resistance to organisational change. [IJMIS]. *International Journal of Management & Information Systems, 17*(2), 113–116.

Baum, S. D. (2020). Social choice ethics in artificial intelligence. *AI \& SOCIETY, 35*(1), 165–176.

Beaudoin, P., Moore, M. A., & Goldsmith, R. E. (2000). Fashion leaders' and followers' attitudes toward buying domestic and imported apparel. *Clothing & Textiles Research Journal*, *18*(1), 56–64. doi:10.1177/0887302X0001800106

Beghetto, V., Bardella, N., Samiolo, R., Gatto, V., Conca, S.; Sole, R., Molin, G., Gattolin, A., Ongaro, N. (2021). By-products from mechanical recycling of polyolefins improve hot mix asphalt performance. *Journal of Cleaner Production*, *318*, 128627.

Beghetto, V., Sole, R., Buranello, C., Al-Abkal, M., & Facchin, M. (2021). Recent advancements in plastic packaging recycling: A mini-review. *Materials*, *14*, 4782.

Behl, A., Sampat, B., Gaur, J., Pereira, V., Laker, B., Shankar, A., Shi, Y., & Roohanifar, M. (2024). Can gamification help green supply chain management firms achieve sustainable results in servitized ecosystem? An empirical investigation. *Technovation*, *129*, 102915. doi:10.1016/j.technovation.2023.102915

Bell, J. and Loane, S., (2010). New-wave global firms: Web 2.0 and SME internationalization. *Journal of Marketing Management, 26*(3), 213-229.

Belmejdoub, A. (2017). *MANAGING ORGANISATIONAL COMMUNICATION: An Analysis of Communication Knowledge*. Stakeholder Requirements and Barriers to Effective Communication in the Workplace.

Bendor-Samuel, P. (2017). The power of digital transformation in a data-driven world. *Forbes*. https://www.forbes.com/sites/peterbendorsamuel/2017/07/21/the-power-of-digital-transformation-in-a-data-driven-world/?sh=cc5e2523f2c3

Beske, P., Land, A., & Seuring, S. (2014). Sustainable supply chain management practices and dynamic capabilities in the food industry: A critical analysis of the literature. *International Journal of Production Economics*, *152*, 131–143. doi:10.1016/j.ijpe.2013.12.026

Bharathi, K., & Sasikumar, M. (2021). Power flow control based on bidirectional converter for hybrid power generation system using microcontroller. *Microprocessors and Microsystems*, *82*, 103950. doi:10.1016/j.micpro.2021.103950

Bhattacharya, S. (2023). Localising the gender equality goal through urban planning tools in South Asia. *Journal of South Asia*, *2*, 45.

Bhimaraju, A., Mahesh, A., & Nirbheram, J. S. (2023). Feasibility study of solar photovoltaic/grid-connected hybrid renewable energy system with pumped storage hydropower system using abandoned open cast coal mine: A case study in India. *Journal of Energy Storage*, *72*, 108206. doi:10.1016/j.est.2023.108206

Bhuiyan, M. R. A. (2022). Overcome the future environmental challenges through sustainable and renewable energy resources. *Micro & Nano Letters*, *17*(14), 402–416. doi:10.1049/mna2.12148

Blair, R. A., Morse, B. S., & Tsai, L. L. (2017). Public health and public trust: Survey evidence from the Ebola Virus Disease epidemic in Liberia. *Social Science & Medicine*, *172*, 89–97. doi:10.1016/j.socscimed.2016.11.016 PMID:27914936

Bley, K., Leyh, C., & Schaffer, T. (2016). *Digitization of German Enterprises in the Production Sector-Do they know how digitized they are?* AISEL. https://aisel.aisnet.org/amcis2016/EntSys/Presentations/9/

Blohm, M., & Dettner, F. (2023). Green hydrogen production: Integrating environmental and social criteria to ensure sustainability. *Smart Energy*, *11*, 100112. doi:10.1016/j.segy.2023.100112

Boca, G. D., & Saraçlı, S. (2019). Environmental education and student's perception, for sustainability. *Sustainability (Basel)*, *11*(6), 1553. doi:10.3390/su11061553

Bodrow, W. (2017). Impact of Industry 4.0 in service oriented firm. *Advances in Manufacturing*, *5*(4), 394–400. http://link.springer.com/10.1007/s40436-017-0196-3

Boenig-Liptsin, M., Tanweer, A., & Edmundson, A. (2022). Data Science Ethos Lifecycle: Interplay of ethical thinking and data science practice. *Journal of Statistics and Data Science Education : An Official Journal of the of the American Statistical Association, 30*(3), 228–240. doi:10.1080/26939169.2022.2089411

Bogers, M. & West, J. (2012). Managing Distributed Innovation: Strategic Utilization of Open and User Innovation. *Types of Organizations & Organizational Behavior E-Journal.*

Bonil, J., Calafell, G., Granados, J., Junyent, M., & Tarín, R. M. (2012). A training model for progress in curriculum greening. *Profesorado. Revista de Currículum y Formación del Profesorado, 16*(2), 145–163.

Borangiu, T., Trentesaux, D., Thomas, A., Leitão, P., & Barata, J. (2019). Digital transformation of manufacturing through cloud services and resource virtualization. *Computers in Industry*. Elsevier. https://linkinghub.elsevier.com/retrieve/pii/S0166361519300107

Bordia, P., Hunt, E., Paulsen, N., Tourish, D., & DiFonzo, N. (2004). Uncertainty during organisational change: Is it all about control? *European Journal of Work and Organizational Psychology, 13*(3), 345–365. doi:10.1080/13594320444000128

Bostrom, N., & Yudkowsky, E. (2018). The ethics of artificial intelligence. In *Artificial intelligence safety and security* (pp. 57–69). Chapman and Hall/CRC. doi:10.1201/9781351251389-4

Boudreau, M. C., & Watson, R. T. (2006). Internet advertising strategy alignment. *Internet Research, 16*(1), 23–37. doi:10.1108/10662240610642523

Boyd, D. (2012). 6. Participating in the Always-On Lifestyle. In *The social media reader* (pp. 71–76). New York University Press. doi:10.18574/nyu/9780814764077.003.0010

Branson, C. M. (2008). Achieving organisational change through values alignment. *Journal of Educational Administration, 46*(3), 376–395. doi:10.1108/09578230810869293

Braun, K., & Kropp, C. (2023). Building a better world? Competing promises, visions and imaginaries-in-the-making of the digitalization of architecture and construction. *Futures, 154*, 103262. doi:10.1016/j.futures.2023.103262

Bravo, R., Segura, M. G., Temowo, O., & Samaddar, S. (2022). How does a pandemic disrupt the benefits of ecommerce? a case study of small and medium enterprises in the US. *Journal of Theoretical and Applied Electronic Commerce Research, 17*(2), 522–557. doi:10.3390/jtaer17020028

Brockhaus, S., Petersen, M., Michael Knemeyer, A. (2019). The promise: signaling sustainability in supply chain relationships. *Logistik im Wandel der Zeit – Von der Produktionssteuerung zu vernetzten Supply Chains (Changing times - from production control to networked supply chains)*. Springer Fachmedien Wiesbaden, Wiesbaden.

Browning, M. H., & Rigolon, A. (2019). School green space and its impact on academic performance: A systematic literature review. *International Journal of Environmental Research and Public Health, 16*(3), 429. doi:10.3390/ijerph16030429 PMID:30717301

Brunei: social media penetration 2022 (2022). Statista. https://www.statista.com/statistics/883777/brunei-social-media-penetration/

Bruneians rank high in social media usage . (2020). Borneo Bulletin Online. https://borneobulletin.com.bn/bruneians-rank-high-social-media-usage/

Bryant, M. (2006). Talking about change: Understanding employee responses through qualitative research. *Management Decision, 44*(2), 246–258. doi:10.1108/00251740610650229

Buettner, R. (2017). Predicting user behavior in electronic markets based on personality-mining in large online social networks: A personality-based product recommender framework. *Electronic Markets, 27*(3), 247–265. doi:10.1007/s12525-016-0228-z

BughinJ. R.KretschmerT.van ZeebroeckN. (2019). Experimentation, learning and stress: The role of digital technologies in strategy change. *Available at* SSRN 3328421. doi:10.2139/ssrn.3328421

Burda, M. &Wyplosz, C. (2009). Macroeconomics: A European text. Oxford: Oxford University Press.2,28.

Butt, J. (2020). A Conceptual Framework to Support Digital Transformation in Manufacturing Using an Integrated Business Process Management Approach. *Designs 4.3, 17.*

Cai, W. J., Loon, M., & Wong, P. H. K. (2018). Leadership, trust in management and acceptance of change in Hong Kong's Civil Service Bureau. *Journal of Organizational Change Management, 31*(5), 1054–1070. doi:10.1108/JOCM-10-2016-0215

Camarinha-Matos, L. M., Fornasiero, R., Ramezani, J., & Ferrada, F. (2019). Collaborative Networks: A Pillar of Digital Transformation. *Applied Sciences.* MDPI. https://www.mdpi.com/2076-3417/9/24/5431

Canover, R. S., & Kartikasari, D. (2021). Penetration of imported products on e-commerce platform in indonesia and strategies for improving local product competitiveness. [IJEBAR]. *International Journal of Economics, Business, and Accounting Research, 5*(1), 23–33. doi:10.29040/ijebar.v5i1.1328

Cao, Y., Lu, Y., Gupta, S., & Yang, S. (2015). The effects of differences between ecommerce and m-commerce on the consumers' usage transfer from online to mobile channel. *International Journal of Mobile Communications, 13*(1), 51. doi:10.1504/IJMC.2015.065890

Celine Dorathy, M. B. (2011). Carbon Emission-An Emerging Issue in Corporate Governance. *Journal of Commerce and Management Thought, 2*(3), 451–461.

Chakraborty, S. (2023). Human Rights and Artificial Intelligence: Issues and Challenges. *Dynamics of Dialogue, Cultural Development, and Peace in the Metaverse,* 1–14.

Chandra, S., & Kumar, K. N. (2018). Exploring factors influencing organizational adoption of augmented reality in e-commerce: Empirical analysis using technology–organization–environment model. *Journal of Electronic Commerce Research, 19*(3), 237–265.

Chanias, S. (2017). *Mastering digital transformation: The path of a financial services provider towards a digital transformation strategy.* AISnet. https://aisel.aisnet.org/ecis2017_rp/2/

Chatterjee, S. (2015). Assessing India's Progress in Achieving the Millennium Development Goals: Key Drivers of Inter-state Variations. *United Nations Economic and Social Commission for Asia and the Pacific (ESCAP). South and South-West Asia Office, 20,* 25.

Chauhan, C., Parida, V., & Dhir, A. (2022). Linking circular economy and digitalisation technologies: A systematic literature review of past achievements and future promises. *Technological Forecasting and Social Change, 177,* 121508. doi:10.1016/j.techfore.2022.121508

Chau, N. T., & Deng, H. (2018). Critical determinants for mobile commerce adoption in Vietnamese SMEs: A conceptual framework. *Procedia Computer Science, 138*(1), 433–440. doi:10.1016/j.procs.2018.10.061

Cheah, J. H., Amaro, S., & Roldán, J. L. (2023). Multigroup analysis of more than two groups in PLS-SEM: A review, illustration, and recommendations. *Journal of Business Research, 156.* doi:10.1016/j.jbusres.2022.113539

Cheah, J. H., Thurasamy, R., Memon, M. A., Chuah, F., & Ting, H. (2020). Multigroup analysis using smartpls: Step-by-step guidelines for business research. *Asian Journal of Business Research*, *10*(3), I–XIX. doi:10.14707/ajbr.200087

Cheatham, B., Javanmardian, K., & Samandari, H. (2019). Confronting the risks of artificial intelligence. *The McKinsey Quarterly*, 1–9.

Chee, L. S., Suhaimi, B. A., & Quan, L. R. (2016). Understanding the determinants of e-commerce adoption: Evidence from manufacture sector in West Malaysia. *Indian Journal of Science and Technology*, *9*(10), 1–8. doi:10.17485/ijst/2016/v9i10/88075

Chel, A., & Kaushik, G. (2011). Renewable energy for sustainable agriculture. *Agronomy for Sustainable Development*, *31*(1), 91–118. doi:10.1051/agro/2010029

Chen, Y.-Y. K., Jaw, Y.-L., & Wu, B.-L. (2016). Effect of digital transformation on organisational performance of SMEs. *Internet Research*, *26*(1). 186–212. https://www.emerald.com/insight/content/doi/10.1108/IntR-12-2013-0265/full/html

Chesbrough, H.W. (2009). *Open Innovation: The New Imperative for Creating and Profiting from Technology*. Harvard Business School Press.

Chesbrough, H.W., (2003). The Era of Open Innovation. *MIT Sloan Management Review*, *44*.

Chisom, O. N., Biu, P. W., Umoh, A. A., Obaedo, B. O., Adegbite, A. O., & Abatan, A. (2024). Reviewing the role of AI in Environmental Monitoring and Conservation: A data-driven revolution for our planet. *World Journal of Advanced Research and Reviews*, *21*(1), 161–171. doi:10.30574/wjarr.2024.21.1.2720

Choi, D. & Valikangas, L. (2001). Patterns of strategy innovation. *European Management Journal*. Elsevier.

Chowdhury, S., Dey, P. K., Rodríguez-Espíndola, O., Parkes, G., Tuyet, N. T. A., Long, D. D., & Ha, T. P. (2022). Impact of organisational factors on the circular economy practices and sustainable performance of small and medium-sized enterprises in Vietnam. *Journal of Business Research*, *147*, 362–378. doi:10.1016/j.jbusres.2022.03.077

Christensen, C. M. (1997). *The Innovator's Dilemma*. Harvard Business School Press.

Christopherson, S., Kitson, M., & Michie, J. (2008, July). Christopherson,S., Kitson,M., Michie,J. (2008). Innovation, networks and knowledge exchange. *Cambridge Journal of Regions, Economy and Society*, *1*(2), 165–173. doi:10.1093/cjres/rsn015

Chwelos, P., Benbasat, I., & Dexter, A. S. (2001). Empirical test of an electronic data interchange adoption model. *Information Systems Research*, *12*(3), 304–321. doi:10.1287/isre.12.3.304.9708

Cillo, V., Petruzzelli, A. M., Ardito, L., & Del Giudice, M. (2019). Understanding sustainable innovation: A systematic literature review. *Corporate Social Responsibility and Environmental Management*, *26*(5), 1012–1025. doi:10.1002/csr.1783

Claxton, D. B. (2009). Data for Principals, Parents, and Other Stakeholders in Physical Education: Statistical Assessment Made Easy with Excel. *Strategies (Reston, VA)*, *22*(5), 20–24. doi:10.1080/08924562.2009.10590836

Clohessy, T., Acton, T., & Morgan, L. (2017). The Impact of Cloud-Based Digital Transformation on IT Service Providers. *International Journal of Cloud Applications and Computing*, *7*(4). http://services.igi-global.com/resolvedoi/resolve.aspx?doi=10.4018/IJCAC.2017100101

Commission, E. (2019). *AI: Ethics Guidelines for Trustworthy AI*. High-Level Expert Group on AI.

Connelly, C. E., Zweig, D., Webster, J., & Trougakos, J. P. (2012). Knowledge hiding in organizations. *Journal of Organizational Behavior*, *33*(1), 64–88. doi:10.1002/job.737

Constatinades, E., Romero, C. L., & Gomez, M. A. (2010). *Effects of web experience on consumer choice: a multicultural approach.*

Cortez, L. A. B., Larson, D. L., & Da Silva, A. (1997). Energy and exergy evaluation of ice production by absorption refrigeration. *Transactions of the American Society of Agricultural Engineers, 40*, 395–403.

Craig, T., & Campbell, D. (2012). *Organisations and the business environment.* Routledge. doi:10.4324/9780080454603

Creswell, J. W. J.C. (2017). *Research design: Qualitative, quantitative, and mixed methods approaches.* Amazon. https://www.amazon.in/Research-Design-Qualitative-Quantitative-Approaches/dp/1452226105

Criado, J. I., Sandoval-Almazan, R., Valle-Cruz, D., & Ruvalcaba-Gómez, E. A. (2021). Chief information officers' perceptions about artificial intelligence: A comparative study of implications and challenges for the public sector. *First Monday.*

Criteo. (2020). *Comportamento Degli Utenti di Appnel 2020: Italia (Report).* Criteo. https://www.criteo.com/it/wpcontent/uploads/sites/9/2020/07/Deck-GlobalAppSurvey- IT.pdf

Davis, F. D. (1986). Perceived usefulness, perceived ease of use, and user acceptance of information technology. *Management Information Systems Quarterly, 13*(3), 319–340. doi:10.2307/249008

Davis, F. D., Bagozzi, R. P., & Warshaw, P. R. (1989). User Acceptance of Computer Technology: A Comparison of Two Theoretical Models. *Management Science, 35*(8), 982–1003. https://www.jstor.org/stable/2632151. doi:10.1287/mnsc.35.8.982

de Bem Machado, A., Souza, M. J., & Catapan, A. H. (2019). Systematic Review: Intersection between Communication and Knowledge. *Journal of Information Systems Engineering & Management, 4*(1), em0086.

De Nobile, J. (2016). Organisational communication and its relationships with job satisfaction and organisational commitment of primary school staff in Western Australia. *Educational Psychology, 37*(3), 380–398. doi:10.1080/01443410.2016.1165797

de Nobrega, V. M. (2022). A Diverse (AI) World: How to Make Sure That the Digital World Reflects the Richness and Diversity of Our World. In Impact of Women's Empowerment on SDGs in the Digital Era (pp. 180–204). IGI Global.

de Oliveira Neto, G. C., Teixeira, M. M., Souza, G. L. V., Arns, V. D., Tucci, H. N. P., & Amorim, M. (2022). Assessment of the Eco-Efficiency of the Circular Economy in the Recovery of Cellulose from the Shredding of Textile Waste. *Polymers (20734360), 14*(7), 1317. doi:10.3390/polym14071317

de Oliveira, R. T., Ghobakhloo, M., & Figueira, S. (2023). Industry 4.0 Towards Social and Environmental Sustainability in Multinationals: Enabling Circular Economy, Organizational Social Practices and Corporate Purpose. *Journal of Cleaner Production, 430*, 139712. doi:10.1016/j.jclepro.2023.139712

DESA FSDO. (2024), Financing for Development. *Financing for Sustainable Development Report 2024.* UN. https://desapublications.un.org/publications/financing-sustainable-development-report-2024

Dharmayanti, N., Ismail, T., Hanifah, I. A., & Taqi, M. (2023). Exploring Sustainability Management Control System and eco-innovation Matter Sustainable Financial Performance: The role of supply chain management and digital adaptability in Indonesian context. *Journal of Open Innovation, 9*(3), 100119. doi:10.1016/j.joitmc.2023.100119

Di Vaio, A., Syriopoulos, T., Alvino, F., & Palladino, R. (2020). *"Integrated thinking and reporting" towards sustainable business models: A concise bibliometric analysis.* Meditari Account. Res.

Diamantopoulos, A., Davydova, O., & Arslanagic-Kalajdzic, M. (2019). Modeling the role of consumer xenocentrism in impacting preferences for domestic and foreign brands: A mediation analysis. *Journal of Business Research, 104*, 587–596. doi:10.1016/j.jbusres.2018.12.007

Dihni, V. A. (2021). *Penjualan E-Commerce Indonesia Diproyeksi Paling Besar di Asia Tenggara pada 2021*. KataData. https://databoks.katadata.co.id/datapublish/2021/09/21/penjualan-e-commerce-indonesia-diproyeksi-paling-besar-di-asia-tenggara-pada-2021

Dillon, E. J., Hennessy, T., & Hynes, S. (2010). Assessing the sustainability of Irish agriculture. *International Journal of Agricultural Sustainability, 8*(3), 131–147. doi:10.3763/ijas.2009.0044

Dobbe, R., Gilbert, T. K., & Mintz, Y. (2021). Hard choices in artificial intelligence. *Artificial Intelligence, 300*, 103555. doi:10.1016/j.artint.2021.103555

Doherty, N. F., Champion, D., & Wang, L. (2010). An holistic approach to understanding the changing nature of organisational structure. *Information Technology & People, 23*(2), 116–135. doi:10.1108/09593841011052138

Dolata, U. (2017). *Apple, Amazon, Google, Facebook, Microsoft: market concentration-competition-innovation strategies.*

Dringoli, A. (2009). *Creating Value Through Innovation*. Edward Elgar Publishing.

Drucker, P. F. (1993). The rise of the knowledge society. *The Wilson Quarterly, 17*(2), 52–72.

Dües, C. M., Tan, K. H., & Lim, M. (2013). Green as the new Lean: How to use Lean practices as a catalyst to greening your supply chain. *Journal of Cleaner Production, 40*, 93–100. doi:10.1016/j.jclepro.2011.12.023

Dyer, J. H., & Nobeoka, K. (2000). Creating and managing a high-performance knowledge-sharing network: The Toyota case. *Strategic Management Journal, 21*(3), 345–367. doi:10.1002/(SICI)1097-0266(200003)21:3<345::AID-SMJ96>3.0.CO;2-N

Ebert, C. (2019). Digital transformation. *IEEE Softw*. IEEE. https://www.chcduarte.com/dx2018.pdf

Edugraph (September 30, 2024). *National Education Policy recommends pedagogy training for Anganwadi workers to raise teaching standards*. https://www.telegraphindia.com/edugraph/national-education-policy-recommends-pedagogy-training-for-anganwadi-workers-to-raise-teaching-standards/cid/1969946.

Effendi, M. I., Sugandini, D., & Istanto, Y. (2020). Social media adoption in SMEs impacted by COVID-19: The TOE model. *Journal of Asian Finance. Economics and Business, 7*(11), 915–925. doi:10.13106/jafeb.2020.vol7.no11.915

Eid, R., & El-Gohary, H. (2011). The impact of emarketing use on small business enterprises' marketing success. *Service Industries Journal*.

Ekaputri, S., Sudarwanto, T., & Marlena, N. (2018). Peran Lingkungan Industri, Perilaku Kewirausahaan, Dan Kemampuan Manajerial Terhadap Kinerja Perusahaan Pada Usaha Logam Skala Mikro. *JRMSI-Jurnal Riset Manajemen Sains Indonesia, 9*(1), 1–21. doi:10.21009/JRMSI.009.1.01

Elangovan, N., & Sundaravel, E. (2021). Method of preparing a document for survey instrument validation by experts. *MethodsX, 8*(April), 1–9. doi:10.1016/j.mex.2021.101326 PMID:34434840

Elia, G., Petruzzelli, A.M., & Urbinati, A. (2020). Implementing Open Innovation Through Virtual Brand Communities: A Case Study Analysis in The Semiconductor Industry. *Technological Forecasting and Social Change*.

Elkadeem, M. R., Kotb, K. M., Sharshir, S. W., Hamada, M. A., Gabr, I. K., Hassan, M. A., Worku, M. Y., Abido, M. A., Ullah, Z., Hasanien, H. M., & Selim, F. F. (2024). Optimize and analyze a large-scale grid-tied solar PV-powered SWRO system for sustainable water-energy nexus. *Desalination, 579*, 117440. doi:10.1016/j.desal.2024.117440

Ercantan, O., & Eyupoglu, S. (2022). How do green human resource management practices encourage employees to engage in green behavior? perceptions of university students as prospective employees. *Sustainability (Basel), 14*(3), 1718. doi:10.3390/su14031718

Etikan, I., Musa, S. A., & Alkassim, R. S. (2016). Comparison of convenience sampling and purposive sampling. *American Journal of Theoretical and Applied Statistics, 5*(1), 1–4. doi:10.11648/j.ajtas.20160501.11

Etzioni, A., & Etzioni, O. (2017). Incorporating ethics into artificial intelligence. *The Journal of Ethics, 21*(4), 403–418. doi:10.1007/s10892-017-9252-2

European Commission. (2024a), *European Climate Pact.* EC. https://climate-pact.europa.eu/priority-topics/green-skills_en

European Commission. (2024a). *Digital European Plan (2021-2027).* EC. https://education.ec.europa.eu/focus-topics/digital-education/action-plan

Fakheri, S., Bahrami-Bidoni, Z., Makui, A., Pishvaee, M. S., & Gonzalez, E. D. S. (2022). A sustainable competitive supply chain network design for a green product under uncertainty: A case study of Iranian leather industry. *Socio-Economic Planning Sciences, 84*, 101414. doi:10.1016/j.seps.2022.101414

Fan, L., Liu, X., Wang, B., & Wang, L. (2017). Interactivity, engagement, and technology dependence: understanding users' technology utilisation behaviour. *Behaviour \& Information Technology, 36*(2), 113–124.

Fearis, P. (1995). *The polaroid experience: Countdown to market.* WCDM, World Class Design to Manufacture. https://www.proquest.com/scholarly-journals/polaroid-experience-countdown-market/docview/207943859/se-2

Feller, J., Finnegan, P., and Nilsson, O. (2011). Open Innovation and Public Administration: Transformational Typologies and Business Model Impacts. *European Journal of Information Systems.*

Feng, H., Wang, F., Song, G., & Liu, L. (2022). Digital transformation on enterprise green innovation: Effect and transmission mechanism. *International Journal of Environmental Research and Public Health, 19*(17), 10614. doi:10.3390/ijerph191710614 PMID:36078329

Fidan, F. Ş., Aydoğan, E. K., & Uzal, N. (2021). Fidan, F.,S., Aydo"gan, E.K., and Uzal, N (2021). An integrated life cycle assessment approach for denim fabric production using recycled cotton fibers and combined heat and power plant. *Journal of Cleaner Production, 287*, 125439. doi:10.1016/j.jclepro.2020.125439

Financial Express. (2024). *Deputy CM of Rajasthan Diya Kumari of Rajasthan approved the transformation of 6204 mini Anganwadis into model centres.* https://www.financialexpress.com/jobs-career/education-deputy-cm-of-rajasthan-diya-kumari-of-rajasthan-approved-the-transformation-of-6204-mini-anganwadis-into-model-centres-3407650/..

Financing for Development. (2015). *Report of the third International Conference on Financing for Development,* http://www.undocs.org/A/CONF.227/20

Fishbein, M., & Ajzen, I. (1975). *Belief, attitude, intention and behavior: An introduction to theory and research.*

Fishbein, M., & Ajzen, I. (1975). *Belief, Attitude, Intention, and Behavior: An Introduction to Theory and Research.* Addison-Wesley.

Fjeld, J., Achten, N., Hilligoss, H., Nagy, A., & Srikumar, M. (2020). Principled artificial intelligence: Mapping consensus in ethical and rights-based approaches to principles for AI. *Berkman Klein Center Research Publication, 2020–1.*

Foerster-Metz, U. S., Marquardt, K., Golowko, N., Kompalla, A., & Hell, C. (2018). Digital Transformation and its Implications on Organizational Behavior. *Journal of EU Research in Business.* https://ibimapublishing.com/articles/JEURB/2018/340873/

Forni, A. (2016). *Gartner reveals top predictions for IT organizations and users in 2017 and beyond.*

Furstenau, L. B., Sott, M. K., Kipper, L. M., Machado, E. L., Lopez-Robles, J. R., Dohan, M. S., Cobo, M. J., Zahid, A., Abbasi, Q. H., & Imran, M. A. (2020). Link between sustainability and industry 4.0: Trends, challenges and new perspectives. *IEEE Access : Practical Innovations, Open Solutions, 8,* 140079–140096. doi:10.1109/ACCESS.2020.3012812

Furst, S. A., & Cable, D. M. (2008). Employee resistance to organisational change: Managerial influence tactics and leader-member exchange. *The Journal of Applied Psychology, 93*(2), 453–462. doi:10.1037/0021-9010.93.2.453 PMID:18361644

Garbarino, E., & Strahilevitz, M. (2004). Gender differences in the perceived risk of buying online and the effects of receiving a site recommendation. *Journal of Business Research, 57*(7), 768–775. doi:10.1016/S0148-2963(02)00363-6

Garon, M. (2012). Speaking up, being heard: Registered nurses' perceptions of workplace communication. *Journal of Nursing Management, 20*(3), 361–371. doi:10.1111/j.1365-2834.2011.01296.x PMID:22519614

Gassman, O. (2006) Opening up the innovation process towards an agenda. *R&D Management 36*(3), 223-228.

Gatell, I. S., & Avella, L. (2024). Impact of Industry 4.0 and circular economy on lean culture and leadership: Assessing digital green lean as a new concept. *European Research on Management and Business Economics, 30*(1), 100232. doi:10.1016/j.iedeen.2023.100232

George, B., Walker, R. M., & Monster, J. (2019). Does Strategic Planning Improve Organizational Performance? A Meta-Analysis. *Public Administration Review, 79*(6), 810–819. https://onlinelibrary.wiley.com/doi/abs/10.1111/puar.13104

Ghasemy, M., Teeroovengadum, V., Becker, J. M., & Ringle, C. M. (2020). This fast car can move faster: A review of PLS-SEM application in higher education research. *Higher Education, 80*(6), 1121–1152. doi:10.1007/s10734-020-00534-1

Ghezzi, A., Cavallo, A., Sanasi, S., Rangone, A. (2021). Opening Up to Startup Collaborations: Open Business Models and Value Co-creation in SMEs. *Competitiveness Review: An International Business Journal.*

Ghobakhloo, M., Arias-Aranda, D., & Benitez-Amado, J. (2011). Adoption of e-commerce applications in SMEs. *Industrial Management & Data Systems, 111*(8), 1238–1269. doi:10.1108/02635571111170785

Gibson, N. (2018). *An Analysis of the Impact of Social Media Marketing on Individuals' An Individuals' Attitudes and Perceptions at NOVA Community A Community College.*

Gobbo Junior, J. A(2007). Inter-firm manufacturing strategy. *Congresso Brasileiro de Engenharia de Fabricação.*

Golightly, J., Ford, C., Sureka, P., and Reid, B. (2012). *Realising the Value of Open Innovation.* BIG Innovation Centre. The Work Foundation, Lancaster University.

Gomber, P., Koch, J.-A., & Siering, M. (2017). Digital Finance and FinTech: Current research and future research directions. *Journal of Business Economics, 87*(5), 537–580. doi:10.1007/s11573-017-0852-x

Gopalan, B. and Natarajan, R. (2014). Analytical models for Open Innovation and Value Co-creation. *Proceedings of the Decision Sciences Institute (DSI) Conference* in Tampa, Florida (USA).

Gray, P. H., Parise, S. & Iyer, B., (2011). Innovation impacts of using social bookmarking systems. *MIS Quarterly* (35:3), pp. 629-643.

Greenan, N. (2003). Organisational change, technology, employment and skills: An empirical study of French manufacturing. *Cambridge Journal of Economics, 27*(2), 287–316. doi:10.1093/cje/27.2.287

Griffin, R. W., Phillips, J. M., & Gully, S. M. (2014). *Organisational Behaviour: Managing People and Organisations* (12th ed.). Cengage.

Griswold, W. (2013). Community education and green jobs: Acknowledging existing connection. *Adult Learning, 24*(1), 30–36. doi:10.1177/1045159512467322

Group, W. B. (2016). World Development Report 2016: Digital Dividends. *World Bank Group flagship report.* World Bank Publications. https://books.google.co.in/books?id=dAl-CwAAQBAJ

Grover, V. & Kohli, R. (2012). Cocreating IT Value: New Capabilities and Measures for Multifirm Environments. *MIS Quarterly, 36*(1), 225-232.

Guan, L., Li, W., Guo, C., & Huang, J. (2023). Environmental strategy for sustainable development: Role of digital transformation in China's natural resource exploitation. *Resources Policy, 87*, 104304. doi:10.1016/j.resourpol.2023.104304

Guan, T., Meng, K., Liu, W., & Xue, L. (2019). Public attitudes toward Sustainable Development Goals: Evidence from five Chinese cities. *Sustainability (Basel), 11*(20), 57–93. doi:10.3390/su11205793

Gulamhuseinwala, I., Bull, T. & Lewis, S. (2015). FinTech is gaining traction and young, high-income users are the early adopters. *Journal of Financial Perspectives, 3*.

Haidt, J. & Allen, N. (2020). *Scrutinizing the effects of digital technology on mental health.*

Hair, H. G. T. M., Ringle, C. M., & Sarstedt, M. (2017). A Primer on Partial Least Squares Structural Equation Modeling (PLS-SEM) (2nd ed.). Sage Publications Ltd.

Hair, R. J. J., Sarstedt, M., & Ringle, C. M. (2018). When to use and how to report the results of PLS-SEM. *European Business Review, 31*(1), 2–24. https://doi.org/10.1108/EBR-11-2018-0203

Hair, J. F., Black, W. C., Babin, B. J., & Anderson, R. E. (2019). *Multivariate Data Analysis* (8th ed.). Cengage., doi:10.1002/9781119409137.ch4

Hair, J. F., Hult, G. T. M., Ringle, C. M., & Sarstedt, M. (2014). *A Primer on Partial Least Squares Structural Equation Modeling (PLS-SEM).* SAGE Publications Ltd.

Hair, J. F. Jr, Hult, G. T. M., Ringle, C. M., Sarstedt, M., Danks, N. P., & Ray, S. (2021). *Partial least squares structural equation modeling (PLS-SEM) using R: A workbook.* Springer Nature. doi:10.1007/978-3-030-80519-7

Haleem, A., Javaid, M., Singh, R. P., Suman, R., & Qadri, M. A. (2023). A pervasive study on green manufacturing towards attaining sustainability. *Green Technologies and Sustainability, 1*(2), 100018. doi:10.1016/j.grets.2023.100018

Hamdan, M., Ahmad, N., Jaidin, J. H., & Anshari, M. (2020). Internationalisation in Brunei's higher education and its policy implications: Case study of Universiti Brunei Darussalam. *TEST Engineering and Management, 83*, 764–779.

Han, H., & Zhou, Z. (2024). The rebound effect of energy consumption and its determinants in China's agricultural production. *Energy, 290*, 129961. doi:10.1016/j.energy.2023.129961

Hanson, Ranson, M. K., Oliveira-Cruz, V., & Mills, A. (2023). Expanding access to priority health interventions: A framework for understanding the constraints to scaling-up. *Journal of International Development, 15*(1), 1–14. doi:10.1002/jid.963

Hapuwatte, B. M., & Jawahir, I. S. (2021). Closed-loop sustainable product design for circular economy. *Journal of Industrial Ecology, 25*(6), 1430–1446. doi:10.1111/jiec.13154

Hartványi, T., Huszár, V., & Palásthy, I. (2023). Pilot Research & Development of a Multifunctional and Multi-Purpose Sports Equipment - Automotive Technologies for the Olympics. *Acta Technica Corviniensis - Bulletin of Engineering, 16*(1), 1–5.

Hasmawati, F., Samiha, Y. T., Razzaq, A., & Anshari, M. (2020). Understanding nomophobia among digital natives: Characteristics and challenges. *Journal of Critical Reviews*, 7(13), 122–131.

Hassan, Q., Sameen, A. Z., Salman, H. M., & Jaszczur, M. (2023). Large-scale green hydrogen production via alkaline water electrolysis using solar and wind energy. *International Journal of Hydrogen Energy*, 48(88), 34299–34315. doi:10.1016/j.ijhydene.2023.05.126

Hawkridge, D., Armellini, A., Nikoi, S., Rowlett, T., & Witthaus, G. (2010). Curriculum, intellectual property rights and open educational resources in British universities—And beyond. *Journal of Computing in Higher Education*, 22(3), 162–176. doi:10.1007/s12528-010-9036-1

Hazen, B. T., Russo, I., Confente, I., & Pellathy, D. (2021). Supply chain management for circular economy: Conceptual framework and research agenda. *International Journal of Logistics Management,* 32(2), 510-537. doi:10.1108/IJLM-12-2019-0332

Heavin, C., & Power, D. J. (2018). Challenges for digital transformation – towards a conceptual decision support guide for managers. *Journal of Decision Systems*, 27. https://www.tandfonline.com/doi/full/10.1080/12460125.2018.1468697

Heeks, R. (2017). *Information and communication technology for development (ICT4D)*. Routledge. doi:10.4324/9781315652603

Heilig, L., Schwarze, S., & Vos, S. (2017). *An analysis of digital transformation in the history and future of modern ports*. AISNET. https://aisel.aisnet.org/hicss-50/da/decision_support_for_scm/2/

Hernandez, A. A. (2020). Green IT adoption practices in education sector: a developing country perspective. In Waste Management: Concepts, Methodologies, Tools, and Applications (pp. 1379-1395): IGI Global. doi:10.4018/978-1-7998-1210-4.ch063

Hess, T., Matt, C., Benlian, A., & Wiesböck, F. (2016). Options for formulating a digital transformation strategy. *MIS Quarterly Executive*. http://search.ebscohost.com/login.aspx?direct=true&profile=ehost&scope=site&authtype=crawler&jrnl=15401960&AN=115879199&h=QyVwVRj0ZlOg7sMRTNzRQApgAyeYo204HYsgFcdVL6%2FJdayO%2BXl7oLQDQO3IHOPYd%2BopvZ8Kw8unktp8OPzeHA%3D%3D&crl=c

Hettiarachchi, B. D., Brandenburg, M., & Seuring, S. (2022). Connecting additive manufacturing to circular economy implementation strategies: Links, contingencies and causal loops. *International Journal of Production Economics*, 246, 108414. doi:10.1016/j.ijpe.2022.108414

Hinings, B., Gegenhuber, T., & Greenwood, R. (2018). Digital innovation and transformation: An institutional perspective. *Information and Organization*, 28(1), 52–61. https://linkinghub.elsevier.com/retrieve/pii/S1471772718300265

Hmoud, H., Al-Adwan, A. S., Horani, O., Yaseen, H., & Zoubi, J. Z. A. (2023). Factors influencing business intelligence adoption by higher education institutions. *Journal of Open Innovation*, 9(3), 100111. doi:10.1016/j.joitmc.2023.100111

Ho, H. (2021). COVID-19 in Brunei Darussalam: How Does the Small Nation Cope? | *Heinrich Böll Foundation | Southeast Asia Regional Office*.

Hoang, T. D. L., Nguyen, H. K., & Thu, N. H. (2021). Towards an economic recovery after the COVID-19 pandemic: Empirical study on electronic commerce adoption of small and medium enterprises in Vietnam. *Management & Marketing*, 16(1), 47–68. doi:10.2478/mmcks-2021-0004

Hodkiewicz, M., Klüwer, J. W., Woods, C., Smoker, T., & French, T. (2020). Digitalization and reasoning over engineering textual data stored in spreadsheet tables. *IFAC-PapersOnLine, 53*(3), 239–244. https://linkinghub.elsevier.com/retrieve/pii/S2405896320301853

Hoffmann, E. A. (2007). Open-ended interviews, power, and emotional labor. *Journal of Contemporary Ethnography*, *36*(3), 318–346. doi:10.1177/0891241606293134

Holtzhausen, D. (2002). The effects of a divisionalised and decentralised organisational structure on a formal internal communication function in a South African organisation. *Journal of Communication Management (London)*, *6*(4), 323–339. doi:10.1108/13632540210807152

Homburg, C., Wielgos, D., & Kühnl, C. (2019). *Digital business capability and its effect on firm performance*. MaDoc. https://madoc.bib.uni-mannheim.de/48903/?rs=true&

Hossain, M. B., Dewan, N., Senin, A. A., & Illes, C. B. (2023). Evaluating the utilization of technological factors to promote e-commerce adoption in small and medium enterprises. *Electronic Commerce Research*. doi:10.1007/s10660-023-09692-7

Hou, F., Bi, F., Jiao, R., Luo, D., & Song, K. (2020). Gender differences of depression and anxiety among social media users during the COVID-19 outbreak in China: A cross-sectional study. *BMC Public Health*, *20*(1), 1648. doi:10.1186/s12889-020-09738-7

Hsu, S. H., Chen, W. H., & Hsieh, M. J. (2006). Robustness testing of PLS, LISREL, EQS and ANN-based SEM for measuring customer satisfaction. *Total Quality Management & Business Excellence*, *17*(3), 355–372. doi:10.1080/14783360500451465

Huang, C., Zhang, Z., Mao, B., & Yao, X. (2022). An overview of artificial intelligence ethics. *IEEE Transactions on Artificial Intelligence*, *4*(4), 799–819. doi:10.1109/TAI.2022.3194503

Huang, Y., Shi, Y., & Xu, J. (2023). Integrated district electricity system with anaerobic digestion and gasification for bioenergy production optimization and carbon reduction. *Sustainable Energy Technologies and Assessments*, *55*, 102890. doi:10.1016/j.seta.2022.102890

Huda, M., Anshari, M., Almunawar, M. N., Shahrill, M., Tan, A., Jaidin, J. H., & Masri, M. (2016). Innovative teaching in higher education: The big data approach. *Tojet*, 1210-1216.

Husain, Z. (2013). Effective communication brings successful organisational change. *The Business & Management Review*, *3*(2), 43.

Husgafvel, R., & Sakaguchi, D. (2022). Circular Economy Development in the Construction Sector in Japan. *World (2673-4060)*, *3*(1), 1–26. doi:10.3390/world3010001

Hussain, A., Shahzad, A., & Hassan, R. (2020). Organizational and Environmental Factors with the Mediating Role of E-Commerce and SME Performance. *Journal of Open Innovation*, *6*(4), 196. doi:10.3390/joitmc6040196

Hussain, S. T., Lei, S., Akram, T., Haider, M. J., Hussain, S. H., & Ali, M. (2018). Kurt Lewin's change model: A critical review of the role of leadership and employee involvement in organisational change. *Journal of Innovation & Knowledge*, *3*(3), 123–127. doi:10.1016/j.jik.2016.07.002

Immelt, J. R., Govindarajan, V., & Trimble, C. (2009). How GE is disrupting itself. *Harvard Business Review*, *87*(10), 56–65.

Imran, M., & Hameed, W. (2018). Influence of Industry 4.0 on the Production and Service Sectors in Pakistan: Evidence from Textile and Logistics Industries. *Social Sciences*, *7*(12), 246. https://www.mdpi.com/2076-0760/7/12/246

Inglehart, R. (1995). Public support for environmental protection: Objective problems and subjective values in 43 societies. *PS, Political Science & Politics*, *28*(1), 57–72. doi:10.2307/420583

International Monetary Fund. (2021). *World Economic Outlook: managing divergent recoveries*. IMF. https://www.imf.org/en/Publications/WEO/weo-database/2021/April

Ipe, M. (2003). Knowledge sharing in organizations: A conceptual framework. *Human Resource Development Review*, *2*(4), 337–359. doi:10.1177/1534484303257985

Iqbal, A., Latif, F., Marimon, F., Sahibzada, U. F., & Hussain, S. (2019). From knowledge management to organizational performance. *Journal of Enterprise Information Management*, *32*(1), 36–59. https://www.emerald.com/insight/content/doi/10.1108/JEIM-04-2018-0083/full/html

Iqbal, A., Melhem, Y., & Kokash, H. (2012). Readiness of the university students towards entrepreneurship in Saudi private university: An exploratory study. *European Scientific Journal*.

Irani, Z., & Sharp, J. M. (1997). Integrating continuous improvement and innovation into a corporate culture: A case study. *Technovation*, *17*(4), 199–223. doi:10.1016/S0166-4972(96)00103-4

Irianto, D., & Kartikasari, D. (2020). Fan Loyalty toward International Football Team : The Role of Brand Image. *International Journal of Applied Business Research*, *2*(1), 58–72. doi:10.35313/ijabr.v2i01.95

Islam, M. S., Islam, M. S., Khan, T., Akhter, R., Rahman, S. M., Ara, H., Thurasamy, R., & Hoque, I. (2023). Umbrella Review in Green Supply Chain Management (GSCM): Developing Models for adoption and sustaining GSCM. *Environmental Challenges*, 100820.

Itten, R., Hischier, R., Andrae, A. S. G., Bieser, J. C. T., Cabernard, L., Falke, A., Ferreboeuf, H., Hilty, L. M., Keller, R. L., Lees-Perasso, E., Preist, C., & Stucki, M. (2020). Digital transformation—life cycle assessment of digital services, multifunctional devices and cloud computing. *The International Journal of Life Cycle Assessment*, *25*(10). 2093–2098. http://link.springer.com/10.1007/s11367-020-01801-0

Ivanova, V. V., Kazakova, E., Lezina, T. A., Martyanova, V. N., Saltan, A. A., Anette, S., & Dirk, S. (2015). *Comparing bachelor studies in business informatics at universities in Russia and Germany*. Cyberleninka. https://cyberleninka.ru/article/n/16415853

Iverson, R. D. (1996). Employee acceptance of organisational change: The role of organisational commitment. *International Journal of Human Resource Management*, *7*(1), 122–149. doi:10.1080/09585199600000121

Jalil, F., Yang, J., Al-Okaily, M., & Rehman, S. U. (2024). E-commerce for a sustainable future: integrating trust, green supply chain management and online shopping satisfaction. *Asia Pacific Journal of Marketing and Logistics*. doi:10.1108/APJML-12-2023-1188

Jaman, S. F. I., & Anshari, M. (2021). Facebook as marketing tools for organizations: Knowledge management analysis. In *Research Anthology on Strategies for Using Social Media as a Service and Tool in Business* (pp. 117–131). IGI Global. doi:10.4018/978-1-7998-9020-1.ch007

James, A. T., Kumar, G., James, J., & Asjad, M. (2023). Development of a micro-level circular economy performance measurement framework for automobile maintenance garages. *Journal of Cleaner Production*, *417*, 138025. doi:10.1016/j.jclepro.2023.138025

James, R. (2013). *Student Feature Male and Female Attitudes to Online Shopping*. Women in Society.

Janssen, O. (2004). The barrier effect of conflict with superiors in the relationship between employee empowerment and organizational commitment. *Work and Stress*, *18*(1), 56–65. doi:10.1080/02678370410001690466

Japar, D. F. I. P. M., & Anshari, M. (2023). Potential and challenges of the Metaverse on future businesses. In *Metaverse applications for new business models and disruptive innovation* (pp. 102-119). IGI Global.

Jarlbrink, J., & Snickars, P. (2017). Cultural heritage as digital noise: nineteenth century newspapers in the digital archive. *Journal of Documentation, 73*(6), 1228–1243. https://www.emerald.com/insight/content/doi/10.1108/JD-09-2016-0106/full/html

Jat, H. S., Datta, A., Choudhary, M., Sharma, P. C., & Jat, M. L. (2021). Conservation Agriculture: Factors and drivers of adoption and scalable innovative practices in Indo-Gangetic plains of India–a review. *International Journal of Agricultural Sustainability, 19*(1), 40–55. doi:10.1080/14735903.2020.1817655

Javaid, M., Haleem, A., Singh, R. P., & Suman, R. (2022). Artificial intelligence applications for industry 4.0: A literature-based study. *Journal of Industrial Integration and Management, 7*(01), 83–111. doi:10.1142/S2424862221300040

Jayani, D. H. (2020). *Orang Indonesia Habiskan Hampir 8 Jam untuk Berinternet.* Katadata. https://databoks.katadata.co.id/datapublish/2020/02/26/indonesia-habiskan- hampir-8-jam-untuk-berinternet

Jayani, D. H. (2021). *UMKM Indonesia bertambah 1,98% pada 2019.* databoks. https://databoks.katadata.co.id/datapublish/2021/08/12/umkm-indonesia-bertambah-198-pada-2019

Jenifer, R. D., & Raman, G. P. (2015). Cross-cultural communication barriers in the workplace. *International Journal of Management, 6*(1), 348–351.

Jennings, K. E. (2010). Developing creativity: Artificial barriers in artificial intelligence. *Minds and Machines, 20*(4), 489–501. doi:10.1007/s11023-010-9206-y

Jobin, A., Ienca, M., & Vayena, E. (2019). The global landscape of AI ethics guidelines. *Nature Machine Intelligence, 1*(9), 389–399. doi:10.1038/s42256-019-0088-2

Jody, B. J., Daniels, E. J., Duranceau, C. M., Pomykala, J. A., & Spangenberger, J. S. (2011). *End-of-life vehicle recycling: State of the art of resource recovery from shredder residue.* https://doi.org/ doi:10.2172/1010492

Johannsdottir, L., Olafsson, S., & Davidsdottir, B. (2015). Leadership role and employee acceptance of change: Implementing environmental sustainability strategies within Nordic insurance companies. *Journal of Organizational Change Management, 28*(1), 72–96. doi:10.1108/JOCM-12-2013-0238

John, K. N. (2018). Importance of Communication to Stakeholders in all Organisations.

Joo, T. M., & Teng, C. E. (2016). use of Social Media in PR: A Change of Trend. World Academy of Science, Engineering and Technology. *International Journal of Humanities and Social Sciences.*

Jordan, M. I. (2019). Artificial intelligence—The revolution hasn't happened yet. *Harvard Data Science Review, 1*(1).

Kabeer, N. (2016). Leaving No One Behind: The Challenge of Intersecting Inequalities. ISSC, IDS and UNESCO, Challenging Inequalities: Pathways to a Just World, *World Social. Scientific Reports, 22*, 55–58.

Kaiser, H. F. (1960). The application of electronic computers to factor analysis. *Educational and Psychological Measurement, 20*(1), 141–151. doi:10.1177/001316446002000116

Kam, A. J. Y., & Tham, S. Y. (2022). Barriers to e-commerce adoption: Evidence from the retail and food and beverage sectors in Malaysia. *Asian-Pacific Economic Literature, 36*(2), 32–51. doi:10.1111/apel.12365

Kane, G. C., Palmer, D., Philips Nguyen, A., Kiron, D., & Buckley, N. (2015). Strategy, Not Technology, Drives Digital Transformation. *MIT Sloan Management Review.* Deloitte. https://sloanreview.mit.edu/projects/strategy-drives-digital-transformation/

Kannan, P. K., & Li, H. (2017). Digital marketing: A framework, review and research agenda. *International Journal of Research in Marketing, 34*(1), 22–45. doi:10.1016/j.ijresmar.2016.11.006

Kartikasari, D., Almunawar, M. N., Anshari, M., & Sumardi, W. H. (2023). Foreign versus Domestic Products in Cross-border E-commerce: a Conceptual Framework. *Jurnal Bisnis Dan Manajemen (JBM), 19*(2), 44–59. https://doi.org/ https://doi.org/10.23960/jbm.v19i2.91

Kashyap, A., & Agrawal, R. (2020). Scale development and modeling of intellectual property creation capability in higher education. *Journal of Intellectual Capital, 21*(1), 115–138. doi:10.1108/JIC-09-2018-0168

Kaufmann, L., & Gaeckler, J. (2015). A Structured Review of Partial Least Squares in Supply Chain Management Research. *Journal of Purchasing and Supply Management, 21*(4), 259–272. doi:10.1016/j.pursup.2015.04.005

Kay, R. (2006). Addressing gender differences in computer ability, attitudes and use: The laptop effect. *Journal of Educational Computing Research, 34*(2), 187–211. doi:10.2190/9BLQ-883Y-XQMA-FCAH

Kemenkopukm, H. (2022). *MenKopUKM kolaborasi dengan Jagoan Internet Marketer bantu UMKM go digital*. https:// kemenkopukm.go.id/read/menkopukm-kolaborasi-dengan-jagoan-internet-marketer-bantu-umkm-go-digital

Khalid, M. (2024). Smart grids and renewable energy systems: Perspectives and grid integration challenges. *Energy Strategy Reviews, 51*, 101299. doi:10.1016/j.esr.2024.101299

Khan, A. G., Hasan, N., & Ali, M. R. (2023). Unmasking the Behavioural Intention of Social Commerce in Developing Countries: Integrating Technology Acceptance Model. *Global Business Review, 09721509231180701*, 09721509231180701. doi:10.1177/09721509231180701

Khin, S., & Ho, T. C. (2019). Digital technology, digital capability and organizational performance. *International Journal of Innovation Science, 11*(2), 177–195. https://www.emeraldinsight.com/doi/10.1108/IJIS-08-2018-0083

Khwaji, A., Alsahafi, Y., & Hussain, F. K. (2022). Conceptual Framework of Blockchain Technology Adoption in Saudi Public Hospitals Using TOE Framework. *International Conference on Network-Based Information Systems*. Kwansei Gakuin University, Japan. 10.1007/978-3-031-14314-4_8

Kieslich, K., Keller, B., & Starke, C. (2022). Artificial intelligence ethics by design. Evaluating public perception on the importance of ethical design principles of artificial intelligence. *Big Data & Society, 9*(1), 20539517221092956. doi:10.1177/20539517221092956

Kiesling, M., Wilke, H., & Kolbe, L. M. (2010). *Overcoming challenges for managing IT innovations in non-IT companies*. AMCIS. https://core.ac.uk/download/pdf/301344818.pdf

Kim, G., Shin, B., & Kwon, O. (2012). Investigating the value of sociomaterialism in conceptualizing IT capability of a firm. *Journal of Management Information Systems, 29*(3), 327–362. doi:10.2753/MIS0742-1222290310

Kim, W., Jeong, O.-R., & Lee, S.-W. (2010). On social Web sites. *Information Systems, 35*(2), 215–236. doi:10.1016/j. is.2009.08.003

Kioupi, V., & Voulvoulis, N. (2020). Sustainable Development Goals (SDGs): Assessing the contribution of higher education programmes. *Sustainability (Basel), 12*(17), 67–71. doi:10.3390/su12176701

Knickel, K., Ashkenazy, A., Chebach, T. C., & Parrot, N. (2017). Agricultural modernization and sustainable agriculture: Contradictions and complementarities. *International Journal of Agricultural Sustainability, 15*(5), 575–592. doi:10.10 80/14735903.2017.1373464

Kock, N. (2022). WarpPLS User Manual : Version 8.0. In ScriptWarp Systems.

Kock, N. (2015). Common method bias in PLS-SEM: A full collinearity assessment approach. *International Journal of e-Collaboration, 11*(4), 1–10. doi:10.4018/ijec.2015100101

Kock, N. (2016). Hypothesis Testing with Confidence Intervals and P Values in PLS-SEM. *International Journal of e-Collaboration, 12*(3), 1–6. doi:10.4018/IJeC.2016070101

Kogut B. and Almeida P. (1999). Localization of knowledge and the mobility of engineers in regional networks. *Management Science, 45*, 905-917.

Koksalmis, G. H., & Gozudok, A. (2021). What Impacts E-Commerce Acceptance of Generation Z? A Modified Technology Acceptance Model. In M. Al-Emran & K. Shaalan (Eds.), *Recent Advances in Technology Acceptance Models and Theories* (pp. 57–77). Springer International Publishing. doi:10.1007/978-3-030-64987-6_5

Koohafkan, P., Altieri, M. A., & Gimenez, E. H. (2012). Green agriculture: Foundations for biodiverse, resilient and productive agricultural systems. *International Journal of Agricultural Sustainability, 10*(1), 61–75. doi:10.1080/1473 5903.2011.610206

Korenkova, M., Maros, M., Levicky, M., & Fila, M. (2020). Consumer Perception of Modern and Traditional Forms of Advertising. *Sustainability (Basel), 12*(23), 9996. doi:10.3390/su12239996

Kotsev, E., & Stoycheva, B. (2024). AIP Conference Proceedings: Vol. 3063. *Antecedents of individual innovativeness: Exploring gender, age and job nature.* AIP Publishing.

Krakowski, A., Greenwald, E., Hurt, T., Nonnecke, B., & Cannady, M. (2022). Authentic Integration of Ethics and AI through Sociotechnical, Problem-Based Learning. *Proceedings of the AAAI Conference on Artificial Intelligence, 36*(11), 12774–12782. doi:10.1609/aaai.v36i11.21556

Krasnova, A., Veltri, N., Eling, N., & Buxmann, P. (2017). Why men and women continue to use social networking sites: The role of gender differences. *The Journal of Strategic Information Systems, 26*(4), 261–284. doi:10.1016/j.jsis.2017.01.004

Kriebitz, A., & Lütge, C. (2020). Artificial intelligence and human rights: A business ethical assessment. *Business and Human Rights Journal, 5*(1), 84–104. doi:10.1017/bhj.2019.28

Kroculick, J. B. (2022). Enabling Green Digital Transformation through a Sustainable Systems Engineering Leadership Model. *Paper presented at the INCOSE International Symposium.* INCOSE. 10.1002/iis2.12896

Krupa, T., & Ostrowska, T. (2012). Decision-making in flat and hierarchical decision problems. *foundations of management, 4*(2), 23-36.

Kuckertz, A., Brändle, L., Gaudig, A., Hinderer, S., Morales Reyes, C. A., Prochotta, A., Steinbrink, K. M., & Berger, E. S. C. (2020). Startups in times of crisis – A rapid response to the COVID-19 pandemic. *Journal of Business Venturing Insights, 13*(April), e00169. Advance online publication. doi:10.1016/j.jbvi.2020.e00169

Kumar, D. S., & Purani, K. (2018). Model Specification Issues in PLS-SEM: Illustrating Linear and Non-linear Models in Hospitality Services Context. *Journal of Hospitality and Tourism Technology, 9*(3), 338–353. doi:10.1108/JHTT-09-2017-0105

Kurniawan, T. A., Maiurova, A., Kustikova, M., Bykovskaia, E., Othman, M. H. D., & Goh, H. H. (2022). Accelerating sustainability transition in St. Petersburg (Russia) through digitalization-based circular economy in waste recycling industry: A strategy to promote carbon neutrality in era of Industry 4.0. *Journal of Cleaner Production, 363*, 132452. doi:10.1016/j.jclepro.2022.132452

Kurniawan, T. A., Othman, M. H. D., Hwang, G. H., & Gikas, P. (2022). Unlocking digital technologies for waste recycling in Industry 4.0 era: A transformation towards a digitalization-based circular economy in Indonesia. *Journal of Cleaner Production, 357*, 131911. doi:10.1016/j.jclepro.2022.131911

Kurniawan, T. A., Othman, M. H. D., Liang, X., Goh, H. H., Gikas, P., Kusworo, T. D., Anouzla, A., & Chew, K. W. (2023). Decarbonization in waste recycling industry using digitalization to promote net-zero emissions and its implications on sustainability. *Journal of Environmental Management*, *338*, 117765. doi:10.1016/j.jenvman.2023.117765 PMID:36965421

Lal, B., & Chavan, C. R. (2019). A road map: E-commerce to world wide web growth of business world. *Global Journal of Management and Business Research*, *19*(11), 32–36.

Lampert, M., & Papadongonas, P. (2016). *Towards 2030 Without Poverty: increasing knowledge of progress made and opportunities for engaging frontrunners in the world population with the global goals*. OxFamSol. https://oxfamsol.be/sites/default/files/documents/towards_2030_without_poverty-glocalities2016-2-new.pdf

Landaeta, R. E., Mun, J. H., Rabadi, G., & Levin, D. (2008). Identifying sources of resistance to change in healthcare. *International Journal of Healthcare Technology and Management*, *9*(1), 74–96. doi:10.1504/IJHTM.2008.016849

Lasi, H., Fettke, P., Kemper, H.-G., Feld, T., & Hoffmann, M. (2014). Industry 4.0. *Business & Information Systems Engineering*, *6*(4), 239–242. doi:10.1007/s12599-014-0334-4

Lattu, A. and Maulana, A. (2023). Determinant Factors of Personal Innovativeness in Information Technology of Ride-Hailing New Brand: The Role of Gender. *International Journal of Health Engineering and Technology (IJHET)*, 2.

Lazariuc, C., & Lozovanu, E. (2021). Intellectual property in the context of global ethics. [EEJRS]. *Eastern European Journal for Regional Studies*, *7*(1), 218–229. doi:10.53486/2537-6179.7-1.11

Le Meunier-Fitzhugh, K., & Piercy, N. F. (2008). The Importance of Organisational Structure for Collaboration between Sales and Marketing. *Journal of General Management*, *34*(1), 19–36. doi:10.1177/030630700803400102

Leal Filho, W., Will, M., Salvia, A. L., Adomssent, M., Grahl, A., & Spira, F. (2019). The role of green and Sustainability Offices in fostering sustainability efforts at higher education institutions. *Journal of Cleaner Production*, *232*, 1394–1401. doi:10.1016/j.jclepro.2019.05.273

Lerman, L. V., Benitez, G. B., Müller, J. M., de Sousa, P. R., & Frank, A. G. (2022). Smart green supply chain management: A configurational approach to enhance green performance through digital transformation. *Supply Chain Management*, *27*(7), 147–176. doi:10.1108/SCM-02-2022-0059

Lewin, K. (1951). *Field theory in social science: selected theoretical papers* (D. Cartwright, Ed.).

Lezina, T., Nissen, V., Reimer, K., & Saltan, A. (2016). The Role and Tasks of IT in Russian Companies A Survey of the Status Quo. In: *GSOM Emerging Markets Conference 2016*. PurePortal. https://pureportal.spbu.ru/en/publications/the-role-and-tasks-of-it-in-russian-companies-a-surveyof-the-stat

Lian, A. T. G., Lily, J., & Cheng, C. T. (2022). The Study of SMEs' E-Commerce Adoption in Sabah and Sarawak. *International Journal of Academic Research in Business & Social Sciences*, *12*(7), 314–326. doi:10.6007/IJARBSS/v12-i7/13900

Lim, Y., Cheng, B., Cham, T., Ng, C., & Tan, J. (2019). Gender Differences in Perceptions and Attitudes Toward Online Shopping: A Study of Malaysian Consumers. [JMAP]. *Journal of Marketing Advances and Practices*, *1*(2), 12–15.

Lindquist, J. D., Vida, I., Plank, R. E., & Fairhurst, A. (2001). The modified CETSCALE: Validity tests in the Czech Republic, Hungary, and Poland. *International Business Review*, *10*(5), 505–516. doi:10.1016/S0969-5931(01)00030-0

LiouJ. J.JiangC.LiuS.JiangH.ShaoT. (2024). Selecting Green Suppliers for E-Commerce Enterprises Based on a Hybrid Multiple-Criteria Decision-Making Model. *Available at* SSRN, 1-43. doi:10.2139/ssrn.4770626

Liu, X., He, M., Gao, F., & Xie, P. (2008). An empirical study of online shopping customer satisfaction in China: A holistic perspective. *International Journal of Retail & Distribution Management, 36*(11), 919–940. doi:10.1108/09590550810911683

Liu, Y., Yu, Y., Huang, Y., & Guan, W. (2024). Utilizing the resources efficiency: Evidence from the impacts of media industry and digitalization. *Resources Policy, 88*, 104346. doi:10.1016/j.resourpol.2023.104346

Lombardi, R. (2019). Knowledge transfer and organizational performance and business process: past, present and future researches. *Business Process Management Journal, 25*(1), 2–9. https://www.emerald.com/insight/content/doi/10.1108/BPMJ-02-2019-368/full/html

Long, F., Bhuiyan, M. A., Aziz, N. A., & Rahman, M. K. (2022). Predicting young Chinese consumers' intentions to purchase Western brands: Structural model analysis. *PLoS ONE, 17*, 1–17. doi:10.1371/journal.pone.0267563

Lozano, R. (2006). Incorporation and institutionalization of SD into universities: Breaking through barriers to change. *Journal of Cleaner Production, 14*(9–11), 787–796. doi:10.1016/j.jclepro.2005.12.010

Lozano, R., Lukman, R., Lozano, F. J., Huisingh, D., & Lambrechts, W. (2023). Declarations for sustainability in higher education: Becoming better leaders, through addressing the university system. *Journal of Cleaner Production, 48*, 10–19. doi:10.1016/j.jclepro.2011.10.006

Lundvall, B.-A. (2009). Innovation as an interactive process: user-producer interaction to the national system of innovation. *African Journal of Science, Technology, Innovation and Development, 1*(2_3), 10–34.

Lunenburg, F. C. (2010). Communication: The process, barriers, and improving effectiveness. *Schooling, 1*(1), 1–10.

Lu, Y., Nakicenovic, N., Visbeck, M., & Stevance, A.-S. (2015). Policy: Five priorities for the UN Sustainable Development Goals. *Nature, 520*(7548), 433. doi:10.1038/520432a PMID:25903612

Ma, J., & Poursoleiman, R. (2022). Optimization of the home energy system in presence of price fluctuation and intermittent renewable energy sources in grid-connected and islanded modes. *Sustainable Energy Technologies and Assessments, 54*, 102875. doi:10.1016/j.seta.2022.102875

Makarius, E. E., Mukherjee, D., Fox, J. D., & Fox, A. K. (2020). Rising with the machines: A sociotechnical framework for bringing artificial intelligence into the organization. *Journal of Business Research, 120*, 262–273. doi:10.1016/j.jbusres.2020.07.045

Makin, S. (2018). *Searching for digital technology's effects on well-being*. Outlook.

Maksan, M. T., Kovačić, D., & Cerjak, M. (2019). The influence of consumer ethnocentrism on purchase of domestic wine: Application of the extended theory of planned behaviour. *Appetite, 142*, 104393. doi:10.1016/j.appet.2019.104393

Malhotra, N. K. (2009). *Riset Pemasaran Pendekatan Terapan*. PT. Indeks Kelompok Gramedia.

Manoo, M. U., Shaikh, F., Kumar, L., & Arıcı, M. (2024). Comparative techno-economic analysis of various stand-alone and grid connected (solar/wind/fuel cell) renewable energy systems. *International Journal of Hydrogen Energy, 52*, 397–414. doi:10.1016/j.ijhydene.2023.05.258

Marczewska, M., & Kostrzewski, M. (2020). Sustainable Business Models: A Bibliometric Performance Analysis. *Energies, 13*(22), 6062. doi:10.3390/en13226062

Marius, C., & Schmidt, S. (2022). A formal framework for conceptions of sustainability – a theoretical contribution to the discourse in sustainable development. *Sustainable Development, 20*(6), 400–410.

Maroufkhani, P., Iranmanesh, M., & Ghobakhloo, M. (2022). Determinants of big data analytics adoption in small and medium sized enterprises (SMEs). *Industrial Management & Data Systems, 122*(9), 1–24. doi:10.1108/IMDS-11-2021-0695

Martínez, J. L., Marco, J. N., & Moya, B. R. (2020). Analysis of the adoption of customer facing InStore technologies in retail SMEs. *Journal of Retailing and Consumer Services*, *57*(1), 102225. doi:10.1016/j.jretconser.2020.102225

Martin, J.-L., Maris, V., & Simberloff, D. S. (2016). The need to respect nature and its limits challenges society and conservation science. *Proceedings of the National Academy of Sciences of the United States of America*, *113*(22), 6105–6112. doi:10.1073/pnas.1525003113 PMID:27185943

Mastrocinque, E., Ramírez, F. J., Honrubia-Escribano, A., & Pham, D. T. (2022). Industry 4.0 enabling sustainable supply chain development in the renewable energy sector: A multi-criteria intelligent approach. *Technological Forecasting and Social Change*, *182*, 121813. doi:10.1016/j.techfore.2022.121813

Mathew, D., Brintha, N. C., & Jappes, J. T. W. (2023). Artificial intelligence powered automation for industry 4.0. In *New Horizons for Industry 4.0 in Modern Business* (pp. 1–28). Springer. doi:10.1007/978-3-031-20443-2_1

Matt, D. T., Pedrini, G., Bonfanti, A., & Orzes, G. (2023). Industrial digitalization. A systematic literature review and research agenda. *European Management Journal*, *41*(1), 47–78. doi:10.1016/j.emj.2022.01.001

Ma, X., Pan, Y., Zhang, M., Ma, J., & Yang, W. (2024). Impact of carbon emission trading and renewable energy development policy on the sustainability of electricity market: A stackelberg game analysis. *Energy Economics*, *129*, 107199. doi:10.1016/j.eneco.2023.107199

Maxwell, G., & Steele, G. (2003). Organisational commitment: A study of managers in hotels. *International Journal of Contemporary Hospitality Management*, *15*(7), 362–369. doi:10.1108/09596110310496006

Maya, Y., Putri, R. W., & Davey, O. M. (2023, May). Toward the Legal Aspect on Developing Academics Intellectual Property Rights in University. In *3rd Universitas Lampung International Conference on Social Sciences (ULICoSS 2022)* (pp. 17-29). Atlantis Press. 10.2991/978-2-38476-046-6_3

Mazzucato, M. (2018). Mission-oriented research & innovation in the European Union. *European Commission*. https://www.obzor2020.hr/userfiles/Mazzucato Report Missions_2018.pdf

McFarland, S. G. (1981). Effects of question order on survey responses. *Public Opinion Quarterly*, *45*(2), 208–215. doi:10.1086/268651

McHugh, M.L. (2013). The chi-square test of independence. *Biochemia Medica, Medicinska naklada, 23*(2), 143–149.

Memon, M. A., Ramayah, T., Cheah, J., Ting, H., Chuah, F., & Cham, T. H. (2021). PLS-SEM Statistical Programs: A Review. *Journal of Applied Structural Equation Modeling*, *5*(1), i–xiv. doi:10.47263/JASEM.5(1)06

Mersita, D., Fathoni, A., & Wulan, H. S. (2019). Analysis of Empowerment of Human Resources in Efforts to Optimize The Potential of Human Capital in UMKM. *Journal of Management Information Systems*, *5*(5), 1–8.

Messinger, P. R., Stroulia, E., Lyons, K., Bone, M., Niu, R. H., Smirnov, K. & Perelgut, S. (2009). Virtual worlds - past, present, and future: New directions in social computing. *Decision Support Systems, 47*(3), 204-228.

Meyerson, G., & Dewettinck, B. (2012). Effect of empowerment on employees performance. *Advanced Research in Economic and Management Sciences*, *2*(1), 40–46.

Mikalef, P., & Pateli, A. (2017). Information technology-enabled dynamic capabilities and their indirect effect on competitive performance: Findings from PLS-SEM and fsQCA. *Journal of Business Research*, *70*, 1–16. doi:10.1016/j.jbusres.2016.09.004

Milosevic, N., Dobrota, M., & Barjaktarovic Rakocevic, S. (2018). *Digital economy in Europe: Evaluation of countries' performances*, *36*(2), 861–880. https://hrcak.srce.hr/index.php?show=clanak&id_clanak_jezik=312156

Mint, (August 14, 2023). *Indian agriculture must balance profits with sustainable practices.* https://www.livemint.com/opinion/first-person/indian-agriculture-must-balance-profits-with-sustainable-practices-11691889108165.html(Accessed on: December 18, 2023).

Modgil, S., Gupta, S., Sivarajah, U., & Bhushan, B. (2021). Big data-enabled large-scale group decision making for circular economy: An emerging market context. *Technological Forecasting and Social Change, 166,* 120607. doi:10.1016/j.techfore.2021.120607

Moll, I. (2022). The fourth industrial revolution: A new ideology. *TripleC: Communication, Capitalism & Critique. Open Access Journal for a Global Sustainable Information Society, 20*(1), 45–61.

Moniruzzaman, M., Yassine, A., & Benlamri, R. (2023). Blockchain and cooperative game theory for peer-to-peer energy trading in smart grids. *International Journal of Electrical Power & Energy Systems, 151,* 109111. doi:10.1016/j.ijepes.2023.109111

Morris, D. R. (1991). Exergy analysis and cumulative exergy consumption of complex chemical processes:The industrial chlor-alkali processes. *Chemical Engineering Science, 46,* 459–465.

Mubarak, M. F., Yusoff, W. F. W., Mubarik, M., Tiwari, S., & Kaya, K. A. (2018). Nurturing Entrepreneurship Ecosystem in a Developing Economy: Myths and Realities. *Journal of Technology Management and Business, 6*(1). https://publisher.uthm.edu.my/ojs/index.php/jtmb/article/view/4251

Mubarak, M. F., Shaikh, F. A., Mubarik, M., Samo, K. A., & Mastoi, S. (2019). The Impact of Digital Transformation on Business Performance. *Engineering, Technology &. Applied Scientific Research, 9*(6), 5056–5061.

Mugge, P., & Gudergan, G. (2017). The Gap Between the Practice and Theory of Digital Transformation, Whitepaper. *The 50th Hawaiian International Conference of System Science.* IEEE.

Mulyani, M. A., Razzaq, A., Sumardi, W. H., & Anshari, M. (2019, August). Smartphone adoption in mobile learning scenario. In *2019 International Conference on Information Management and Technology (ICIMTech)* (Vol. 1, pp. 208-211). IEEE..

Mulyani, M. A., Yusuf, S., Siregar, P., Nurihsan, J., Razzaq, A., & Anshari, M. (2021, August). Fourth industrial revolution and educational challenges. In *2021 International Conference on Information Management and Technology (ICIMTech)* (Vol. 1, pp. 245-249). IEEE. 10.1109/ICIMTech53080.2021.9535057

Munir, M. T., Li, B., Naqvi, M., & Nizami, A. S. (2023). Green loops and clean skies: Optimizing municipal solid waste management using data science for a circular economy. *Environmental Research,* •••, 117786. PMID:38036215

Muqadas, F., Rehman, M., Aslam, U., & Ur-Rahman, U. (2017). Exploring the challenges, trends and issues for knowledge sharing. *VINE Journal of Information and Knowledge Management Systems, 47*(1), 2–15. doi:10.1108/VJIKMS-06-2016-0036

Musa, M. I., Nurhaidah (2015). Dampak pengaruh globalisasi bagi kehidupan bangsa indonesia. *Jurnal Pesona Dasar, 3*(3)

Musakwa, M. T., & Odhiambo, N. M. (2019). THE impact of remittance inflows on poverty in Botswana: an ARDL approach. *Journal of Economic Structures, 8*(1), 42. https://journalofeconomicstructures.springeropen.com/articles/10.1186/s40008-019-0175-x

Nabila, M., Purwandari, B., Nazief, B. A. A., Chalid, D. A., Wibowo, S. S., & Solichah, I. (2018). Financial Technology Acceptance Factors of Electronic Wallet and Digital Cash in Indonesia. *2018 International Conference on Information Technology Systems and Innovation, ICITSI 2018 - Proceedings,* (pp. 284–289). IEEE. 10.1109/ICITSI.2018.8696091

Nabity-Grover, T., Cheung, C., & Bennett Thatcher, J. (2020). Inside out and outside in: How the COVID-19 pandemic affects self-disclosure on social media. *International Journal of Information Management, 55*, 102188. doi:10.1016/j.ijinfomgt.2020.102188

Nadeem, A., Abedin, B., Cerpa, N., & Chew, E. (2018). Editorial: Digital Transformation & Digital Business Strategy in Electronic Commerce - The Role of Organizational Capabilities. *Journal of theoretical and applied electronic commerce research, 13*(2). https://www.scielo.cl/scielo.php?script=sci_arttext&pid=S0718-18762018000200101&lng=en&nrm=iso&tlng=en

Nainggolan, R. (2016). Gender, Tingkat Pendidikan dan Lama Usaha Sebagai Determinan Penghasilan UMKM Kota Surabaya. *Jurnal Kinerja, 20*(1), 1–12. doi:10.24002/kinerja.v20i1.693

Nastase, M., Giuclea, M., & Bold, O. (2012). The impact of change management in organizations-a survey of methods and techniques for a successful change. *Revista De Management Comparat International, 13*(1), 5.

Nasution, M. D. T. P., Rafiki, A., Lubis, A., & Rossanty, Y. (2021). Entrepreneurial orientation, knowledge management, dynamic capabilities towards e-commerce adoption of SMEs in Indonesia. *Journal of Science and Technology Policy Management, 12*(2), 256–282. doi:10.1108/JSTPM-03-2020-0060

Nelissen, P., & van Selm, M. (2008). Surviving organisational change: How management communication helps balance mixed feelings. *Corporate Communications, 13*(3), 306–318. doi:10.1108/13563280810893670

Nilsson, M., Griggs, D., & Visbeck, M. (2016). Policy: Map the interactions between Sustainable Development Goals. *Nature, 534*(7607), 320–322. doi:10.1038/534320a PMID:27306173

Nissen, V., & Termer, F. (2014). Business IT-Alignment Ergebnisse einer Befragung von IT-Fuhrungskraften in Deutschland. *HMD Praxis der Wirtschaftsinformatik, 51*(5), 549–560. https://link.springer.com/article/10.1365/s40702-014-0060-x

Nissen, V., & Von Rennenkampff, A. (2015). *Measuring and managing IT agility as a strategic resource-examining the IT application systems landscape, 6*(60). https://cyberleninka.ru/article/n/17214559

Nwankpa, J. K., & Roumani, Y. (2016). *IT Capability and Digital Transformation: A Firm Performance Perspective.* AISEL. https://aisel.aisnet.org/icis2016/ISStrategy/Presentations/4/

O'Byrne, D., Dripps, W., & Nicholas, K. A. (2015). Teaching and learning sustainability: An assessment of the curriculum content and structure of sustainability degree programs in higher education. *Sustainability Science, 10*(1), 43–59. doi:10.1007/s11625-014-0251-y

Ocloo, C. E., Xuhua, H., Akaba, S., Shi, J., & Worwui-Brown, D. K. (2020). The Determinant Factors of Business to Business (B2B) E-Commerce Adoption in Small- and Medium-Sized Manufacturing Enterprises. *Journal of Global Information Technology Management, 23*(3), 1–26. doi:10.1080/1097198X.2020.1792229

Omar, A. M., & Anshari, M. (2023). Super Smart Society 5.0: Innovation in Public Policy Post-Industry 4.0. In Digital Transformation for Business and Society (pp. 91-110). Routledge.

On-Piu Chan, J. (2020). Digital Transformation in the Era of Big Data and Cloud Computing. *International Journal of Intelligent Information Systems, 9*(3). http://www.sciencepublishinggroup.com/journal/paperinfo?journalid=135&doi=10.11648/j.ijiis.20200903.11

Ordoñez de Pablos, P. (2023). Digital innovation and green economy for more resilient and inclusive societies: Understanding challenges ahead for the green growth. *Journal of Science and Technology Policy Management, 14*(3), 461–466. doi:10.1108/JSTPM-05-2023-193

Ordóñez de Pablos, P. (2024). Digital transformation, innovation and competitiveness: Some insights from Asia. *Journal of Science and Technology Policy Management, 15*(1), 1–5. doi:10.1108/JSTPM-01-2024-222

Ordóñez de Pablos, P., Almunawar, N., & Anshari, M. (2023a). *Developing Skills and Competencies for Digital and Green Transitions*. IGI-Global. doi:10.4018/978-1-6684-9089-1

Ordóñez de Pablos, P., Almunawar, N., & Anshari, M. (2023b). *Perspectives on the Transition Toward Green and Climate Neutral Economies in Asia*. IGI-Global. doi:10.4018/978-1-6684-8613-9

Organisation-for-Economic-Co-operation-and-Development. (2019). *The impact of artificial intelligence on the future of work*. OECD.

Organizer. (2020). *Cabinet Approves NEP 2020 – Paves way for transformational reforms in school and higher education in the country*. https://organiser.org/2020/07/29/129578/bharat/cabinet-approves-national-education-policy-2020-paving-way-for-transformational-reforms-in-school-and-higher-education/..

Orlikowski, W. (2001). *The Duality of Technology. The Contemporary Giddens, Social Theory in a Globalizing Age. CGA Bryant and D. Jary*. Palgrave.

Page, J., Hinshaw, D., & McKay, B. (2021). What We Know About the Origins of Covid-19. *Wall Street Journal*. https://www.wsj.com/articles/what-we-know-about-the-origins-of-covid-19-11624699801

Pal, P., & Mukherjee, V. (2021). Off-grid solar photovoltaic/hydrogen fuel cell system for renewable energy generation: An investigation based on techno-economic feasibility assessment for the application of end-user load demand in North-East India. *Renewable & Sustainable Energy Reviews, 149*, 111421. doi:10.1016/j.rser.2021.111421

Pandita, D., Singh, M., & Choudhary, S. (2019). The Changing Dynamics of Manager-Subordinate Relationships in Organizations: An Empirical Study. *European Business Review, 00–00*. doi:10.1108/EBR-04-2017-0072

Pan, Y. (2016). Heading toward Artificial Intelligence 2.0. *Engineering (Beijing), 2*(4), 409–413. doi:10.1016/J.ENG.2016.04.018

Park, H. J., & Kitty, G. D. (2002). Attitudes, Subjective Norms and Behavioral Intentions toward Purchasing Imported Casual Clothing. *Journal of the Korean Society of Clothing and Textiles, 26*(12), 1791–1803.

Peng, H. (2013). Why and when do people hide knowledge? *Journal of Knowledge Management, 17*(3), 398–415. doi:10.1108/JKM-12-2012-0380

Percy, L. (2018). *Strategic integrated marketing communications. (2018)*. Taylor & Francis Group. doi:10.4324/9781315164342

Perkumienė, D., Atalay, A., Safaa, L., & Grigienė, J. (2023). Sustainable Waste Management for clean and safe environments in the recreation and tourism sector: A case study of Lithuania, Turkey and Morocco. *Recycling, 8*(4), 56. doi:10.3390/recycling8040056

Pham-Truffert, M., Metz, F., Fischer, M., Rueff, H., & Messerli, P. (2020). Interactions among Sustainable Development Goals: Knowledge for identifying multipliers and virtuous cycles. *Sustainable Development (Bradford), 28*(5), 1236–1250. doi:10.1002/sd.2073

Picaud-Bello, K., Schiele, H., Koch, V., & Francillette, M. (2024). Innovation through sustainability: Identifying purchaser skills fostering green innovation. *Cleaner Logistics and Supply Chain, 10*, 100136. doi:10.1016/j.clscn.2023.100136

Piccolo, R., Romeo, E. F., & Zarić, S. (2024). Green marketing, brand development and digital strategies: Forging a sustainable future. *KNOWLEDGE-International Journal, 63*(1), 15–20.

Pinto, L. (2023). *Investigating the relationship between green supply chain purchasing practices and firms'*.

Pinto, L. (2023, February 15). performance. *Journal of Industrial Engineering and Management, 16*(1), 78–101. doi:10.3926/jiem.3686

Pipitwanichakarn, T., & Wongtada, N. (2021). Leveraging the technology acceptance model for mobile commerce adoption under distinct stages of adoption. *Asia Pacific Journal of Marketing and Logistics, 33*(6), 1415–1436. doi:10.1108/APJML-10-2018-0448

Piribauer, B., Bartl, A., & Ipsmiller, W. (2021). Piribauer, B.; Bartl, A.; Ipsmiller, W. Enzymatic textile recycling—Best practices and outlook. [PubMed]. *Waste Management & Research, 39*(10), 1277–1290. doi:10.1177/0734242X211029167

Podder, S. K., Karuppiah, M., Thomas, B., & Samanta, D. (2022). Research initiative on sustainable education system: Model of balancing green computing and ict in quality education. Paper presented at the *2022 Interdisciplinary Research in Technology and Management (IRTM)*. IEEE. 10.1109/IRTM54583.2022.9791758

Porter, M.E. & Kramer, M.R. (2011). Creating shared value. *Harvard Business Review*.

Pousttchi, K., Gleiss, A., Buzzi, B., & Kohlhagen, M. (2019). Technology Impact Types for Digital Transformation. In: *2019 IEEE 21st Conference on Business Informatics (CBI)*. IEEE. https://ieeexplore.ieee.org/document/8807798/

Pradhan, P., Costa, L., Rybski, D., Lucht, W., & Kropp, J. P. (2017). A systematic study of Sustainable Development Goal (SDG) Interactions. *Earth's Future, 5*(11), 1169–1179. doi:10.1002/2017EF000632

Prahalad, C. K. and Ramaswamy, V. (2004). Co-creation experiences: The next practice in value creation. *Journal of Interactive Marketing, 18*(3), 5-14.

Pratiwi, A. C., Pertiwi, N. R. L., & Al Baihaqi, A. H. (2023). The Importance of Understanding Intellectual Property Rights from a Legal Perspective and Its Benefits for Society. *Proceedings vof Islamic Economics. Business, and Philanthropy, 2*(2), 100–120.

Prester, J. (2020). *Emerging Leaders in Digital Work: Toward a Theory of Attentional Leadership*. AISEL. https://aisel.aisnet.org/icis2020/is_workplace_fow/is_workplace_fow/12/

Pretty, J., Smith, G., Goulding, K. W. T., Groves, S. J., Henderson, I., Hine, R. E., King, V., Van Oostrum, J., Pendlington, D. J., Vis, J. K., & Walter, C. (2008). Multi-year assessment of Unilever's progress towards agricultural sustainability II: Outcomes for peas (UK), spinach (Germany, Italy), tomatoes (Australia, Brazil, Greece, USA), tea (Kenya, Tanzania, India) and oil palm (Ghana). *International Journal of Agricultural Sustainability, 6*(1), 63–88. doi:10.3763/ijas.2007.0323

Prime Minister's Office. (2021), *Brunei Darussalam Sustainable Development Goals Annual Report 2021*. Prime Minister's Office.

Purvis, B., Mao, Y., & Robinson, D. (2019). Three pillars of sustainability: In search of conceptual origins. *Sustainability Science, 14*(3), 681–695. doi:10.1007/s11625-018-0627-5

Purwandari, B., Otmen, B., & Kumaralalita, L. (2019). Adoption factors of e-marketplace and instagram for micro, small, and medium enterprises (MSMEs) in Indonesia. *Proceedings of 2019 2nd International Conference on Data Science and Information Technology*, Seoul, Republic of Korea. 10.1145/3352411.3352453

Putra, P. O. H., & Santoso, H. B. (2020). Contextual factors and performance impact of e-business use in Indonesian small and medium enterprises (SMEs). *Heliyon, 6*(1), 1–10. doi:10.1016/j.heliyon.2020.e03568 PMID:32211544

Putri, F. S., Purwosaputro, R., Putri, S. K. M., & Ananda, A. S. (2023). Analysis of the influence of perceived value on browsing behavior in C2C E-Commerce with depth of review as antecedent. *International Journal of Data and Network Science*, 7(4), 1613–1626. doi:10.5267/j.ijdns.2023.8.002

Qalati, S. A., Li, W., Ahmed, N., Mirani, M. A., & Khan, A. (2021). Examining the factors affecting SME performance: The mediating role of social media adoption. *Sustainability (Basel)*, 13(75), 1–24. doi:10.3390/su13010075

Qiu, Y., Chen, Q., & Ng, P. S. J. (2023). Research on the Spillover Effects of Digital Transformation on the Sustainable Growth of Green Schools. *Proceedings of Business and Economic Studies*, 6(6), 16–23. doi:10.26689/pbes.v6i6.5749

Rabiee, F. (2004). Focus-group interview and data analysis. *The Proceedings of the Nutrition Society*, 63(4), 655–660. doi:10.1079/PNS2004399 PMID:15831139

Rafiq M. Y., & Javeid H. M. U. (2018). *Impact of Gender Differences on Online Shopping Attitude of University Students*, 1-9.

Rai, A., Pavlou, P., Im, G. and Du, S., 2012. Interfirm IT capability profiles and communications for cocreating relational value: Evidence from the logistics industry. *MIS Quarterly, 36*(1), 233-262.

Rajendra, P., Kumari, M., Rani, S., Dogra, N., Boadh, R., Kumar, A., & Dahiya, M. (2022). Impact of artificial intelligence on civilization: Future perspectives. *Materials Today: Proceedings, 56*, 252–256. doi:10.1016/j.matpr.2022.01.113

Rakesh Kumar, M. (2015), National Implementation of the SDG. *SDG Monitoring India 2015*. UN. https://unstats.un.org/sdgs/.../Presentation--4.3-Implementation-of-SDG-Monitoring--I

Ramadanty, M. L., & Kartikasari, D. (2020). Purchase Intention of e-Payment : The Substitute or Complementary Role of Purchase Intention of E-Payment : The Substitute or Complementary Role of Brand, Sales Promotions, and Information Quality. *2nd International Conference on Applied Economy and Social Science, October*, (pp. 298–308). ScitePress. 10.5220/0010355402980308

Ramaswamy, V. & Gouillart, F. (2010). Building the Co-Creative Enterprise. *Harvard Business Review, 88*(10), 100-109.

Rani, K. U. (2016). Communication barriers. *Journal of English Language and Literature, 3*(2), 74–76.

Rashid, Z. A., Sambasivan, M., & Rahman, A. A. (2004). The influence of organisational culture on attitudes toward organisational change. *Leadership and Organization Development Journal*.

Rasidah, H.A.B. (2020). COVID-19 drives 116% growth in interbank fund transfers: AMBD. *The Scoop*.

Rasoolimanesh, S. M., Ali, F., & Jaafar, M. (2018). Modeling residents' perceptions of tourism development: Linear versus non-linear models. *Journal of Destination Marketing & Management, 10*(May), 1–9. doi:10.1016/j.jdmm.2018.05.007

Ray, C. M., Sormunen, C., & Harris, T. M. (1999). Men's and women's attitudes toward computer technology: A comparison. *Office Systems Research Journal*.

Raynor, M. E., & Christensen, C. M. (2003). Innovating for growth: Now IS the time. *Ivey Business Journal, 68*(1), 1–9.

Razzaq, A., Samiha, Y. T., & Anshari, M. (2018). Smartphone habits and behaviors in supporting students self-efficacy. *International Journal of Emerging Technologies in Learning, 13*(2), 94. doi:10.3991/ijet.v13i02.7685

Religia, Y. (2022). The effect of environmental pressures and the covid19 pandemic on the adoption of TikTok by MSMEs: Can MSME engagement moderate? *Journal of International Conference Proceedings, 5*(5), 285–300. doi:10.32535/jicp.v5i5.2031

Religia, Y., Surachman, Rohman, F., & Indrawati, N. K. (2020). The antecendence of e-commerce adoption by micro, small, and medium sized enterprise (MSME) with e-commerce training as moderation. *Solid State Technology*, *63*(2), 335–346.

Religia, Y., Surachman, S., Rohman, F., & Indrawati, N. (2021). *E-commerce adoption in SMEs: A literature review. Proceedings of the 1st International Conference on Economics Engineering and Social Science (InCEESS 2020)*, Bekasi, Indonesia. 10.4108/eai.17-7-2020.2302969

Ren, F., & Kwan, M. (2009, April). (2008). The Impact of Geographic Context on E-shopping Behavior. *Environment and Planning. B, Planning & Design*, *36*(2), 262–278. doi:10.1068/b34014t

Riedel, C., Blohm, I., Leimeister, J.M. and Krcmar, H., (2013). The Effect of Rating Scales on Decision Quality and User Attitudes in Online Innovation Communities. *International Journal of Electronic Commerce, 17*(3), 7-36.

Ritala, P., Baiyere, A., Hughes, M., & Kraus, S. (2021). Digital strategy implementation: The role of individual entrepreneurial orientation and relational capital. *Technological Forecasting and Social Change*, *171*, 120961. doi:10.1016/j.techfore.2021.120961

Riyanto, A. D. (2022). *Hootsuite (We are Social): Indonesian Digital Report 2022.*. Hoot Suite. https://andi.link/hootsuite-we-are-social-indonesian-digital-report-2022

Rodríguez-García, A.-M., López Belmonte, J., Agreda Montoro, M., & Moreno-Guerrero, A.-J. (2019). Productive, structural and dynamic study of the concept of sustainability in the educational field. *Sustainability (Basel)*, *11*(20), 5613. doi:10.3390/su11205613

Rogers, E. M. (1995). *Diffusion of innovations* (Vol. 12).

Rogers, E. M., & Cartano, D. G. (1962). Methods of Measuring Opinion Leadership. *Public Opinion Quarterly*, *26*(3), 435–441. https://www.jstor.org/stable/2747233. doi:10.1086/267118

Roser, T., Samson A., Humphreys, P. and Cruz-Valdivieso, E. (2009). Co-creation: new pathways to value: An overview. *Promise Corporation.*

Ross, J. (2017). How to develop a great digital strategy. *MIT Sloan Management Review, 58*(2).

Rubel, A. (2016). The Black Box Society: The Secret Algorithms that Control Money and Information, by Frank Pasquale. Cambridge: Harvard University Press, 2015. 320 pp. ISBN 978–0674368279. *Business Ethics Quarterly*, *26*(4), 568–571. doi:10.1017/beq.2016.50

Rudhumbu, N., Svotwa, D., Munyanyiwa, T., & Mutsau, M. (2016). *Attitudes of Students towards Entrepreneurship Education at Two Selected Higher Education Institutions in Botswana: A Critical Analysis and Reflection.* Academic Journal Of Interdisciplinary Studies., doi:10.5901/ajis.2016.v5n2p83

Rumaizi, I. H., Anshari, M., Almunawar, M. N., & Masri, M. (2023). Maslow's Hierarchy of Needs and Digital Wallet Usage Among Youth. In *Digital Psychology's Impact on Business and Society* (pp. 179–202). IGI Global. doi:10.4018/978-1-6684-6108-2.ch008

Ryu, J. S. (2011). Consumer attitudes and shopping intentions toward pop-up fashion stores. *Journal of Global Fashion Marketing*, *2*(3), 139–147. doi:10.1080/20932685.2011.10593092

Sachs, J. D. (2021). Sustainable Development Report 2021: the decade of action for the Sustainable Development Goals. Cambridge University Press.

Sachs, J. D. (2012). From millennium development goals to sustainable development goals. *Lancet*, *379*(9832), 832–2206. doi:10.1016/S0140-6736(12)60685-0 PMID:22682467

Sahebi, H., Khodoomi, M., Seif, M., Pishvaee, M., & Hanne, T. (2023). The benefits of peer-to-peer renewable energy trading and battery storage backup for local grid. *Journal of Energy Storage*, *63*, 106970. doi:10.1016/j.est.2023.106970

Saini, H., Upadhyaya, A., & Khandelwal, M. K. (2019). *Benefits of cloud computing for business enterprises: A review. Proceedings of International Conference on Advancements in Computing & Management (ICACM)*. IEEE. 10.2139/ssrn.3463631

Sait, M. A., Almunawar, M. N., Anshari, M., & Masri, M. (2023). Digital Wallet Adoption in Supporting Financial Inclusion: A Conceptual Framework. *2023 International Conference on Sustainable Islamic Business and Finance (SIBF)*. IEEE. 10.1109/SIBF60067.2023.10380043

Sait, M. A., & Anshari, M. (2021). Industrial Revolution 4.0: A New Challenge to Brunei Darussalam's Unemployment Issue. [IJABIM]. *International Journal of Asian Business and Information Management*, *12*(4), 33–44. doi:10.4018/IJABIM.20211001.oa3

Sakaria, D., Maat, S. M., & Mohd Matore, M. E. E. (2023). Examining the Optimal Choice of SEM Statistical Software Packages for Sustainable Mathematics Education: A Systematic Review. *Sustainability (Basel)*, *15*(4), 3209. doi:10.3390/su15043209

Samaranayake, S. U., & Takemura, T. (2017). Employee readiness for organizational change: A case study in an export oriented manufacturing firm in Sri Lanka. *Eurasian Journal of Business and Economics*, *10*(20), 1–16. doi:10.17015/ejbe.2017.020.01

Samiha, Y. T., Handayani, T., Razaq, A., Fithriyah, M., Fitri, A., & Anshari, M. (2022, March). Implementation of Education 4.0 as sustainable decisions for a sustainable development. In *2022 International Conference on Decision Aid Sciences and Applications (DASA)* (pp. 846-850). IEEE. 10.1109/DASA54658.2022.9765080

Samiha, Y. T., Handayani, T., Razzaq, A., Fitri, A., Fithriyah, M., & Anshari, M. (2021, November). Sustainability of Excellence in Education 4.0. In *2021 Sustainable Leadership and Academic Excellence International Conference (SLAE)* (pp. 1-5). IEEE. 10.1109/SLAE54202.2021.9788095

Sanchez-García, E., Martínez-Falcó, J., Marco-Lajara, B., & Manresa-Marhuenda, E. (2024). Revolutionizing the circular economy through new technologies: A new era of sustainable progress. *Environmental Technology & Innovation*, *33*, 103509. doi:10.1016/j.eti.2023.103509

Šapić, S., Kocić, M., & Filipović, J. (2018). Brand and consumer characteristics as drivers of behaviour towards global and local brands. *Zbornik Radova Ekonomskog Fakulteta u Rijeci*, *36*(2), 619–645. doi:10.18045/zbefri.2018.2.619

Saridakis, G., Lai, Y., Mohammed, A. M., & Hansen, J. M. (2018). Industry characteristics, stages of E-commerce communications, and entrepreneurs and SMEs revenue growth. *Technological Forecasting and Social Change*, *128*(1), 56–66. doi:10.1016/j.techfore.2017.10.017

Sarstedt, M., Ringle, C. M., & Hair, J. F. (2017). Treating Unobserved Heterogeneity in PLS-SEM: A Multi-method Approach. In *Partial Least Squares Path Modeling*. (pp. 197–217). Springer International Publishing. http://link.springer.com/10.1007/978-3-319-64069-3_9 doi:10.1007/978-3-319-64069-3_9

Sartori, L., & Theodorou, A. (2022). A sociotechnical perspective for the future of AI: Narratives, inequalities, and human control. *Ethics and Information Technology*, *24*(1), 4. doi:10.1007/s10676-022-09624-3

Sarvgyan (2024). *Top Features of New Education Policy (NEP) 2020*. https://news.sarvgyan.com/new-education-policy-nep-2020-features..

Sattiraju, V. K., Pandey, R., Pallela, R., Sircar, A., Ligade, V. S., Muragundi, P. M., & Janodia, M. D. (2022). Intellectual property rights policies of higher education institutions (HEIs) in India: A cross-sectional study. *Journal of Science and Technology Policy Management, 13*(4), 837–848. doi:10.1108/JSTPM-01-2021-0002

Schallmo, D. R. A., & Williams, C. A. (2018). *Digital Transformation Now*. Springer. https://www.springer.com/gp/book/9783319728438

Schildt, H. (2017). Big data and organizational design – the brave new world of algorithmic management and computer augmented transparency. *Innovation, 19*(1), 23–30. https://www.tandfonline.com/doi/full/10.1080/14479338.2016.1252043

Schlosser, A. E. (2003). Experiencing Products in the Virtual World: The role of goal and imagery in influencing attitudes versus purchase intentions. *The Journal of Consumer Research, 30*(2), 184–198. doi:10.1086/376807

Schober, P., Boer, C., & Schwarte, L. A. (2018). Correlation coefficients: Appropriate use and interpretation. *Anesthesia and Analgesia, 126*(5), 1763–1768. doi:10.1213/ANE.0000000000002864 PMID:29481436

Schwab, K. (2017). *The fourth industrial revolution*. Currency.

Schwertner, K. (2017). Digital transformation of business. *Trakia Journal of Science, 15* (Suppl.1), 388–393. http://tru.uni-sz.bg/tsj/TJS_Suppl.1_Vol.15_2017/65.pdf

Scoones, I. (1999). New ecology and the social sciences: What prospects for a fruitful engagement. *Annual Review of Anthropology, 28*(1), 479–507. doi:10.1146/annurev.anthro.28.1.479

Shah, B. B. P. (2018). *Assessing digital transformation capabilities*. MIT. https://dspace.mit.edu/handle/1721.1/121798

Shahadat, M. M. H., Nekmahmud, M., Ebrahimi, P., & Fekete-Farkas, M. (2023). Digital Technology Adoption in SMEs: What Technological, Environmental and Organizational Factors Influence in Emerging Countries? *Global Business Review, 09721509221137199*. doi:10.1177/09721509221137199

Shahbaz, M. S., Chandio, A. F., Oad, M., Ahmed, A., & Ullah, R. (2018). No Title. *International Journal of Sustainable Construction Engineering and Technology, 9*(2). https://publisher.uthm.edu.my/ojs/index.php/IJSCET/article/view/3579

Shahbaz, M. S., Sohu, S., Khaskhelly, F. Z., Bano, A., & Soomro, M. A. (2019a). A Novel Classification of Supply Chain Risks. *Engineering, Technology &. Applied Scientific Research, 9*(3), 4301–4305.

Shahbaz, M. S., Soomro, M. A., Bhatti, N. U. K., Soomro, Z., & Jamali, M. Z. (2019b). The impact of supply chain capabilities on logistic efficiency for the construction projects. *Civil Engineering Journal, 5*(6), 1249–1256. doi:10.28991/cej-2019-03091329

Shah, N., Irani, Z., & Sharif, A. M. (2017). Big data in an HR context: Exploring organizational change readiness, employee attitudes and behaviors. *Journal of Business Research, 70*, 366–378. doi:10.1016/j.jbusres.2016.08.010

Shang, S. S. C., Li, E. Y., Wu, Y. & Hou, O. C. L. (2011). Understanding Web 2.0 service models: A knowledge-creating perspective. *Information & Management, 48*(5), 178-184.

Sharma, H. B., Vanapalli, K. R., Samal, B., Cheela, V. S., Dubey, B. K., & Bhattacharya, J. (2021). Circular economy approach in solid waste management system to achieve UN-SDGs: Solutions for post-COVID recovery. *The Science of the Total Environment, 800*, 149605. doi:10.1016/j.scitotenv.2021.149605 PMID:34426367

Shimp, T. A., & Sharma, S. (1987). Consumer Ethnocentrism: Construction and Validation of the CETSCALE. *JMR, Journal of Marketing Research, XXIV*(9), 280–289. doi:10.1177/002224378702400304

Shukla, R. K. (2016). *Coordination Practices in Supply Chain Management, 16*(1), 44–54. https://web.a.ebscohost. com/abstract?direct=true&profile=ehost&scope=site&authtype=crawler&jrnl=09725814&asa=Y&AN=117524981 &h=kdg%2B0rzQUfc2d7vKDCs%2FmxcD12t%2BaXWAqe4UX3qKO2VUkHxdd75I%2B7tf6dzUuzwnNxen6CiEB 7G6SQLKfUzuMA%3D%3D&crl=c&resultNs=AdminWebAuth&resultLocal=ErrCrlNotAuth&crlhashurl=login.asp x%3Fdirect%3Dtrue%26profile%3Dehost%26scope%3Dsite%26authtype%3Dcrawler%26jrnl%3D09725814%26asa% 3DY%26AN%3D117524981

Sieber, A. (2019). Does facebook violate its users' basic human rights? *NanoEthics, 13*(2), 139–145. doi:10.1007/ s11569-019-00345-4

Singh, P. K., Khatake, P., Gori, Y., Parmar, A., Shivakumar, P., Anandhi, R. J., & Kareem, S. H. (2023). Harmonizing innovation: The path to sustainable design and production. *E3S Web of Conferences.* IEEE. doi:10.1051/e3sconf/202345301025

Singh, N., & Sinha, N. (2020). How perceived trust mediates merchant's intention to use a mobile wallet technology. *Journal of Retailing and Consumer Services, 52*, 101894. doi:10.1016/j.jretconser.2019.101894

Smith, H. (2021). Clinical AI: opacity, accountability, responsibility and liability. *AI \& SOCIETY, 36*(2), 535–545.

Smith, I. (2005). Achieving readiness for organisational change. *Library Management, 26*(6/7), 408–412. doi:10.1108/01435120510623764

Son, J., Jin, B., & George, B. (2013). Consumers' purchase intention toward foreign brand goods. *Management Decision, 51*(2), 434–450. doi:10.1108/00251741311301902

Specker Sullivan, L., & Reiner, P. (2021). Digital wellness and persuasive technologies. *Philosophy \& Technology, 34*, 413–424.

Spowart, J. E., Gupta, N., & Lehmhus, D. (2018). Additive Manufacturing of Composites and Complex Materials. *JOM: The Journal of The Minerals, Metals & Materials Society* (TMS), *70*(3), 272–274. doi:10.1007/s11837-018-2742-2

Staab, N. (2016). *P. and & Oliver.* Digitalisierung der Dienstleistungsarbeit. https://edoc.unibas.ch/57929/

Stahl, B. C., Rodrigues, R., Santiago, N., & Macnish, K. (2022). A European Agency for Artificial Intelligence: Protecting fundamental rights and ethical values. *Computer Law \& Security Review, 45*, 105661.

Stare, A. (2011). The impact of the organisational structure and project organisational culture on project performance in Slovenian enterprises. *Management, 16*(2), 1–22.

Štefko, R., & Steffek, V. (2018). Key Issues in Slow Fashion: Current Challenges and Future Perspectives. *Sustainability (Basel), 10*(7), 2270. doi:10.3390/su10072270

Steinle, C., & Schiele, H. (2008). Limits to global sourcing? Strategic consequences of dependency on international suppliers: Cluster theory, resource-based view and case studies. *Journal of Purchasing & Supply Management, 14*, 3-14. doi:10.1016/j.pursup.2008.01.001

Stephen, A. T. (2016). The role of digital and social media marketing in consumer behavior. *Current Opinion in Psychology, 10*, 17–21. doi:10.1016/j.copsyc.2015.10.016

Stevens, J. (1996). *Applied multivariate statistics for the social sciences.* Lawrence Erlbaum.

Stjepić, A.-M., Pejić Bach, M., & Bosilj Vukšić, V. (2021). Exploring risks in the adoption of business intelligence in SMEs using the TOE framework. *JRFM, 14*(2), 58. doi:10.3390/jrfm14020058

Sullivan, W., Sullivan, R., & Buffton, B. (2001). Aligning individual and organisational values to support change. *Journal of Change Management, 2*(3), 247–254. doi:10.1080/738552750

Sun, L., Li, X., & Wang, Y. (2024). Digital trade growth and mineral resources In developing countries: Implications for green recovery. *Resources Policy*. 88, pp. 104338. S&P Global, (August 3, 2023). *Future Farming: Agriculture's Role in a More Sustainable India*. https://www.spglobal.com/en/research-insights/featured/special-editorial/look-forward/future-farming-agriculture-s-role-in-a-more-sustainable-india (Accessed on: December 18, 2023).

Sun, W., Guo, Z., Yang, Z., Wu, Y., Lan, W., Liao, Y., Wu, X., & Liu, Y. (2022). A Review of Recent Advances in Vital Signals Monitoring of Sports and Health via Flexible Wearable Sensors. *Sensors (14248220), 22*(20), N.PAG. doi:10.3390/s22207784

Sun, S., Hall, D. J., & Cegielski, C. G. (2020). Organizational intention to adopt big data in the B2B context: An integrated view. *Industrial Marketing Management, 86*, 109–121. doi:10.1016/j.indmarman.2019.09.003

Sun, X., Zhou, X., Wang, Q., Tang, P., Law, E. L. C., & Cobb, S. (2021). Understanding attitudes towards intellectual property from the perspective of design professionals. *Electronic Commerce Research, 21*(2), 521–543. doi:10.1007/s10660-019-09378-z

Suryono, P., & Pitoyo, A. J. (2013). Kesesuaian Tingkat Pendidikan dan Jenis Pekerjaan Pekerja di Pulau Jawa: Analisis Data Sakernas Tahun 2010. *Jurnal Bumi Indonesia*, 2(1), 59–68.

Sven Cravotta, M. G. (2019). Digitalization in German family firms – some preliminary insights. *Revistes, 4*(1). https://revistes.ub.edu/index.php/JESB/article/view/j051

Syaifullah, J., & Syaifullah, M., Sukendar, Mu, & Junaedi, J. (2021). Social Media Marketing and Business Performance of MSMEs During the COVID-19 Pandemic. *The Journal of Asian Finance. Economics and Business, 8*(2), 523–531. doi:10.13106/JAFEB.2021.VOL8.NO2.0523

Tan, M. (2004). Nurturing scientific and technological literacy through environmental education. *Kokusai Kyoiku Kyoryoku Ronshu, 7*(1), 115–131.

Tay, H. L., & Low, S. W. K. (2017). Digitalization of learning resources in a HEI – a lean management perspective. *International Journal of Productivity and Performance Management, 66*(5), 680–694. https://www.emerald.com/insight/content/doi/10.1108/IJPPM-09-2016-0193/full/html

Taylor, S., & Todd, P. A. (1995). Understanding information technology usage: A test of competing models. *Information Systems Research, 6*(2), 144–176. doi:10.1287/isre.6.2.144

Teo, T. S. (2001). Demographic and motivation variables associated with Internet usage activities. *Internet Research, 11*(2), 125–137. doi:10.1108/10662240110695089

The Indian Express. (2024). Maharashtra plans integration of Anganwadis and primary schools as per NEP recommendation. https://indianexpress.com/article/cities/mumbai/maharashtra-integration-anganwadis-primary-schools-nep-8900571.

The News India Express. (August 18, 2023). *India's agriculture sustainability at risk*. https://www.newindianexpress.com/xplore/2023/aug/18/indiasagriculture-sustainability-at-risk-2606814.html (Accessed on: December 18, 2023).

The Sunday Guardian. (October 14, 2023). *The Green Revolution in India: Harnessing Electric Tractors for Sustainable Agriculture*. https://sundayguardianlive.com/business/the-green-revolution-in-india-harnessing-electric-tractors-for-sustainable-agriculture (Accessed on: December 18, 2023).

The Times of India. (2022). *Implementation of NEP 2020: Focusing on early childhood learning*. https://timesofindia.indiatimes.com/blogs/voices/implementation-of-nep-2020-focusing-on-early-childhood-learning..

The Times of India. (2023). *15 anganwadis in Indore to be turned into pre-schools*. https://timesofindia.indiatimes.com/city/indore/15-anganwadis-in-indore-to-be-turned-into-pre-schools/articleshow/98109116.cms. (Accessed on: April 4, 2024).

The Times of India. (May 4, 2023). *Embracing sustainable agriculture: A virtuous cycle of prosperity.* https://timeso-findia.indiatimes.com/blogs/voices/embracing-sustainable-agriculture-a-virtuous-cycle-of-prosperity/ (Accessed on: December 18, 2023).

The Wire. (July 21, 2023). *How Natural Farming Can Revive India's Farmlands and Ensure Sustainable Agriculture.* https://thewire.in/agriculture/how-natural-farming-can-revive-indias-farmlands-and-ensure-sustainable-agriculture (Accessed on: December 18, 2023).

The World Bank Group. (2022a). *Individuals using the Internet (% of population) – Brunei Darussalam.* World Bank Group. https://data.worldbank.org/indicator/IT.NET.USER.ZS?locations=BN

The World Bank Group. (2022b). *Mobile cellular subscriptions – Brunei Darussalam.* The World Bank Group. https://data.worldbank.org/indicator/IT.CEL.SETS?end=2020&locations=BN&start=2010

Thelwall, M. (2014). Heart and soul: Sentiment strength detection in the social web with sentistrength, 2017. *Cyberemotions: Collective Emotions in Cyberspace.*

The-Royal-Society. (2018). *The future of privacy: A review of the ethical and legal challenges.* The Royal Society.

Thomas, D., Deblecker, O., & Ioakimidis, C. S. (2018). Optimal operation of an energy management system for a grid-connected smart building considering photovoltaics' uncertainty and stochastic electric vehicles' driving schedule. *Applied Energy, 210,* 1188–1206. doi:10.1016/j.apenergy.2017.07.035

Thorlakson, T., De Zegher, J. F., & Lambin, E. F. (2018). Companies' contribution to sustainability through global supply chains. *Proceedings of the National Academy of Sciences of the United States of America, 115*(9), 2072–2077. doi:10.1073/pnas.1716695115 PMID:29440420

Tornatzky, L. G., & Fleischer, M. (1990). *The processes of technological innovation.* Lexington Books.

Tripopsakul, S. (2018). Social media adoption as a business platform: an integrated TAM-TOE framework. *PJMS, 18*(2), 350-362. doi:10.17512/pjms.2018.18.2.28

Truant, E., Giordino, D., Borlatto, E., & Bhatia, M. (2024). Drivers and barriers of smart technologies for circular economy: Leveraging smart circular economy implementation to nurture companies' performance. *Technological Forecasting and Social Change, 198,* 122954. doi:10.1016/j.techfore.2023.122954

Truter, I. (2006). Barriers to communication and how to overcome them: management. *South African Pharmaceutical Journal. Suid-Afrikaanse Tydskrif vir Apteekwese, 73*(7), 55–58.

Tsolakis, N. K., Keramydas, C. A., Toka, A. K., Aidonis, D. A., & Iakovou, E. T. (2014). Agrifood supply chain management: A comprehensive hierarchical decision-making framework and a critical taxonomy. *Biosystems Engineering, 120,* 47–64. https://doi.org/ stems eng.2013.10.014. doi:10.1016/j.biosy

Tulloch, C. (2010). Style-Fashion- Dress : From Black to Post-Black. *Fashion Theory, 14*(3), 273–304. doi:10.2752/175174110X12712411520179

Ullah, Z., Qazi, H. S., Alferidi, A., Alsolami, M., Lami, B., & Hasanien, H. M. (2024). Optimal energy trading in cooperative microgrids considering hybrid renewable energy systems. *Alexandria Engineering Journal, 86,* 23–33. doi:10.1016/j.aej.2023.11.052

UN DESA & UNFCCCA. (2024). Reinforcing the 2030 Agenda and eradicating poverty in times of multiple crises: the effective delivery of sustainable, resilient and innovative solutions. *Global Expert Group Meeting in preparation for HLPF.* UN. https://sdgs.un.org/sites/default/files/202401/Draft%20CN_EGM%20for%20SDG13%20at%202024%20HLPF_as%20of%2031%20Jan.pdf

United Nations General Assembly. (2023), Economic and Social Council Progress towards the Sustainable Development Goals: Towards a Rescue Plan for People and Planet, *United Nations General Assembly report 2023*, 143, https://sdgs.un.org/sites/default/files/202304/SDG_Progress_Report_Special_Edition_2023_ADVANCE_UNEDITED_VERSION.pdf

United Nations. (2014). *The Millennium Development Goals Report 2014.* UN. https://unctad.org/en/PublicationsLibrary/wir2014_en.pdf

Upadhyay, A., Balodi, K. C., Naz, F., Di Nardo, M., & Jraisat, L. (2023). Implementing industry 4.0 in the manufacturing sector: Circular economy as a societal solution. *Computers & Industrial Engineering, 177*, 109072. doi:10.1016/j.cie.2023.109072

Urbach, N., Drews, P., & Ross, J. (2017). Digital business transformation and the changing role of the IT function. *MIS Quarterly Executive, 16* (2), 1–4. https://www.researchgate.net/profile/Nils_Urbach/publication/318113029_Digital_Business_Transformation_and_the_Changing_Role_of_the_IT_Function/links/595bb148458515117741b2a0/Digital-Business-Transformation-and-the-Changing-Role-of-the-IT-Function.pdf

Vabø, M., & Hansen, H. (2016). Purchase intentions for domestic food: A moderated TPB-explanation. *British Food Journal, 118*(10), 2372–2387. doi:10.1108/BFJ-01-2016-0044

Valencia, A., Qiu, J., & Chang, N. B. (2022). Integrating sustainability indicators and governance structures via clustering analysis and multicriteria decision making for an urban agriculture network. *Ecological Indicators, 142*, 109237. doi:10.1016/j.ecolind.2022.109237

Valle-Cruz, D., Criado, J. I., Sandoval-Almazán, R., & Ruvalcaba-Gomez, E. A. (2020). Assessing the public policy-cycle framework in the age of artificial intelligence: From agenda-setting to policy evaluation. *Government Information Quarterly, 37*(4), 101509. doi:10.1016/j.giq.2020.101509

Valle-Cruz, D., García-Contreras, R., & Gil-Garcia, J. R. (2023). Exploring the negative impacts of artificial intelligence in government: The dark side of intelligent algorithms and cognitive machines. *International Review of Administrative Sciences*, 00208523231187051.

Van den Hooff, B., & de Ridder, J. A. (2004). Knowledge sharing in context: The influence of organisational commitment, communication climate and CMC use on knowledge sharing. *Journal of Knowledge Management, 8*(6), 117–130. doi:10.1108/13673270410567675

Vatican News. (December 04, 2023). *COP28: Sustainable agriculture is antidote to climate change.* https://www.vaticannews.va/en/world/news/2023-12/cop28-sustainable-agriculture-antidote-to-climate-change.html (Accessed on: December 18, 2023).

Vermeulen, S. J., Campbell, B. M., & Ingram, J. S. I. (2012). Climate change and food systems. *Annual Review of Environment and Resources, 37*(1), 195–222. . doi:10.1146/annurev-environ-020411-130608

Version, P. (2018). *Artificial Intelligence & Human Rights : O PPORTUNITIES & R ISKS.*

Vial, G. (2019). Understanding digital transformation: A review and a research agenda. *The Journal of Strategic Information Systems, 28*(2), 118–144. https://linkinghub.elsevier.com/retrieve/pii/S0963868717302196

Vinoth, V. K. & Muthuvelayutham, C. (2020). "Study on Sustainable Supply chain Implementation in Business Organisations". *International Journal of Research Culture Society, 16*, 192-196.

Visco, A., Scolaro, C., Facchin, M., Brahimi, S., Belhamdi, H., Gatto, V., & Beghetto, V. (2022). Agri-Food Wastes for Bioplastics: European Prospective on Possible Applications in Their Second Life for a Circular Economy. *Polymers (20734360), 14*(13), 2752–N.PAG. https://doi.org/ doi:10.3390/polym14132752

Wagner, C. and Majchrzak, A. (2007). Enabling customer-centricity using wikis and the wiki way. *Journal of Management Information Systems, 23*(3), 17-43.

Wall, G. (2010). On exergy and sustainable development in environmental engineering. *The Open Environmental Engineering Journal, 3,* 21–32.

Wamba, S. F., Gunasekaran, A., Akter, S., Ren, S. J., Dubey, R., & Childe, S. J. (2017). Big data analytics and firm performance: Effects of dynamic capabilities. *Journal of Business Research, 70,* 356–365. doi:10.1016/j.jbusres.2016.08.009

Wang, H., Feng, J., Zhang, H., & Li, X. (2020). The effect of digital transformation strategy on performance. *International Journal of Conflict Management, 31*(3), 441–462. https://www.emerald.com/insight/content/doi/10.1108/IJCMA-09-2019-0166/full/html

Wang, C., Yan, G., & Ou, J. (2023). Does digitization promote green innovation? Evidence from China. *International Journal of Environmental Research and Public Health, 20*(5), 3893. doi:10.3390/ijerph20053893 PMID:36900903

Wang, J., Shu, T., Zhao, W., & Zhou, J. (2022). Research on Chinese Consumers' Attitudes Analysis of Big-Data Driven Price Discrimination Based on Machine Learning. *Frontiers in Psychology, 12*(February), 1–15. doi:10.3389/fpsyg.2021.803212 PMID:35178011

Wang, Y. F., Chen, S.-P., Lee, Y.-C., & Tsai, C.-T. S. (2013). Developing green management standards for restaurants: An application of green supply chain management. *International Journal of Hospitality Management, 34*(1), 263–273. doi:10.1016/j.ijhm.2013.04.001

Wang, Y., McKee, M., Torbica, A., & Stuckler, D. (2019). Systematic literature review on the spread of health-related misinformation on social media. *Social Science & Medicine, 240,* 112552. doi:10.1016/j.socscimed.2019.112552 PMID:31561111

Wang, Z., Huang, Y., Ankrah, V., & Dai, J. (2023). Greening the knowledge-based economies: Harnessing natural resources and innovation in information and communication technologies for green growth. *Resources Policy, 86,* 104181. doi:10.1016/j.resourpol.2023.104181

Weber, R. H. (2010). Internet of Things--New security and privacy challenges. *Computer Law \& Security Review, 26*(1), 23–30.

Webster, F., Rice, K., & Sud, A. (2020). A critical content analysis of media reporting on opioids: The social construction of an epidemic. *Social Science & Medicine, 244,* 112642. doi:10.1016/j.socscimed.2019.112642 PMID:31731136

Wertz, J. (2018). *Digital Transformation Is Critical For Business Development.*

Wessel, L., Baiyere, A., Ologeanu-Taddei, R., Cha, J., & Blegind Jensen, T. (2021). Unpacking the Difference Between Digital Transformation and IT-Enabled Organizational Transformation. *Journal of the Association for Information Systems, 22*(1), 102–129. https://aisel.aisnet.org/jais/vol22/iss1/6/

Wilhelm, M. and Kohlbacher, F. (2011). Co-opetition and knowledge co-creation in Japanese supplier-networks: The case of Toyota. *Asian Business & Management, 10*(1), 66-86.

Wognum, P. M. N., Bremmers, H., Trienekens, J. H., Van Der Vorst, J. G. A. J., & Bloemhof, J. M. (2010). *Advanced engineering informatics systems for sustainability and transparency of food supply chains—Current status.*

Wong, J., Koh, W. C., Alikhan, M. F., Abdul Aziz, A. B. Z., & Naing, L. (2020). Responding to COVID-19 in Brunei Darussalam: Lessons for small countries. *Journal of Global Health, 10*(1), 010363. doi:10.7189/jogh.10.010363 PMID:32566154

Wooldridge, A. (2010). The World Turned Upside Down. London: *The Economist*.

Xin, L., & Seo, S. (2020). The role of consumer ethnocentrism, country image, and subjective knowledge in predicting intention to purchase imported functional foods. *British Food Journal*, 122(2), 448–464. doi:10.1108/BFJ-05-2019-0326

Xu, J., Liu, Q., Wider, W., Zhang, S., Fauzi, M. A., Jiang, L., Udang, L. N., & An, Z. (2024). Research landscape of energy transition and green finance: A bibliometric analysis. *Heliyon*, 10(3), e24783. doi:10.1016/j.heliyon.2024.e24783 PMID:38314294

Yahya, A. (2020). *Effects of COVID-19 outbreak on Brunei's economy*.

Yakavenka, V., Mallidis, I., Vlachos, D., Lakavou, E. and Eleni, Z. (2020). Development of a multi-objective model for the design of sustainable supply chains: the case of perishable food products. *Annals of Operations Research*, 294, 593–621. doi:10.1007/s10479-019-03434-5

Yang, M., Chen, L., Wang, J., Msigwa, G., Osman, A. I., Fawzy, S., Rooney, D. W., & Yap, P.-S. (2022). Circular Economy Strategies for combating climate change and other environmental issues. *Environmental Chemistry Letters*, 21(1), 55–80. doi:10.1007/s10311-022-01499-6

Yang, T., Xun, J., & Chong, W. K. (2022). Complementary resources and SME firm performance: The role of external readiness and E-commerce functionality. *Industrial Management & Data Systems*, 122(4), 1128–1151. doi:10.1108/IMDS-01-2022-0045

Yan, X., Han, Z., Zou, C., & Cheng, C. (2024). Assessing the role of emerging green technology transfer in sustainable development and identification of key regions in Yangtze River Delta region. *Technological Forecasting and Social Change*, 200, 123099. doi:10.1016/j.techfore.2023.123099

Yeng, S. K., Osman, A., Haji, O. Y., & Safizal, M. (2015). E-Commerce adoption among Small and Medium Enterprises (SMEs) in Northern State of Malaysia. *Mediterranean Journal of Social Sciences*, 6(5), 37–43. doi:10.5901/mjss.2015.v6n5p37

Yildirim, C., & Correia, A.-P. (2015). Exploring the dimensions of nomophobia: Development and validation of a self-reported questionnaire. *Computers in Human Behavior*, 49, 130–137. doi:10.1016/j.chb.2015.02.059

Yildiz Çankaya, S., & Sezen, B. (2019). Effects of green supply chain management practices on sustainability performance. *Journal of Manufacturing Technology Management*, 30(1), 98–121. doi:10.1108/JMTM-03-2018-0099

Yin, L., Hassan, H., & Mokhtar, M. (2021). Application of SPSS Data Processing Technology in International Education in China. *Proceedings - 2021 2nd International Conference on Education, Knowledge and Information Management*, (pp. 570–573). IEEE. 10.1109/ICEKIM52309.2021.00130

Yu, A. (2023). Research and prospect of enterprise digital transformation and green innovation. *Industrial Engineering and Innovation Management*, 6(11), 12–22.

Zain, M., Yusob, A., & Ang, S. (2012). The key principles of managing people: The Brunei perspective. *Educational Research*, 3, 594–602.

Zamani, S. Z. (2022). Small and Medium Enterprises (SMEs) facing an evolving technological era: A systematic literature review on the adoption of technologies in SMEs. *European Journal of Innovation Management*, 25(6), 735–757. doi:10.1108/EJIM-07-2021-0360

Zhang, H., & Xie, Y. (2024). Assessing natural resources, rebounding trends, digital economic structure and green recovery dynamics in China. *Resources Policy*, 88, 104482. doi:10.1016/j.resourpol.2023.104482

Zhang, L., Li, D., Cao, C., & Huang, S. (2018). The influence of greenwashing perception on green purchasing intentions: The mediating role of green word-of-mouth and moderating role of green concern. *Journal of Cleaner Production*, *187*, 740–750. doi:10.1016/j.jclepro.2018.03.201

Zhang, M., Yang, J., Yu, P., Tinajero, G. D. A., Guan, Y., Yan, Q., Zhang, X., & Guo, H. (2024). Dual-Stackelberg game-based trading in community integrated energy system considering uncertain demand response and carbon trading. *Sustainable Cities and Society*, *101*, 105088. doi:10.1016/j.scs.2023.105088

Zhang, Y., & Jin, S. (2023). How does Digital Transformation Increase Corporate Sustainability? the moderating role of top management teams. *Systems*, *11*(7), 355. doi:10.3390/systems11070355

Zhao, M., & Dholakia, R. R. (2009). A multi-attribute model of web site interactivity and customer satisfaction: An application of the Kano model. *Managing Service Quality*, *19*(3), 286–307. doi:10.1108/09604520910955311

Zhou, Y., & Lund, P. D. (2023). Peer-to-peer energy sharing and trading of renewable energy in smart communities - trading pricing models, decision-making and agent-based collaboration. *Renewable Energy*, *207*, 177–193. doi:10.1016/j.renene.2023.02.125

Ziaee Bigdeli, A., Baines, T., Bustinza, O. F., & Guang Shi, V. (2017). Organisational change towards servitization: A theoretical framework. *Competitiveness Review*, *27*(1), 12–39. doi:10.1108/CR-03-2015-0015

Zisopoulos, F. K., Moejes, S. N., Rossier-Miranda, F. J., Van Der Goot, A. J.,& Boom, R.M. (2015). Exergetic comparison of food waste valorization in industrial bread production. *Energy*, *82*, 640–649.

Zuboff, S. (2019). *The age of surveillance capitalism: The fight for a human future at the new frontier of power: Barack Obama's books of 2019*. Profile books.

Zuiderveen Borgesius, F. J. (2020). Strengthening legal protection against discrimination by algorithms and artificial intelligence. *International Journal of Human Rights*, *24*(10), 1572–1593. doi:10.1080/13642987.2020.1743976

Zuliarni, S., Kartikasari, D., Hendrawan, B., & Windrayati Siregar, S. S. (2023). The impact of buying intention of global fashion on local substitute: The role of product design and price. *Heliyon*, *9*(11), e22160. doi:10.1016/j.heliyon.2023.e22160 PMID:38045170

Zuti, B. (2018). *Digitalization, regional competitiveness and the governments of the future*. Sznet Istvan University. http://publicatio.bibl.u-szeged.hu/13581/7/13581.pdf

About the Contributors

Patricia Ordóñez de Pablos is a professor in the Department of Business Administration in the Faculty of Business and Economics at The University of Oviedo, Spain. She completed her education in The London School of Economics, UK. Her teaching and research interests focus on the areas of strategic management, knowledge management, organizational learning, intellectual capital and information technologies, with special interest in Asia (Bhutan, China, Laos, Myanmar). She is Editor-in-Chief of the International Journal of Learning and Intellectual Capital (IJLIC) and International Journal of Asian Business and Information Management (IJABIM), respectively. She has edited books for IGI Global, Elsevier, Routledge, and Springer. In 2021, 2022 and 2023, she earned placement on Stanford University's "Ranking of the World Scientists: World's Top 2% Scientists" list. Additionally she is listed in World Top Scientists of Research.com in the Areas of Social Science and Humanities in Spain.

Muhammad Anshari has been named on the Stanford University List of Top 2% World Researchers in 2022 for the categories of ICT, Business & Management. Currently, he serves as Deputy Director Institute of Policy Studies and Academic Staff at School of Business & Economics, Universiti Brunei Darussalam. His professional experience started when he was IT Business Analyst at Astra International. Research Fellowship from The Government Republic of China (Taiwan) at National Taiwan University (Jan-Dec, 2014). Research Fellowship from King Saud University - the Kingdom of Saudi Arabia 2009. Senior Associate Researcher of Informatics Department, Universitas Islam Negeri Yogyakarta, Indonesia.

Haji Mohammad Nabil Almunawar is currently an associate professor at the School of Business and Economics, Universiti of Brunei Darussalam (UBDSBE), Brunei Darussalam. He was the former dean of UBDSBE. He received his bachelor's degree in 1983 from Bogor Agricultural University, Indonesia, master's degree (MSc) from the Department of Computer Science, University of Western Ontario, London, Canada in 1991, and Ph.D in Computer Science/Information Systems from the University of New South Wales in 1998. Dr. Almunawar has published more than 150 papers in refereed journals, books, book chapters, encyclopedias, and international conference proceedings. He has more than 30 years of teaching experience in the area of information systems. His overall research interests include applications of IT in management, e-business/commerce, digital marketplace/platform, digital business ecosystem, health informatics, information security, and cloud computing. Currently, he focuses his research on digital transformation, digital marketplace, digital platform, and digital business ecosystem.

Annie Dayani is a lecturer at the School of Business and Economics UBD since 2001. She graduated from UBD with a Bachelor of Business Administration. Under UBD study exchange program, she has also earned a Diploma in European Management Science from University Kent, Canterbury UK. Her Masters Degree is in Applied Information Technology from Monash University Australia. In 2013, she completed her PHD in Communication Technology at University of Queensland, Australia. Research interests include business and management, information systems, media and communication and e-government as well as knowledge management.

Jatin Anand is a driven individual from Ranchi. He has a passion for writting book chapter. With a background in renewable chapter, Jatin strives for excellence in all his endeavors. Outside of his work, he enjoys designing.

Jatin Anand belongs from Ranchi, Jharkhand and currently pursuing Bachelor of technology from Asansol Engineering College in Electrical Engineering (2021-2025). His area of interest is exploring the fields of science and technology.

K. Balaji, currently working as Assistant Professor in Commerce and Economics, Presidency University, Bangalore. He did Ph.D. from KLU Business School, KL University, Vijayawada. He is having 12 years of teaching experience. He has to his credit 23 Research Articles published in reputed National and International Journals. He has participated and presented more than 12 papers in both National and International Seminars/Conferences and also attended more than 50 workshops/FDPS organized by various reputed organizations. He has also participated in more than 50 seminars / webinars organized by various reputed organizations. He has also attended in 6 Short Term Training programs.He has successfully conducted 3 webinars, one 5 day FDP and one International Conference on Reimaging marketing in New Normal. He is a ratified as Assistant Professor by both JNTUH, JNTU Anantapur and Sri Venkateswara University, Tirupati. His specialized areas include, Accounting and Financial management, Marketing Management, Retailing Management, Consumer Behavior studies, Entrepreneurship and Business Laws.

Thuraya Farhana Said is a lecturer at Universiti Brunei Darussalam School of Business and Economics, Brunei Darussalam. Her current research interests lie within a larger field of study of strategic management, performance management, organisational development and entrepreneurship. She has contributed articles to international journals such as the International Journal of Public Sector Performance Management and the Knowledge Management Research and Practice Journal. Additionally, she authored a case study for the book 'Case Studies in Work, Employment and Human Resource Management,' published by Edward Elgar Publishing. Since 2017, she has been an active member of the University's team dedicated to entrepreneurship development.

Balaji Gopalan is an Assistant Professor in the area of Production, Operations and Logistics Management at the Department of Decision Sciences and works at the CMS Business School, Bangalore (India).

Zuraihan Masri, with over 15 years of experience in the telecommunications industry, has demonstrated a remarkable career trajectory spanning various domains. Beginning in operational roles, Zuraihan Masri swiftly transitioned into product management, leveraging expertise in understanding market demands and driving innovation. This led to an exploration of international business, broadening horizons to global markets and strategic partnerships. Zuraihan Masri holds a Master of Business Administration (MBA) degree from the esteemed University Brunei Darussalam, where a solid foundation in business principles and leadership was honed. Currently, Zuraihan Masri is pursuing a part-time Ph.D. in Management, with a focus on digital transformation, technology evolution, change management, innovation, and technology. This academic pursuit reflects a commitment to staying at the forefront of industry advancements and driving organizational growth through cutting-edge strategies.

Irfan Khan is working as Regional Manager-ASEAN at Supreme & Co. Pvt. Ltd., India. His area of interest includes Automation and Sustainable Development in T & D Sector.

Rupesh Kumar Sinha is working as an Associate Professor with the CMS Business School, Bangalore (India) in the area of Decision Science. He is with the Department of Decision Sciences.

Vinoth Kumar is an Assistant Professor In the Department of Decision Sciences at the CMS Business School, Bangalore (India).

Dharmbir Prasad was born in 1986 at Nalanda, Bihar, India. He received his B.Tech. degree in electrical engineering from Hooghly Engineering & Technology College (under West Bengal University of Technology), Hooghly, India and M.Tech. in Power System from Dr. B.C. Roy Engineering College (under West Bengal University of Technology), Durgapur, India, respectively. Currently, he is working in the capacity of assistant professor in the department of electrical engineering, Asansol Engineering College, Asansol, West Bengal, India. Now, he has pursued Ph.D. degree from Indian School of Mines, Dhanbad, Jharkhand, India. His research interest includes economic operation of power system.

Fairul Rizal Rashid is a Lecturer of Management at the School of Business and Economics, Universiti Brunei Darussalam. He has completed his PhD in 2014 from the University of Southampton, United Kingdom. His area of expertise revolves around the topic of performance management and strategic management. He has also been actively involved in consultancy works in his fields of research and holds various administrative positions at the same institution.

Ranadip Roy is Seeking opportunities for further research and academic collaboration Experienced Ph.D. holder from Indian Institute of Technology with over 12 years in academia, specializing in renewable energy optimization, soft computing, and power system optimization. Currently an Associate Professor and Dean of Students' Affairs at Sanaka Educational Trust's Group of Institutions, Durgapur, West Bengal. Recognized for receiving the Best Researcher Award twice and as the Best Coordinator, Eastern Region (MoE, NDLI, IIT Kharagpur). Actively involved in Ministry of Education initiatives as an Evaluator (SIH) and Innovation Ambassador for MoE, India. More than 30+ research papers, book chapters, patent and conferences at various SCI, Scopus and IEEE indexed journals and other platforms. Skilled reviewer for esteemed journals and IEEE conferences.

Muhammad Azmi Sait is a young researcher and doctoral candidate in Management at the University Brunei Darussalam. Holding a Master's degree in Management from Universiti Brunei Darussalam and a Bachelor's degree in Petroleum Engineering from the University of New South Wales, he brings a multidisciplinary perspective to his work. His current research focuses on understanding the dynamics of technology adoption, discontinuance, and resistance behavior in developing economies. With an enthusiastic passion for exploring the impact of technology on society and business, Muhammad Azmi is particularly interested in research that involves advancing digital inclusion and literacy within societies. Beyond academia, he actively participates in community service initiatives aimed at promoting social cohesion and development. His dedication to advancing knowledge, paired with his proficiency in data analysis and communication, positions him as a valuable contributor to the discourse on digital transformation and inclusive growth.

Rodrigo Sandoval-Almazan is Associate Professor of Social and Political Sciences Faculty of the Autonomous University of the State of Mexico (UAEM) based in Toluca, México. He has been professor of the Graduate School of Public Administration (EGAP) and Business Administration (EGADE) of the Institute of Technology and Superior Studies of Monterrey (ITESM), Campus Estado de Mexico. He is a member of the National Researchers System Level 2. He has authored or coauthored more than 30 research papers and the book Building Digital Government Strategies (2017). In 2013 he won the 2nd Latin American Award for Public Administration (INAP). Dr. Sandoval Almazan is a member of Mexican Academy of Science and some editorial boards of e-government journals such as Government Information Quarterly, IJPADA. His research interests include e-government metrics, public innovation, information technology organizations, social media in government, and open government.

Rudra Pratap Singh was born in 1983 at Chittaranjan, Burdwan, West Bengal, India. He received his B. Tech. and M. Tech degree in electrical engineering from Asansol Engineering (under the West Bengal University of Technology), Asansol, West Bengal, India and MBA in Power Management from the University of Petroleum and Energy Studies, Dehradun, Uttrakhand, India, respectively. He received his Ph.D. degree from the Indian School of Mines, Dhanbad, Jharkhand, India. Currently, he is working in the capacity of assistant professor in the department of electrical engineering, Asansol Engineering College, Asansol, West Bengal, India. His research interest includes the application of state estimation and optimization techniques in various fields of engineering.

David Valle-Cruz, Ph.D., MInf, BEng, is an Assistant Professor in the Science Department at the Universidad Autónoma del Estado de México and is a member of the Mexican National System of Researchers. David is a Computer Engineer, he holds a Master of Informatics, and a Ph.D. in Economics and Management. He has been a visiting researcher at the Center for Technology in Government (CTG), SUNY Albany, NY, and at the Computer Science and Multi-Agent Systems Laboratory of CINVESTAV, Guadalajara, Mexico. His articles have been published in leading journals, including Government Information Quarterly, Cognitive Computation, First Monday, Information Polity, and International Journal of Public Sector Management (among others). His research interests are related to Applied Artificial Intelligence, Social Media, and Emerging Technologies in the Public Sector.

314

Index

Operations Management 130, 148
Organisational Change 214-220, 223-227, 229-230, 233, 235-239
organization 22, 39, 76, 108-112, 115, 118-119, 121-122, 129, 148, 152, 160, 167, 169, 171-174, 177-181, 184-186, 189, 198, 223, 231, 239
Organization Performance 169, 185
Outsourcing 128, 131, 148

P

Partial Least Squares 123-124, 191, 240-241, 257, 261
Path Coefficients 240, 247, 255, 260
Path Models 240, 255, 260-261
personal innovativeness to information technology 263, 265
Place of Residence 194, 196, 199, 202-203, 207-208
PLS-SEM (Partial Least Square Structural Equation Modeling) 260
Poverty Alleviation 1, 15, 22
Process 4, 42, 56, 73-74, 79, 81, 83, 100, 115, 122, 128, 135-137, 139, 142, 144, 148, 161-163, 167, 172-173, 176, 178-179, 187, 190, 197, 200-201, 204, 206, 215-217, 219-221, 223, 227, 231, 238, 242, 251-252, 263, 270
Procurement 83, 148, 173
Product Lifecycle Management 27, 148
Production 6, 13-15, 20, 22, 27, 31, 33, 37-41, 43-49, 53, 56-58, 81, 85, 87, 96, 103-104, 115, 126-130, 133-138, 141-144, 147-148, 154, 159, 173, 180, 186-187, 189
Production Design 148
Productivity 34, 39-40, 76, 148, 177, 185, 187, 192, 226
Project 11-12, 14, 38, 56, 75, 78, 87-88, 93-94, 129-130, 134, 138, 148, 180, 228, 233, 239
Public Policy 1, 22, 191
Purchase Intention 243, 253, 255, 258, 260

R

Rapid Prototyping 148
Reliability 43, 94, 115-116, 136, 148, 240, 244-246, 248, 251-252, 255, 260-261, 265, 270
Reliability vs. Validity 260
Resilient future 23-24, 27-29, 75
Reverse Engineering 128, 148
revolution 12, 30-31, 33, 35, 38, 40, 59, 69-70, 72-73, 76, 78-81, 151, 153, 166-167, 181, 187, 191, 235, 239
Robustness 165, 240, 252-253, 255, 257, 261, 269

S

SEM (Structural Equation Modeling) 261
Services 10-11, 14-15, 22, 24, 28, 30, 53, 63, 76, 78-79, 111, 114-115, 125, 127-130, 132-134, 138, 140, 142, 148, 152-154, 156, 172-174, 180, 187-189, 199-200, 203, 205-208, 235, 254, 257, 259-260, 263, 271
Singularity 151
SmartPLS 114, 241-249, 251-253, 255-256, 261
SMEs 39, 108-115, 117-126, 144, 174, 186-188
SNI (Subjective Norms Toward Imports) 261
Social 1-3, 5, 8-13, 18, 20-22, 25-28, 30-31, 33, 35, 38-39, 57-59, 62, 65, 69-70, 72, 74-76, 79-81, 84, 89, 91, 103-106, 115, 120, 122-126, 132, 143-145, 150-153, 155, 157-168, 170-172, 178-179, 187-189, 193-198, 200-201, 203-205, 209-212, 215, 224, 235, 237-238, 242-243, 253-256, 258-259, 261, 263, 265, 269
Social Justice 1, 5, 22
Standardization 128, 130, 134, 141, 148
Statistical Technologies 240-241, 244, 247, 249, 252-253, 255
Structural Equation Modeling 123, 241-242, 251, 257-261
Supply Chain Management 30-32, 78, 85, 104, 107, 124, 127-130, 134, 136, 141-142, 144-148, 192
Sustainability 1-3, 5, 9-11, 17, 19-21, 23-33, 35, 37-40, 43, 46, 49, 52, 54, 57-59, 69-70, 73-74, 76-78, 81-85, 87, 91-92, 95, 103-106, 109, 114, 120, 125, 129, 134, 141, 143, 147-148, 170, 186, 209, 211-212, 218, 238, 258
Sustainable 1-31, 33-35, 37-40, 43-44, 46, 56-60, 70, 73-89, 91, 93, 95-107, 109, 121, 124-125, 127, 130, 140, 142, 144-147, 152, 167, 187-188, 190, 192, 194, 225, 258, 271
Sustainable Development Goals (SDGs) 1-4, 6-9, 16-20, 22, 25
sustainable education 74, 85-86
Sustainable Synergy 23-25, 27-29

T

technology 2, 8, 11-13, 16-19, 24-26, 29-33, 38, 41, 43, 61-62, 64-70, 72-74, 76-81, 83-85, 87, 92, 106-113, 115, 118-126, 128-130, 134, 140, 142-144, 150, 152, 154, 156-158, 160, 162-163, 166-169, 171, 173-175, 177, 179, 185-192, 195, 197, 199-201, 206, 208-212, 225, 235-238, 241, 257, 259,

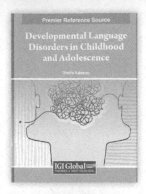

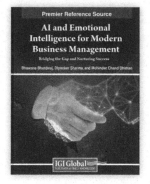

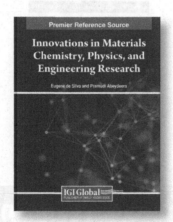
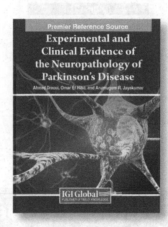
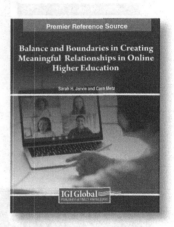

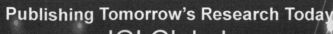

 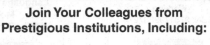

Individual Article & Chapter Downloads

US$ 37.50/each

Easily Identify, Acquire, and Utilize Published Peer-Reviewed Findings in Support of Your Current Research

- Browse Over ***170,000+ Articles & Chapters***
- ***Accurate & Advanced*** Search
- Affordably Acquire ***International Research***
- ***Instantly Access*** Your Content
- Benefit from the ***InfoSci® Platform Features***

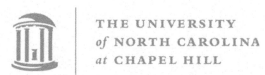

THE UNIVERSITY
of NORTH CAROLINA
at CHAPEL HILL